MW00895319

# CAPITALIZING ON CULTURE
## Critical Theory for Cultural Studies

# CAPITALIZING ON CULTURE

## Critical Theory for Cultural Studies

*Shane Gunster*

UNIVERSITY OF TORONTO PRESS
Toronto Buffalo London

Toronto Buffalo London
Printed in Canada

ISBN 0-8020-3693-7

Printed on acid-free paper

---

**National Library of Canada Cataloguing in Publication**

Gunster, Shane
Capitalizing on culture : critical theory for cultural studies / Shane Gunster.

ISBN 0-8020-3693-7

1. Popular culture – Economic aspects. 2. Popular culture – Study and teaching. I. Title.

CB427.G85 2004 306.4 C2003-907031-X

---

An earlier version of chapter 1 appears as 'Revisiting the Culture Industry Thesis: Mass Culture and the Commodity Form,' *Cultural Critique* 45 (Spring 2000).

University of Toronto Press acknowledges the financial assistance to its publishing program of the Canada Council for the Arts and the Ontario Arts Council.

This book has been published with the help of a grant from the Canadian Federation for the Humanities and Social Sciences, through the Aid to Scholarly Publications Programme, using funds provided by the Social Sciences and Humanities Research Council of Canada.

University of Toronto Press acknowledges the financial support for its publishing activities of the Government of Canada through the Book Publishing Industry Development Program (BPIDP).

# Contents

# Acknowledgments

First, I would like to acknowledge the support and assistance of David McNally. He provided help and encouragement throughout this project, as well as inspiration and guidance by way of a consistent willingness to engage critically with the issues, problems, and ideas arising out of the commodification of culture. I also thank Asher Horowitz, Scott Forsyth, and Colin Mooers for their generous help while I was researching and writing this book. The Social Sciences and Humanities Research Council of Canada has my gratitude for its generous financial support in the form of doctoral and postdoctoral fellowships. At University of Toronto Press, my editors Chris Bucci, Siobhan McMenemy, Frances Mundy, and Matthew Kudelka provided expert advice and encouragement, making this a better book than it would have otherwise been.

Many friends and colleagues in the Political Science Department at York University played a greater role than they may ever know in providing a supportive and stimulating critical environment. I am especially glad to have shared my experiences as a graduate student with Cam Bodnar, Peter Fargey, Adam Harmes, Derek Hrynyshyn, Michel Roy, Stephanie Ross, Christine Saulnier, and Andrej Zaslove. In this regard, a special mention goes to the weekly 'Freud/Adorno' reading group in the form of Andrew Biro and Steven Hayward, which served as a refuge from the demands of writing and also as a truly remarkable intellectual exercise. Beyond York's windswept campus, I want to thank Tom Glenne, Don MacLean, Paul Saurette, and Kathy Trevenen for their friendship while I was writing this book, and the crew from Saturday morning hockey for letting me score an easy goal every now and then.

Finally, I want to thank my family for their patience throughout a process that often enough seemed endless. Mom, dad, and sister cheered me on from afar. Adrienne was a source of support and inspiration from beginning to end, and many of the ideas in this book were first expressed on our evening walks – at first just the two of us, and later with Andreas and now also Lauren. My son's birth marked the initial emergence of book from dissertation, and my daughter arrived just in time for the finishing touches. I dedicate this work to them.

CAPITALIZING ON CULTURE

Critical Theory for Cultural Studies

# Introduction: Culture as Commodity

In the not too distant past, juxtaposing the terms 'culture' and 'commodity' inevitably summoned two very different constellations of meaning and value: the latter denoted the economic, commercial, and industrial logic and activities associated with the capitalist marketplace, while the former signified – in one sense or another – just about any human thought or action that kept its distance from, or even deliberately opposed, the instrumental rationality associated with the commodity form. From the sublime heights of great art to the everyday rituals of folklore and custom, culture traced a set of practices and experiences that were insulated against rule by the profit motive. As Raymond Williams explains, under the tutelage of Romanticism, culture was broadly conceptualized as a necessary sanctuary from 'abstract rationalism' and from the '"inhumanity" of current industrial development.'[1] Today, however, any lingering normative sentiments that culture and commodity ought to be kept separate are rarely taken seriously: at best, such sentiments are perceived as either utopian musings or nostalgic longings for a 'golden age' that has long since passed; more often, they appear as the desperate and self-serving efforts of cultural bureaucrats and their beneficiaries to defend various government cultural programs against the disciplinary cutbacks of neoliberalism; at worst, they are attacked as harbingers of an irrational and even millenarian fundamentalism.

As a result of the expansionary inertia of the culture industry, the conceptual distance that once separated these two terms is rapidly shrinking: more than ever before, culture exists as a commodity. Global media corporations are aggressively appropriating cultural practices both new and old in order to ensure that their products are as ubiquitous as possible, the point being to maximize the extent to which access to culture must pass through the circuits of exchange. It is impossible to measure with any precision the extent to which human cultural activities are actually commodified; we can, however, say that the systemic pressure to harmonize culture with commodity is inescapable. As quickly as new cultural styles and technologies emerge, they are courted, seized, and replicated by capital as new modes of producing marketable forms of difference. The breathtaking speed at which new information technologies have been integrated into networks of capitalist production, distribution, and consumption bears witness to this logic. To be sure, the appropriation of media networks such as the Internet and the World Wide Web continues to be a highly uneven and unstable process; many aspects of these systems evade and even defy regulation by market mechanisms. Yet there is little doubt that the commodity form plays a far more dominant role in shaping and defining these new technologies now than it did at their inception a mere decade ago.[2] As cultural producers and consumers, individuals can and do resist this pressure in many ways, some more successful than others; but these tactics ultimately have done little to change the overall inertia of the system. One can disagree with the unequivocal and exclusionary tone of one critic's stark assessment – 'culture's status as a commodity is the most fundamental fact about it, deeply affecting its form and inherent ideology'[3] – but it is difficult to deny that the commodity form now exercises a profound influence over contemporary forms of culture.

Yet many who are working today in the field of cultural studies take exception to claims like this, especially insofar as they are used to ground speculation about the broader social, political, and ideological effects of mass culture.[4] First, they argue that bringing the concepts *culture* and *commodity* into close proximity summons the spectre of a Marxist economic reductionism – one that displaces the heterogeneous specificity of different cultural objects as well as the diverse practices through which individuals and groups use these objects, and replaces it all with the crude notion that culture's ideological significance arises from the fact that it is produced as a commodity. Second, many believe that tracking the meaning or effect of culture to its identity as a commodity inevitably leads us down the path to an elitist hermeneutics that divides culture between the 'bad' mass-produced commodities of the culture industry and the 'good' work of serious aesthetic practice; such an approach thereby invokes a condescending pedagogy that is fundamentally antidemocratic and unlikely to have any popular resonance at all. In contrast to this unjustified elevation of the 'productive moment' in the assessment of contemporary culture, most forms of cultural studies insist on a more balanced, sophisticated, and empirical consideration of the real complexity of cultural practices. Culture, under this approach, is broadly defined as the signs, objects, activities, structures, and institutions through which we take meaning and pleasure from our social and material environment, express and define ourselves, and communicate with others. Culture evolves, in part, through our creative interaction and engagement with cultural commodities: it does not spring forth from those commodities, discrete and fully formed at the point of production. In fact, cultural studies tends to reverse the focus on production by insisting that the effects of cultural phenomena are best understood by looking to the many practices, habits, thoughts, feelings, and desires that shape, define, and give substance to everyday life. Most research in the field is oriented toward investigating this complex and fluid intersection of cultural forces, including the particular ways in which groups or individuals adapt the products of the culture industry to better fit their own needs, interests, and desires.

In other words, the analytic gaze of cultural studies becomes most intense at those moments and in those spaces when a cultural object's identity as commodity recedes from view. As cultural objects are disarticulated from networks of promotion and distribution, isolated from broader patterns of consumption, and integrated into particular environments, the perceptible gap between their intended use, meaning, and pleasure (derived, for example, from the class interests of those who own the means of cultural production) and how they are actually used, understood, and enjoyed takes on a revelatory epistemological significance, confirming that these differences are the most important fact when it comes to understanding the real effects of mass culture. The intentions supposedly built into a mass-cultural object at the point of production are often equated with its identity as a commodity. Hence, the discovery that such intentions are often subverted as a cultural commodity is 'read' in very different ways by different people is taken as incontrovertible evidence that the cultural significance of an object depends only peripherally on its existence as a commodity. As culture and commodity are conceptually divided, the relevance of the latter category begins to fade and in many cases slips out of sight altogether.

Over the past two decades, the commitment of cultural studies to this separation has been most clearly expressed in the field's 'debate' with political economy. Alarmed by the possibility of reducing the effects of the mass media to the class interests of those who own them, cultural studies has championed a conception of culture as relatively autonomous from the economy. In a prominent exchange on the respective merits of these two modes of analysis, Lawrence Grossberg – arguably the leading theorist of cultural studies in the United States today – attacks the simple equation of economic and ideological power:

> Certainly economic practices and relations determine the distribution of practices and commodities (although not entirely by themselves), but do they determine which meanings circulate and which do not? I doubt it. Those articulations are much more complex and difficult to describe. The fact that certain institutions (and individuals) would like to control how people interpret texts or what they do with them does not mean that such 'intentions' actually determine what people do and think, that is, the effects of practices.[5]

Consideration of culture as a commodity is conceptually subsumed beneath the consideration of culture as a simple form of class ideology: for cultural studies, the former necessarily implies the latter. It follows that lying behind the 'return to production' advocated by political economy is not only a greater focus on economic processes but also the old bogeyman of left-wing elitism, 'the desire to return to a simpler model of domination in which people are seen as passively manipulated "cultural dupes."'[6] Grossberg and others in cultural studies are certainly right to criticize the facile belief that those who own the media can and do easily and effectively control the hearts and minds of those who consume the media. However, this principled line of argument creates a rather acute theoretical gap in the field insofar as it has the intellectual effect of censoring investigation into the specific properties that culture acquires as a commodity. One is left, in other words, with a rather strange paradox in contemporary cultural studies: at the same time as the commodity form grows ever more prominent in ordering the cultural field, those most carefully engaged in investigating this field engage in an almost wilful disregard of culture's existence as a commodity for fear of sacrificing theoretical sophistication and independence to much cruder models of ideological critique. Those looking for theoretical insight into the commodification of culture must seek it elsewhere.

Crossing to the other side of this analytic divide, political economists of culture and those conducting critical media studies tend to be far more willing to engage with the evolving relationship between culture and capitalism. An extensive body of work has evolved that thoroughly and systematically describes how broader economic and political processes both define the operating principles and priorities of the mass media, and are, in turn, shaped and influenced by it.[7] This work focuses on state and corporate structures and how their synchronization with a capitalist economic system exerts significant pressure on media institutions to produce very specific kinds of culture and communication. Responding to Grossberg's claim that 'there is little or nothing that is commercially unthinkable,'[8] Nicholas Garnham – a prominent advocate of political economy – agrees that this is probably true, 'but there are certainly some meanings that are thought and others that are not; political economy argues that this pattern is not entirely random or culturally determined in the narrow sense.'[9] For political economy, tracing these patterns usually involves two types of investigation: a comprehensive accounting of the economic and political context in which culture is produced, promoted, distributed, and consumed; and an ideological critique of the systemic biases that this context inscribes in the content of the mass media, especially insofar as it offers a vision of the world in which liberal capitalism displaces all alternatives as the best possible means of organizing human societies.

Attending to the macro level of analysis, however, leaves political economy little time to explore how, independent of specific ideological content, commodified culture affects patterns of thought, being and desire at the level of individuals.[10] Instead, it has largely ceded that territory to cultural studies, perhaps fearful that prolonged attention to how culture is received or consumed would inevitably privilege an overly expansive account of human agency. 'By focusing on consumption and reception and on the moment of interpretation,' Garnham writes, 'cultural studies has exaggerated the freedoms of consumption and daily life.'[11] In the same manner that cultural studies ritualistically slays the dragon of economic reductionism to justify its exclusionary theoretical practice, many in political economy exaggerate the celebratory jubilance of those in cultural studies as a warning against the dangers of straying too far from the macro level of production. Such caricatures do conceptual injustice to the complexity and sophistication that characterize the best efforts of both camps; they also foster a profound reluctance among each to cross into the conceptual territory claimed by the other. As an intellectual consequence, neither approach has proven willing or able to develop a theoretical framework that speculates on the effects that culture as a commodity has on patterns of thought, experience, and pleasure. Hardening disciplinary boundaries and continuing mutual hostility make it unlikely that such a framework will emerge from either camp in the near future.

In this book I propose to address this gap by drawing on the critical theory of Theodor Adorno and Walter Benjamin to theorize the relationship between culture, commodity, and human experience. Critical theory is perfunctorily dismissed by many in cultural studies and is largely untapped (albeit acknowledged) by most in political economy, yet it offers us an avenue for rethinking the commodification of culture in important new ways. Outside the relatively narrow confines of critical theory scholarship, Adorno and Benjamin often appear as antagonists in a sharp dispute over the emancipatory potential of mass culture: the former's bristling condemnation of the culture industry in *Dialectic of Enlightenment* and other pieces is inevitably contrasted with the latter's sympathetic reading of film and photography in the fabled 'The Work of Art in the Age of Its Technological Reproducibility.' There is little doubt that their relationship was characterized by considerable intellectual tension; that said, we can deploy their differences productively by reading them as expressive of the dialectical complexity that their shared mode of theorizing brings to the investigation of human culture and society. My principal aim in the pages that follow is to mobilize this complexity in aid of rethinking the effects that commodified forms of culture have on the potential for different types of human experience. Specifically, I have three objectives. The first is to develop a clear and succinct account of the depth and sophistication of Adorno's critique of mass culture that will lay the foundations for its rescue from the conceptual oblivion to which it is so often hastily condemned when considered in isolation from the broader project of critical theory. The second is to arrange Benjamin's work around the problematic of culture, commodity, and experience so as to reconstruct the speculative theoretical narrative at its core that can most effectively bring his explosive musings into contact with our own time. The third is to read Adorno and Benjamin together on these themes, with the goal of producing a dialectical theory of mass culture that not only registers and explores the contradictions that cultural commodities impose on human experience, but also attends to the transformative possibilities coiled within those contradictions.

More than fifty years ago, Adorno and Horkheimer coined the term

*Kulturindustrie* to denote the systematic application of the principles, procedures, and values of industrial capitalism to the creation and marketing of mass culture.[12] They argued that entertainment corporations were churning out a never-ending supply of films, radio programs, magazines, newspapers, and books, following the same Fordist, assembly-line logic that governed the production of other consumer commodities such as automobiles, clothing, or furniture. In the early 1960s, reflecting on the origins of the phrase 'culture industry,' Adorno explained that it had been chosen over the more conventional 'mass culture' in order to 'exclude from the outset the interpretation agreeable to its advocates: that it is a matter of something like a culture that arises spontaneously from the masses themselves, the contemporary form of a popular art.' Such a formulation, he explained, had to be opposed 'in the extreme.'[13] One suspects they also hoped to produce a measure of critical energy through the novel union of two signifiers – culture and industry – that would have been viewed by many at the time as nonsensical and even as referencing fundamentally opposed social logics. Today, generally, these two concepts are no longer perceived as dissonant – a perverse confirmation of the remarkable prescience of Adorno and Horkheimer in forecasting many of the tendencies that have come to structure contemporary cultural production and consumption. Far from being a stimulus to critical reflection, the phrase has morphed into a means of describing a part of the economy. A neologism no longer, the culture industry is something to be encouraged, promoted, and enjoyed. Conceptually, the discursive contradictions of the term have been subsumed beneath a 'realistic' accounting of the status quo, a development that Adorno and Horkheimer themselves prophesied in their famous essay: 'Films and radio no longer need to present themselves as art. The truth that they are nothing but business is used as an ideology to legitimize the trash they intentionally produce. They call themselves industries.'[14]

As rhetorically productive as the term *industry* might once have been in challenging idealized notions of autonomous cultural creation and use by juxtapositioning them with the sameness, drudgery, and discipline of the factory, the governing logic of the culture industry for Adorno and Horkheimer is provided not by the organizational structures or techniques of industrial production *per se* but rather by the capitalist social relations in which they are embedded. In other words, it is commodification – not industrialization – that lies at the heart of the culture industry thesis. 'Cultural entities typical of the culture industry,' notes Adorno, 'are no longer *also* commodities, they are commodities through and through. This quantitative shift is so great that it calls forth entirely new phenomena.'[15] At its core, the thesis provides a rigorous and systematic analysis of these 'new phenomena' both in terms of the effects of the commodity form on cultural objects and practices and, more broadly, in terms of the consequences of this intersection on human beings and society as a whole. Operating at an extremely high level of abstraction, this framework dispenses with class-based accounts of ideological domination in favour of exploring how the logic of the commodity form – independent of the intentions of those who produce, control or distribute mass culture – imposes itself on cultural objects and how those objects in turn shape and define the parameters of human experience. Unlike many in cultural studies and political economy, Horkheimer and Adorno reject the view that the impact of these objects depends on the extent to which consumers believe the explicit messages and ideological content of mass culture. Instead, they theorize cultural commodities in terms of their impact on patterns of thought and desire and, above all, on how they affect the human capacity for autonomy and experience. In short, the culture industry thesis strives to answer two questions: What specific properties does culture develop when it is produced and sold as a commodity? And what must human beings become in order to maximize the meaning and pleasure taken from cultural commodities?

Many question the contemporary relevance of a theoretical framework that was developed to explain a cultural formation that now seems so distant from our own: after all, the products and practices of the culture industry have changed significantly over the past fifty years. Even sympathetic critics contend that the catalyst for Adorno's cultural pessimism was the historically specific fusion of mass culture, liberal democracy, and Fordist capitalism that emerged in the 1930s and grew to maturity after the Second World War. In an era of disorganized capitalism and postmodern cultural diversity, many tenets of the culture industry thesis – especially its ruthless insistence on the sameness of commodified culture – must be questioned and revised.[16] This caution is reflected in the relatively small role that Adorno's writings on mass culture have played in the recent renaissance of first-generation critical theory.[17] Questions of aesthetics and philosophy figure prominently in this theorizing; at the same time, the culture industry thesis has largely been met with an uncomfortable silence: its fiercely polemic tone seems embarrassingly out of place amidst the more tentative and localized analyses offered by cultural studies.[18] When the work on mass culture is taken up, the emphasis tends to be on a close reading of Adorno's infamous critique of jazz.[19] Such efforts are often highly effective at tracing the limits and historical specificity of this encounter, but they also restage Adorno's broader critique of mass culture as a misguided attack on a particular musical tradition: his failure to engage fairly with the genuine complexity and diversity of jazz effectively indicts the culture industry thesis in its entirety.

Conversely, my own treatment of Adorno's work on mass culture grounds its contemporary relevance in a complex, detailed theoretical account of the pressures and limits that the commodity form relentlessly imposes on culture and, by extension, on the capacity for critical thought and experience. Although the banality of mass culture in the interwar years provided Adorno with inspiration for his critique, he did not conceive that critique as an empirical study of existing cultural practices, nor did he execute it as one.[20] Although Adorno admits the value of empirically testing his speculative propositions,[21] he steadfastly refuses to subordinate theoretical speculation to the mere positivist accounting of the status quo; indeed, he regards speculative excess as the requisite element in a critical dialectical thought that seeks to keep alive historical potential in an administered society. Essential to thought 'is an element of exaggeration, of over-shooting the object, of self-detachment from the weight of the factual.'[22] Like modernist art, Adorno's work deliberately employs exaggeration as a technique for casting into bold relief the secret authoritarian tendencies of a culture that proclaims itself to be nothing less than the cultural instantiation of freedom and democracy. The essential force of his argument is not directed at the particular failings of early mass culture, nor should it be tied to them; instead, it is driven by the need to theorize the logic of commodification, a logic that has only become clearer in the past fifty years. And this is precisely what the culture industry thesis delivers with such unique force and potency. Thus, contrary to those who suggest that updating Adorno depends on cleansing his work of its vigorous polemic in the interests of greater sensitivity to postmodern cultural diversity, I believe the more important task must involve the exegetical foregrounding of those elements which attend most deeply to the effects of the commodity form. In chapter 1, my aim is to distill and organize these elements into a coherent critique of commodified culture as distinct from the more sweeping account of Enlightenment reason and historical progress beneath which they are often subsumed.

The many years that separate Adorno's time from our own are often cited as evidence of his obsolescence; actually, this distance offers a chance for us to estrange aspects of our present that most contemporary scholars would otherwise let pass without notice. At the time Adorno was writing, many people could still remember when culture and commodity were distinct entities; thus, he was able to draw from alternative aesthetic frameworks and traditions to bring into bold relief the limitations and specificity of the culture industry as a means of organizing human expression and communication. It has become common sense to fault Adorno for offering no way out; actually, his deep pessimism offers a necessary first step in building a visceral awareness that culture need not be the way it is today, that other forms of culture are possible even though they may be difficult to conceive. Ironic and exaggerated claims are meant to (negatively) innervate the utopian moments that lie behind them so as to all the more powerfully shock us into an awareness of the extent to which they are actually true. Writing about the curious smile that lingered on the death mask of Gustav Mahler, Adorno wondered whether

> we might conclude that the unfathomable sorrow of his last works had undercut all hope in order to avoid succumbing to illusion, rather as if hope were not unlike the superstitious idea of tempting fate, so that by hoping for something you prevent it from coming true. Could we not think of the path of disillusionment described by the development of Mahler's music as by no other as an example of the cunning not of reason but of hope?[23]

It takes little imagination to reposition this eulogy in an autobiographical vein. At one level, this rigorous denial of hope cleaves to the tradition of the *Bilderverbot*, the ban on images of the future or the divine invoked by both Marxism and Judaism. Yet this does not mean that hope for a different future plays no role in Adorno; rather, that hope lies hidden at the core of his critique. In a letter to Benjamin, he once observed that Franz Kafka's unsettling prose 'represents a photograph of our earthly life from the perspective of a redeemed life, one which merely reveals the latter as an edge of black cloth.'[24] A decade later in *Minima Moralia*, this sentiment reappears as an ethical imperative: 'The only philosophy which can be responsibly practised in the face of despair is the attempt to contemplate all things from the standpoint of redemption.'[25] Adorno's uncompromising critique restores a profound sense of the *systemic* contingency that underlies the totality of the culture industry; contrast this with the much shallower and individualized variant that cultural studies attaches to the fate of specific cultural objects.

A full exploration of the contours of this contingency, however, requires an openness to theoretical speculation that Adorno, admittedly, is both unwilling and unable to provide in the context of mass culture. His work on aesthetics offers a highly sophisticated discussion of how culture might emancipate human experience from the restrictions of capitalist modernity, yet he steadfastly refuses to consider whether mass culture itself might contain any similar possibilities. Instead, his tone and his mode of analysis are relentlessly negative and polemical; he denounces mass culture as repetitive and standardized, with the differences between products being little more than calculated deviations to ensure marketability and to gratify the illusion of individual taste. This has led some to suggest that his critique, while useful in terms of highlighting the shortcomings of the culture industry, ought to be balanced with a more sensitive assessment of those critical openings which do exist. In a seminal essay defining cultural studies, for example, Richard Johnson argues that Adorno's sweeping generalizations must be contextualized with greater attention to how people actually take up mass culture. This claim has become accepted though not necessarily practised wisdom in the field.[26] Douglas Kellner, one of the few practitioners of cultural studies who draws deeply from the Frankfurt School, makes the case for a 'multi-perspectival' approach, one in which models and concepts from both fields are selectively deployed to overcome each other's deficiencies.[27] Others have adopted a more philosophical frame of reference, pointing to the 'affirmative' materialism of postmodern thinkers as providing a useful counterpoint to Adorno's negativity. Jane Bennett, for instance, explores how Foucault, Deleuze, and Guattari identify and valorize fragments of enchantment in mass culture that can energize an ethical disposition in ways far too quickly dismissed by Adorno and Horkheimer.[28] And although Robert Miklitsch cautions that Deleuze and Guattari's positivity ultimately serves as a mirror image of Adorno's negative orientation, he frames the encounter of these two traditions as decisive in the movement toward a dialectical form of critique that is simultaneously sceptical and affirmative.[29] Undoubtedly, projects such as these generate valuable insights regarding the limitations of these competing frameworks. However, they are generally less successful at using the friction of these encounters to energize the production of novel theoretical configurations that move beyond these limitations in any coherent fashion. One might say that the epistemological gaps and normative political differences between cultural studies and postmodern philosophy on the one hand, and critical theory on the other, are simply too broad to produce a fruitful theoretical partnership.

But it is unnecessary to look beyond critical theory for conceptual resources that can help broaden and deepen Adorno's account of culture and commodity. Where Adorno theorizes this moment as little more than disastrous for humanity, Benjamin actively (re)constitutes it as a collective threshold experience – for, as he notes in *The Arcades Project*, 'we have grown very poor in threshold experiences'[30] and he remains acutely sensitive to the contradictions that permeate this experience, to the possibilities as well as the dangers that it represents. As scholarship on critical theory has long recognized, Adorno and Benjamin shared an extremely productive intellectual relationship, with each having a profound impact on the theoretical evolution of the other.[31] Their disagreements about the social effects of mass cultural technologies unfold within a shared theoretical framework and normative political orientation that, above all, is shaped by the desire of both to rescue the possibilities for critical thought and experience in a world where such possibilities are increasingly eviscerated by instrumental reason and capitalist social relations. Benjamin himself once offered: 'It seems to me that our respective investigations, like two different headlamps trained upon the same object from opposite directions have served to reveal the outline and character of contemporary art in a more thoroughly original and much more significant manner than anything hitherto attempted.'[32] Both believe that the commodity form poses an enormous danger to critical thought and action and severely damages the human capacity for experience. Benjamin, however, is far more willing to speculate on the utopian potential simultaneously generated by capitalism's destruction of traditional forms of experience and culture. For example, he looks to new cultural technologies – most notably film – as opening up new kinds of experiences that might serve as the basis for transformative collective social action. 'What I should like to postulate,' Adorno repeatedly demanded of Benjamin in their correspondence, 'is *more* dialectics.'[33] Yet this is precisely what the former's writings offer the latter – a theoretically adventurous and open-ended exploration of the contradictions that attend the commodification of culture and experience. Benjamin's work helps restore a dialectical quality to the culture industry thesis – in particular, a capacity for immanent critique – by looking to how the objects and activities of mass culture, markers of a degraded and ravaged experience in their current incarnation, can also serve as traces of the utopian potential that lies petrified within human society.

Writing about the mode of dialectical thinking urged on us by Marx, Fredric Jameson explains that 'we are somehow to lift our minds to a point at which it is possible to understand that capitalism is at one and the same time the best thing that has ever happened to the human race, and the worst.'[34] In other words, dialectical analysis does not emerge out of a comprehensive description of all that is good and bad in the world, a fair-minded accounting of the positive and the negative aspects of all objects and practices, or a teleology of contradictions that inevitably leads from one set of conditions to another. Instead, we are enjoined to think and feel the immense potential of the social world so that the failure to release and activate it is inscribed deeply on our minds and bodies as a loss of catastrophic proportions. 'The crisis consists precisely in the fact that the old is dying,' wrote Antonio Gramsci, 'and the new cannot be born.'[35] Constellating Adorno and Benjamin excavates this logic at the intersection of culture and commodity form. This task involves neither a synthesis of their differences into a unified framework nor a retroactive adjudication of the respective merits of their positions. Instead, it requires the selective arrangement and suspension of their differences within a shared theoretical space oriented toward a dialectical understanding of the contradictions that define not only cultural commodities but also their effects on human experience.

The intensely heterogeneous quality of Benjamin's writings, magnified by the collection of fragments and theoretical aphorisms in *The Arcades Project*, enables multiple and often contrasting points of entry into his work. It also sustains a substantial amount of excellent work that puzzles through the intellectual genealogy of this complex thinker, a productive form of exegetical 'brooding' over the many possible constellations that can be generated by arranging these different fragments in various ways. Reflecting the desire that animated Benjamin's own intellectual disposition, contemporary scholars often frame these encounters in terms of a desire to bring Benjamin into contact with the needs and interests – theoretical or otherwise – of today. The introduction to one recent collection puts it: 'What previously unrecognized cognitions will flash up from our new encounter with *The Arcades*

*Project*, as cognitions about Benjamin's work that make available something new of the dangers and the dreams, the forgotten and the remembered, of his time, but also and simultaneously of our own?'[36] In Chapters Two and Three, I likewise deploy Benjamin in exploring a set of questions that have only grown more intense in the decades since his passing. In particular, how does the commodification of cultural life redefine the possibilities for human experience? I am guided, in other words, less by the aim of patiently deducing his 'true' intentions and tracing their chronological evolution and more by the hope of using his condensed theoretical fragments to stimulate an innovative (re)thinking of the relationship between culture and commodity. For as Michael Jennings persuasively argues, privileging this theme is consistent with the core project of Benjamin's final years, an unfinished treatise on the nineteenth-century French poet Charles Baudelaire. The 'theoretical armature' of this book (and of the broader *Passagenwerk*), titled 'The Commodity as a Poetic Object,' was to present a theory of commodified human experience: 'The book on Baudelaire,' notes Jennings, 'argues with remarkable intensity that the structure of human experience in the mid-nineteenth century was, without exception, determined by the nature of its most prevalent object: the commodity.'[37] My reconstruction of this 'theoretical armature' unfolds through a reading of key themes in Benjamin's work, themes that include capitalism and second nature, mimesis, competing types of experience (*Erfahrung* and *Erlebnis*), voluntary and involuntary memory, new cultural technologies, and an innovative form of revolutionary pedagogy known as the 'dialectical image.'

Throughout, a dialogue with Adorno sustains the tensions that *redialecticize* our understanding of culture as commodity. In the second and third chapters, Benjamin occupies the bulk of our attention because the fertile psychoanalytic architecture he develops furnishes the conceptual resources necessary to mediate the more rigid culture industry thesis described in the first chapter. Yet this mediation must not be misconstrued as simply moderating the bristling tone and totalizing nature of the culture industry thesis. The (postmodern) transformation of Benjamin into a cunning archivist or collector of cultural and experiential fragments that escape or resist the logic of commodification does a profound injustice to the core dynamic of his work. Above all, his words must not be recruited in the service of banal assurances that cultural commodities are never as bad as pessimists like Adorno believe, that there is always something more to culture than its existence as a commodity. Benjamin does argue that the commodification of culture opens up fantastic new possibilities for human experience which demand the supersession of capitalism; but in the end he remains horrified by how these demands are continually suppressed, ignored, or colonized by an emerging consumer society. As a theorist of the dialectical image, he develops a highly speculative theory of how the latent contradictions of the logic of capitalism, as they have accumulated historically, might be intensified and exploded from within. But this requires an intensified awareness and a literally visceral awareness of the monumental impoverishment of experience at the hands of capital.

The relentless negativity of the culture industry thesis has an important role to play in such an endeavour. Adorno's pessimism sharpens and deepens the contradiction between the potential lying within commodified culture and how that potential is currently repressed. Except in highly compressed fragments, this polemic force is either lacking or cryptically disguised in Benjamin's work. Indeed, it has led many outside the field of critical theory to interpret it – usually based on selective readings of certain pieces, especially the 'Work of Art' essay – as providing an optimistic assessment of the democratic possibilities of mass culture. It is not uncommon for Benjamin to be appended to the most celebratory strains of cultural studies as their intellectual progenitor. For example, both Angela McRobbie and Susan Willis suggest that John Fiske – arguably the most famous of those who argue that shopping and watching television constitute legitimate forms of cultural resistance – is the most faithful contemporary interpreter of Benjamin's work.[38] Similarly, Don Slater and Fran Tonkiss finger Benjamin (with Georg Simmel) as the most significant theoretical inspiration behind work in cultural studies on the diverse pleasures and freedoms of shopping.[39] Such readings are troubling insofar as they completely miss the critique of capitalism that lies at the heart of Benjamin's writings. Adorno repeatedly champions *The Arcades Project* as developing the motif of Hell to describe how an explosion of commodities transformed nineteenth-century Paris – the *ur*-form of contemporary urban society – into a phantasmagorical wasteland in which death (the inorganic) was literally worshipped through the repetitive rituals of consumption. That such a vision could somehow be marshalled in support of a facile consumerism is an index of the contemporary need for Adorno's bleak vision to anchor the often cryptic fragments left by Benjamin. 'Pessimism all along the line,' Benjamin once declared in an essay on surrealism that foreshadowed the rapid darkening of his hope for humanity during the 1930s. As I make use of Benjamin to add a dialectical complexity to Adorno's work on mass culture, Adorno will be equally important in ensuring that the normative force which energizes that dialectic – namely, a desperate fear that the moment to realize the potential coiled within humanity will pass unnoticed in favour of a slide into barbarism – remains powerful and vibrant.

The most significant opposition to critical theory's emphasis on the commodification of culture lies within cultural studies. Despite the initial 'underground' appeal of *Dialectic of Enlightenment* to the counterculture movement of the 1960s and the widespread popularity of the more accessible version of critical theory developed by Herbert Marcuse in *One Dimensional Man*,[40] the culture industry thesis gradually fell out of favour with those engaged in the critical study of culture. Its uncompromising disdain seemed ineffective as a proselytizing strategy; moreover, it appeared insensitive to the possibilities for social emancipation encouraged by the postwar transformation of popular culture. In the late 1960s and 1970s a much different kind of critical cultural analysis grew out of a cross-fertilization of French structuralism, Marxist semiotics, the empirical tradition of the British culturalists, and Antonio Gramsci's conception of hegemony. Led by Stuart Hall, the Centre for Contemporary Cultural Studies at Birmingham University insisted on the conditional independence of cultural practices from economic structures as well as the polysemic nature of commodified cultural processes: people could and did use the cultural forms provided by late capitalism to resist and critically engage with oppressive and exploitative social, political, and economic systems. Combining ethnography, textual analysis, and ideological critique, the cultural theorists of the Birmingham School explicitly rejected what they perceived to be the elitist biases of the Frankfurt School. Instead of starting with the economy and moving toward culture, their theoretical framework encouraged a concentration on the specificities of the cultural sphere as 'relatively autonomous' from the requirements of capital. The agency of specific 'sub-cultures' in negotiating a meaningful cultural existence was used as a model for thinking through how people actively appropriated the raw materials of the hegemonic culture to produce their own. While broader questions of structural political economy (i.e., class) played a major role in the early work of the Birmingham scholars, the influence of contemporary social theory shifted the centre's priorities toward the analysis of localized cultural practices, the reception of culture, and the role of cultural formations in the production of subjectivity.

The fourth chapter takes up this tradition to get a better sense of why cultural studies has been both unable and unwilling to focus on the intersection of culture and commodity as a defining feature of the contemporary cultural environment. My intent is not to produce yet another polemic decrying the jubilant populist excesses of cultural studies;[41] rather, I return to one of its founding moments to explore why it rejected the claims of critical theory with so much vigour. There are a number of reasons why a systematic engagement with Hall and the Birmingham School is both important and timely. First, they are widely accepted as providing the theoretical foundations for contemporary cultural studies, especially those whose work explores the relationship between culture, power, and society. Unlike literary variants of cultural studies, which aspire to deconstruct key literary and theoretical texts, the Birmingham scholars are well-known for their desire and ability to analyse the wider social implications of cultural phenomena. Thus it becomes especially important to assess the capacity of their conceptual apparatus to make sense of the lines of force running between cultural and economic processes. Second, it has become common to attribute the conservative sins of cultural studies to its Americanization: the radical political sensibilities of Birmingham – so the argument goes – were tragically diluted as they crossed the Atlantic to be institutionalized in a largely depoliticized American academy.[42] Casting a critical eye toward the theoretical origins of cultural studies at the centre helps us avoid the simplified perspective that such narratives have inspired. Third, despite their well-publicized hostility to Adorno, the Birmingham School once held a great deal in common with critical theory; most crucially, both developed a critical Marxist problematic to investigate the role of contemporary culture in maintaining the hegemony of liberal democratic capitalism. Why, then, did they ultimately take such divergent paths? And what are the implications that attend those theoretical choices? Finally, in the face of decades of casual dismissal at the hands of cultural studies, a critical interrogation of the Birmingham School guided by the work of Adorno and Benjamin is long overdue. After all, no sustained exchange between these two traditions has ever taken place; instead, critical theory was generally viewed by the centre as offering little more than an example of how *not* to do cultural studies. The time has come for a more substantive and fair-minded reckoning between these two schools of cultural theory. The question of how to adequately theorize commodified culture offers an ideal point of departure for such an encounter.

My inquiry into cultural studies begins with Hall and the Birmingham School but does not end there. As an emergent discipline, cultural studies exploded out of Birmingham and has moved in many different directions beyond the initial paradigm established by the centre. A comprehensive engagement with the many facets of contemporary cultural studies is beyond the scope of this project, and, thankfully, the discipline's abundant reflexivity makes such an effort unnecessary: few other fields of scholarship expend as much time and effort documenting and reflecting on their own history and development as cultural studies.[43] Instead, a more productive route winds through a deeper engagement with the work of those who have deliberately moved beyond the constraints of Birmingham to develop new ways of understanding the relations between culture and economy. In this regard, the work of Lawrence Grossberg has been exemplary. Grossberg is critical of the idealistic excesses that often attend the study of culture in isolation from other social processes, and he has led the way in developing a sophisticated theoretical model for tracing the role of culture in producing effects within and being produced by other areas of social life. Revising the concept of articulation, he suggests that the multiple emotional, physical, and libidinal energies that are generated by and invested in specific cultural practices can be either associatively transferred to political and ideological projects or isolated from those projects, depending on how these practices are articulated in certain ways within a particular social formation. In Grossberg's work, this approach has been especially productive in looking at the cultural dimensions of neoconservatism. Might it also be used to map out the direct effects of the commodity form on culture? Chapter 5 opens with an extended discussion of the concept of articulation as developed by Grossberg, and investigates the very real possibilities it holds, both in terms of reconsidering the effects of commodification and in terms of facilitating a substantive exchange with critical theory.

The book closes with a sober assessment of the differences that divide cultural studies and critical theory and with some possible points of contact between them. Notwithstanding his iconoclastic revisiting of many of the founding assumptions of cultural studies, Grossberg has proven largely unwilling to apply his innovative theoretical framework in bridging the gap with political economy or critical theory. Yet there are some intriguing parallels between his work and that of Adorno, and this raises the possibility of a dialogue between critical theory and cultural studies. In the second half of chapter 5, I briefly lay out the main arguments of Grossberg and Hall in dismissing the relevance of commodification to the study of culture and its effects. The essence of their position, I argue, boils down to two complementary assumptions: first, language and culture are inherently polysemic, and second, cultural consumption is an active and creative process, which ensures that there is always a great deal more to culture than its existence as a commodity. I then work through how Adorno and Benjamin might respond to these claims by examining some of the common misreadings of critical theory by cultural studies, recasting their critical stance as one that for the most part does not reject the possibility that culture may exceed its economic function but rather insists that this relation be explicitly theorized. I end the chapter by looking at how elements of Grossberg's analysis of difference and affect in postmodernity echo Adorno's fears about our own half-conscious complicity with the culture industry. These parallels suggest that the commodification of difference offers an ideal theme through which critical theory and cultural studies might engage in a more cooperative investigation of contemporary cultural phenomena.

Adorno's writings are occasionally praised for furnishing a sobering blast of pessimism, one that constitutes a timely reminder of the limitations of the fashionable cynicism which often masquerades as critique in a postmodern cultural environment. Yet brought together with Benjamin, he provides much more than a merely ornamental counterpart to the excessive optimism of cultural studies. Both theorists offer a complex and sophisticated framework for thinking through how the commodification of culture systematically transforms our ability to experience the world. Among the first to observe that cultural practices have effects beyond their power to represent social reality in particular ways, they look at how these practices not only condition cognitive capacities but also work through and on the body and the unconscious. Alongside the labour process, culture is understood as having complementary importance in terms of inscribing economic structures and patterns onto our bodies, minds, and social relations. Besides acting as an ideological mouthpiece for liberal capitalism, the culture industry actually binds individuals directly to the exchange relation itself through a series of cognitive, libidinal, somatic, and affective pathways. Exploring how this happens opens up important insights into the construction, maintenance, and extension of capitalism as a hegemonic system based on a broad, 'consensual' foundation of social support. Yet Benjamin also delivers a profound sense of the immense social potential set in motion by the fusion of culture and commodity insofar as it opens up entirely new types of experience, memory, and subjectivity. Like Marx, he looks directly into the heart of capital to find the means to overcome it. A world in which the commodity form grows ever stronger calls for an acute sensitivity to both the possibilities and the limitations it brings to cultural life. It is my hope that reading Adorno and Benjamin together offers us the opportunity to develop such a sensitivity by thinking through some of the most important questions in contemporary cultural theory.

# 1
# Mass Culture and the Commodity Form: Revisiting the Culture Industry Thesis

... the splinter in your eye is the best magnifying glass.

Theodor Adorno, *Minima Moralia*

Adorno once observed that what distinguished Freud's analysis of mass behaviour from earlier efforts was 'the absence of the traditional contempt for the masses' and that 'instead of inferring from the usual descriptive findings that the masses are inferior per se and likely to remain so, he asks in the spirit of true enlightenment: what makes masses into masses?'[1] One might argue that Adorno was similarly inspired in his examination of the structure, characteristics, and effects of the culture industry. As 'mass deception,' the culture industry has long played an architectonic role in the transformation of human and natural potential into the modern barbarism of late capitalism. The extension of capitalist social relations and their identitarian logic to the production, distribution, and consumption of cultural goods not only destroys the emancipatory possibilities traditionally harboured by art and culture, thus sabotaging human capacities for experience and critical thought, but also binds individuals somatically, cognitively, and libidinally to the exchange relation itself. Unfortunately, Adorno often shrouds his penetrating analyses in a dense, fatalistic prose and spends as much time mourning the death of autonomy as he does explaining why it has occurred. Moreover, his essays are filled with evocative and poetic aphorisms and with paratactic sentences that repudiate logical structure – fertile ground for the hermeneutic manufacture of clichés that make it difficult to grapple with the arguments he makes. In other words, the manner in which he expresses the culture industry thesis often gets in the way of the substantive claims he makes. Much of the literature surrounding this thesis reflects this tendency.[2] The result has often been a sterilization of the debate that historically has raged around Adorno's more provocative phrases. Are people really the cultural victims that he so often makes them out to be? Obviously, this question is very important. But it is often discussed with only marginal attention paid to how Adorno actually theorizes the effect of the commodity form on culture – the cornerstone of his analysis of the culture industry.

In this chapter, I hope to change all this. Whatever value Adorno's work may hold, it certainly does not provide a measured, precise, and balanced account of contemporary cultural practices. And condemning him on this basis is neither fair nor a particularly interesting exercise. I want to lay out as clearly as possible the basic tenets of the culture industry thesis as they bear on the commodification of culture. What is it about the combination of culture and capitalism that so alarms Adorno? How does the commodification of culture work its lethal magic on individuals in a capitalist society? What part do commodified cultural practices play in the ongoing production and maintenance of the hegemony of capitalist social relations? By considering these questions, we should be able to avoid a premature dismissal of Adorno's conclusions in favour of first investigating how and why he reaches them. Below, I foreground the theme of commodification, which should clear a path into Adorno's work that has become overgrown with cliché, invective, and polemic.

## Particular and Universal, Detail and Whole: The False Unities of Mass Culture

Adorno offers his clearest description of mass culture in 'On Popular Music,' an essay he wrote in English with the assistance of an American sociologist, George Simpson, while a member of the Princeton Radio Research project.[3] On the one hand, he argues, the 'fundamental' property of popular music is that it is unremittingly standardized: 'Every detail is substitutable; it serves its function only as a cog in a machine.'[4] Popular songs all share a common underlying musical structure; each is written according to the same formulaic pattern to ensure that it fits smoothly into pre-existing listening habits. On the other hand, marketability demands that this repetition be hidden beneath the illusion of individuality, difference, and novelty. The dialectic between new and old is a constant feature of all forms of culture; however, the culture industry sets in motion a promotional logic that enforces a premature resolution of this tension. 'To be plugged, a song-hit must have at least one feature [i.e., a "hook"] by which it can be distinguished from any other, and yet possess the complete conventionality and triviality of all others.'[5] Both within and across cultural products, the inconsequential or 'pseudo-individual' variations must be deliberately foregrounded and exaggerated – a necessary correlate to the growing tyranny of dominant styles. David Kendall, a television producer with Warner Bros., echoes Adorno's diagnosis almost exactly. In pitching an idea, he notes, 'you'd always say it is unique. You would say it is a unique twist.' Yet at the same time he asserts that there is no such thing as 'great, original, breakthrough television [because] it is all about reacting to other things.' Of the network executives who ultimately control which programs are financed and aired, he observes: 'The only thing they know that works is something that has worked. So they will try and clone what has happened before and keep the writers and producers in the reins.'[6] Kendall reiterates Horkheimer and Adorno almost exactly: the culture industry 'rejects anything untried as a risk. In film, any manuscript which is not reassuringly based on a best-seller is viewed with mistrust.'[7] The description 'pseudo-individuation' has often been attacked as signifying an elitist disposition because it seemingly requires the superior judgment of a critic to distinguish between 'true' and 'false' difference. However, Adorno proposes this term less as a strategy of cultural critique and more as a means of defining the structural pressures that commodification imposes on all forms of cultural production.

Unfortunately, terms such as 'standardization' and 'pseudo-individuation' can tilt the analytic priorities of the culture industry thesis away from exploring how those pressures function toward a totalizing dismissal of all mass culture as exactly the same. Moreover, the use of industrial imagery to indict mass culture as little more than another form of assembly line production does not help us explore the specific qualities of culture as commodity as opposed to culture as industry.[8] Simple denunciations of mass culture as standardized too easily invoke caricatures of the culture industry as a factory mechanistically churning out identical products according to the autocratic dictates of executives. They suggest a rigid, cumbersome, and bureaucratic apparatus with a hierarchical chain of command in which the formulas and licensed deviations of mass culture are unilaterally determined and imposed by senior management. There is little doubt that Adorno often champions this perspective, but it hardly exhausts his analytic engagement with mass culture and it can actually obscure the more sophisticated elements of that engagement. So I want to temporarily set aside this problematic in favour of another – one that equally vexed Adorno although it rarely attracts much attention in discussions of the culture industry thesis.

What is the relation between individual elements of cultural goods? How are these elements combined to create a discrete and coherent cultural 'text'? How do such texts participate in and challenge the aesthetic or cultural traditions out of which they emerge? When we attend to Adorno's treatment of these questions, we encounter a more supple and engaged form of cultural analysis than is commonly attributed to him. This is an important first step in freeing the culture industry thesis from its (now) stifling association with the historical specificity of Fordist cultural production. In other words, this approach reveals that Adorno's primary concern is not a centralized form of bureaucratic cultural production, but rather the effect of commodification *per se* on culture. This lays the foundations for exploring the homologies between cultural objects and the forms of experience they produce: the relation between detail and whole in mass culture both generates and reflects an equivalent relation between specific events and episodes as they are integrated into the broader experiential and mnemic patterns of an individual's life history. This dialectic between cultural objects and experience becomes especially important when we set out to chart the parallels between Adorno and Benjamin in their work on mass culture.

Adorno privileges music as a medium for theorizing this relation. Music played a very important role in his life: he studied composition with Alban Berg in Vienna and wrote extensively on the subject throughout his career.[9] Given his understanding of and commitment to serious music as a medium of expression and critical cognition, he was horrified by its systematic corruption by the culture industry. Indeed, one might argue that for him, popular music (*especially* jazz) serves as a kind of archetype for all products of the culture industry, and that he uses it to demonstrate everything that is regressive, affirmative, and harmful in mass culture. Instead of jumping into the controversy about the validity of Adorno's analysis of jazz, I want to deploy his work heuristically as a means for sketching out what he believed to be the essential qualities of mass cultural forms. His own words serve as guidance here:

'Jazz is not what it "is" ... Rather, it is what it is used for.'[10] Adorno grounds the aesthetic potential of music in its unique capacity to express, explore and problematize the relationship between the particular and the whole in a sensuous manner that escapes the tyranny of purely conceptual forms of thought. Describing the symphonic form, he observes that 'every detail, however spontaneous in emphasis, is absorbed in the whole by its very spontaneity and gets its true weight only by its relation to the whole, as revealed finally by the symphonic process. Structurally, one hears the first bar of a Beethoven symphonic movement only at the very moment when one hears the last bar.'[11]

For example, by way of relaxing the grip of musical forms over their constituent parts, the composers of the eighteenth and nineteenth centuries aesthetically expressed, celebrated, and participated in the political, economic, and social triumphs of liberalism. As the rationalization and commodification of human life advanced in the twentieth century, serious composers such as Arnold Schönberg and Alban Berg again restructured the relation between detail and whole in order to express and criticize these broader social processes. The point is that music's critical potential depends on its capacity to sustain the tension between the distinct pieces of a musical composition and their assembly in the creation of a unified whole.

Conversely, in the music of the culture industry the tension between detail and whole has been altogether destroyed: 'Lacking both contrast and relatedness, the whole and the detail look alike. Their harmony, guaranteed in advance, mocks the painfully achieved harmony of the great bourgeois works of art.'[12] Time and historical development – the gatekeepers of memory, difference, and 'otherness' in serious music – vanish and are replaced by the 'spatialized temporality of the ever same.'[13] This development was foreshadowed in Richard Wagner's development of the *leitmotif*, a simple musical phrase specifically designed to be easily remembered independent of its place in the larger composition.[14] Once individual details appear completely detached from the whole, they lose their capacity to express particularity in a meaningful way; only within the express tension between part and whole can the former's conditional liberation from the latter, and its distinction from other parts, be truly experienced as an emancipatory and critical moment. 'The romantic dissolution of the preconceived unity into its details, something which once pressed the right of the individual against the inflexibility of the totality, nevertheless harboured its opposite, the process of mechanization, in its very principle: the emancipated detail first becomes an effect and finally a trick.'[15] Following a path blazed by Wagner – though by no means predetermined by his music – popular music dissolves into the serial agglomeration of memorable musical phrases that are no longer consciously mediated through a coherent whole. Detail is separated from the whole both within individual pieces (i.e., the structural relation between a certain sound and the progression of a song) and within the broader aesthetic traditions of which a particular piece is a part (i.e., how a piece takes up, develops and challenges the rules and principles of a musical style). The detail is seemingly comprehended in an instant instead of being mediated through its relation to the whole.

The cognitive aspect of musical consumption disappears as a consequence, and once it does, individual details take on a new primary function: to provide immediate sensual gratification. Pop music relies on simple harmonies, conventional tonalities, and sheer volume to 'jazz up' its constituent elements; once serious music is (re)arranged to isolate and accentuate particular musical passages:

> Because they were originally defined only as moments of the whole, the instants of sensory pleasure which emerge out of the decomposing unities are too weak even to produce the sensory stimulus demanded of them in fulfillment of their advertised role. The dressing up and puffing up of the individual erases the lineaments of protest, sketched out in the limitation of the individual to himself over and against the institution, just as in the reduction of the large-scale to the intimate, sight is lost of the totality in which bad individual immediacy was kept within bounds in great music.[16]

'Classical music,' for example, is marketed to and consumed by a mass audience through the 'greatest hits' of particular composers, collections organized around particular themes, or the inclusion of fragments in movie soundtracks. Similarly, Adorno notes that performers, orchestras, and instruments have been fetishized to the point where the worship of them entirely displaces listening to and thinking about the music itself. Designed to produce an immediate effect, the individual details of mass culture lose their specificity and thereby become interchangeable. In a movie soundtrack, for example, a specific piece of music that excites a certain emotional response (e.g., rage, excitement, sadness) can be easily replaced by any other that has a similar effect. Analysed in structural terms, pop music songs exhibit a similarly limited range of musical techniques, which are endlessly rearranged. As a consequence, a narrow catalogue of devices evolves – one that is called on again and again in the production of standardized compositions. Tautologically, the most successful forms are imitated in a circle of never-ending repetition. It is not the lack of complexity of musical details that draws Adorno's ire: stock jazz arrangements, he admits, are often more technically sophisticated than serious modern music.[17] Similarly, it is not the presence of repetition itself that he views as a problem; indeed, 'musical analyses ... have shown that even the most diffuse and dissociated (that is, least repetitious) creations contain similarities, that certain parts are related to others in terms of some specific characteristics, and that, generally, the intended nonidentity is realized only through reference to such identities.'[18] Rather, what he objects to so strongly is the standardized deployment of musical details – a deployment that makes no effort to express, develop, or even acknowledge a relation of details with one another, with the whole composition of which they are a part, or the larger aesthetic context from which they have evolved.

Yet this apparently carefree disposition does not guarantee the autonomy of the detail: insofar as its freedom is taken lightly, it is lost. Exaggerated attention to fragments serves mainly to *conceal* the whole, not to excise it. In the music of the culture industry, the tyranny of the whole is generally imposed and sustained metrically: songs are composed around simple rhythmic patterns and even their more complex elements must constantly subordinate themselves to the 'beat.' The musical content seems to change constantly; however the quiet domination of rhythm binds that content to a pattern that repeats itself over and over again. It follows that pop music is especially insidious because it successfully hides its repetitive base beneath a seemingly free style. Adorno's favourite examples for demonstrating 'pseudo-individuation' are the techniques of syncopation and vibrato in jazz. He is notoriously hostile to jazz, describing it as a musical form 'which fuses the most rudimentary melodic, harmonic, metric and formal structure with the ostensibly disruptive principle of syncopation, yet without ever really disturbing the crude unity of the basic rhythm, the identically sustained metre, the quarter-note.'[19] Syncopation refers to a temporary displacement in the metric accents of a musical passage and is typically secured by stressing the weak beat while vibrato indicates slight, rapid variations in pitch that can add warmth and 'expressiveness' to an instrument or voice. These musical devices seem to disturb and break apart the dominant repetitive rhythmic patterns and are praised for just that reason when jazz identifies itself as a vital and spontaneous musical form; however, they are only momentary diversions, and they quickly fall back into line once the beat reasserts itself, which it inevitably does. Adorno reads this 'resistance' in Oedipal terms as nothing more than 'a kind of backtalk to the father in which readiness to knuckle under is already implied.'[20] Even the improvisations themselves are quickly standardized and integrated into the repertoire of the culture industry; they are there to provide, as required, the semblance of spontaneity, vitality, individuality, and/or rebellion against authority.[21] The forms by which interruptions are subordinated to a 'master-code' vary within and between different cultural mediums. In the content of most films, for example, any contradictions or tensions that surface are 'magically' resolved at their conclusion: 'and they all lived happily ever after.' Variations are permitted but only on the condition that they ultimately be trumped by a standardized norm.

Mass culture is fixated on detail and deceptively creates the sensation of immediacy in a world where everything is mediated through exchange.[22] Popular music 'leaves no room for conceptual reflection between itself and the subject and so it creates an illusion of immediacy in the totally mediated world, of proximity between strangers, of warmth for those who come to feel the chill of unmitigated struggle of all against all.'[23] The more that human social relations are abstracted and reified, the more people must be assured of their continued capacity for feeling and emotion. Hardened against the innumerable shocks of everyday life, we are moved to tears by a sentimental melody that reassures us that we still have our humanity. Divested of any relationship with the whole or other elements, the individual detail effectively exaggerates its facticity, its concreteness: it appears as something that simply is – something that should be enjoyed, felt, experienced as is – and one is discouraged from giving any thought to its origin, history, or potential. When we are engaged with these details, it often seems as if we *directly* experience them in a way that touches something deep within us, arousing, for example, 'pure' emotions of love, fear, desire, happiness and so on. Yet for Adorno, such an elision of the distance between subject and object is an entirely ideological moment: 'thought may only hold true to the idea of immediacy by way of the mediated, but it becomes the prey of the mediated the instant it grasps directly for the unmediated.'[24] Instead of demonstrating the impossibility of such experience as modern art struggles to do, mass culture assumes the position of its gatekeeper: by consuming its products we are fooling ourselves into thinking, believing, and feeling that we are still able to have real experiences. As the real impoverishment of human existence grows, the culture industry must continually strive, by way of technology, to expand its capacity to deliver ever more powerful stimuli directly to all the human senses at once. Hence the Wagnerian ideal of the *Gesamtkunstwerk* – the fusion of all arts into one work – comes to fruition in mass culture: 'The accord between word, image, and music is achieved so much more perfectly than in *Tristan* because the sensuous elements, which compliantly document only the surface of social reality, are produced in principle within the same technical work process, the unity of which they express as their true content.'[25] The need for better and more totalizing sensory stimulus – one of the driving forces behind the evolution of entertainment technology – is rooted in the ever-increasing difficulty of cultivating a sense of immediacy in a thoroughly administered and mediated world.

One might expect that such technology would facilitate an escapist mass culture that seeks to hide the drudgery of contemporary existence. A mere glance at the content of much mass culture could lead one to this opinion; however, a deeper analysis of the structures and forms used in its production leads to the conclusion that under capitalism there is actually a growing concordance between the products of the culture industry and everyday life. Horkheimer and Adorno explain how the culture industry increasingly reproduces the world outside: 'The more densely and completely [the film's] techniques duplicate empirical objects, the more easily it creates the illusion that the world outside is a seamless extension of the one which has been revealed in the cinema.'[26] Mass culture has become a 'poetry of its own nourished upon the work ethic.'[27] As we shall see in Chapter Three, Benjamin thinks that film can be a progressive medium – that surrealistic techniques such as montage can be mobilized to shock audiences out of a state of complacency. In a critique of these views, Adorno notes that 'when I spent a day in the studios at Neubabelsberg a couple of years ago, what impressed me most of all was how *little* montage and all the advanced techniques [Benjamin] emphasize[s] were actually used; rather, it seems as though reality is always *constructed* with an infantile attachment to the mimetic and then "photographed."'[28] Instead of shocking audiences, technological advances in areas such as film are deployed by the culture industry to systematically reduce and ultimately eradicate the distance between art and life. Some might argue that the iconic character of film necessarily predisposes it toward this collapsing of sign and referent; however, as avant-garde cinema clearly demonstrates, many sophisticated techniques such as discontinuous editing, slow motion, and special effects exist that could easily be used to destabilize the relation between film and what it depicts. Yet such disruption rarely appears in the films of the culture industry. For example, sound – both music and speech – is used to reduce rather than accentuate the shock and discomfort aroused by the mediation of the real through technology.[29] The labelling of modern films as 'escapist' is deeply ironic for Adorno, because all the consumers of these films actually escape from is the possibility of imagining another life: 'It is not because they turn their back on washed-out existence that escape films are so repugnant, but because they do not do so energetically enough, because they are themselves just as washed-out, because the satisfactions they fake coincide with the ignominy of reality, of denial. The dreams have no dream.'[30] Similarly, any imaginative tendency present in music such as jazz is permitted only on the condition that it 'tirelessly strive to remake itself in the image of reality, to repeat the latter's commands to itself, to submit to them.'[31] In short, any tension or contradiction between culture and reality has been steadily eroded by the increasingly sophisticated technology and primitive aesthetic techniques of the culture industry.

The striking unity of culture and reality, of detail and whole, of cultural object and artistic style, that Adorno describes furnishes a model of mass culture: 'the false identity of universal and particular.'[32] True aesthetic creativity in both the production and the reception of art feeds on the structural tension that lingers between individual details, artworks, and the styles of which they are more than mere examples. In the bourgeois period, great art did not arise out of the flawless construction of unity or the effortless imposition of aesthetic form on the raw material of sound, matter, or words. Such material is never 'raw' or natural for Adorno; it is never a *tabula rasa* on which the artist freely imposes her will. Rather, it is always embedded in a socio-historical context and presents the artist with a set of demands and possibilities that can only be expressed, developed, and satisfied as they are mediated through (*not* subsumed by) aesthetic styles that represent – albeit in a condensed form – tradition, history, and the accumulation of human experience. The culture industry abandons this model of cultural creation, and flees as it does so the necessary failures that inevitably accompany the truthful, passionate striving for reconciliation in bourgeois art and the associated mental and physical suffering that such failure inspires.[33] Mass cultural practices gorge themselves on the illusion that they have escaped these dilemmas; they exchange unfulfilled longing for the pleasures of immediate gratification. However, the illusion of total freedom is but the mirror image of total captivity. The seeming absence of style becomes nothing but its complete and utter victory. And, 'being nothing other than style, [the culture industry] divulges style's secret: obedience to the social hierarchy.'[34]

## The Commodification of Culture: Exchange-Value Triumphant

Initially, the extension of capitalist social relations to aesthetic production and distribution had an emancipatory effect: freed from the direct bondage of religious service and patronage, artists were allowed a greater opportunity to focus exclusively on the immanent logic of their products. 'The purposelessness of the great modern work of art is sustained by the anonymity of the market. The latter's demands are so diversely mediated that the artist is exempted from any particular claim.'[35] Thus capitalism gives birth to the autonomous art of the eighteenth and nineteenth centuries, which comes to pride itself on its capacity to turn its back on the issues and problems of the day and to create art for the sake of art itself. However, this newly found aesthetic autonomy does not come without a price: the relationship between art and society does not disappear; rather, it migrates into questions of form. The human capacity for cultural creation was originally born from the separation of mental and physical labour, and all cultural activities bear the mark of this original sin: their utopian claims to beauty and transcendence have ever since rested on the misery and suffering of humanity. As Benjamin famously puts it. 'There is no document of culture which is not at the same time a document of barbarism.'[36] By virtue of their freedom from the direct tutelage of feudal social relations wrought by commodification, the masterpieces of bourgeois art are finally able to express this 'guilt' of art in its purest form. The historical quality of its material and the sociality of the labour through which it 'works' on this material force autonomous art to take the contradictions of social, political, and economic structures into its very core as mediated through aesthetic styles. In the very best works, such incorporation is ultimately a toxic act, necessarily poisoning the dreams of identity and reconciliation harboured by all cultural objects. But only in failure can art give true expression to real human suffering: 'that is the secret of aesthetic sublimation: to present fulfillment in its brokenness.'[37] Unfortunately, the moment of aesthetic freedom initially provided by the commodity form was all too brief; in the twentieth century that freedom quickly eroded as cultural production was increasingly organized as a profit-making industry.

For Adorno, the extension of capitalist social relations is not simply the displacement of one type of economic production by another. It also represents the culmination of a 'dialectic of enlightenment' that traces out a universal history 'leading from the slingshot to the megaton bomb.'[38] Initially born out of desperate attempts to control a hostile and terrifying nature, human societies gradually develop an instrumental reason that increases their capacity to predict, manipulate, and dominate the natural environment. Conventional wisdom charts this transition as a move from myth to enlightenment; for their part, Horkheimer and Adorno theorize these two seemingly distinct human eras as dialectically intertwined. Mythic forms already embodied the human desire to dominate nature and foreshadowed the identitarian logic of the Enlightenment *vis-à-vis* substitution through sacrifice; the illusion of modern thinking – whether in its positivist or idealist varieties – that it has entirely purified itself of the contaminants of natural history delivers enlightenment back into the world of myth. Thus, 'myth is already enlightenment, and enlightenment reverts to mythology.'[39] One of the primary sins of modern thought is its tendency to assume that real, material, historical subjects and objects can be adequately and completely represented through concepts: humanity accommodates its fear of the unknown by conceptually liquidating anything that cannot be integrated into its own rational structures: 'Nothing is allowed to remain outside, since the mere idea of the "outside" is the real source of fear.'[40] Anything that can be classified and/or quantified can be theoretically subjected to human knowledge and control; anything that cannot serves only to dramatize the limits of knowledge and experience, summoning memories of a time when humans lived in terror of an uncontrollable environment. That which is other must be integrated, abolished, or banished to the sphere of art and fantasy.

Needless to say, these processes do not occur in the mind alone. The 'will to identity' has embedded itself in many different social structures and institutions throughout human history. That being said, the commodity form is the most perfect manifestation of this logic. As Jameson explains, Adorno is persuaded by Marx of the terrifying power of commodification to subsume all particularities, all non-identity, all 'use-value,' beneath the all-encompassing category of exchange:

> How is it, when the consumption (or 'use') of any specific object is unique, and constitutes a unique and incomparable event in our own lives as well, that we are able to think of such things as 'the same'? Sameness here is not merely the concept of the category of this particular object (several different things being steaks, cars, linen, or books) but also, and above all, the equivalence of their *value*, the possibility we have historically constructed of comparing them (one car for so many pounds of steak), when in terms of experience or consumption – in other words, of use value – they remain incomparable and speculation is incapable of weighing the experience of eating this particular steak against that of a drive in the country. Exchange value, then, the emergence of some third, abstract term between two incomparable objects ... constitutes the primordial form by which identity emerges in human history.[41]

The penetration of the commodity form into aesthetic production is, therefore, particularly damaging to an activity which, for Adorno, was especially suited to the affirmation and expression of sensuous particularity. Insofar as the logic of identity penetrates the creation and reception of art through commodification, it effectively dissolves art's ability to reflect social contradictions through the tension between detail and whole. Instead, culture becomes the false identity of the particular and the universal; its internal relations, techniques, and forms are restructured around equivalence, calculability, and effect. The false resolution or erasure of contradictions displaces their sophisticated exploration: every thing comes to be perfectly integrated with every other thing. Parallel to the totalitarian positivism that dominates science, Adorno argues that the obsession with identity ultimately drains all time, history, and potential from cultural objects in terms of both their forms and the material that is mediated through them. Although it once freed art from the direct bondage of feudal relations, commodification quickly becomes an even more effective taskmaster, imposing the most precise, extensive, and insidious controls over cultural activity that have ever existed.

At its most obvious level, such control is exercised through the rational organization of cultural production into the culture industry. Initially guided by Friedrich Pollock's analysis of the massive organizational power of democratic state capitalism,[42] Horkheimer and Adorno select this term to draw attention to how culture is produced and ordered from the top down:

> The culture industry fuses the old and familiar into a new quality. In all its branches, products which are tailored for consumption by masses, and which to a great extent determine the nature of that consumption, are manufactured more or less according to plan. The individual branches are similar in structure or at least fit into each other, ordering themselves into a system almost without a gap. This is made possible by contemporary technical capabilities as well as economic and administrative concentration. The culture industry intentionally integrates its consumers from above.[43]

The creation of such an industry is driven by the objective of making a profit from the sale of culture. References to products being manufactured 'according to plan' and to 'economic and administrative concentration' that 'intentionally integrates its consumers from above' summon the spectre of a totalitarian system under which information ministries disseminate propaganda to brainwash a helpless population. In the 1940s, this sort of rhetoric played a key role in illuminating the ideological similarities between liberal democracies and authoritarian governments in the mid-twentieth century. It also alluded to the more visible, direct, and extensive forms of control required to ensure that cultural production conformed to the logic of commodification at a time when the memory of cultural practices that were something other than commodities was still potent. Today, the pervasiveness of commodification and of corporate cultures organized around the quest for 'synergies' means that such controls have largely been internalized by most cultural producers, who are fully cognizant of – if not always entirely sympathetic to – the need for mass culture to turn a profit easily and quickly. As Bill Ryan's excellent study of corporate cultural production shows,

> the interests of capital are not something external to an otherwise independent labour process. The rules of valorisation and realisation enter into its very constitution, as personified by creative management and realised through their decisions and directions ... The imperatives of accumulation are *built into* functional relations between the different types of workers which comprise the [creative] team itself.[44]

Rigid lines of bureaucratic authority have been replaced by flexible networks of coordination which ensure that information and resources are directed into the production of material that can be smoothly integrated into existing patterns of distribution, promotion, and consumption.

It is not the mere sale of cultural products that Adorno finds so offensive: as noted earlier, the initial commodification of art was limited to the sale of finished works in the marketplace. Just as the commodification of labour power does not immediately result in the direct control of capitalists over the labour process, so too the artist initially had substantial liberty in creating discrete products, which were then sold. However, the incentive to realize a profit has led to the increasing application of rationalized techniques to production itself, and this has sounded the death knell for autonomous art. The development of the immanent problems of a particular work, which is precisely how art is able to also express broader social issues, is sacrificed in favour of the production of something that has a marketable effect on its audience and can therefore be quickly sold. The initial imposition of this schematic on the chaotic and unruly practices of popular culture, and the guarded autonomy of serious art, required the formation of a hierarchical culture industry. Gradually, though, this schematic has been internalized so that it has become almost impossible to conceptualize the creation of culture – even at the most basic level – as guided by anything other than its potential effect on others. For Adorno, 'no work of art, regardless of what its maker thinks of it, is directed toward an observer, not even toward a transcendental subject of apperception; no artwork is to be described or explained in terms of the categories of communication.'[45] The organizing principle of aesthetic creation and cultural criticism ought to be guided by how and why aesthetic objects are produced, not how they are received. Yet this is exactly what occurs under capitalism: the effect of a particular work on an audience comes to take precedence over its truth content. Culture is made specifically for the purpose of being sold; production is subordinated to distribution, and the promise of art is thereby dissolved.

It is the process of capital formation itself (i.e., the need to make a profit through the circulation of goods) that introduces, maintains, and enforces the structural equivalence between different cultural products: 'This [capitalist] work process integrates all the elements of production, from the original concept of the novel, shaped by its sidelong glance at film, to the last sound effect. It is the triumph of invested capital. To impress the omnipotence of capital on the hearts of expropriated job candidates as the power of their true master is the purpose of all films, regardless of the plot selected by the production directors.'[46]

This is most obvious in capital/technology-intensive forms of cultural production such as film, which are forced to adopt the techniques of production pioneered in other industries.[47] The creation of cultural products is efficiently divided into its constituent parts, which can then be individually perfected to extract the desired response from the audience. The detachment of specific parts from the whole facilitates the maximum extraction of surplus value, since each component can be repeatedly cycled through the marketplace. For instance, a film generates revenue not only through its initial distribution, but also through the extraction, packaging, and reselling of its images, sounds, and stories in an ever-expanding consumptive cycle. For example, *The Lion King* (1994) earned $300 million at the box office but generated a total profit of over $1 billion via the reprocessing of its images, music, and characters through the vast array of media that form the Disney empire as well as through licensing arrangements to 'brand' commodities from fast food to children's clothing.[48] For Adorno, forms of cultural production and reception that fixate on the detail and the isolated fragment are simply incompatible with the free development of the internal logic of a particular aesthetic object. They 'purge the life-process of all that is uncontrollable, unpredictable, incalculable in advance and thus deprive it of what is genuinely new.'[49] The application of profit-driven mass-production techniques to aesthetic activities leaves a frozen, synchronic, and lifeless cultural landscape in its wake.

One of the cornerstones of Marx's theory of commodity fetishism is the way that exchange in a market environment disguises the labour that originally produced the commodity, that gave it 'value.' The commodity itself is assumed to naturally possess properties that are in fact the result of and properly attributed to human activity. Thus, the social nature of the good – the fact that it was made by human beings for others – is ultimately lost. 'All reification is a forgetting,' notes Adorno. 'Objects become purely thing-like the moment they are retained for us without the continued presence of their other aspects: when something of them has been forgotten.'[50] This dynamic is no less valid for cultural products than for the goods and services of the industrial system. It helps transform cultural objects and processes – and more important, the world they depict – into autonomous, independent entities and structures that cannot be controlled by human beings. For Adorno, one of the most important qualities of modern art is that it foregrounds its synthetic genesis through an increasingly abstract form: it explicitly highlights the fact that it is an object *without* an apparent function that has been deliberately made by human labour. When we watch a film or listen to the radio, however, little indication is provided to us regarding how the offering was composed, directed, or performed. Instead, curiosity about these aspects of culture is pervasively channelled into an obsessive fascination with gossip about the lives, habits, and scandals of cultural celebrities. Put another way, one of the priorities of cultural technology is to excise the memory of human activity in mass culture. For example, special effects in film are deemed praiseworthy insofar as they merge effortlessly with the realist narrative, and they are disparaged if they break up this continuity and remind us of the artifice of culture. The content of popular culture is not necessarily translated directly into everyday life, but people are encouraged to organize and interpret their experiences in an equally rigid and mechanical fashion.[51] Consequently, cultural objects are fetishized insofar as they discretely assume qualities that are more properly attributable to the nexus of social relations, human beings, and the material practices that create them. Moreover, the world that is faithfully duplicated by mass culture similarly becomes reified as an autonomous entity beyond human control, as a 'second nature' to which individuals have no choice but to adapt and submit. Just as dead labour comes back to haunt the living in the form of capital, the filtration of culture's production and distribution through the commodity form helps erase its human origins, reifying it into an external entity that stands over and against those who originally made it.

This dynamic takes on particular significance for Adorno insofar as the main quality that is fetishized in the exchange process is exchange-value itself. The culture industry thesis proposes that commodification reaches its most extreme in the objects of mass culture, with use-value being *entirely* replaced by exchange-value.[52] At its most basic level, this can be understood as referring to the fact that people are now only capable of evaluating aesthetic objects based on their value in the marketplace: 'The unified standard of value consists in the level of conspicuous production, the amount of investment put on show.'[53] In going to a concert, for example, the consumer is not appreciating the music on its own terms, but only 'worshipping the money that he himself has paid for the ticket.'[54] Pleasurable participation in culture is thereby regulated by and even confined to the act of exchange. However the *open* displacement of use-value by exchange-value is but one, relatively minor, aspect of Adorno's claim. The culture industry does not hide the fact that its products are designed for sale; furthermore, it markets them as satisfying the needs and desires of its customers. Indeed, much of the system's success rests on its ability to combine these two claims. After all, culture seems to be something that one 'uses' immediately through various perceptive and tactile faculties. Most of us, following the act of purchase, believe and feel that we are engaged in a relation of immediacy or pure use with the culture industry's products. However, for Adorno, 'quick reactions, unballasted by a mediating constitution, do not restore spontaneity, but establish the person as a measuring instrument deployed and calibrated by a central authority.'[55] Cultural consumption takes place in a market environment in which the only thing that is actually being used is the exchange-value of the commodity:

> The appearance of immediacy takes possession of the mediated exchange-value itself. If the commodity in general combines exchange-value and use-value, then the pure use-value, whose illusion the cultural goods must preserve in completely capitalist society, must be replaced by pure exchange-value, which precisely in its capacity as exchange-value deceptively takes over the function of use-value ... The feelings which go to the exchange value create the appearance of immediacy at the same time as the absence of a relation to the object belies it ... The more inexorably the principle of exchange-value destroys use-values for human beings, the more deeply does exchange-value disguise itself as the object of enjoyment.[56]

In other words, the consumption of mass culture conditions people to think and feel that the only real, natural, or pleasurable use-value of an object lies in its exchange-value. In a terrifying reversal of fortune, the very same characteristics that once guarded the promise of culture – its self-isolation from the utilitarian functionalism of the 'practical' world – now serve as the foundation for its utter betrayal. The appearance that culture can separate itself from other social spheres is precisely what constitutes its exchange-value in the first place: it is the illusion of immediacy and 'pure' experience that is being sold. Historically, there is a real basis for both folk culture and serious art to be consumed in this way: each once provided, in its own unique fashion, a temporary, ideological, and conditional but still real emancipation from the drudgery of social existence. However, the production of cultural goods is now utterly dominated by the commodity form itself, and the emancipatory immediacy they cultivate is based exclusively on the pure mediation of exchange. We might think or feel that we are escaping the world by losing ourselves in a film or popular music, but really, we are being trained to derive pleasure from exchange-value itself. As culture – one of the main activities from which human beings derive pleasure – is thoroughly commodified, capitalism itself starts to *feel* good.

This is not simply an instrumental deduction rooted in the market's capacity to deliver all manner of cultural delights; more important, it feels good because the very forms of these cultural goods, and, consequently, the patterns of human cognition and experience needed to enjoy them, are based on the logic of identity and exchange: 'Now equivalence itself becomes a fetish.'[57] Interchangeability, repetition, pseudo-individuation: the categories through which culture is conceived, produced and consumed are now determined by capital. The aesthetic 'problems' with which culture now occupies itself are entirely subservient to the profit motive. The cultural object becomes little more than an aesthetic after-effect of the logic of exchange. In consuming these objects and structuring our cognitive, somatic, and affective patterns accordingly, we are literally consuming exchange value – and not simply in the banal sense that the product is purchased, but because its structure is so thoroughly defined by the commodity form. In fact, this 'structure of feeling' is so deeply embedded in late capitalism that cultural goods no longer even need to be bought and sold: '[Culture] is so completely subject to the law of exchange that it is no longer exchanged; it is so blindly equated with use that it can no longer be used. For this reason it merges with the advertisement.'[58] And just as advertising helps lock us into certain forms of consumptive behaviour, a commodified culture takes on that function for capitalism at large: 'It has been asked what the cement is which still holds the world of commodities together. The answer is that this transfer of the use-value of consumption goods to their exchange-value contributes to a general order in which eventually every pleasure which emancipates itself from exchange-value takes on subversive features. The appearance of exchange-value in commodities has taken on a specific cohesive function.'[59]

A thing is not valued or 'useful' until after it has been marketed and distributed as a commodity: 'Advertising today is a negative principle, a blocking device: anything which does not bear its seal of approval is economically suspect.'[60] Any properties of an object – and increasingly of subjects themselves – that defy this logic are either suspect and excluded or gradually transformed into exchange-value itself. In Andreas Huyssen's apt terms, 'the commodification of art ends up in the aestheticization of the commodity.'[61] The fetish character of cultural commodities helps produce a particular kind of 'one-dimensional' consciousness. Goods, services, and people are not to be – and for many, can no longer be – understood in any sense other than their value in the marketplace. This legitimation of exchange-value and the consequent eradication of use-value that is at once openly admitted and deeply hidden is one of the most important ways that the culture industry enhances the social cohesion of late capitalist society.

As one might expect, cultural objects and activities that are dominated by the commodity form bear substantial affinities with the organization of productive labour under capitalism. As humanity devotes fewer and fewer resources to socially necessary labour, it has greater time away from the workplace. However, this separation of work and leisure is largely illusory, since the kinds of activities that people practise in their free time secretly reproduce the conditions of work. The drugging rhythms of the machine are the industrial counterpart to the repetitive structures of jazz and modern film: the commodity form binds them tightly together. The commodification and rationalization of labour has led to an increasingly precise control over the minds and bodies of workers. Human activity is subordinated to the demands of efficient production: it must adapt itself to the needs of the machine.[62] On the one hand, bored by the endless repetition of the assembly line or sales counter, people want novelty in their leisure time; on the other hand, the exhaustion inherent in the labour process means that most are either unwilling or unable to devote the concentration that would be required to truly break from the patterns of thought and experience to which they have become accustomed at work: 'They want standardized goods and pseudo-individuation, because their leisure is an escape from work and at the same time is molded after those psychological attitudes to which their workaday world exclusively habituates them.'[63] While leisure masquerades as 'free time,' it is an open secret that its true purpose is to replenish one's working energies. And the ability to submit once again to the machine, to the 'system,' is only possible if the memory of that machine doesn't stray too far from body and mind: 'The only escape from the work process in factory and office is through adaptation to it in leisure time. This is the incurable sickness of all entertainment. Amusement congeals into boredom, since, to be amusement, it must cost no effort and therefore moves strictly along the well-worn grooves of association.'[64] Conscious subordination to the machine may be relaxed, but the secret, subconscious discipline imposed by production cannot simply be shrugged off through inactivity: it can only be displaced by the conscious effort to adopt a different way of thinking and being. Such activity does not leave one refreshed for the next day's work; furthermore, it makes it that much more difficult to switch back to the forms of behaviour and thought required in the workplace: 'No spark of reflection is allowed to fall into leisure time, since it might otherwise leap across to the workaday world and set it on fire.'[65] Work and leisure are bound together in an unholy alliance: the culture industry openly celebrates its independence from production, selling its products as 'freedom' from the drudgery of the everyday, all the while secretly delivering its consumers ever-deeper into the clutches of a world from which they so anxiously desire to escape.[66]

## Mass Culture and Cognition: The End of Autonomy

What kind of cognitive patterns does such a culture produce? What type is required in order for it to become a *mass* culture? How does the culture industry structure the way people see, think about, and experience the social and material environment? For Horkheimer and Adorno, the idealist philosophy of Kant ironically provides one of the clearest testaments to the fate of thought and experience as it passes through the dialectic of enlightenment. In *Critique of Pure Reason*, Kant describes how raw sensory data are processed and synthesized into human experience based on certain *a priori* transcendental categories. Data are subsumed under various concepts in order to allow human beings to make conceptual sense of their environment. The schematic through which we understand the world is one that we ourselves bring to it. For Kant, this schematic of apperception is timeless and ahistorical. Inspired by Hegel's dialectical critique of Kant's synchronic philosophical system, Georg Lukacs famously argues that these transcendental categories of cognition are, in fact, historically specific and dependent on socioeconomic structures. In late capitalism, for example, categories of perception and understanding are broadly constructed according to the functions of equivalence (exchange) and calculability (rationalization). Building on Lukacs's critique, Adorno is sharply critical of Kant's hypostatization of the historical conditions of the emerging bourgeoisie as timeless and existential for the human species. Nevertheless, he also believes that Kant's system is a model for understanding how the culture industry – and more broadly, capitalism itself – forms and structures human experience: 'The senses are determined by the conceptual apparatus in advance of perception; the citizen sees the world as made *a priori* of the stuff from which he himself constructs it. Kant intuitively anticipated what Hollywood has consciously put into practice: images are precensored during production by the same standard of understanding which will later determine their reception by viewers.'[67] It is not transcendental reason that defines the categories of cognition; rather, it is the culture industry as dominated by the commodity form. Instead of challenging the logic of production, which remains the ever-present potential of aesthetic activity, contemporary mass cultural consumption actually helps forge the fetters that lock us into the restrictive cognitive patterns imposed by capitalism.

Adorno is fond of noting that mass culture does our thinking for us: we are fed 'predigested' products that have already been conceptually organized and processed for easy consumption: 'The active contribution which Kantian schematism still expected of subjects – that they should, from the first, relate sensuous multiplicity to fundamental concepts – is denied to the subject by [the culture] industry. It purveys schematism as its first service to the customer.'[68] For Kant, the cognitive process involves the active subsumption of raw, sensory data into the various concepts of understanding. For Adorno, true experience – both aesthetic and otherwise – arises out of the tension or dialectic between the familiar and the unfamiliar; it forces us to actively think about what we are seeing and feeling in light of our past and our future, and even to speculate on alternatives to the present. However, the 'data' provided by the culture industry have already been organized and classified. One does not have to impose stereotypes on the movies, songs, and stories of mass culture, comparing them to other experiences or analyzing them to see how they both fit into and challenge existing conceptual frameworks. Rather, in the ultimate triumph of style, they come prepackaged for immediate consumption. Films and television programs, radio broadcasts, and popular music have already been so extensively organized, sorted, and classified that there is nothing left for people to schematize. Cultural difference becomes, first and foremost, a function of the marketplace: 'Sharp distinctions like those between A and B films, or between short stories published in magazines in different price segments, do not so much reflect real differences as assist in the classification, organization, and identification of consumers. Something is provided for everyone so that no one can escape; differences are hammered home and propagated.'[69] The cognitive dimension of cultural experience is limited to the mere sorting of sensations into a crude schematic according to the labels firmly stamped on them at the point of production: 'The composition hears for the listener.'[70] At best, anything that ventures outside these stereotypes is ignored; at worst, it inspires a combination of fear and hatred that demands the destruction of that which remains outside one's understanding and control. Thus, the capacity to have new experiences, to critically reflect on things that do not fit into a predetermined cognitive schematic, is fatally damaged.

Adorno recognizes that mass culture needs to compensate for its arbitrary restriction of the cognitive process. It does this through the increasingly sophisticated use of modern entertainment technology to multiply the force and type of sensual stimuli with which it can bombard consumers. The profusion of such stimuli requires constant attentiveness to process the visual, aural, and tactile sensations that are produced at any given moment. Sustained thought on any particular aspect is impossible because of the sheer volume of details that must be absorbed and sorted. People must learn to react automatically, rapidly processing the details without thinking, and doing so according to the cues provided, or they will inevitably be left behind:

> The wither of imagination and spontaneity in the consumer of culture today need not be traced back to psychological mechanisms. The products themselves, especially the most characteristic, the sound film, cripple those faculties through their objective makeup. They are so constructed that their adequate comprehension requires a quick, observant, knowledgeable cast of mind but positively debars the spectator from thinking, if he is not to miss the fleeting facts ... The required qualities of attention have become so familiar from other films and other culture products already known to him or her that they appear automatically. The power of industrial society is imprinted on people once and for all.[71]

This is more than merely an echo of the traditional arguments of cultural conservatives – arguments which assert that a restriction of cognition is a necessary corollary of mass culture's technological capacity to flood the senses with a dazzling array of sensations. Film, television, and music do not have to be this way. Instead, their current shortcomings are attributed mainly to the restrictions imposed through the domination of cultural production and society at large by the commodity form. Technology is mobilized to produce the interchangeable parts needed by the culture industry instead of the considerable variation demanded by modern aesthetics.

Contemporary cultural products are not the only victims of this dynamic. Even the most critical works of art and their reception are colonized through their endless repetition: 'Anyone who would decide to paint cubistically in 1970 would be safe providing posters useful for advertisements.'[72] It is not the mere passage of time that dulls the critical edge of serious art. Rather, it is the capacity of the culture industry to swallow these works and disgorge them in a context that aligns them with the consumptive patterns of mass culture. Memories of the aesthetic styles that these artworks once rebelled against have been dissolved, inevitably dulling the critical impulse that once honed its edge against the grindstone of tradition. The commodification of serious art actually leads to (the perception of) constitutional changes in the objects themselves: 'They become vulgarized. Irrelevant consumption destroys them. Not merely do the few things played again and again wear out, like the Sistine Madonna in the bedroom, but reification affects their internal structure. They are transformed into a conglomeration of irruptions which are impressed on the listeners by climax and repetition, while the organization of the whole makes no impression whatsoever.'[73]

In this way, the commodification of culture directs people's attention to the smallest and most insignificant details, ostensibly offering satisfaction of the intense desire for the new that is a constant companion to life in a world of the ever-same. We are both unable and unwilling to perceive and contemplate the relation between these fragmented moments and the whole; as a result, our attention is captured by whatever the spotlight illuminates. The current moment completely absorbs our attention; then, as our attentiveness is displaced to the next set of sensations, the previous set becomes little more than an abstract memory. 'Channel-surfing' – the privileged mode of contemporary interaction with television, and thus, perhaps the dominant cultural activity in advanced capitalist societies – perfectly expresses this basic logic. Concordantly, the mode of apperception becomes synchronic, static, and dehistoricized, entirely preoccupied with the singular detail as detached from any kind of context. To satisfy a never-ending appetite for novelty, the culture industry must constantly 'jazz up' these individual fragments in order to sustain attention and promote consumption; the impoverished sense of experience that inevitably accompanies the compartmentalization of thinking, feeling, and existing must be compensated for by the spiralling intensification of cultural sensations from moment to moment.

The pervasiveness of this type of cultural consumption in everyday life has profound cognitive implications. Among the most important is that people are increasingly unable to recognize, understand, and experience contradictions in their lives *as* contradictions. The perception of contradictions requires the capacity to bring two or more sensations, ideas, or objects into a comparative relationship in which their dissimilarities can be examined within a shared whole. In existential terms, it requires that experience be organized temporally into an overarching narrative continuum of both personal and collective self-identity. As this temporal dimension is effectively spatialized in mass culture – each cultural object repeats the patterns of the preceding object as though it were doing so for the first time – and as cognitive patterns are adjusted accordingly, we in effect sacrifice our capacity to experience and reflect on the contradictions that exist within and between things and social relations:

> Whatever problems of psychological fate the film may present, through parading the events past the viewer on the screen the power of the oppositions involved and the possibility of freedom within them is denied and reduced to the abstract temporal relationship of before and after. The eye of the camera which has perceived the conflict before the viewer and projected it upon the unresisting smoothly unfolding reel of film has already taken care that the conflicts are not conflicts at all.[74]

Once again, this is not a technological determinism; rather, it is a social one imposed by the logic of the commodity form. Film does not have to reproduce reality as a series of abstract temporal moments: this formal dynamic is forced upon it by the culture industry. And so the culture industry ideologically realizes the task that Kant had originally ascribed to reason itself: 'This harmony of nature with our cognitive faculty is presupposed *a priori* by the Judgement.'[75] This is not to say that conflict itself and the suffering imposed by socioeconomic contradictions are absent from mass culture; indeed, many of its genres are rooted in their depiction. That being said, the repetitive cultural forms through which these images and ideas are unceasingly expressed reinforce cognitive patterns that are incapable of sustaining any critical thought on the subject at hand: 'If an astrologer urges his readers to drive carefully on a particular day, that certainly hurts no one; they will, however, be harmed indeed by the stupefaction which lies in the claim that advice which is valid every day and which is therefore idiotic, needs the approval of the stars.'[76] Anger, frustration, and misery at social injustice may boil up into a rage at one moment, then dissipate in the next, replaced by a different set of emotions solicited by another set of stimuli. In his analysis of astrology columns from The *Los Angeles Times*, Adorno calls this behaviour 'bi-phasic.'[77] The 'healthy' citizen must necessarily become schizophrenic, distributing the contradictory requirements of life over different periods of the day. Social conflict is managed by taking 'the individual apart as it were, into adaptive and autonomous components, thus implicitly endorsing the actual impossibility of much praised "integration."'[78] The ephemeralization of experience that results from this is in part an entirely rational response to a social reality in which individuals are increasingly powerless to effect change: Why be troubled by a world that cannot be changed anyway? However, the tentative, defensive character of such reasoning is inevitably displaced by a serialized process of cognition that functions *a priori* to prevent contradictions themselves from entering one's consciousness.[79]

In short, both the products of the culture industry and the manner in which they are generally consumed militate against the kind of mediation that is needed for critical thought. Horkheimer and Adorno summarize these changes in the cognitive process: 'Knowledge does not consist in mere perception, classification, and calculation but precisely in the determining negation of whatever is directly at hand. Instead of such negation, mathematical formalism, whose medium, number, is the most abstract form of the immediate, arrests thought at mere immediacy. The actual is validated, knowledge confines itself to repeating it, thought makes itself mere tautology.'[80]

Critical cognition requires the 'determinate negation' of immediacy. In its Hegelian form, this refers to the projection of human will onto objects external to it: human beings fully actualize themselves only through conscious and reflective interaction with products made through the mixing of human labour – conceptual or otherwise – with nature. Adorno is sharply critical of the idealist, totalitarian flavour of Hegel's philosophy; in Hegel, the subject comes to completely dominate the object by ultimately seeing only itself, in the form of *Geist*, in it. However, he does recognize that the critical, intentional 'determinate negation' of immediate reality through conceptual reflection is the only means by which one can truly explore the barriers to thought and thus negatively grasp for the changing essence of the object, as well as help to emancipate the potential frozen within objects by an institutionalized logic of identity. Awareness that an object might be something other than it is constitutes the emancipatory core of linguistic and other forms of expression: primitive animistic traditions foreshadow a dialectical semiotics that enables the determinate negation of the immediacy of the status quo; this in turn makes possible the introduction of a temporal and spatial counter-factual or speculative dimension to the contemplation of the existent:

> If the tree is addressed no longer as simply a tree but as evidence of something else, a location of *mana,* language expresses the contradiction that it is at the same time itself and something other than itself, identical and not identical. Through the deity speech is transformed from tautology to language. The concept, usually defined as the unity of the features of what it subsumes, was rather, from the first, a product of dialectical thinking, in which each thing is what it is only by becoming what it is not.[81]

As cultural forms and 'reality' increasingly come to mirror each other, this speculative dimension of semiotic expression is lost. In other words, the products of the culture industry do not allow people to reflexively secure the intellectual distance that is necessary for them to think critically about – to determinatively negate – the world around them. In *Minima Moralia,* Adorno writes that 'the value of a thought is measured by its distance from the continuity of the familiar. It is objectively devalued as this distance is reduced; the more it approximates to the pre-existing standard, the further its antithetical function is diminished.'[82] In the reception of mass culture, a false or premature sense of immediacy is cultivated that encourages a direct identification with the cultural product. Adorno does not believe that culture must only be thought and never felt; rather, he senses that serious aesthetic practice offers a unique opportunity for the tentative, partial, and momentary reunification of the mental and physical qualities of human *praxis* that have been pried apart by the dialectic of enlightenment. The affective sensations aroused by art ought to inspire concentration on the mimetic rationalities – and their objects – which make these sensations possible;

similarly, critical analysis of these alternative rationalities enables an enhanced appreciation and experience of culture's affective dimension. Conversely, the sensual temptations of the culture industry only appear thus: 'In the mechanical rigor of their repetition, the functions copied by the rhythm are themselves identical with those of the production processes which robbed the individual of his original body functions.'[83] Exhausted by the labour process and tempted by the culture industry's easy promises to bypass such reflection and proceed directly to existence, nature, self, and pure 'being,' people sacrifice the reflexive distance afforded by thought, submerge themselves in the 'pseudo-immediacy' of the moment, and are delivered all the more completely into the reified, mediated world of late capitalism. In this way pleasure becomes 'nature's vengeance.' As critical thought is sacrificed for submersion in the immediacy of the moment, society delivers itself into the hands of a 'second nature' that takes revenge for the horror wreaked upon the first.

Indeed, cognition becomes even less than an activity of classifying, schematizing, or mediating experience through different concepts; instead, it becomes simple recognition by way of a single conceptual framework. Given how the steady repetition of work and play short-circuits cognition, the only activity left for thought is the appreciation of the familiar: 'The familiarity of the piece is a surrogate for the quality ascribed to it. To like it is almost the same thing as to recognize it.'[84] Programs for musical appreciation and the social venues in which music is often consumed encourage this reaction: 'The [NBC] Music Appreciation Hour conceives of the "fun" one gets out of music as being practically identical with recognition.'[85] The act of recognition is not without its own species of benefits. At its most basic level, the sudden recognition of a piece – 'that's it!' – confirms that the object has not changed over time; this cultivates an illusory sense of stability, order, and self-identity. In addition, when we place a cultural object within a particular genre, we gain the satisfaction of belonging to a larger social group: 'One not only identifies [a particular work] innocently as being this or that, subsuming it under this or that category, but by the very act of identifying it, one also tends unwittingly to identify *oneself* with the objective social agencies of the power of those individuals who made this particular event fit into this pre-existing category and thus "established" it.'[86]

The act of integrating an object – an external entity – into a conceptual framework also carries with it the (sadistic) pleasures of ownership: the object effectively becomes the individual's property to do with as he or she wishes. Cultural curiosity of this kind, note Horkheimer and Adorno, 'is the anthropological sediment of that monopolistic compulsion to handle, to manipulate, to absorb everything, the inability to leave anything beyond itself untouched.'[87] In fact, the hidden appeal of the culture industry's pseudo-individuation stems from this dynamic. Deviations from standard forms fool us into thinking that we are getting something new; not only that, but they afford the consumer a vicarious disciplinary gratification as these deviations are conceptually forced back into line in the act of reception. In other words, mass culture cultivates a fictional sense of agency and participation by encouraging the listener or viewer to impose a predetermined structure on its products:

> In jazz the amateur listener is capable of replacing complicated rhythmical or harmonic formulas by the schematic ones which they represent and which they still suggest, however adventurous they appear. The ear deals with the difficulties of hit music by achieving slight substitutions derived from the knowledge of the patterns. The listener, when faced with the complicated, actually hears only the simple which it represents and perceives the complicated only as a parodistic distortion of the simple.[88]

More simply, 'every extravagant sonority must be so produced that the listener can recognize it as a substitute for a "normal" one.'[89] People are encouraged to misrecognize their subordination to formulaic patterns of cognition narcissistically – that is, as expressions of their own cultural savvy. Finally, this puerile fun is largely fetishized: the gratifications that accompany the process of identification (i.e., a particular kind of relation between subject and object) are associated exclusively with the objects themselves and their purchase. Thus, for Adorno, the buying and selling of culture becomes little more than the buying and selling of the practices of identification.

## 'Psychoanalysis in Reverse': The Psychodynamics of the Culture Industry

But why do these practices feel good? How are the standardized, repetitive, and pseudo-individualistic products of the culture industry able to give pleasure to their consumers? What needs do they satisfy? To answer these questions, we must look to the psychological underpinnings of mass culture. Beyond logic, rationality, and self-interest, Adorno relies on a Freudian conception of the psyche to understand why human beings continue to participate in a mass culture that perpetually degrades, ridicules, and ravages both their thinking and their capacity for experience.[90] 'Without psychology, in which the objective constraints are continually internalized anew, it would be impossible to understand how people passively accept a state of unchanging destructive irrationality and, moreover, how they integrate themselves into movements that stand in rather obvious contradiction to their own interests.'[91] For the purposes of this inquiry, the most important component of this model is the relationship between the ego and the id. Crudely put, the id contains the basic instinctual drives while the ego represents the imposition of controls over those drives. A measure of psychic, motivational, or erotic energy ('libido') cyclically builds up in the id; this energy must then be discharged ('cathected') upon specific objects or through certain activities. Prior to the formation of the ego, the discharge of libidinal energy is immediate, unfocused, and highly mobile: the id, being unable to distinguish between external reality and its internal perceptions (e.g., memories, hallucinations), cathects libidinal energy upon any image that is similar to the drive object. Unfortunately, this often results in actions that do not adequately satisfy basic needs: the image of food, for instance, does not satisfy hunger. To better realize these needs, an ego is formed that limits the immediate discharge of energy, 'neutralizes' it, and then channels it into activities that, while not instantly gratifying, are more effective at satisfying various needs. Infantile omnipotence is shed as the child learns the painful lesson that the world cannot be (re)made according to his or her wants; instead, these desires must sometimes be reined in – sublimated at best, suppressed at worst – in order to take into account environmental realities, including the needs of others. Libido is gradually transformed from a narcissistic force – where the subject only interacts with other objects insofar as it can subordinate them to its own desires – to a truly dialogic or other-seeking force: 'A dialogue relationship is a true object-libidinal relationship with some autonomous external entity: a person or a group, a craft, a science, or a symbol system. A dialogue relationship is the opposite of a pure phantasy ("omnipotent") relationship in which the real characteristics of the object are distorted so that it can serve "merely as a peg on which to hang" primary process displacements.'[92]

The cultivation of such object-libidinal relationships is indicative of the subordination of 'primary process cognition,' whereby the discharge of libidinal energy takes place immediately and upon any object – hallucinatory or otherwise – that might satisfy the drive to 'secondary processes.' In secondary processes, libidinal energy is sublimated into non-instinctual activities that are only indirectly related to the drive object. These latter processes are needed for more abstract human activities such as genuine social interaction, critical thought, and artistic creation. For Freud, the eventual result is civilization. Human beings learn to trade off the uncontrolled discharge of libidinal energy for its sublimation into more socially acceptable activities.

Even when it occurs successfully, ego formation is hardly a pleasant process. The resolution of the Oedipus complex and the displacement of the pleasure principle by the reality principle – the key stages in the formation of the ego, which constitutes the modern, autonomous subject – are psychic transitions inspired and governed by self-deprivation, frustration, and sheer terror.[93] They involve the painful sacrifice of basic desires for happiness and self-gratification in exchange for the possibility of controlling ourselves and our environment. For Horkheimer and Adorno, the adventures of Odysseus represent of the ascetic evolution of modern subjectivity: again and again, the Greek captain sacrifices his instinctual desires, violently forgoing the sensual pleasures of the Lotus-eaters, Circe, and the Sirens, in order to become a self and maintain his identity against the danger of being swallowed up by the forces of myth: 'Humanity had to inflict terrible injuries on itself before the self – the identical, purpose-directed, masculine character of human beings – was created, and something of this process is repeated in every childhood. The effort to hold itself together attends the ego at all stages, and the temptation to be rid of the ego has always gone hand-in-hand with the blind determination to preserve it.'[94]

The sublimation of libidinal energy does allow for its partial discharge through non-instinctual activities, but this is never as fully gratifying as its release through basic instinctual activities. Even after it has been constructed, the ego must constantly maintain itself against the ever-present temptation of regressing to a state where the basic desires for libidinal gratification – which are never eliminated, only disciplined – once again take control. An ego that has been well formed in a social environment that facilitates the sublimation of libidinal energies into socially acceptable pursuits is well placed to manage this tension and maintain itself. However, as these processes are damaged, the possibility of regression grows.[95]

Adorno believes that the transition from liberal to monopoly capitalism has damaged the formation of the ego within the bourgeois family. In large part, this perspective emerged as a consequence of extensive empirical and theoretical research conducted in the 1930s by the Frankfurt School into patterns of authority in the family.[96] At the height of the classical bourgeois era, the family served as the crucible where the autonomous ego was forged in a dialectic of submission to and rebellion against the father. It provided individuals with the resources to accommodate as well as withstand the socializing forces of society. In the words of Horkheimer, the family 'was a kind of second womb, in whose warmth the individual gathered the strength necessary to stand alone outside of it.'[97] The process of ego formation depends greatly on the father's ability to successfully and independently procure a living from the marketplace and thereby occupy a position of strong patriarchal authority within the home. This economic form has been replaced with monopoly capitalism, under which the father has evolved into a manipulated and administered object of larger social structures and institutions; as a result, his strength and influence have been compromised. In Freudian terms, this prevents the Oedipus complex from ever being fully or satisfactorily resolved: the patriarchal authority that ought to have been internalized is largely absent, leaving the individual without a foundation on which to construct an ego. Only through the initial submission to and internalization of the father's authority do children acquire the strength to later criticize and resist irrational social processes. Absent this process, the individual emerges from the family with a stunted ego that craves authority in the form of a surrogate father figure.

In the mass society of the twentieth century, the easiest and most tempting way for weak individuals to escape the rigours of ego maintenance is to become part of a larger group. In his investigation of mass behaviour, Freud notes that 'it is a pleasurable experience for those who are concerned to surrender themselves so unreservedly to their passions and thus to become merged in the group and to lose the sense of the limits of their individuality.'[98] Joining a group allows one to shrug off some of the self-control through which the release of psychic energies is repressed, sublimated, and otherwise disciplined. The group – more particularly its leader – functions as an externalized ego, and this 'frees' individual members to discharge the energies of the id as allowed by the group or leader. In Freud's words, 'the leader of the group is still the dreaded primal father; the group still wishes to be governed by unrestricted force; it has an extreme passion for authority; in Le Bon's phrase, it has a thirst for obedience. The primal father is the group ideal, which governs the ego in the place of the ego ideal.'[99] The bond between the individual and the group is libidinized through the mechanism of identification. At its most primitive level, this is symptomatic of an infantile narcissism whereby the child's ego is only able to love itself insofar as it projects the perfection it strives for within itself onto other objects: in loving the object, it thinks it is loving itself.

Adorno thinks that a similar dynamic operates in contemporary society among adults. In capitalism, people are constantly frustrated with their inability to autonomously and freely direct their activities in accordance with the ideal of the independent bourgeois ego, which continues to possess considerable social authority through the favourable and routine depiction of autonomous and powerful characters in culture and ideology. Repeated failure to meet these standards generates a need for people to satisfy their narcissistic impulses through loving others. But this 'loving of others' remains at an unconscious level, where it is subsequently screened by and/or projected upon a specific image, process, or individual. For the fascist, 'by making the leader his ideal he loves himself, as it were, but gets rid of the stains of frustration and discontent which mar his picture of his own empirical self.'[100] Individuals identify all that they value within themselves with the leader and the collective, its practices and its symbols, and in so doing perversely affirm their identity in the only way they can – by submitting to the leader's authority. Behaviour that is essentially weak and masochistic is psychically and culturally *mis*represented as an indication of strength and self-affirmation.

In capitalist societies, identification with the fascist leader is largely replaced with the cult of celebrity – a cult that is constructed around not only actors but also athletes, media personalities, politicians, businesspeople, and any others on whom the media's fawning gaze tends to fall. This identification is often intensified by its pseudo-collective nature: forms of community are constructed that are based mainly on a shared subordination to and/or imitation of the values, beliefs, style, and image of particular celebrities: 'For the individual, life is made easier through capitulation to the collective with which he identifies. He is spared the cognition of his impotence; within the circle of his own company, the few become the many.'[101] Describing the 'inarticulate followers' of jazz, Adorno notes that 'they could just as well get together in clubs for worshipping film stars or for collecting autographs. What is important to them is the sense of belonging as such, identification, without their paying particular attention to its content ... Merely to be carried away by anything at all, to have something of their own, compensates for their impoverished and barren existence.'[102] At his most extreme, Adorno compares jazz to primitive castration rituals in which one gives up one's sexual identity in order to join the group. In the absence of a strong ego, genuine individuality is experienced not as freedom or autonomy, but rather as a lonely isolation punctuated by moments of helpless terror. The culture industry slips in to fill the void, offering the individual comfort within the mass in exchange for the psychic and largely subconscious sacrifice of his or her autonomy: 'The committees and stars function as ego and superego, and the masses, stripped of even the semblance of personality, are molded far more compliantly by the catchwords and models than ever the instincts were by the internal censor.'[103]

In modern societies, direct participation in a collective is hardly the only or even the main way in which libidinal pressure is released. As social relations are commodified, they are mediated through specific objects and practices that take on properties more properly attributed to the relations themselves. The libidinal pleasures of identification are simulated effectively through the purchase and consumption of particular commodities; for example, in consuming a certain kind of music, individuals identify themselves with a larger community. Furthermore, the culture industry can facilitate libidinal discharge in other ways besides integrating individuals into a group. Mass culture is filled with objects, events, and practices that are designed specifically to solicit, accommodate, and attract the fantasies of its consumers. 'If there were such a thing as a commodity-soul (a notion that Marx occasionally mentions in jest),' notes Benjamin, 'it would be the most empathetic ever encountered in the realm of souls, for it would be bound to see every individual as a buyer in whose hand and house it wants to nestle.'[104] Thus the poetic style of allegory is a perfect match for the superficial polyvalence of the commodity: just as allegories are determined by the subject (any object can be made a sign for any other object), commodities seemingly become what their consumers wish them to be. This sort of empathy is greatest in cultural commodities, which, more than any other objects, need to ingratiate themselves with the affective and libidinal patterns of their buyers. Hence, the products of the culture industry combine simplistic forms with a seemingly infinite range of content: they require minimal mental effort to process, understand, and consume, and they come in an extended range of shapes and sizes onto which the consumer can effortlessly project his or her own fantasies. By offering itself as a surface on which desires can easily be inscribed, mass culture actually promotes cognitive patterns that bear a striking resemblance to primary processes. Within the culture industry, the ego compensates for the endless frustration of social existence, wilfully regressing beyond the *de*centred self-conception of maturity and thereby forgetting the lesson that the world cannot be anything it wants it to be. In this infantile state, ideas, images, and sensations are understood mainly according to their relation to self-gratification: objects enter one's consciousness insofar as they can serve as a site for the immediate cathexis of libidinal energies. Freud thought that primary process cognition is dominant within the unconscious (dream thought), in magical, animistic, and autistic states (pre-historic thought), and in individuals with psychopathological conditions. To this list, Adorno adds the culture industry. Not only does this type of cognition perfectly describe how individuals process and experience mass culture, but it also summarizes the template that organizes the creation of cultural goods at the point of production: they are designed primarily for rapid, easy, and pleasurable consumption.

The structural equivalence that is imposed on cultural production by the commodity form facilitates the mobility of libidinal energies across the field of cultural objects: their underlying 'sameness' makes it easier to construct the associative connections that permit the discharge of libido onto an image as a substitute for its proper drive object. Diversity can only ever be lightly traced over the unchanging products of the culture industry: 'real' differences would require true concentration to comprehend, and such concentration necessarily demands the disciplined and unpleasurable subordination of libido into more abstract cognitive processes. The iconic fidelity of mass culture to the underlying patterns and forms of everyday life only enhances this effect. But what really lies at its core is the commodity form itself. As exchange relations and the logic of identity make all things seem alike, they become all the more readily available for narcissistic projection: 'With the vitiation of their use value, the alienated things are hollowed out and, as ciphers, they draw in meanings.'[105] The projection of desire upon objects, followed by their narcissistic consumption or integration, is the psychological underbelly of identitarian thinking: it is one of the main reasons why identity comes to feel good and how it is *affectively* charged. The grid of equivalence that exchange imposes across human society doubles as a conduit for the primary discharge of libidinal energies as managed by the culture industry. When objects are identified through exchange, their specificities are effectively sacrificed so that we might use them to service our own needs: hence Sade over Kant as the true prophet of the Enlightenment. By way of the object's commodification, any social, historical, and material qualities it has – including any human labour mixed with it – that might interfere with the projection of fantasy upon it are effectively erased. As primary processes increasingly supplant secondary ones in the consumption of culture, reality testing and the concordant use of logic seem like needlessly labourious processes; in fact, they actually get in the way of the pleasures served up by the culture industry. The Orson Welles 'panic broadcast' 'showed that the elimination of the distinction between image and reality has already advanced to the point of a collective sickness.'[106] In the monopoly stage of capitalism, self-control over the instincts is no longer so important (the culture industry can perform this function itself through its 'committees' of stars); instead, what is needed is the control and suppression of critical consciousness. Thus, the shedding of one's attachment to the logical, reality-testing components of the ego through culture matches the alienation of *praxis* that characterizes the labour process. The micromanagement of human activity engendered by capitalism makes the autonomous, self-directed ego redundant in the workplace; not only that, but it makes the sublimated discharge of libidinal energy through waged labour almost impossible. People return home from work desperate for the relaxed amusement of mass culture, through which the psychic pressures built up during the day can be most effectively released.

Whatever we might think or experience, this is not merely a regression to infantile or pre-historic patterns of behaviour and cognition in aid of blowing off a little psychosexual steam. In the case of jazz, for example,

> a disenfranchized subjectivity plunges from the commodity world into the commodity world; the system does not allow for a way out. Whatever primordial instinct is recovered in this is not a longed-for freedom, but rather a regression through suppression ... It is not old and repressed instincts which are freed in the form of standardized rhythms and standardized explosive outbursts; it is new, repressed, and mutilated instincts which have stiffened into masks of those in the distant past. The modern archaic stance of jazz is nothing other than its commodity character.[107]

Let us briefly recall the changing relation between use-value and exchange-value in the culture industry. For Adorno, the latter comes to entirely replace the former. But *vis-à-vis* consumptive patterns, this transpositioning remains a secret: 'The more inexorably the principle of exchange-value destroys use-values for human beings, the more deeply does exchange-value disguise itself as the object of enjoyment.'[108] The vehicle through which the group is identified and on which libido is discharged is always mediated through the market. In other words, the 'object' that people are really identifying with and using to gratify themselves is actually exchange-value itself: 'Now equivalence itself has become a fetish.'[109] We are not fooled into believing that use-value remains in the object; rather, it is the capacity to represent exchange-value, and to be consumed as such, that becomes the use-value of mass culture.

The contemporary obsession with celebrity reflects this dynamic perfectly. It may appear that beauty, vitality, happiness, power, skill, charisma, wealth, and/or other attributes are the objects of mass affection; in fact, it is the easy translation of these apparent virtues into commodities – or aspects of a hyper-commodified self – that is worshipped. In other words, it is a particular attribute *as exchange value* – not the use-value of the attribute *per se* – that is valorized. The commodity form fetishizes this process of exchange: the qualities of human social relations are attached to and appear as the natural properties of an object and are then directly consumed. Just as in Sade's sadomasochistic fantasies, 'the means is fetishized: it absorbs pleasure.'[110] Feelings themselves are displaced into exchange value.[111] Culture is uniquely situated to organize the fusion of pleasure and exchange because it is an activity in which human beings often engage without an overtly instrumentalist orientation; it is so appealing because it feels good and appears to give pleasure in and of itself. Consider sports, for example. The very real enjoyment that people take in collectively engaging in a physical activity for its own sake can be harnessed to broader social processes as this activity is rationalized and commodified:

> By dint of the physical exertion exacted by sport, by dint of the functionalization of the body in team-activity, which interestingly enough occurs in the most popular sports, people are unwittingly trained into modes of behaviour which, sublimated to a greater or lesser degree, are required of them by the work process ... Frequently it is in sport that people first inflict upon themselves (and celebrate as a triumph of their

> own freedom) precisely what society inflicts upon them and what they must learn to enjoy.[112]

The progressive mediation of these types of activities by the commodity form is one of the most insidious and effective means by which it can secretly penetrate human thought and action. Participation in the act of exchange becomes a direct source of pleasure itself, rather than simply an instrument to be used in the acquisition of pleasure. Conversely, we become incapable of achieving pleasure unless the practices and activities from which it is derived are mediated through the market: the exchange process becomes the gatekeeper for any and all forms of satisfaction, extracting our half-conscious loyalties as its toll. One is left with a broad, collective libidinal investment in the core economic structures of modern society; this buttresses the staying power of capitalism beyond anything Marx might have once envisaged.

But the cathexis fostered by mass culture and commodities is ultimately unsuccessful. For Freud, the primary cognitive processes of the infant and of pre-historic human beings inevitably arouse anger, frustration, and disappointment because they facilitate the discharge of motivational energy upon drive objects (images, memories) that are unable to satisfy the drives. This frustration is the basic propellor for ego formation and for the gradual sublimation of the drives into non-instinctual forms of behaviour. Mass culture similarly fails to 'deliver the goods': hallucinatory pleasures are false agents for gratification. It is only ever capable of partially satisfying impulses in a distorted manner: 'The culture industry endlessly cheats its consumers out of what it endlessly promises. The promissory note of pleasure issued by plot and packaging is indefinitely prolonged: the promise, which actually comprises the entire show, disdainfully intimates that there is nothing more to come, that the diner must be satisfied with reading the menu.'[113]

Here, however, the failure to satisfy does not lead to the eventual renovation of the damaged ego – a renovation that might facilitate a more satisfactory resolution of basic needs. Instead, libidinal energies that cannot be discharged effectively are systematically repressed by the endless repetition of the rituals and practices (i.e., consumption) through which we are promised their release. In this way society collectively enacts, through the culture industry, the basic repetition compulsion associated with psychological neuroses: 'This Sisyphean labour of every individual's psychic economy of drives is today socialized, and directly controlled by the institutions of the culture industry.'[114] Again and again people go to a blockbuster film, buy the latest hit CD, or watch the newest television sit-com or drama in the hope that maybe this time they will be different, this time they will actually satisfy the needs and desires they have stimulated. Such products rarely, if ever, do satisfy. In fact, cynicism and discontent with mass culture have been smoothly integrated into the industry itself, spawning entire genres that do little other than mock the banality of what passes for culture these days. Yet to act on this realization and 'cure' ourselves of these infantile compulsions would require both a therapeutic moment of catharsis and a collective, 'revolutionary' moment in which the broader social environment was radically changed. It is not simply a matter of telling people that mass culture is cognitively and psychologically bankrupt: they already know it. But in their weakened state, they are often incapable of imposing this realization on their libidinal economies. Instead, these energies contantly demand release along the only paths that are available in the reified world of late capital.[115]

Neurotic repression through repetition does not always succeed in completely managing the rage, frustration, and disappointment aroused by the broken promises of the culture industry and capitalism itself. One of the most frightening characteristics of the dialectic of enlightenment is that it transforms the anger it has inspired into a critical source of strength. For Horkheimer and Adorno, the prototypical modern example of such reversal is fascist anti-Semitism. The Jews represent 'happiness without power, reward without work, a homeland without frontiers, religion without myth'[116] – attributes that people secretly desire but are forbidden from pursuing by the socioeconomic structures of society. Identitarian logic, as institutionalized through the market, through bureaucratic institutions, and through patterns of self-discipline, denies the satisfaction of basic human needs – a satisfaction that lies tantalizingly within reach: the punishments once suffered by the mythic denizens of Hades have become our own. Horkheimer, Adorno, and Benjamin are fond of citing the tortures of Tantalus and Sisyphus as reborn in the never-ending circle by which desire is invoked by capitalism only to be constantly denied. When the rage and frustration inspired by this contradiction break through the barriers erected by the repetition compulsion, they are redirected away from that which causes them toward more helpless targets: 'Because [the sick subject] cannot acknowledge desire within itself, it assails the other with jealousy or persecution.'[117] As organized by fascism, people collectively engage in what Freud calls 'projection': repressed desires are projected upon others, who are then hated as a means of coping with (i.e., repressing) those desires. Just as one loves oneself by loving the leader and the group, so too one deals with the disappointment of failed expectations by hating the outsider who appears to have realized them. Responsibility for managing one's own desires and self-identity – traditionally the function of the ego – is thereby displaced to social processes which, as their psychological elements remain at a subconscious level, can easily be manipulated by fascist practices and institutions. Fascist xenophobia is *mis*directed anger at the system itself – 'Hitler wants the Jew to be treated as the great exploiter ought to have been treated'[118] – channelled into the hatred of others by a ruling group eager to control this anger for its own purposes.

While xenophobia is certainly an important tool in the repertoire of the culture industry, that industry's own transformative devices are far more sophisticated, insidious, and automatic than those of fascism. As noted earlier, the commodification of culture leads to the exclusion of many critical impulses that had previously been nurtured by aesthetic practice. And yet the effects of commodification are not exclusively repressive; indeed, they do much more than merely prohibit. The authority to exclude critical forces is one thing; the ability to strip them of their subversive potency and incorporate them within is much more. The culture industry's 'victory is twofold: what is destroyed as truth outside its sphere can be reproduced indefinitely within it as lies.'[119] This latter power largely flows out of how a commodified culture is conceptualized by its audience. One of the most terrifying qualities of the culture industry is that most people know that it is a lie or, at the very least, thoroughly instrumentalized and subordinated to business interests, and yet still they take part:

> If it guarantees them even the most fleeting gratification they desire a deception which is nonetheless transparent to them. They force their eyes shut and voice approval, in a kind of self-loathing, for what is meted out to them, knowing fully the purpose for which it is manufactured. Without admitting it they sense that their lives would be completely intolerable as soon as they no longer clung to satisfactions which are none at all.[120]

Belief continues because it is one of the only things that makes life bearable. Success and comfortable survival demand self-deception in an irrational world beyond human control: 'What I like may be bad, a fraud, and fabricated to dupe people, but I don't want to be reminded of that and in my free time I don't want to exert myself or get upset.'[121] Furthermore, mass culture teaches how to behave, how to 'fit in': 'People give their approval to mass culture because they know or suspect that is where they are taught the mores they will surely need as their passport in a monopolized life. This passport is only valid if paid for in blood, with the surrender of life as a whole and the impassioned obedience to a hated compulsion.'[122]

According to Adorno, we actively participate in cultural activities that we know are a lie because self-deception is necessary in a world of lies: irrational behaviour is more than merely reasonable – it is an essential skill for self-preservation when enlightenment itself has once again become myth. Notwithstanding this 'practical value' as an instructor in social mores, the culture industry also has a very real monopoly on pleasure: as elusive, temporary, and false as these pleasures turn out to be, they are the only real option for gratification afforded to those who spend their working days governed by the machines, institutions, and practices of modern capitalism. Everybody knows at one level or another that the whole culture industry is nothing but one big swindle; indeed, the industry itself proudly proclaims this fact as an excuse for its products and thereby excuses them from critical examination – 'It's *only* fun!' And yet it also makes sense *vis-à-vis* our psychological needs for us to deceive ourselves in order to derive some kind, *any kind*, of pleasure from the culture industry, however minimal or ephemeral. Hence the chilling conclusion to the chapter on mass culture in *Dialectic of Enlightenment*: 'That is the triumph of advertising in the culture industry: the compulsive imitation by consumers of cultural commodities which, at the same time, they recognize as false.'[123] One of the few truths left is the knowledge that it is sometimes easiest not to think too much.

This dynamic is crystallized most perfectly in how the culture industry uses humour. For Adorno, laughter at its best expresses the escape of human beings from power and danger. At its worst, it announces the impossibility of escape and celebrates instead the complete submission to and identification with power: 'Fun is a medicinal bath which the entertainment industry never ceases to prescribe. It makes laughter the instrument for cheating happiness.'[124] As the promised happiness of the culture industry is revealed as false, laughter is routinely used to smother and defuse the explosive rage that could otherwise attend such a revelation. People can tolerate and even enjoy the puerile, fraudulent pleasures served up by mass culture only by regularly laughing at themselves. A masochistic humour short-circuits the cognitive process by which personal degradation might be transformed into social and political action: 'It is probably correct to assume that most listeners, in order to comply with what they regard as social desiderata and to prove their "citizenship," half-humorously "join" the conspiracy as caricatures of their own potentialities and suppress bringing to awareness the operative mechanisms by insisting to themselves and to others that the whole thing is only good clean fun anyhow.'[125]

The capacity for self-mockery is a key weapon in the arsenal of today's mutilated subjects – that is, an important means for people to protect themselves against the psychic shocks that accompany the masochistic pleasures of the culture industry: 'His bad taste, his fury, his hidden resistance, his insincerity, his latent contempt for himself, everything is cloaked by "humor" and therewith neutralized.'[126] At its most extreme, things reach a point where, in the prescient words of Benjamin, humanity can experience its own destruction as 'a supreme aesthetic pleasure.'[127] And lurking in the shadows of this self-deprecation is the more sinister *Schadenfreude* – the extraction of sadistic pleasure from laughing at the misfortunes of others. Once we learn to mock and repress our own desires for happiness, it becomes that much easier to be gratified by the sufferings of others.

All things provided by the culture industry, then, are treated with a kind of half-conscious, tolerant, instrumental, and even amused scepticism. This includes values that were originally opposed to such an industry: 'Amusement itself becomes an ideal, taking the place of the higher values it eradicates from the masses by repeating them in an even more stereotyped form than the advertising slogans paid for by private interests.'[128] For example, every time 'justice' or 'freedom' figures prominently in the conventional plot of a film or television show, it transforms the original ideal into a mere vehicle of amusement, thereby dissolving any critical potential the concept might once have had. These ideals are gradually treated no different than any other plot device of the entertainment industry and are thus viewed with the same scepticism as other parts of the industry. Repeat something often enough and in the right context and no one will believe it. In an act of ideological jujitsu, the culture industry turns the ever-present scepticism about itself against those ideas and concepts that might have once presented a challenge to its illusory pleasures: 'To identify culture solely with lies is more fateful than ever, now that the former is really becoming totally absorbed by the latter, and eagerly invites such identification in order to compromise every opposing thought.'[129] Given its monopoly over the production and distribution of cultural objects, the marketplace is able to colonize and integrate aesthetic dissidence. The commodification of all channels of social communication means that even those who consciously set out to resist 'the system' must mediate their work through it in order to reach others. Once they do so, they are done: 'Anyone who resists can survive only by being incorporated. Once registered as diverging from the culture industry, they belong to it as the land reformer does to capitalism.'[130]

Horkheimer and Adorno are not simply talking about co-optation here, although it remains an ever-present danger. They are also speaking to how the culture industry is able to use the legitimate scepticism properly directed against itself to emasculate any critical messages that pass through its circuits while, at the same time, pointing to the existence of such messages as proof of its own pluralist practices. In other words, mass culture perfects the mimetic defences once employed by primitive humanity: by taking its enemies into itself, it effectively disarms them. Even social documentaries and critical realism, which try to document the horrors of modernity, can succumb to this dynamic. In the first place, the desire to communicate an event, narrative, or issue helps sustain the myth that humans do continue to have experiences that they can share with one another. A 'tragic' event, no matter how horrible, assures us that meaning does continue to survive in a world where it has long since vanished: 'To all it grants the solace that human fate in its strength and authenticity is possible even now and its unflinching depiction inescapable. The unbroken surface of existence, in the duplication of which ideology consists solely today, appears all the more splendid, glorious, and imposing the more it is imbued with necessary suffering. It takes on the aspect of fate.'[131]

The 'unflinching depiction' of suffering sponsors the purging of emotions; it also acknowledges unhappiness and suffering as permanent and unchanging in a cruel, inhospitable, and naturalized environment: 'It is katharsis for the masses, but katharsis which keeps them all the more firmly in line. One who weeps does not resist any more than one who marches. Music that permits its listeners the confession of their unhappiness reconciles them, by means of this "release," to their social dependence.'[132] The lingering ego-ideal of the bourgeois subject tells people that they should have feelings, and the cathartic discharge inspired by mass culture allows them to feel something. Only in feelings' absence – as memory, as the unfulfilled longing for release – could a desire for them be critically deployed by culture. But as immediacy, feeling serves as little more than the lie that meaningful experiences still exist in a world constituted by their scarcity. Furthermore, the mediation of human experience through the commodity form necessarily introduces a toxic agent into that experience itself: 'Language which appeals to mere truth only arouses impatience to get down to the real business behind it. Words which are not means seem meaningless, the others seem to be fiction, untruth.'[133] When the representation of something is sold for profit, one grows a little more sceptical, a little more hardened, not only against the process of representation but also toward that which is being represented. As the gap between culture and the status quo dissolves and cultural technology comes increasingly to dominate the sensual environment, these two spheres start to blend into each other. Remember the dynamic of capitalist film: 'The moviegoer ... perceives the street outside as a continuation of the film he has just left, because the film seeks strictly to reproduce the world of everyday perception.'[134] The cognitive and psychological processes through which one learns to 'experience' mass culture are then applied to how life itself is experienced. We expect to be disappointed by culture, having learned that potentiality itself, whether individual or social, cultural, political, or economic, is nothing but a cheap trick designed to fool us into laying down our money one more time. Consequently, the real potential frozen within subjects and objects and their relations/experiences that cultural practice might have helped emancipate, is similarly written off as a sham.

### 'Back to the Future': The Culture Industry and the 'dialectic of enlightenment'

I close this chapter with a brief discussion of how Adorno conceives of the cognitive, psychological, and social effects of the culture industry as they fit into the broader dialectic of enlightenment in which humanity now finds itself entangled. Mass culture is no longer ideological in the traditional sense of the word. In a positivistic sense, its products no longer need to misrepresent or distort the 'truth' about reality. Rather, the representational fidelity of the culture industry to everyday life is increasingly enhanced by technology. This does not mean that the culture industry tells 'the truth' about reality. It *does* in the sense that it presents an image modelled after a positivist experience of the world; but it *doesn't* insofar as it fails to perceive and represent the dialectical potential that lies repressed within that world. Thus, from the perspective of dialectical social theory, mass culture's iconic fidelity to the world is combined with misrepresentations about the meaning of the images it provides: 'Ideology is split between the photographing of brute existence and the blatant lie about its meaning, a lie which is not articulated directly but drummed in by suggestion.'[135] As noted earlier, this has the ideological effect of destroying the capacity of individuals to imagine anything different – the speculative dimension of aesthetics, fantasy, and utopia is crushed: 'Reality becomes its own ideology through the spell cast by its faithful duplication.'[136] In the past, ideology was required by ruling classes to legitimate their dominant social position. This need gave some kind of voice to suffering: it had to be justified with the promise of otherwordly or future redemption. In terms of critique, then, ideology provided an Archimedean point *within* society against which one could pry to the surface of consciousness those mute contradictions that boiled within the social mass. With the loss of formal ideology, another tool has been sacrificed with which people might think reflexively about their own social system by asking to what extent its ideals are realizable in the present day. Immanent critique is thereby seriously and perhaps fatally compromised. Instead, reality and mass culture are locked together in a parasitic circle of repetition that leads each to constantly strengthen the other. Ultimately, this leads to the reification of human society and its institutions, relations, and practices as a second nature over which people can have no control. Constant repetition of the ever-same effectively transmits the truth that no intention or action can ever possibly alter the world, other than by changing the circumstances of an individual's life. It generates a quiescent attitude that is more effective than even the most brutal fascist propaganda. This fits precisely into the broader thesis of the *Dialectic of Enlightenment* that myth is already enlightenment and enlightenment, as we have known it, reverts to myth:

> The arid wisdom which acknowledges nothing new under the sun, because all the pieces in the meaningless game have been played out, all the great thoughts have been thought, all possible discoveries can be construed in advance, and human beings are defined by self-preservation through adaptation – this barren wisdom merely reproduces the fantastic doctrine it rejects: the sanction of fate which, through retribution, incessantly reinstates what always was.[137]

In accord with this 'dialectic,' mass culture helps return humanity to a mythic state in which individuals, filled with a half-conscious terror, desperately seek membership in an omnipotent society (second nature) that cannot be rationally directed or even understood, but only worshipfully imitated. Mass culture becomes 'a kind of training for life when things have gone wrong,'[138] preparing rational beings for life in a world gone mad.

Initially, the bourgeois ego provided some with the capacity to stand independently against the structures and institutions of 'reality.' A privileged few were able to engage in activities such as aesthetics and thereby symbolically challenge the world with its own potential. Space for critical thought was in this way preserved. However, just like our distant ancestors, we are once again confronted with a mythical power to which we must adapt in order to survive. And the only option available for adaptation is submissive identification. The egos of primitive human beings existed only in an embryonic state; our own are seemingly damaged beyond repair, and as such, our motives are really no different from theirs – fear of being left outside, abandoned and tossed aside by power to perish in isolation: 'Nothing is allowed to remain outside, since the mere idea of the "outside" is the real source of fear.'[139] Just as ancient peoples imitated the weather and wild predators in a desperate attempt to gain some control over them, people today are equally driven to find some way of propitiating forces that lie beyond human influence, and to thereby become one with them. This is precisely where the culture industry steps in to fulfil and manipulate this infantile need. Admittedly, there are no more shamanistic rituals to bring one from the outside to the inside; instead, we willingly lose ourselves in the 'iron rhythms' of mass culture. 'The imitative assimilation to commodity models,' notes Adorno, 'is intertwined with folkloristic customs of imitation.'[140] Individuals sacrifice their autonomy in order to bring themselves inside, to integrate themselves into the broader social mass. As Alexis de Tocqueville suspected, to repudiate such puerile gratification carries its own punishment in modern society: 'The ruler no longer says: 'Either you think as I do or you die.' He says: 'You are free not to think as I do; your life, your property – all that you shall keep. But from this day on you will be a stranger among us.'[141] We appear helpless before a reality mediated by the culture industry; not only that, but the sole viable mode of response – imitative submission – ends up reproducing and reinforcing those social relations, structures of cognition, and patterns of behaviour that led us into this quagmire in the first place.

# 2
# Capitalism, Mimesis, Experience: Legacies of the Commodity Fetish

> Heaven and hell, however, hang together.
>
> Adorno and Horkheimer, *Dialectic of Enlightenment*

Simultaneously terrified and offended by the seeming finality of Adorno's verdict on mass culture and its consumers, many seek intellectual refuge in the more forgiving theoretical fragments of Walter Benjamin. Without question, the modesty and ambiguity of Benjamin's later work offer more comfort to contemporary cultural and academic sensibilities than do Adorno's bitter, totalizing polemic. Where Adorno offers only despair, Benjamin gives us hope; for example, in his often read 'The Work of Art in the Age of Its Technological Reproducibility' he offers an account of photography and film that concentrates on the emancipatory possibilities that attend their displacement of more traditional art forms. Adorno throws up his hands in frustration at the masses' incomprehension and even hatred of Beckett and Schönberg; in contrast, Benjamin looks for and finds an equivalent 'de-familiarization' in their eager reception of Chaplin. In the puerile objects and images of industrial capitalism, he sees not only the dreams that keep humanity in a stupefying slumber, but also the desires, imagination, and creative resources that may one day be used to build a new social order. Many have grown sceptical that we will ever see the collective, radical economic and political change needed to challenge the culture industry and capitalism itself; Benjamin, for his part, seems to offer a more 'balanced' approach to cultural analysis – one that can satisfy itself with the fragments of redemptive potential scattered throughout the everyday. As visions of a new social order sink below the postmodern horizon, Benjamin's attempt to thaw our frozen hopes and desires can easily be turned into platitudes about the ubiquity of cultural resistance; dialectical analysis melts into an essentialist pluralism by which we assure ourselves that the hegemony of the culture industry is never as complete, never as final, as Adorno's paranoid fantasies would have us believe.

Needless to say, simplistic, binary reconstructions such as these have repeatedly been criticized by scholars of critical theory. In the first place, the fertile theoretical tension that exists between them owes much of its existence to the broader philosophical project – 'the dialectical self-dissolution of myth'[1] – shared by both. 'For to read Adorno is to sense Benjamin between every other line,' notes Irving Wohlfarth. 'Each of them, after all, considered his own position to be the dialectical corrective of the other.'[2] According to the synchronic, positivist and one-dimensional logic often used in mainstream social science, their positions are mutually exclusive: one is right and the other is wrong. But one of the cornerstones of critical theory is its critique and rejection of precisely these kinds of analytic systems.[3] What if it is the object of analysis itself – in this case, mass culture – that bears the contradictions within it? Indeed, this is precisely the point of dialectical social thought: in exploring the complexities of an object, structure or process, it is vitally important to register and express the multiple and contradictory properties across time and space possessed by that which is being studied. The counter-factual existence of an object – the potential 'other' forms it could take – will necessarily stand in contradiction to its actual existence. This, however, is a contradiction that cannot be resolved analytically unless a unified schematic is imposed on the object from the outside by the subject. In other words, descriptions of an object that do not agree logically may nevertheless accurately reflect its real qualities. In this sense, the famous debates between Benjamin and Adorno are better conceptualized as an ongoing dialogue in which the different elements, possibilities, and dangers of mass culture are continuously developed and theorized. Reading one without the other is like trying to understand a conversation by listening only to one participant.

My goal in this chapter, then, is to bring Adorno's focused polemic into the different context afforded by the writings of Benjamin. A coherent synthesis of their *logically* irreconcilable positions is not my goal; nor do I wish to deploy the latter's work as a mere palliative to moderate or soften Adorno's sharp words. Instead, I want to understand the tension between them as symptomatic of the dangers and opportunities that attend the commodification of culture. It is easy to misunderstand the culture industry thesis as a one-dimensional polemic against the evils of the commodity form. While Adorno admits that the clock cannot be turned back to the autonomous fantasies of *l'art pour l'art,* he doesn't seem to offer much in the way of a dialectical analysis of the culture industry. For him, the only dialectic that seems to have any force is the infamous 'dialectic of enlightenment' that got us into this mess in the first place: 'If "enlightenment is totalitarian," his own impressive account of its own dialectic is itself significantly airless; and if myth is suction, repetition and labyrinthine complication, then the hermetic intricacy of his philosophy is itself not without a mythical undertow.'[4] His criticism of commodification leaves one convinced of its dangers but largely fails to explore any immanent dynamic within this social process that might play a part in its dialectical supersession. As Benjamin observes of French revolutionary Louis-August Blanqui's equally visceral indictment of eternity as the endless repetition of the ever-same, 'The unconscious irony of [his] elaborate enterprise is that the terrible accusation he directs against society takes on the form of unconditional acquiescence to its tendencies.'[5] If one accepts Adorno's devastating analysis, it becomes hard not to fall back into one of many *un*dialectical positions: a nostalgic collapse into the tainted, tragic pleasures of a bourgeois past; a fierce, desperate but idealist, abstract, and ultimately paralyzing aspiration to entirely purge the commodity form from cultural activities; or the hypostatization and 'flattening' of culture as the permanent guilty conscience of capitalist society. In the pages that follow, I want to reconstruct three key elements of the dialectic that lies buried at the heart of the culture industry thesis and the commodity form itself. In so doing, I will be laying the foundations for the 're-dialecticization' of the culture industry thesis that awaits in chapter 3.

## The Return of Myth: Capitalism as Hell, Capitalism as Second Nature

The cultural ruins of the nineteenth century fascinate Benjamin because they provide valuable clues to the genesis of capitalism.[6] Like all Marxist aesthetic critics, he focuses on the relationship between the economic base and the superstructure; however, he distances himself from the rather primitive 'reflection' or 'cause and effect' theory that was predominant at the time he was writing: 'Marx lays bare the causal connection between economy and culture. For us, what matters is the thread of expression. It is not the economic origins of culture that will be presented, but the expression of the economy in its culture.'[7] Accordingly, his *Arcades Project* focuses on how the cultural objects of the nineteenth century expressed certain aspects or qualities of a rapidly expanding capitalist economic system. Sketching the urban visage in dark tones, he fingers the detective story as constructing a cultural, phantasmagoric wilderness that helped those who lived in rapidly expanding cities to make sense of their environment. In Baudelaire's words: 'What are the dangers of the forest and the prairie, compared with the daily shocks and conflicts of civilization? Whether a man grabs his victim on a boulevard or stabs his quarry in unknown woods – does he not remain both here and there the most perfect of all beasts of prey?'[8] Both Alexandre Dumas and Honoré de Balzac plundered the primitive imagery of James Fennimore Cooper's *The Last of the Mohicans* to describe the jungle that was Paris. Balzac wrote, for example, that 'The poetry of terror that pervades the American woods, with their clashes between tribes on the warpath – this poetry which stood Cooper in such good stead attaches in the same way to the smallest details of Parisian life.'[9] Urban streets became 'hunting grounds' in which the detective deployed feral cunning to track and capture his quarry. Conversely, the pursued lost themselves without a trace in the tangled, impenetrable forests into which the masses in the form of the 'crowd' were transfigured. In *Les Misérables*, Victor Hugo, the pre-eminent novelist of nineteenth-century France, observes that 'cities, like forests, have their dens in which all their vilest and most terrible monsters hide.'[10] In other words, the most successful and popular literary styles were those which filtered the experience of modern, urban capitalism through images of untamed wilderness. Benjamin uses these cultural forms to highlight the resurgence of natural imagery in the expression of contemporary forms of experience. Unwittingly perhaps, but guided by the irrepressible cunning of an aesthetic reason that transforms cultural objects into monads, these forms compress the immeasurable temporal divide that separates modern humanity from its prehistoric ancestors into more conventional historicist accounts of human evolution. They shred the ideological cloak of progress that has been draped over material and social existence – an existence that is seemingly once again in thrall to 'natural' forces. It would seem that the jungle has once again become our home.

Inspired by Adorno's account of Kierkegaard's spartan philosophy as representative of the retreat of the bourgeoisie inside itself as its transformative social energies exhausted themselves in the late nineteenth century,[11] Benjamin similarly describes the plush, crowded *intérieur* of middle- and upper-class homes of this period as part of a futile struggle by those with means to wall themselves off from the unfathomable chaos that lay outside. Such spaces constituted 'a radical separation from the exterior ... a home in which the bourgeois can dwell and dream undisturbed by the noise, activity, and threats of the street, the space of the masses and of production, a private individual divorced from the community.'[12] Yet under the keen eyes of the detective, popularized by such nineteenth-century authors as Edgar Allan Poe, Wilkie Collins, and Sir Arthur Conan Doyle, these sanctuaries dissolve into pseudo-natural landscapes in which the solving of crimes comes to depend on the meticulous deciphering of petrified traces of human activity. It is as if the detective is the predator, the criminal his prey. Tutored by this expert gaze, Benjamin identifies the deliberate inscription of traces as the secret motive governing the interior:

> Living in these plush compartments was nothing more than leaving traces made by habits. Even the rage expressed when the least little thing broke was perhaps merely the reaction of a person who felt that someone had obliterated the 'traces of his days on earth.' The traces that he had left in cushions and armchairs, that his relatives had left in photos, and that his possessions had left in linings and étuis and that sometimes made these rooms look as overcrowded as halls full of funerary urns.[13]

The reification that transforms the city street from a social into a natural environment similarly drains social relations from the imaginative constitution of subjectivity, and privileges the inert, fossilized remains of human activity over that activity itself. The bourgeoisie sympathetically sought to 'humanize the commodity' by giving it a home in 'covers and cases';[14] in much the same way, it housed itself in dwellings that became shells. The nineteenth century 'conceived the residence as a receptacle for the person, and it encased him with all his appurtenances so deeply in the dwelling's interior that one might be reminded of the inside of a compass case, where the instrument with all its accessories lies embedded in deep, usually violet folds of velvet.'[15] Coexisting with the rise of capitalism in the nineteenth century, then, the signs of a primordial and mythic nature surreptitiously came to reign over most spheres of human existence, even those most proudly and prominently displayed as evidence of civilization, progress, and the distance of humanity from its primitive, natural origins.

Benjamin's identification of the 'natural' essence of what has generally been understood as historical progress is taken up at length by Adorno and Horkheimer in *Dialectic of Enlightenment*: 'As its final result, civilization leads back to the terrors of nature.'[16] Indeed, much of this work is spent grappling with the paradox by which tremendous advances in human productive capacity, traditionally conceptualized as 'progress' or 'enlightenment,' seem to have actually delivered human societies all the more effectively into the hands of powerful forces beyond their understanding or control. Just as Benjamin ferrets out the expression of this social process in nineteenth-century cultural objects, Adorno locates a similar 'natural presence' throughout contemporary mass culture. For instance, the astrology columns of the *Los Angeles Times* attribute a 'metaphysical dignity' to the necessity of adapting oneself to irrational and incomprehensible structures and processes: 'In as much as the social system is the "fate" of most individuals independent of their will and interest, it is projected upon the stars in order thus to obtain a higher degree of dignity and justification in which the individuals hope to participate themselves.'[17] The advice administered by these columns is harmless enough, but the fact that it depends on 'the stars' for its authority both indicates and reinforces a conception of the world as composed of forces beyond human understanding that ought to be obeyed. Astrology teaches anew the lessons of mythology: 'Only those who subject themselves utterly pass muster with the gods.'[18] Modern ideals that once bespoke a critique of human subjection to heteronomous forces are accordingly restructured in aid of its valorization: 'Freedom [now] consists of the individual's taking upon himself voluntarily what is inevitable anyway.'[19] Natural motifs similarly dominate popular music: while Dumas and Balzac invited their readers to lose themselves in an invocation of the city as wilderness; jazz analogously presents itself as a spontaneous, archaic, and natural musical form drawn from the 'primitive' and autochthonous musical traditions of African Americans. In short, both thinkers are struck by the seeming paradox whereby the imagery of untamed nature is deployed again and again by mass culture and used by people to structure and interpret their experience of a world that is utterly social at its core.

For this 'nature' is obviously not the swamps, forests, and plains of the past. A cornerstone of critical theory from Hegel and Marx to the

Frankfurt School is the idea that there is no such entity as a pure, ontological 'nature,' but rather only a physical environment that has been and continues to be socially mediated through human activity. In an early essay deeply inspired by Benjamin, Adorno argues that 'nature' and 'history' must neither be separated into distinct analytic spheres nor collapsed into a singular theoretical framework (i.e., as Heidegger's ontology interprets the essence of nature as historicity). Instead, 'if the question of the relation of nature and history is to be seriously posed, then it only offers any chance of solution if it is possible *to comprehend historical being in its most extreme historical determinacy, where it is most historical, as natural being, or if it were possible to comprehend nature as an historical being where it seems to rest most deeply in itself as nature.*'[20]

Both first and second nature are highly susceptible to this mode of analysis. The former, for example, is often represented, conceptualized, and experienced as a pristine place where one can mystically commune with pure being. But lying at the core of such an experience is history itself. It is only from within society that nature itself can be experienced as beautiful: its epic majesty and grace can only conjure up the sublime when one is socially and historically insulated from its raw physical power.[21] Conversely, the social processes and institutions that are created through human activity are increasingly reified into natural entities. In *Economic and Philosophical Manuscripts*, Marx argues that one of the defining qualities of labour under capitalism is the alienation of the worker from her activity and the products of her activity: 'The *alienation* of the worker in his product means not only that his labour becomes an object, assumes an *external* existence, but that it exists independently, *outside himself*, and alien to him, and that it stands opposed to him as an autonomous power. The life which he has given to the object sets itself against him as an alien and hostile force.'[22] In other words, the mediation of human activity through the commodity form produces a strange and alien world – one which those who produced it can no longer control or even recognize as their own creation: 'Our emancipated technology stands beside contemporary society as a second nature and indeed, as economic crises and wars show, as a no less elemental nature than that confronted by primitive societies.'[23] The fear that has been effectively banished from 'first nature,' allowing us to experience it as sublime, here takes up its residence; the ghost of that which has been repressed and dominated returns with a vengeance to haunt those very devices through which it is so effectively controlled. Market cycles, bureaucratic institutions, and even cultural activities have become the storms, swamps, and jungles of modernity and are experienced as such by a thoroughly alienated population.

This resurgence of nature and natural imagery is accompanied by the return of myth. Both Adorno and Benjamin treat these two phenomena as dialectically intertwined and often conceptualize them almost synonymously. When we are faced with the inscrutable, myth provides the answers, filling in the horrifying emptiness between cause and effect. In particular, nature and myth share a cyclical temporality that stands opposed to the discontinuities, potentiality, and innovation of genuine human history and social praxis. Both are dominated by repetitive temporal patterns and by the never-ending return of the ever-same: 'The essence of the mythical event is return. Inscribed as a hidden figure in such events is the futility that furrows the brow of some of the heroic personages of the underworld (Tantalus, Sisyphus, the Danaides).'[24] The tortures endured by these heroes symbolically re-enact humanity's subordination to an overwhelming nature; the essence of their punishments is not the torture itself but its exact duplication in a cycle without end. It is not only the punitive dispensations of the gods that bear this pattern – in the Homeric myths, time itself is spatially organized:

> The element which shapes and organizes individuality internally, time, is still so weak that the unity of the adventures remains an outward one, their sequence being formed by the spatial changes of scene, the succession of sites of local divinities on which the hero is flung by the storm. Whenever, at later historical stages, the self has again experienced such weakness, or narration has presupposed it in the reader, the manner of depicting life has slipped into the form of successive adventures. Laboriously and revocably, in the image of the journey, historical time has detached itself from space, the irrevocable schema of all mythical time.[25]

This conception of time is unequivocally connected to a social and material experience ruled by natural forces. The recurring patterns of nature are projected onto a mythic pantheon in the vain hope that through their worship and propitiation these cycles might be controlled; hence, repetition is culturally (re)inscribed on primitive human existence. As the 'prototype of the bourgeois individual,'[26] Odysseus momentarily trumps mythic power by deliberately inflicting on himself the punishments that had previously been the purview of the gods. Having thus inoculated himself against myth through self-sacrifice, he acquires the strength to tear himself and his crew out of the unchanging fabric of natural time and to break into the space of history. Yet his victory is short-lived: the wild success with which myth is cast aside paradoxically lays the groundwork for its surreptitious return. Nature secures vengeance for its conquest by humanity, forging its weapons from the very fetters with which it has been bound; in the same way, myth's resurrection is sponsored by the reason and science that once condemned it with such force to oblivion.

In modernity, repetition is hidden beneath the compulsive pursuit of novelty fostered by commodification itself. Or, better stated, the relentless search for the new, which is always *and* never found, *is* the form that recurrence now assumes: 'What is at issue is not that "the same thing happens over and over," and even less would it be a question here of eternal return. It is rather that precisely in that which is newest the face of the world never alters, that this newest remains, in every aspect, the same. – This constitutes the eternity of hell.'[27] The logic of capital demands that commodities continually stimulate a demand that must never be fully or adequately satisfied by their purchase. Instead, each commodity must lay a trail for the next one. In this sense, commodities for Benjamin function as the 'fetishized "wish-image" of change within an unchanged system.'[28] As mediated through the commodity form, needs and desires are embedded in a cycle of expectation and disappointment – a cycle which inflicts the same repetitive patterns that dominate the world of myth. Adorno, for instance, remarks that 'exchange is the rational form of mythical ever-sameness.'[29]

This dynamic is most purely crystallized in fashion: it 'prescribes the ritual according to which the commodity fetish demands to be worshipped.'[30] Initially we are seduced by the commodity's promise – either directly or through advertising – that its purchase will satisfy our desires and allow us to express our identity and individuality. Momentarily perhaps, it often does. But then, almost as if by design, its appeal rapidly fades and our original infatuation with it is replaced by a repulsion that itself is often accompanied by self-loathing that we could have been so easily fooled. In search of something to ease disappointed expectations, our gaze is again captured by the latest style. Again and again, just like the mythic punishments of Tantalus or Sisyphus, we enact this ritual as subjects under the rule of capital. As the social and material environment increasingly appears inscrutable, exploitative, and brutalizing, our desire to escape and transform these rigid forms of life grows more intense. But since we are unable to express and realize these desires directly – for this must await a massive overhaul of social structures – we must displace them through other kinds of activity. Commodities furnish an ideal substitute. They tempt us with the prospect of vicariously realizing dreams of change through participation in the never-ending parade of goods offered by capitalism. Captivated by the trivial differences by which they eagerly proclaim their distinction from one another, we as consumers fail to realize that every act of consumption is, in fact, indistinguishable from those which preceded it and those which will follow.

While the compulsion to repeat is openly acknowledged in ancient myths, no such awareness accompanies its return under capitalism. Like more traditional celebrations of organic natural cycles, for instance, the rituals of fashion are organized mainly around the seasons. Yet unlike those customs, fashion systematically hides its repetitive infrastructure beneath a compulsive obsession with the 'newest' styles and designs: 'The spring rites of fashion celebrated novelty rather than recurrence; they required not remembrance, but obliviousness to even the most recent past.'[31] In other words, those who participate in the repetitious rituals of modernity are not fully aware of them as such. Instead, these rituals are often glorified as the very incarnation of development, progress, and 'the new.' Benjamin and Adorno are both acutely sensitive to the possibilities for social praxis and historical development that lie at the very core of myth and nature. Adorno writes, for example:

> It is evident that the foundation, the mythic-archaic, the supposedly substantial and enduring mythic, is in no way a static foundation. Rather, there is an element of the historically dynamic, whose form is dialectical, in all great myths as well as in the mythical images that our consciousness still carries. The mythic fundamental elements are in themselves contradictory and move in a contradictory manner.[32]

This approach is what propels Adorno and Horkheimer to return to Homeric myth to find the 'prototype of the bourgeois individual.' Just as enlightenment reverts to myth, myth itself contains the principles of enlightenment. Similarly, Benjamin links the possibility of redemption in the *Trauerspiel* plays to the utter degradation of the existent: 'Ultimately in the death-signs of the baroque, the direction of allegorical reflection is reversed; on the second part of its wide arc it returns, to redeem.'[33] However, the awakening of dialectical potential depends on the ability of human beings to *fully* experience their world as mythic, natural, and/or degraded. In the absence of such awareness, this potential remains frozen. Indeed, this is precisely what is so terrifying about the repetition imposed on existence by the commodity form: it is not fully experienced as such by its inhabitants. Benjamin describes capitalism as 'a natural phenomenon with which a new dream-filled sleep came over Europe, and, through it, a reactivation of mythic forces.'[34] While humanity lies in such a state, its desire for happiness and change can be successfully accommodated within the limits of the commodity form. However, if it could be awakened – if it could be brought to a consciousness of its existence in a world dominated by the forces of myth and nature – it might be possible to redeem the utopian energies that have been mistakenly invested in the empty, dead objects furnished by capitalism.

But for Benjamin, the way out does not lie in a systematic, rationalistic exposé of capitalism as myth, nor does it lie in some measured reduction in the power of the commodity form over social life. Rather, it can only come, paradoxically, through the *increase* of this power: 'The first tremors of awakening serve to deepen sleep.'[35] The contrast between the fetishized ideals of change, progress, autonomy, and life, on the one hand, and the reality of repetition, ever-sameness, heteronomy, and death, on the other, must be sufficiently extreme that their imagistic juxtaposition can break the cycle of dream-sleep imposed by capital. The latter emerges directly out of the former. Consider, for example, Benjamin's deduction that the return of neoclassical motifs – specifically, imagery from Greek myth – coincided with the explosive rise of commodification in early nineteenth-century Paris.[36] Under his 'mythicizing' gaze, an innocuous piece of cultural history that has little significance other than as documentation of the nostalgia that often characterizes urban renewal becomes instead a visceral symbol of humanity's petrified desire to escape the bondage of pre- or 'natural-history.' It is the tension generated from the dialectical suspension of these two moments that generates the possibility of revolution. By this Benjamin does not recommend a fatalistic teleology that envisions the automatic generation of revolutionary sentiment through the intensification of the contradictions of capitalism. There is no guarantee that alienation will be experienced *as* alienation; indeed, 'the bourgeois apparatus of production and publication can assimilate astonishing qualities of revolutionary themes – indeed, can propagate them without calling its own existence and the existence of the class that owns it, seriously into question.'[37] Confronted with communicative and conceptual systems that have been almost entirely reified – thereby foreclosing the possibility of rationally expressing alienation – Benjamin turns to the sphere of images to generate, express and mobilize contemporary experiences of alienation. In educating 'the image-making medium within us, raising it to a stereoscopic and dimensional seeing into the depths of historical shadows,'[38] the historical materialist searches for images from the past that can be triggered to illuminate dialectically the horrors and opportunities of the present. The juxtaposition of contemporary capitalism with images of myth and nature represents one such constellation. The creation of such images is, however, by no means sufficient for the generation of critical consciousness. Instead, a unique form of human perception, cognition, and action is required to fuse these images with living experience in order to produce a revolutionary innervation. It is to the mimetic faculty that we now turn.

## Revolutionary Innervation or Death Mask: The Two Faces of Mimesis

Like most concepts deployed by Benjamin and Adorno, the term *mimesis* takes on different meanings depending on the theoretical constellation in which it is embedded. In certain contexts, it is conceptualized as the most emancipatory of human practices; in others, it represents the very pinnacle of degraded experience under capitalism. We begin with the former and conclude with the latter. Benjamin defines mimesis as having two related components: first, it refers to the perception of similarities between objects, and second, it indicates the practice of making oneself like other objects: 'Nature produces similarities; one need only think of mimicry. The highest capacity for producing similarities, however, is man's. His gift for seeing similarity is nothing but a rudiment of the once powerful compulsion to become similar and to behave mimetically.'[39] In 'On the Mimetic Faculty' Benjamin points to the remnants of this faculty in the play of children: not only do they imitate other individuals, but their games also involve 'becoming' the objects around them. This activity renews the possibility of bringing together – if only for a moment – the mimetic and rational faculties that have long been separated through the processes of enlightenment. For most adults, the cognition of an object is organized around its subsumption within a fixed, classificatory system: What are the characteristics by which it can be distinguished from other objects and from oneself? For children, however, the difference between subject and object has not yet frozen into the seemingly insurmountable barrier it will later become for most adults. Instead, the epistemological valence of their cognitive processes orients them in the opposite direction: they try to discover the similarities between themselves and other objects. The absence of abstract semiotic systems, both internal and external, to catalogue these similarities channels their manifestation into mimetic action. In children, the results of mimetic cognition are expressed in an active, physical form: quite literally, they often think by doing. In other words, cognitive success becomes, for them, a function of their capacity to transform themselves into a means of expression for the objects that surround them. Of course, Benjamin was aware of the dangers of idealizing infantile behavioural patterns, which are often marked as much by narcissistic fantasies of omnipotence as by respect for the other.[40] Instead of simply returning to or reproducing such forms of cognition, he uses them heuristically to highlight alternative cognitive possibilities that have largely been suppressed through education, socialization, and adaptation to the instrumental logic of the market and the workplace. The fusion of cognition and action in the child's desire to become the world can open adult eyes to the potential for an emancipatory relationship with the object world that is empowering, pleasurable, *and* non-instrumental.

Benjamin identifies in the art of the surrealists an aesthetic practice that makes use of the mimetic faculty to innervate or (re)charge human existence. In the market and in the workplace, objects tend either to be treated as distinct, discrete, and alien entities or to solicit the narcissistic projection of fantasy, inviting consumers to make of the object what they wish it to be. In each case, the gap between subject and object is confirmed. Conversely, surrealist aesthetic practices such as montage engage the world in a manner that deliberately forsakes formal logic and conventional representational techniques in order to stimulate an expansion of how people are able to experience objects, people, and places, both in and of themselves and with regard to their largely hidden significance in the constitution of subjectivity:

> Only when in technology body and image so interpenetrate that all revolutionary tension becomes bodily collective innervation, and all the bodily innervations of the collective become revolutionary discharge, has reality transcended itself to the extent demanded by the *Communist Manifesto*. For the moment, only the Surrealists have understood its present commands.

> They exchange, to a man, the play of human features for the face of an alarm clock that in each minute rings for sixty seconds.[41]

As Sigrid Weigel observes, this passage, which concludes Benjamin's major essay on surrealism, suggests that its aesthetic strategies culminate 'in a materialization of the image in corporeal innervations, that is, in an enfleshment of expressive matter, whereby the body becomes the material of imagery – a quite literal ... form of embodiment.'[42] On the one hand, the body is (re)configured as a site for aesthetically enacting the explosive physiological innervation that a revolutionary reorganization of technology might produce on a much larger scale. It prefigures a second-order use of cultural technologies to master the abstract and highly self-destructive use of technology that currently prevails. Supplementing humanity's relations with technology with a mimetic rationality opens up the possibility that technology could be used to invent and actualize new forms of social life, rather than in the abstraction, forgetting, and ultimate destruction of that life. On the other hand, the concluding image of this passage – the human face *literally* becomes an alarm clock – signifies the vital (though often repressed) ability of the body's mimetic faculty to register and express the danger to humanity of forms of social organization such as capitalism. For example, an aesthetically mediated mimesis of the degradation and instrumentalization of objects as they are commodified can ignite a re-experiencing of human alienation – in both the workplace and the marketplace – that blazes through the phantasmagoric veil which normally shrouds it within capitalism.

Benjamin argues that in addition to these sensuous forms of mimesis, the mimetic faculty has migrated from the perception and adoption of physical similarities to the 'non-sensuous similitudes' of language.[43] He discerns a mimetic dimension of language whereby it reveals relations and similarities between things in ways that transcend its function as a purely semiotic system. As a means of conceptualizing this dimension of language, he describes how

> graphology has taught us to recognize in handwriting images that the unconscious of the writer conceals in it. It may be supposed that the mimetic process which expresses itself in this way in the activity of the writer was, in the very distant times in which script originated, of utmost importance for writing. Script has thus become, like language, an archive of nonsensuous similarities, of nonsensuous correspondances.[44]

Written words contain *both* semiotic and mimetic elements. A structuralist approach to language teaches that the relations between sign and referent are entirely arbitrary and only acquire meaning and significance within the differences of linguistic systems. Words function purely as signifiers. Conversely, Benjamin insists that 'language never gives *mere* signs.'[45] Careful analysis of the unique ways in which words take shape under the hand of a particular writer can reveal dimensions of an individual's unconscious that might otherwise remain hidden. Beyond the idiosyncratic claims of graphology, however, Benjamin offers the radical speculation that traces of humanity's collective unconscious are similarly inscribed within or, more accurately, may be *activated* by language itself. Notwithstanding the fixed connotation of the term 'archive,' his primary objective in developing this theory is not to excavate static correspondences locked away within accumulations of words. Rather, he understands language as a tool that humanity can use to energize, magnify, and extend the mimetic faculty's ability to perceive similitude beyond iconic visual resemblances and the classificatory regimes of scientific rationality. Furthermore, deducing the mimetic significance of language does not proceed in complete isolation from its expressive and communicative functions. Linguistic meaning initially excites the perception of non-sensuous similitude, but that which is perceived must not then be circumscribed within the boundaries of that meaning: 'The mimetic element in language can, like a flame, manifest itself only through a kind of bearer. This bearer is the semiotic element. Thus the nexus of meaning of words or sentences is the bearer through which, like a flash, similarity appears.'[46]

A full consideration of the significance of mimesis for Benjamin's broader theory of experience must await the third chapter. At this point, it is enough to say that he regards the perception of these 'flashes' of similarity as playing a crucial role in our ability – both as individuals and collectively – to access memory and create a framework for experience that goes beyond the immediate sensations of the present. As we will see, Benjamin is strongly influenced by Freud's understanding of how experience can be deflected from the conscious faculties to the unconscious: memories from the latter will sporadically erupt into the former, but only in a distorted form. In the case of dreams, for example, wishes considered too dangerous to bring into consciousness are permitted expression only on the condition that they be masked in the fantastic images, symbols, and codes of the dream. Weigel notes that the 'readability' of memories is 'structured by the dialectic of consciousness and mnemic traces, and described in terms of a momentary flickering-up or becoming visible.'[47] This 'flickering-up' corresponds to 'flashes' that are mimetically perceived:

> The perception of resemblances thus refers precisely to the instant of the readability of memory traces which Freud described as the flickering up of consciousness in apperception ... A reading of this kind, which is adept at deciphering non-sensuous similitudes and distorted representations and in which language-memory and memory-language converge, constitutes, then, the attitude through which remains, images, things, words, gestures, and graphic images become readable and cognizable as traces. And this is, as Benjamin says, the 'attitude of genuine recollection.'[48]

Mimesis is much more than the archaic residue of primitive rituals that have long been displaced by science and reason. It holds out the possibility for an empowering and innervating relationship with the object world that does not rely on the narcissistic projection or sadistic imposition of human will on the other. The mimetic faculty enables a fuller experience of the social and material environment; it also mobilizes these experiences as it liberates their memory from the unconscious to flash through and energize minds and bodies in times of opportunity and danger.

Mimetic practices do not, however, inevitably lead to human emancipation and the redemption of the object. They bear the hopes of the past, but they are also scarred by its violence. The 'powerful compulsion to become like something else' to which Benjamin alludes is none other than terror of the unknown and the desperate struggle for self-preservation. Humans once imitated a wild, unpredictable, and all-powerful nature in the hope of assimilating themselves to it. In becoming one with their physical environment, they actively sacrificed a latent subjectivity that threatened to cut them off from that environment. These practices appear as the antithesis of enlightenment, but they also contain within them its germ cell – namely, the willingness and capacity of human beings to change (i.e., sacrifice) themselves in order to acquire power over nature. As science and reason strip the world of its enchantment, the mimetic cognition that dominated primitive humanity is seemingly left behind or confined to aesthetics and childhood. Yet mimesis is not so much abandoned as perfected. The animistic qualities attributed to nature by earlier societies – the result of anthropomorphic projection – introduced a feedback loop into mimetic rituals that compromised man's ability to fully become the inanimate world. Once this distortion is removed, mimesis of nature can proceed without hindrance: 'Only deliberate adaptation to it brings nature under the power of the physically weaker. The reason that represses mimesis is not merely its opposite. It is itself mimesis: of death. The subjective mind which disintegrates the spiritualization of nature masters spiritless nature only by imitating its rigidity, disintegrating itself as animistic.'[49]

In the past, human beings sought power by making themselves resemble a nature populated by spirits, demons, and gods; today, cognitive processes are molded after an environment composed of inert matter that is thoroughly subjected to the rule of science and instrumental reason: 'In technology the adaptation to lifelessness in the service of self-preservation is no longer accomplished, as in magic, by bodily imitation of external nature, but by automating mental processes, turning them into blind sequences.'[50] The rigid, static, and instrumental logic of identity must be adopted in order to take possession of nature *as* inert matter. Mimetically, human perception is radically impoverished: 'The manifold affinities between existing things are supplanted by the single relationship between the subject who confers meaning and the meaningless object.'[51] The evolution of science, technology, and social structures through which this new power over nature is organized and managed is contingent on the self-transformation of human beings into inanimate matter: 'Thought is reified as an autonomous, automatic process, aping the machine it has itself produced, so that it can finally be replaced by the machine.'[52] Thus humanity enacts the lessons learned by Odysseus so long ago: only by sacrificing itself does it continue to live.

For Benjamin, Marx's political economy offers convincing testimony to the ongoing mimesis of death endured by the worker under capitalism. As noted earlier, Marx described how the commodification of labour-power sponsors the alienation of labour and its eventual return, in the form of capital, to further tyrannize and dominate the worker – that which is living is forced to submit and adapt to that which is dead:

> The article being assembled comes within the worker's range of action independently of his volition, and moves away from him just as arbitrarily. 'It is a common characteristic of all capitalist production ...,' wrote Marx, 'that the worker does not make use of the working conditions. The working conditions make use of the worker; but it takes machinery to give this reversal a technologically concrete form.' In working with machines,

workers learn to coordinate 'their own movements with the uniformly constant movements of an automaton.'[53]

Instead of the empowering, innervating experience that self-directed mimesis makes possible, this imposed adaptation to the machine is the example *par excellence* of the insular, defensive function of mimesis. Instead of opening up avenues to the external world, 'apotropaic mimesis'[54] closes them down in order to protect the individual against physical harm and excessive shock. This defensive use of the mimetic faculty, argues Benjamin, is hardly confined to the factory floor: it saturates the totality of modern urban experience. Analysing a description of a city scene by Edgar Allen Poe, Benjamin observes that 'his pedestrians act as if they had adapted themselves to machines and could express themselves only automatically. Their behaviour is a reaction to shocks. "If jostled, they bowed profusely to the jostlers."'[55] Just as the worker has no choice within capitalism but to submit to the machine, so too is the urban inhabitant left without any option but to propitiate the forces in his or her environment through mimetic adaptation. The *flâneur* who demands elbow room as he strolls along is a dying breed. Even the human face – among the most adept parts of the human body for expressing and registering similarities – succumbs to these defensive strategies: the smile that settles on the passer-by now functions as little more than a 'mimetic shock absorber.'[56]

Even more terrifying is the capacity of commodified cultural practices to libidinize apotropaic mimesis, transforming it into an activity that is experienced as pleasurable. Once again, Benjamin chooses fashion to illustrate this dynamic, constellating with death that which conventionally signifies life, vitality, and renewal: 'Fashion prescribed the ritual by which the commodity fetish demands to be worshipped ... Fashion stands in opposition to the organic. It couples the living body to the organic world. To the living, it defends the rights of the corpse. The fetishism that succumbs to the sex appeal of the inorganic is its vital nerve. The cult of the commodity presses such fetishism into its service.'[57]

The ritual that fashion prescribes for the worship of the commodity fetish is the relentless pursuit of novelty through patterns of repetitious consumption that never end. Such is the mythic dynamic that lies at the heart of the commodity form. The satirical sketches of Grandville – in which commodities are rendered as human – explore in images the perversity with which things appear to take on a life of their own under capitalism. Conversely, in the case of fashion, that which actually does have life – the human, primarily the female, body – is treated as an inanimate object that can only acquire life by draping itself in the newest fashions of the day. Benjamin would hardly have been surprised by the violence to which people increasingly subject their bodies in pursuit of the synthetic ideals that dominate the mass media. Indeed, his comment that fashion 'defends the rights of the corpse' could hardly be more fitting to describe the emaciated, skeletal bodies of most of the women positioned by mass culture as objects of desire. The fragmentation of the human body into fetishized pieces – into the corpse – is prefigured in *The Origin of German Tragic Drama* as necessary for the body to assume an allegorical role in mourning plays.[58] Similarly, the fetishization of the human body that occurs under capitalism is a necessary condition for its continuing commodification. Fashion becomes 'the dialectical exchange between woman and ware – between carnal pleasure and the corpse.'[59] Inanimate objects displace human relationships as the privileged sites of libidinal discharge; in the phantasmagoria of capitalism, sexual pathology fuses with the fetishism of commodities as the seemingly autonomous life of the object assumes a 'sex appeal.' The quality of sexual attractiveness attaches itself to clothes, style, and image as a facsimile of the person: 'Erotic desire, instinctual desire itself, and also those forces of fantasy-life that might imagine a better society are cathected onto commodities. Trapped within capitalism, they become its enthusiastic source of support.'[60] As commodities are brought to the consumer through the marketplace, the act of exchange is vicariously libidinized: the commodity form itself becomes the privileged site for the arousal, management, and satisfaction of human desire. The commodification of sexuality reinforces this dynamic as the expression and discharge of desire is linked to sameness and identity: 'With the exhibition of girls in rigidly uniform dress at a later period, the music hall review explicitly introduced the mass-produced article into the libidinal life of the big city dweller.'[61] Yet the belief that one is entering into a relation of immediacy with these objects is a double illusion: not only are the fantasies they offer an objective delusion generated by the fetishism of the commodity, but access to them is always mediated through the market. Cruelly deceived, our mimesis of the life that we come to believe lies outside ourselves, reverses into a mimesis of death.

For Benjamin, the figure of the gambler is perhaps the clearest representation of this reversal. At first glance, games of chance would seem to have little in common with the drudgery experienced on the assembly line: each time the dice are thrown or the cards are reshuffled, the intoxicating promise of the new and unexpected becomes almost palpable. But in a nineteenth-century lithograph of a gambling club, Benjamin identifies the defensive, reactive mimesis that both activities share: 'The figures presented show us how the mechanism to which gamblers entrust themselves seizes them body and soul, so that even in their private sphere, and no matter how agitated they may be, they are capable only of reflex actions. They behave like the pedestrians in Poe's story. They live their lives as automatons.'[62]

In much the same way as Adorno describes the hidden parallels between work and mass culture, Benjamin locates gambling in a constellation of phenomena such as world exhibitions and fun fairs, where people are trained to take pleasure from activities that are normally experienced as exhaustive drudgery. The gambler enjoys to the point of addiction a repetitious and monotonous set of processes that arouse boredom, frustration, and hatred in other environments. Writing about jazz, Adorno explains that 'the compulsion to adjust to mechanized production evidently requires the conflict between that mechanization and the living body to be repeated, neutralized and imitated, in the body's leisure time. Something like a reconcilement between helpless body and machinery, human atom and collective power, is symbolically celebrated.'[63] Together with Horkheimer, he traces this type of adaptive mimesis back to mythic sacrifice: 'The venerable belief in sacrifice is probably itself a behavior pattern drilled into the subjugated, by which they reenact against themselves the wrong done to them in order to be able to bear it.'[64] In contemporary capitalism, such sacrifice is organized, rationalized and, most importantly, libidinized by the culture industry: its practices function to inoculate individuals mimetically against the shocks experienced by living organisms that are forced to adapt themselves to inorganic objects, processes, and structures. By voluntarily giving the events in his life a 'shock-like' quality,[65] the gambler unwittingly but effectively prepares his mind and body for a modern existence saturated with shocks. By secretly replicating the cognitive patterns and physical behaviour from which one flees during 'free time,' the rituals of mass culture exercise mimetic faculties in the defensive strategies needed for survival under capitalism.

As advertising and the display of commodities become more and more dominant, actual purchase of the good is often no longer required to cement this empathy with the commodity. Simply in gazing upon the object or its representation, we lose ourselves in the fantasies it inspires. In a prescient anticipation of the function of advertising, Benjamin describes world fairs as 'schools where the masses, forced away from consumption, learned how to empathize with exchange value.'[66] And as he himself acknowledges, this argument shares much with Adorno's claim that in mass culture it is exchange-value itself that is now enjoyed as use-value:

> Empathy with the commodity presents itself to self-introspection or inner experience as empathy with inorganic matter ... Basically, however, empathy with the commodity is probably empathy with exchange-value itself. And in fact, one can hardly imagine the 'consumption' of exchange-value as anything else but an empathy with it ... Empathy with exchange-value can turn guns into articles of consumption more attractive than butter.[67]

Empathy, in this case, is closely connected with the mimetic faculty: one empathizes with an other by imagining what it must be like to *be* that other. As capitalism makes an increasingly diverse array of commodities available for speculative and real consumption, mimesis is one of the dominant practices through which people participate in the hopes, desires and dreams offered for sale. With ever greater intensity, bodies and lives are desperately modelled after commodities that promise a pleasure unavailable in the alienated labour and reified social relations of capitalist society. In a sinister doubling of the commodification of labour, people empathize with commodities, desiring to become commodities themselves in the hope of partaking of some of the independence, autonomy, and 'life' that they seem to possess. Hence Benjamin fingers Baudelaire's genius in positioning the prostitute as the *ur*-figure of urban capitalism. A mimetic instinct that once offered the body as a sensuous instrument for the inscription, expression, and performance of similarities – thereby challenging the limitations of purely instrumental forms of reason – is historically reoriented toward the production of a subjectivity in which the human being is imagined first and foremost as a marketable commodity, a collection of features that might solicit the interested gaze of a buyer.

As Miriam Hansen notes, Adorno similarly identifies a mimetic dialectic that enjoins consumers to imitate those whom they see on the screens of the culture industry. Once again, Wagner's musical forms prefigure the direction that is eventually perfected by mass culture:

'What [he] has done with artistic rationality is to conjure up and manipulate a half-submerged and forgotten collective world of images.'[68] Art's capacity to work through images and thereby cultivate a mimetic relation between subject and object is simultaneously the basis for its emancipatory potential *and* its use as an ideological instrument *par excellence*. On the one hand, the mimetic impulse can temporarily destabilize the narcissism of the ego, opening the subject up to a non-instrumental relation with the object. On the other hand, as images, culture can tap directly into the unconscious and activate latent mimetic impulses to copy what is seen. In *Minima Moralia*, Adorno writes that 'the human is indissolubly linked with imitation: a human being only becomes human at all by imitating other human beings.'[69] As the culture industry grows to fill the empty spaces of social life, it increasingly provides the model for the mimetic genesis of individuals. We learn who we are and are not through the images in mass culture: 'The movements which the film presents are mimetic impulses which, prior to all content and meaning, incite the viewers and listeners to fall into step as if in a parade.'[70] Benjamin, as we will see, views this suspension of consciousness and its associated 'censorship' mechanisms as a potent opportunity for the synthetic generation of experience (*Erfahrung*). Adorno, in contrast, views this evasive penetration of the unconscious as 'psychoanalysis in reverse'[71] – as enabling defensive psychological mechanisms that, remaining hidden, ultimately close off the possibility for experience. Even worse, those mechanisms enable the 'push-button behaviour patterns'[72] of late capitalism and fascism. As the iconic fidelity of mass cultural forms is perfected through modern technology – signified for Adorno and Horkheimer by the transition from silent to sound film – the essence of those forms as writing, as synthetic creations, disappears entirely from vision and consciousness. However, their scriptural character returns all the more powerfully at the level of the subconscious in the form of an injunction to be like those on the screen:

> Simulating immediacy, individuality, and intimacy, the 'characters' of mass culture spell out norms of social behaviour – ways of being, smiling, and mating. Regardless of the explicit messages touted via dialogue and plot, the viewer is ceaselessly asked to translate image into script, to read the individual appearance of a star as an imperative of identity – 'to be like her' – and to articulate the most subtle nuances in terms of the binary logic of 'do and don't.'[73]

And so Adorno can lament that 'every visit to the cinema leaves me, *against all vigilance*, stupider and worse.'[74] This 'image-writing' is not a conscious strategy of clever manipulation on the part of culture industry managers; rather, it takes shape within the parameters specified by the commodity form. Thus, its 'talking masks,'[75] entirely constructed by the commodified productive apparatus of the culture industry, have been stripped of their humanity: 'As far as mass culture is concerned reification is no metaphor: it makes the human beings that it reproduces resemble things even where their teeth do not represent toothpaste and their care-worn wrinkles do not evoke cosmetics.'[76] Cinema goers are driven by the perennial hope of finding life; nevertheless, they obey the mimetic injunction to become what they see: 'They assimilate themselves to what is dead.'[77] A burgeoning product-placement industry ensures that this desire for assimilation is efficiently channelled into the consumption of commodities.

Even the happiness supposedly sold by the culture industry succumbs to this dynamic: 'Mimesis explains the enigmatically empty ecstacy of the fans in mass culture. Ecstacy is the motor of imitation ... When people dance to jazz for example they do not dance for sensuous pleasure or in order to obtain release. Rather they merely depict the gestures of sensuous human beings.'[78] In chapter 1 I explained why Adorno believes that the pleasures promised by the culture industry are never adequately fulfilled: its objects, images, and fantasies are simply incapable of sustaining the discharge of libidinal energy. Accordingly, sensual gratification is itself mimetically copied rather than actually experienced: mass culture leaves its consumers no other choice. This explains the element of self-parody that is increasingly finding its way into the culture industry: 'Its medium is caricature. Dance and music copy stages of sexual excitement only to make fun of them.'[79] Standing 'under the sign of terror,'[80] it is hardly surprising that under such conditions, the mimetic propitiation of forces beyond our control will inevitably be coloured by the artifice that accompanies performance. Fear and joy do not mix. On the one hand, this fear annuls the critical edge that once accompanied satire: laughter now functions not to break the spell of power, but only to erase any chance of escape. On the other hand, the fact that mass culture's pleasures can themselves only be consumed mimetically offers a slender ray of hope. Writing about fascist propaganda, Adorno notes that the masses are not duped by its promises. Rather, their enthusiasm is similarly performed: 'It is through this performance that they strike a balance between their continuously mobilized instinctual urges and the historical stage of enlightenment they have reached, and which cannot be revoked arbitrarily.'[81] The suspension of humanity between these two imperatives keeps alive the hope that the mimetic chains which bind them to the images of the culture industry may perhaps one day be broken. Arguably, what feeds this hope is the memory of a human capacity for experience, which has yet to be entirely closed down.

## The End of Experience? From *Erfahrung* to *Erlebnis*

A central theme in Benjamin's later work is how the capacity of human beings to experience their social and material environment has been transformed by the growth of technology and urbanization in capitalist society. These changes impede the meaningful integration of individual experiences into a historical continuum of memory or 'life-experience' (*Erfahrung*). Instead, people deploy various psychic mechanisms to defend themselves against the shocks of everyday life, and as a result, experience is broken into detached and isolated fragments. Each experience (*Erlebnis*) remains separated from all the others in a serialized chain of compartmentalized and discrete events. Adorno does not deploy this particular framework, but as I argued in the previous chapter, he holds similar views regarding the impoverishment of human experience under the tutelage of the culture industry. In the final section of this chapter I survey Benjamin's conception of the shift from *Erfahrung* to *Erlebnis* so as to make visible the homologies between this experiential continuum and Adorno's analysis of mass culture.

'*Memory*,' writes Benjamin, 'creates the chain of tradition which transmits an event from generation to generation.'[82] He suggests that in the past, personal and communal memories blended together in a tightly woven mnemic field that both enabled and regulated the transmission of cultural knowledge. The experience of specific events was governed by their enforced immersion in this field: nothing was experienced without simultaneously being placed in a network of stories and memories that helped determine its significance and meaning. In large part, the maintenance of this field relied on the desire and capacity of individuals to embed particular events in their own life histories, and, subsequently, to communicate both the event and its narrative integration to others. Both activities are fused in the figure of the storyteller: 'A story does not aim to convey an event per se, which is the purpose of information; rather, it embeds the event in the life of the storyteller in order to pass it on as experience to those listening.'[83] In this process of mnemic integration, the storyteller teaches by example, showing others by way of his or her own active presence within the tale how it is possible to make another's experiences one's own, to blur the lines between that which happens to oneself and that which happens to others. The telling of a story 'submerges the thing into the life of the storyteller, in order to bring it out of him again. Thus, traces of the storyteller cling to a story the way the handprints of the potter cling to a clay vessel.'[84] In this way the chains of tradition are forged. However, the heat of the furnace that forges them is not provided solely by the storyteller's art. It must be fuelled by an audience whose psychic disposition is fundamentally open to receiving the experiences of others, and who are able to use tradition to perceive the resemblances between them and their own, and who are eager to weave the storyteller's experiences into their own memories. Moreover, it is not just the memories of others that are so assimilated; so too are personal experiences: separate events experienced by an individual are similarly fused with and mediated through a mnemic matrix that traces multiple connecting pathways between their particular location in time and space and the broader personal and collective life-experience of which they are a part. Something of this full experience of the world – largely generated and sustained through an expansive use of memory to embed the individual in tradition and history – is what Benjamin hopes to convey with the term *Erfahrung*.

One might expect that this conception of experience requires attentive subjects who vigilantly patrol both their own experiences and those of others for suitable fragments that can be consciously and rationally assimilated with their memory structures. However, quite the opposite is true. *Erfahrung* relies on a kind of experience in which there is a relatively open intercourse between consciousness and the body. The relations among the physical sensations, cognitive perceptions, affective states, libidinal energies, and memories aroused by a particular event are fluid, complementary, and fundamentally equitable. Events are experienced in a more holistic manner as individuals bring into play *all* of their perceptive, sensory, and cognitive faculties. No single faculty is positioned architectonically to govern selectively how events are experienced; rather, the data from each sensory apparatus are placed on a fairly equal footing within consciousness. These full and expansive experiences can then easily be immersed and later embedded in the mnemic field that draws out the countless connections between themselves and the memories that are arrayed within this field. As with experiencing the external environment, this process of immersion is not managed solely by conscious processes. In fact, Benjamin suggests that too much attentiveness will actually compromise the individual's capacity to hear the stories of others and integrate them into his or her own experience and memory: 'This process of assimilation, which takes place in the depths, requires a state of relaxation which is becoming rarer and rarer. If sleep is the apogee of physical relaxation, boredom is the apogee of mental relaxation. Boredom is the dream bird that hatches the egg of experience. A rustling in the leaves drives him away.'[85] In other words, a relaxed, distracted frame of mind is optimal because it maximizes the sensitivity of mnemic systems to the most comprehensive inscription of the story and its consequent linkages with other memories as opposed to its mediation and filtration through conscious perception.

In *Erfahrung*, specific events are never experienced in isolation; they always take on their meaning and significance as they are integrated into a broader individual and social framework of tradition. Benjamin argues that this historical continuity of experiences is one of the primary differences between the story and the novel, with the latter's rise signifying the slow emergence of a very different framework for experience and its communication. The story is based on the instructive exchange of experiences between individuals; in contrast, 'the birthplace of the novel is the individual in his isolation, the individual who can no longer speak of his concerns in exemplary fashion, who himself lacks counsel and can give none. To write a novel is to take to the extreme that which is incommensurable in the representation of human existence.'[86] What is lost here is not the abstract capacity to communicate information about events that have occurred, but rather the ability and desire to make these experiences one's own. The reader of a novel may find its events extremely compelling; even so, they remain events that have happened to another, fixed through printing in time and space. After all, what distinguishes the novel from other forms of prose is the absence of any connection to oral traditions of storytelling.[87] Conversely, stories collapse the distinction between individuals, communities, and even historical epochs. A true story never becomes dated, and its didactic content always remains fresh: it 'does not expend itself. It preserves and concentrates its energy and is capable of releasing it even after a long time ... It is like those seeds of grain that have lain for centuries in the airtight chambers of the pyramids and have retained their germinative power to this day.'[88] Time and space are themselves rendered fluid and permeable by the power of a story. The experiences contained in stories may be separated from the present by vast historical and geographical distances; yet they do not lose their power to affect the present, because of their positioning within the shared memories that continue to mediate and interpret contemporary experience through the influence of tradition: 'For an experienced event is finite – at any rate, confined to one sphere of experience; a remembered event is infinite, because it is merely a key to everything that happened before it and after it.'[89] Not all forms of remembrance, however, possess this power: memory only acquires it when it is fused with experience in the production of *Erfahrung*. Conversely, the novel depicts existence in the form of detached, isolated fragments that are fundamentally dissimilar as well as permanently fixed in specific locations in time and space. The newspaper marks the ultimate triumph of the communication of experience as 'information':

> If it were the intention of the press to have the reader assimilate the information it supplies as part of his own experience, it would not achieve its purpose. But its intention is just the opposite, and it is achieved: to isolate events from the realm in which they could affect the experience of the reader. The principles of journalistic information (newness, brevity, clarity, and, above all, lack of connection between the individual news items) contribute as much to this as the layout of the pages and the style of writing.[90]

What the novel does for individual experiences, the newspaper does for the events of the world. Newspapers are embedded in an explanatory dynamic of their own, and the information they provide seals itself off from immersion in experience, memory, or tradition. Indeed, the only cognitive operation a newspaper leaves to its readers is an external form of objective verifiability: the information may be true or false, but either way it remains closed and distant from the experience of its consumers.

The novel and the newspaper are literary markers for changes in experience wrought by much greater forces. The dominant experience of modern life, argues Benjamin, is that of continual shocks. The fusion of technology, urban space, and the commodity form has produced a social environment in which individuals are subjected to an increasing volume of stimuli that must be rapidly perceived, accommodated, and processed. From the city's streets, factories, and offices to its shopping malls, theatres, and gambling houses, few social spheres are exempt from this social logic. For instance, the casual nineteenth-century stroll of the *flâneur*, who once delighted in taking turtles for walks on urban boulevards to enforce a relaxed pace,[91] has been replaced by the brisk conduct of pedestrians anxious to be on their way: 'Moving through [the traffic of a big city] involves the individual in a series of shocks and collisions. At dangerous crossings, nervous impulses flow through him in rapid succession, like the energy from a battery.'[92] Following Marx's analytic lead, Benjamin discerns a similar dynamic in the transformation of the labour process under capitalism. The self-directed activity of the craftsman has become a thing of the past. Instead, workers are now forced, with increasing precision, to adapt their minds and bodies to the patterns dictated by the machine and/or the institution, actively transforming themselves into the slaves of a technological apparatus that is itself animated and given phantasmagoric life by the relentless drive for capital accumulation. As discussed earlier, one response to this type of environment is the adoption of an apotropaic mimesis whereby the individual automatically subordinates his or her actions and thoughts to the patterns imposed heteronomously by external forces. However, this tactic is useful only insofar as these forces assume relatively stable patterns. In many cases, the shocks of everyday life are not so predictable, in which case other defensive human faculties must be used.

Strongly influenced by Freud's theoretical speculations on the nature of memory in *Beyond the Pleasure Principle*, Benjamin argues that consciousness itself is one of the most potent devices for insulating an individual's cognitive systems from the shocks imposed on its sensory apparatus by the environment. Quoting from this work, he notes that

> 'it would be the special characteristic of consciousness that, unlike what happens in all other systems of the psyche, the excitatory process does not leave behind a permanent change in its elements, but expires, as it were, in the phenomenon of becoming conscious.' The basic formula of this hypothesis is that 'becoming conscious and leaving behind a memory trace are incompatible processes within one and the same system' ... In Freud's view, consciousness as such receives no memory traces whatever, but has another important function: protection against stimuli.[93]

*Erfahrung* constitutes itself through the unification of perception, bodily experience, and memory; the inhabitants of modernity must then separate these elements to guard against toxic stimuli. The individual deploys consciousness to select and filter out various aspects of experience in order to protect his or her psychic apparatus against the dangers of excessive shock. To the extent that consciousness can process and thereby deflect the traumas of everyday life, individuals can shield themselves from the psychic consequences that would accrue if these incidents were fully experienced. Not only is the psyche thereby insulated, but any residue from these waves of shock that does manage to penetrate these defences is absorbed, isolated, and confined to the body and the unconscious. In limiting the interchange among cognitive, psychic, and corporeal systems, the operations of memory in the generation of *Erfahrung* are fundamentally compromised. Memory and experience are effectively cut off from each other, and this radically impoverishes both. The weaving of events into experience requires their immersion in the mnemic field: the world is no longer 'experienced' in such a way that it can enter memory; furthermore, the lines of transmission linking memory, consciousness, and the body that are necessary for this integration have been defensively sterilized. As a result, the fusion of sensory data with mnemic impulses – a fusion required for an individual to 'experience' his or her existence fully – no longer occurs. In this way, *Erfahrung* is displaced by a new type of abstract, impoverished, and disconnected experience that Benjamin calls *Erlebnis*.

In a brilliant discussion of Benjamin's 'Work of Art' essay, Susan Buck-Morss reads this transformation of experience under capitalism through a shift from aesthetics – classically defined as a form of cognition in which the bodily senses occupy a central position – to an *anaesthetic* framework in which the cognitive faculties are reorganized so as to systematically suppress data from the senses. Environmental stimuli that might once have solicited conscious reflection and mnemic immersion have become so dangerous that they must be shunted aside. In this sense, an excessively attentive or alert disposition and an automatized or habitual mimesis share the common goal of restricting the openness of human beings to their world:

> Being 'cheated out of experience' has become the general state, as the synaesthetic system is marshalled to parry technological stimuli in order to protect both the body from the trauma of accident and the psyche from the trauma of shock. As a result the system reverses its role. Its goal is to *numb* the organism, to deaden the senses, to repress memory: the cognitive system of synaesthetics has become, rather, one of *an*aesthetics.[94]

Buck-Morss goes on to link this transformation of experience to Benjamin's rather alarming suggestion at the close of the 'Work of Art' essay that humanity's 'self-alienation has reached the point where it can experience its own annihilation as a supreme aesthetic pleasure.'[95] The rise of *Erlebnis* is marked by such a thorough desensitization to our individual and (more importantly perhaps) our collective existence that it becomes possible for our conscious faculties – effectively divided from the body, the unconscious and the memories (history) that lie buried there – to regard our own degradation and suffering with an almost contemplative detachment. For Benjamin as for Adorno, Kafka's stories tell as much: 'Just as K. lives in the village on Castle Hill, modern man lives in his own body: the body slips away from him, is hostile toward him. It may happen that a man wakes up one day and finds himself transformed into a vermin.'[96] In the most extreme cases – fascism being the obvious example – people derive pleasure from the spectacle of an aestheticized politics as enabled by the rise of new cultural technologies – this, despite its openly self-destructive qualities. More broadly, the ability to 'ignore,' instrumentalize, and often brutalize one's own body in the interests of working and even playing harder is deeply embedded in mass culture: recall Adorno's suggestion that sport trains people to enjoy the functionalization of the body that they must endure at the workplace. And most ominously, 'whoever is hard with himself earns the right to be hard with others.'[97]

One of the most significant elements of this transition from *Erfahrung* to *Erlebnis* is a transformation in how time itself is experienced. The impact of modern shocks on the individual can be dramatically reduced insofar as those shocks are serially processed and recorded. The cumulative impact of contemporary experience is enough to drive one into madness; however, an ability to break time up into a series of disconnected segments organizes this experience into discrete pieces that are possible to manage:[98]

> The greater the shock factor in particular impressions, the more vigilant consciousness has to be in screen stimuli; the more efficiently it does so, the less these impressions enter long experience [*Erfahrung*] and the more they correspond to the concept of isolated experience [*Erlebnis*]. Perhaps the special achievement of shock defense is the way it assigns an incident a precise point in time in consciousness, at the cost of the integrity of the incident's contents. This would be a peak achievement of the intellect; it would turn the incident into an isolated experience [*Erlebnis*].[99]

Moments that have been lived are experienced and recorded in isolation from other moments in one's life. It is not so much that they are subsequently forgotten, though this is often the case; rather, if they are wilfully remembered it is only abstractly, as an incident whose impact on the individual is limited to a particular moment in time and space. Specific experiences are sequentially inscribed in memory; each comes to occupy a compartment divided from the others. Furthermore, the integration of these memories into personal and collective histories is additively managed: narratives take the form of serial packets of information united only by the otherwise contingent fact that they describe events that happened to the same individual or group. The affective, libidinal, and bodily dimensions of experience that may have been bound up in particular events fade into empty, sterile husks in conscious memory as they are starved of that which might have kept them alive – namely, their supra-conscious immersion in an open mnemic field that deploys an expansive, associative logic to create webs and linkages between the past and the present.

This does not mean that *Erlebnis* is necessarily experienced as a dreary, monolithic, and repetitive existence. Indeed, the opposite is largely the case. Recall the image of the gambling club discussed earlier:

> Not one of the individuals in the scene is pursuing the game in ordinary fashion. Each man is dominated by an emotion: ... joy ... distrust ... despair ... belligerence ... All these modes of conduct share a concealed characteristic: the figures presented show us how the mechanism to which gamblers entrust themselves seizes them body and soul, so that even in their private sphere, and no matter how agitated they may be, they are capable only of reflex actions ... They live their lives as automatons and resemble Bergson's fictitious characters who have completely liquidated their memories.[100]

In *Erlebnis* the individual lives for and in 'the moment' and is entirely dominated by that moment and its associated sensations and emotions insofar as they are not contextualized within a broader framework of memory and experience. Even though each game is duplicated again and again, the failure of this exact repetition to register fully in the gambler's experience allows him to live each moment as if it were the first – a form of experience that has now become generalized. And as for the gambler, so too for society: 'The dreaming collective knows no history. Events pass before it as always identical and always new.'[101]

Crudely put, *Erlebnis* wipes clean the slate of experience by reducing the density and breadth of both collective and individual memories that can be made available in experiencing, contextualizing, and giving meaning to a specific event. And let us not forget that *Erlebnis* itself is in large part a consequence of the underlying sameness of lived experience within capitalist social relations: 'The absolute qualitative invariance of the time in which labor that generates exchange value runs its course – such absolute equality is the grayish background against which the gaudy colors of sensation stand out.'[102] In this context, Benjamin describes betting as 'a device for giving events the character of a shock, detaching them from the context of experience.'[103] The shock-like quality of events means that they are processed by consciousness and thereby deflected away from memory. Despite having lived them in the past, the full memories of such experiences are unavailable for understanding similar events in the present and the future. The gambler returns, again and again, eagerly lusting after the promise of novelty, change, and excitement, and he is able to live each identical moment again as if for the first time. Thus Anatole France describes gambling as 'the secret of living a whole lifetime in a few minutes.'[104] Intellectually, perhaps he knows the futility of his actions, but he is unable to deploy his own experiences of past disappointment to break his addiction. A desire for the new that is perpetually inscribed in practices, objects, and relations that never change describes, of course, not only gambling but an entire cultural apparatus that is constructed around the commodity form.

At this point, the homologies between *Erlebnis* and Adorno's propositions regarding the effects of the culture industry on human cognition should be clear. Although Adorno does not theorize the transformation of experience in quite this fashion, he certainly holds a similar set of concerns regarding the effect of mass culture on memory.[105] In a later article, for instance, his contrast between bourgeois art and mass culture regarding their effects on human experience is remarkably similar to Benjamin's *Erfahrung/Erlebnis* continuum: 'Experience – the continuity of consciousness in which everything not present survives, in which practice and association establish tradition in the individual – is replaced by the selective, disconnected, interchangeable and ephemeral state of being informed, which as one can already observe, will promptly be cancelled by other information.'[106]

Similarly, Horkheimer and Adorno repeatedly describe mass cultural products as a serial agglomeration of 'shocks and sensations,' which are nevertheless smoothly integrated into patterns of consumption given the synchronic structure of contemporary cognition: 'The defective power of recall on the part of the consumer furnishes the point of departure: no one is trusted to remember anything that has already happened or to concentrate upon anything other than what is presented to him in the given moment. The consumer is thus reduced to the abstract present.'[107] For Adorno, the spatialization and consequent eradication of the temporal dimension of experience is one of the greatest crimes of the culture industry and of the broader social tendencies of capitalism. Summarizing Adorno's critique of the music of Igor Stravinsky – a favourite target – Calvin Thomas writes that 'The spatialization in his music insures that experience itself is not negotiated within temporal processes, which still preserve the possibility of agency and development, but is conferred only among a random host of disconnected, fragmented, interchangeable forms with no discernable relationship to a whole.'[108] It is not simply that the potential for change and development is erased, but that it is forced into spatialized forms that sponsor the continuing illusion of endless freedom. The compartmentalization of memory ensures that the present is experienced as a novelty even though the truly new can only be developed in dialectical mediation with the past. As Goethe's Mephistopholes notes, the Devil's greatest power is the destruction of memory: 'and it's as good as if it never happened.'[109] Adorno believes that this type of experiential impoverishment stands in a symbiotic relationship with mass culture: each is the necessary corollary of the other. On the one hand, the culture industry depends on consumers whose collective amnesia sponsors the never-ending purchase of commodities that never really change. On the other hand, the enjoyment of these goods – one of the few pleasures left after the exhaustive drudgery of the workplace – requires that experience be actively (re)structured in just such a serialized manner.

For Adorno, this symbiosis is not an autochthonous product of modernity. The desperation with which people partake of the culture industry – of which the mimetic quality of their ecstacy is perhaps the best marker – is driven by their growing desire for novelty, immediacy, and colour in an existence that is becoming more and more alienated: 'Generally speaking there is good reason to assume that all forms of pseudo-activity contain a pent-up need to change the petrified relations of society. Pseudo-activity is misguided spontaneity.'[110] Thus, mass culture assumes a compensatory function; popular music, for example, is designed to 'decorate' the empty, discontinuous time of modern life and thereby provide the illusion of change, progress and becoming: 'The color of the inner sense, the bright, detailed imagery of the flow of time, assures a man that within the monotony of universal comparability there is still something particular.'[111] Contrast this with the rigorous formula of Schönberg's twelve-tone compositions, which raise the repetitive quality of modern life into consciousness. However, the ornamentation furnished by the culture industry is secretly made of the same stuff that it tries to hide. Any attempt to break more substantively with the cognitive and psychological patterns established in the workplace and society at large is met with either incomprehension or frustration at the effort required for thinking 'the new'; neither is very good for business. Furthermore, individuals can be expected to adjust themselves as they try to take pleasure from that which is given to them. In order to partake of these illusions and see them as something other than the repetition of the ever-same, one's own experiential framework must be changed so that it comes to echo the decomposition of time into the discontinuous, shock-like moments that it was originally trying to flee. As it does, the relationship between specific events and the personal and collective life experience of which they are a part takes on similar qualities to the relationship between the particular detail or moment and the whole in the products of the culture industry. In the case of music, for example, 'if the moments of sensual pleasure in the idea, the voice, the instrument are made into fetishes and torn away from any functions which could give them meaning, they meet a response equally isolated, equally far from the meaning of the whole, and equally determined by success in the blind and irrational emotions which form the relationship to music into which those with no relationship enter.'[112]

As the framework for experience 'adjusts' to this pattern of stimulation, individuals become unable to understand, desire, or experience anything different: thus do *Erlebnis* and the culture industry come together in a tautological embrace. Both Benjamin and Adorno, then, share a similar diagnosis of how the growth of capitalism has shattered the traditional capacity of human beings to embed individual experiences in a larger narrative continuum both personal and collective in favour of a disjointed, spatialized temporality in which subjectivity has decayed into a collage of shocks.

# 3

# Dreams of Redemption? Adorno, Benjamin, and the Dialectics of Culture

> The products of false consciousness resemble picture puzzles in which the true subject peeks out from among clouds, foliage and shadows.
>
> Benjamin, 'An Outsider Makes His Mark'

Adorno, despite the fiercely guarded negativity of his analysis, shares with Benjamin the belief that human experience is never fully colonized by the culture industry. It is impossible to read his work on mass culture without encountering occasional fragments of hope scattered throughout the otherwise unbroken polemic. True to form, Adorno argues that such fragments never show themselves directly; instead, we must decipher their inverted reflection out of mass cultural practices that at first glance leave us with little hope. Witness the spin he puts on the inexorable repetition of the culture industry: 'Since as subjects men themselves still represent the ultimate limit of reification,' note Horkheimer and Adorno, 'mass culture must try and take hold of them again and again: the bad infinity involved in this hopeless effort of repetition is the only trace of hope that this repetition might be in vain, that men cannot be wholly grasped after all.'[1] Similarly, the passionate energy with which people perform their integration into mass culture gives an ambiguous inflection to Adorno's otherwise desolate exploration of popular music: 'In order to become a jitterbug or simply to "like" popular music, it does not by any means suffice to give oneself up and to fall in line passively. To become transformed into an insect, man needs that energy which might possibly achieve his transformation into a man.'[2] Empirically, *The Authoritarian Personality* contains examples of those whose low scores on the 'F-scale' demonstrate that more than an insignificant fraction have preserved the capacity for some critical awareness.[3] Chance for redemption is extended even to the most degraded objects of the culture industry: 'Vestiges of the aesthetic claim to be something autonomous, a world unto itself, remain even within the most trivial product of mass culture.'[4] Such words bespeak a hope that, unfortunately, is never developed more fully or systematically in the writings on the culture industry. In large part, this absence can be explained by Adorno's belief that reification, alienation, and commodification are never fully experienced as such in mass culture – a prerequisite to any authentic emancipatory impulse. However, he does think that there are human practices – namely, serious modern art – through which such an experience can be produced. For that reason, I begin this chapter with a short excursus into the famously impenetrable labyrinth of Adorno's aesthetic theory.

**The Promise of Culture: Adorno's Aesthetics**

Notwithstanding the utopian traces that linger there, Adorno's aesthetic theory may seem a strange endpoint for a discussion of the culture industry. At first glance, mass culture and serious art are only the most distant of cousins: the obvious differences between their creative output widen into an apparently insurmountable divide when the broader contexts of production and reception are added to the mix. Reading Adorno's work on aesthetics in the late twentieth century, I cannot help being struck by the extraordinary distance between his descriptions of art and my own cultural experience. I have learned over time to describe and even explain conceptually what 'structural listening' is, but I remain hopelessly inept when it comes to actually trying to listen or even imagine listening to music 'structurally.' Others have noted how *Aesthetic Theory* itself 'presupposes a primitive accumulation of the capital of aesthetic experience,'[5] without which, one is smugly assured, there is really little hope of ever truly grasping the text. Conversely, the cynical, patronizing tone of Adorno's own remarks on the evil banality of mass culture testify rather convincingly to his own inability or unwillingness to experience its pleasures.[6] Battle lines drawn, these differences can and often do harden into the warring camps of populism and elitism. At times, Adorno appears as an eager participant in these cultural skirmishes; but there are other moments when he recognizes their ultimate futility. To Benjamin, for instance, he once remarked that both mass culture and serious art 'bear the stigmata of capitalism, both contain elements of change ... Both are torn halves of an integral freedom, to which, however, they do not add up.'[7] Freedom belongs neither to their simple addition nor to the discrete triumph of one over the other; instead, its possibility emerges in the tension that arises from their juxtaposition. Each serves as the other's guilty conscience, reminding it of promises once made but long since forgotten. While Adorno may not have always heeded this advice himself (i.e., that culture and serious art are equally torn halves of freedom), I propose that we do so now. For a full understanding of the culture industry texts – both the logic of their arguments and their bitter tone – will always elude us in the absence of an encounter with the aesthetic potential against which the measure of mass culture is so ruthlessly taken. And while an inability to have aesthetic experiences as Adorno once did limits the force of his arguments, it need not condemn them to contemporary irrelevance. Adorno's aesthetic propositions are immeasurably dimmed by the gap that separates us from him; nevertheless, they can still function as a kind of negative utopia: instead of giving philosophical shape to aesthetic experiences already had, they can help destabilize our own experience of mass culture by proposing how culture could do so much more than keep us entertained, make us feel good, and help pass the time.

According to Adorno, one of the most important qualities of serious art is its social uselessness, its lack of function. Inspired by Kant's aesthetic theory, and especially by his understanding of art as representing 'purposiveness without purpose,'[8] he regards the true goal of aesthetic creation as the creation of objects that are entirely *useless* in an instrumental sense. In the postwar era, Adorno similarly argues that only because philosophy is 'good for nothing' is it not yet obsolete.[9] As exchange relations and bureaucratic rationalization gradually expand to encompass all spheres of social life, they bring with them an instrumental, utilitarian logic in which all things, activities, and even people take on value only insofar as they are useful for something else: 'The identity of everything with everything is bought at the cost that nothing can at the same time be identical to itself.'[10] In other words, objects and people are barred from expressing their specificity, asserting their autonomy, and/or developing their potentiality, because their existence and – in the case of human beings, their self-awareness – is predicated on their being-for-others. Art protests the seemingly inexorable advance of this logic, tangibly demonstrating that the attribution of worth need not be completely subsumed by the category of use. 'Total purposelessness gives the lie to the totality of purposefulness in the world of domination, and only by virtue of this negation, which consummates the established order by drawing the conclusion from its own principle of reason, has existing society up to now become aware of another that is possible.'[11]

As an entirely rational activity, the creation and reception of art reminds us that human reason can be used purposively without subordinating itself to functional considerations. The refusal of works of art to justify themselves before the inquisition of social utility solicits the rage of many; but for others this mute, helpless arrogance can help destabilize the authority of such questions themselves. Using its own historically specific forms, art is often able to stir something deep within, including, most importantly, a mimetic faculty that is the legacy of human evolution. This faculty is ontogenetically recapitulated in the play of children and scattered throughout human society in a variety of forms such as language. Bourgeois society tries to pre-emptively disarm these dangerously siren-like experiences by banishing the mimetic rationality of art to the harmless purgatory of utopian fantasy. Yet a powerful, non-conceptual affinity with certain artworks makes it difficult for people to simply dismiss them as so much nonsense: 'As a musical composition compresses time, and as a painting folds spaces into one another, so the possibility is concretized that the world could be other than it is.'[12] Once art is experienced in this way, these experiences can be given conceptual expression with the tools provided by critical interpretation and aesthetic philosophy. This reflection concludes that artistic practice fundamentally invalidates instrumental reason's totalitarian claim to encompass reason *per se*; art furnishes tangible evidence of the very different but altogether rational use of the imagination in the arrangement of materials to create objects that are governed by their own alternative, immanent, and mimetic logics. Thus, art's uselessness, its 'purposive purposelessness,' keeps alive the possibility of different kinds of relations between subjects and objects, human beings and nature, and human beings with and among themselves. Most importantly, art's purposive purposelessness performs 'the rescue of nature,' mimetically siding with a suppressed nature 'to which it owes the idea of a purposefulness that is other than that posited by humanity; an idea, obviously, that was undermined by the rise of natural science.'[13] As we are moved by these aesthetic acts, we are reminded of our own affinities with the repressed nature that lies forgotten within.

The mimetic rationality of aesthetics differs from the abstract systems of philosophy and natural science in part because it actively incorporates the sensuous qualities of the world within its very forms: 'Art is the most drastic argument against the epistemological separation of sensuousness and understanding.'[14] It forcibly and palpably reminds us of a materiality that is real but that cannot be adequately represented, subsumed, or abstracted under conceptual systems. 'By virtue of its mimetic structure,' argues Richard Wolin, 'aesthetic truth retains an affinity with the somatic side of things, with that *ineffable* dimension that remains occluded in pure conceptualization, the fact that truth can never be securely and totally grasped by thought.'[15] The most important objective of Adorno's materialist philosophical project is to recognize and preserve moments of non-identity by way of self-reflexively exploring the limitations that necessarily attend thought: 'The name of dialectics says no more, to begin with, than that objects do not go into their concepts without leaving a remainder.'[16] It is not the act of identification *per se* – the subsumption of a particular object within a concept or conceptual system by a subject – that is at issue: indeed, 'to think is to identify.'[17] It is too rarely noted that for Adorno, the moment of identity in thought is not exclusively totalitarian; in fact, it contains the germ cell of critique itself: 'Thought as such, before all particular contents, is an act of negation, of resistance to that which is forced upon it; this is what thought has inherited from its archetype, the relation between labor and material ... The effort implied in the concept of thought itself, as the counterpart of passive contemplation, is negative already – a revolt against being importuned to bow to every immediate thing.'[18]

The problem arises when this act of conceptual subsumption is misrecognized as a complete representation of the object, in terms of both its historical and material facticity and its as yet undeveloped potentialities. The spectacular success with which humanity has expanded its capacity to control and dominate nature – ostensibly in the interests of self-preservation, has largely convinced it of the self-sufficiency of instrumental reason as institutionalized in capitalist and bureaucratic social structures. Anything that cannot be functionally integrated into these structures is dismissed as irrelevant; or, more commonly, it fails to enter human consciousness at all. At its most extreme, this is the logic that informed the Holocaust: 'Genocide is the absolute integration ... Auschwitz confirmed the philosopheme of pure identity as death.'[19]

Conversely, art recalls the existence and dignity of that which history has seemingly cast aside: 'Aesthetic identity seeks to aid the non-identical which in reality is repressed by reality's compulsion to identify.'[20] Works of art foster a different kind of identity, that of the object with itself; to use a theological metaphor of which Benjamin is fond, people make art to continue the task God assigned to Adam – the naming of being:

> There is a language of sculpture, of painting, of poetry. Just as the language of poetry is partly, if not solely, founded on the name language of man, it is very conceivable that the language of sculpture or painting is founded on certain kinds of thing languages, that in them we find a translation of the language of things into an infinitely higher language, which may still be of the same sphere. We are concerned here with nameless, nonacoustic languages, languages issuing from matter.[21]

Beauty, argues Adorno, is the 'characteristic of escaping from the fixed concept.'[22] The sensual, non-conceptual particularity of art keeps alive the memory of an 'indissoluble "something"'[23] that exists beyond all our efforts to give it conceptual expression. Thus, thought is driven to think itself, to become self-reflexive: identification remains as thought's constitutive operation, but thought loses its idealist pretence to omnipotence by recognizing the limitations that inevitably attend all acts of thinking. Most importantly, thought learns to share its control over cognition with other human faculties (e.g., the mimetic), and thereby dramatically expands how we meaningfully experience ourselves, others, and the world around us.

A work of art succeeds, then, if it is able to foster a mimetic relationship between subject and object that fundamentally destabilizes the omnipotent self-understanding of the modern ego:

> The shock aroused by important works is not employed to trigger personal, otherwise repressed emotions. Rather, this shock is the moment in which recipients forget themselves and disappear into the work; it is the moment of being shaken ... Shudder, radically opposed to the conventional idea of experience [*Erlebnis*], provides no particular satisfaction for the I; it bears no similarity to desire. Rather, it is a memento of the liquidation of the I, which, shaken, perceives its own limitedness and finitude.[24]

Although feeding on its memory, this self-liquidation is *not* the passive, terrified mimetic propitiation of our primitive ancestors, who imitated their world in a futile attempt to secure control over it – a propitiation that is reproduced in the ritual mimicry of the culture industry. Rather, 'only the strong and developed subject, the product of all control over nature and its injustice, has the power both to step back from the object and to revoke its self-positing.'[25] Mimetic strategies are used deliberately to construct a non-instrumental relationship with aesthetic material that fosters the emancipation of its immanent potential: the ego is momentarily but repeatedly and necessarily liquidated in the creative process. Freud sponsors such a view of creative activity: 'The artist experiences the creative urge in a passive manner, flooded by a plethora of impressions, thoughts and images surging up from the unconscious, though "ego control is intact."'[26] For Adorno, there simply is no other way to make authentic art. And under conditions of contemporary capitalism, there is no better way to recognize, negatively, the existence of non-identity. This recognition can be fully developed only within the mimetic practices of serious art, in which individuals are able to consciously and reflexively, though temporarily, liquidate their egos – including their own desires for self-gratification – and give themselves up to the object itself. Primitive mimetic practices originated in the terrified attempts of early human beings to save themselves from capricious nature by integrating themselves with it, by making themselves like it. The disciplinary suspension of the instinct for self-preservation helps 'deterrorize' mimesis and thereby transform it into an emancipatory practice through which humans can relearn and thereby move past their own limitations: 'For a few moments the I becomes aware, in real terms, of the possibility of letting self-preservation fall away, though it does not actually succeed in realizing this possibility.'[27] In a systematic reversal of narcissistic omnipotence, aesthetic mimesis involves the thoroughly mediated pleasure of trying to make oneself like the artwork, not make the artwork like oneself: 'The spectator must not project what transpires in himself on to the artwork in order to find himself confirmed, uplifted and satisfied in it, but must, on the contrary, relinquish himself to the artwork, assimilate himself to it, and fulfill the work in its own terms.'[28] This dynamic is, of course, recognizable as a fundamental inversion of the psychodynamics of mass culture, where individuals use culture as a screen on which to project their desires. In a deliberate attempt to short-circuit this process, abstract art refuses to use familiar cultural forms; in this way it prevents the audience from enjoying the narcissistic gratifications that accompany projection. Instead, it facilitates aesthetic mimesis (or reactionary dismissal) by forcing the audience to contemplate the work on its own terms (or not at all).

Incidentally, this description also does justice to Adorno's own prickly style: his texts are expressly designed so that they cannot be quickly or easily consumed. Referring to Adorno's infamous impenetrability, Jameson notes that 'in the realm of philosophy the bristling jargon of seemingly private languages is to be evaluated against the advertising copybook recommendations of "clarity" as the essence of "good writing": whereas the latter seeks to hurry the reader past his own received ideas, difficulty is inscribed in the former as a sign of the effort which must be made to think real thoughts.'[29] We should, therefore, not be surprised when Adorno tells us that the 'final straw' in his decision to return to Germany from the United States was the ongoing attempts by American editors to simplify his prose![30]

Aesthetic mimesis does not take place in a vacuum. As a first condition, the ego must be strong, stable, and well formed; considerable sublimation is required in order to bind libidinal energies to activities that are so far distanced from basic, physical gratification. The underdeveloped egos of late capitalism are ill equipped for genuine aesthetic contemplation and *praxis*. As a second condition, social relations and the distribution of material resources must be organized so that this 'bound' libidinal energy can be freely externalized to interact with other objects. As Gad Horowitz explains, capitalism's alienation of labour short-circuits this interaction: 'Libido, the energy of desire, is prevented from entering into reciprocal interaction with the realities of the external world; frustrated, it is thrown back to the infantile phantasies which in turn remain unmodified by reality, ineffective in reality, and excluded from preconscious awareness.'[31] The transformation of libido from narcissistic to object seeking does not happen automatically: it must be carefully nurtured and supported by specific social practices. In the absence of these practices, the ego still needs some means of discharging the libidinal energy, which it is consequently unable to bind, neutralize, and sublimate. In these situations, the temptation of narcissistic regression, as eagerly solicited, organized, and manipulated by fascism and/or the culture industry, often becomes too much for individuals to withstand.

When it does occur, though, the benefits of the self-directed liquidation of the ego accrue not only to human beings but also to the objects through which these strategies are mediated. Trapped by a reified, administered world, objects can only be brought to speech through the active intervention of the subject. Objectivity in a dialectical, non-positivist sense can only be reached through the total subjective mediation of all aesthetic material: 'For mimesis of what is not administered the subject has no other locus than in the living subject.'[32] Adorno remains hopeful that the human subject is never fully integrated: due to a capacity for physical pain and suffering that can never be fully excised, human beings will always harbour the potential for negation. Thus 'the physical moment tells our knowledge that suffering ought not to be, that things should be different. "Woe speaks: Go."'[33] As such, one can look to the 'inextinguishably idiosyncratic particular subject' whose specificities can still serve as the 'plenipotentiaries of negation.'[34] Yet this is hardly a simple, crude, or naive faith in the irrepressible creative energies of humanity. These idiosyncratic energies are never purely subjective impulses as, for example, psychoanalysis might assert; rather, they always involve the passage of the subjective through the objective as these energies are mediated by the law of form.[35] In the case of lyric poetry, for instance, 'through its configurations it assimilates itself completely into subjective impulses; one would almost think it had produced them. But at the same time language remains the medium of concepts, remains that which establishes an inescapable relationship to the universal and to society.'[36] And so, in art, subject and object enter into relations of true, mutual dependence.

A mimetic, reflexive relationship with the object destabilizes the blinding narcissism of a human species intoxicated by its own power over the natural environment; this is merely the inversion of the primal terror of nature as experienced by prehistoric human beings. On the one hand, we become aware of how nature can offer body and mind so much more stimulation, development, and gratification, so much more 'experience,' as our will to power over it is moderated. On the other hand, we also come to recognize that nature has its own defences, that it extracts a merciless revenge for its surrender: the so-called triumph of the subject is truly a Pyhrric victory in the sense that it can claim its spoils only on the condition of its own unceasing self-repression, self-mutilation, and, ultimately, self-destruction. Art's anamnesis of that which cannot be identified, only repressed, displaces a narrow egocentrism in favour of a more reflective, flexible, and expansive subjectivity that can come to know, feel, and experience something of the world outside itself: 'The reconciled condition would not be the philosophical imperialism of annexing the alien. Instead, its happiness would lie in the fact that the alien, in the proximity it is granted, remains what is distant and different, beyond the heterogeneous and beyond that which is one's own.'[37] In short, the subject comes to know, feel, and experience the limitations and violence to both subject *and* object that necessarily accompany thought and social patterns which forget or repress the moment of non-identity. As for the object, imprisoned in the identitarian prison of exchange-relations, it is only through the conscious intervention of the subject that it can truly develop and express its own potential. Drawing from a mimetic reservoir of alternative rationalities – its 'inextinguishable idiosyncrasies' – the subject is able to challenge the prevailing use and conceptualization of objects and momentarily shatter their heteronomous integration into rationalized and commodified social practices. Consequently, the object is freed to develop in ways that are not predetermined by human convention but that are necessarily enabled by subjective *praxis*. Hence, the subject becomes, if only for a moment, 'the agent, not the constituent, of the object.'[38]

Curiously perhaps, the critical powers of modern art *vis-à-vis* instrumental rationality are not borne out of a complete break with this logic; rather, they are themselves derived largely from the latter's internalization. The concept of internalization as a necessary milestone on the path to resistance is one that looms large in critical theory. Adorno is fond of noting, for example, that 'one must have tradition in oneself, to hate it properly.'[39] More significantly perhaps, Adorno's conception of psychology is similarly structured: the child must internalize the authority of the father in order to eventually develop the capacity to resist him and broader social processes.[40] Just as the primitive mimetic rituals of prehistoric humans were based on the logic of incorporation – taking the essence of that which threatened (e.g., climate, animals, rival tribes) into oneself disarmed the threat by way of familiarization – so too is modern art able to offer a sort of critical inoculation by way of its mimesis of rationalization and commodification. In this context, mimesis does not refer to the straightforward duplication of reality, but rather to the imitation of its structural form. Beckett's plays, Kafka's stories, and Schönberg's music do not serve up the mirror image of human society; rather, they ingest reification into their very forms: 'It is mimesis of the systematic framework which impoverishes experience, not a mimesis of individual impoverished experience which misrepresents such experience as though it were immediate and untouched after all.'[41] In other words, that which is imitated is not a thing but rather a process of rationalization. In so doing, the frozen qualities of social processes that have been objectively produced under conditions of commodity (and concept) fetishism are aesthetically liquefied, and the identity of reason as a *process*, as a social relation and not a thing, can be brought to consciousness.

A strange thing happens to instrumental rationality as it is plucked from the sphere of production and pressed into the creation of an object that exists for itself rather than for others. Stripped of its dignity in an almost carnivalesque fashion, its emptiness, limitations, and absurdity are momentarily revealed. Abstract art turns the conventional values of modernity against themselves. The more an artwork develops itself in accordance with instrumental reason, the more ridiculous it becomes by the standards of this reason: 'Its ridiculousness is, however, also part of a condemnation of empirical rationality; it accuses the rationality of social praxis of having become an end in itself and as such the irrational and mad reversal of means into ends.'[42] In Beckett's *Waiting for Godot*, for instance, the relations of domination and servitude are isolated, exaggerated, and thereby made absurd, giving expression to the absurdity that one's labour continues to be alienated and controlled by others even though collective self-preservation no longer requires such a social system.[43] The deliberately foregrounded 'abstract' techniques of modern art are a mimetic tribute to how abstract social relationships have become in contemporary society: 'Art carries out the eclipse of concretion, an eclipse to which expression is refused by a reality in which the concrete continues to exist only as a mask of the abstract and the determinate particular is nothing more than an exemplar of the universal that serves as its camoflage and is fundamentally identical with the ubiquity of monopoly.'[44] Similarly, the obsolescence of aesthetic styles that desperately thrusts modern art into greater and greater abstraction expresses the ever-widening foreclosure of immediacy in contemporary society.

In much the same way as Benjamin praises Baudelaire, Adorno lauds the French poet for neither portraying reification nor railing against it, but instead for taking it deeply into the very form of his poetic work. This formal engagement with commodification, as opposed to a 'realistic' description of its effects, is what gives modern art its unique, critical force: 'Baudelaire proved to be correct. Emphatic modern art does not thrive in Elysian fields beyond the commodity, but is, rather, strengthened by way of the experience of the commodity, whereas classicality itself becomes a commodity, an exemplary daub.'[45] In this light, we can begin to make sense of Adorno's seemingly paradoxical description of modern art as the 'absolute commodity.'[46] Commodities pretend to exist for others, to act as the mere carriers of use-value, yet their production, distribution, and consumption are actually organized to realize exchange-value: in reality, the satisfaction of human needs is of tertiary importance in the circuit of capital. Modern works of art strip the commodity of its ideological cover not by standing apart from it, but rather by mimetically searing its logic into their very core and thereby rendering it visible: 'The absolute commodity would be free of the ideology inherent in the commodity form, which pretends to exist for-another, whereas ironically it is something merely for-itself. It exists for those who hold power.'[47] Horkheimer and Adorno adopt similar techniques in their praise of Nietzsche and Sade as truthfully pursuing the logic of Kant's philosophical propositions to their horrifying conclusion in the utter instrumentalization of all social relations. Not only do such works reveal the stark brutality of an instrumental reason without limits, but they also negatively establish the foundations for the (re)assertion of collective human control: 'In pursuing the implications of reason still more resolutely than the positivists [Sade and Nietzsche's] secret purpose was to lay bare the utopia which is contained in every great philosophy, as it is in Kant's concept of reason: the utopia of a humanity which, itself no longer distorted, no longer needs distortion.'[48] By aesthetically dominating those rational forms which are accustomed to having the upper hand in everyday life, modern art once again gives expression to the founding wish of the Enlightenment: that humanity might consciously and collectively control its own fate.

In a world in which communication and cultural sharing have been thoroughly commodified and rationalized, modern art must constantly search for new methods for forcing an awareness of reification into the minds of those who have never known anything but the reified social relations of capitalism. The techniques of dissonance and atonality, described by Adorno as the 'de-aestheticization' of art, are used because aesthetic practice can no longer tolerate 'the contradiction between the symbolic reconciliation projected in art and [the] actual unreconciled condition of the world as a whole.'[49] The denunciation and even critical representation of social structures, Adorno believes, is now a capacity only of form, not content:

> Kafka, in whose work monopoly capitalism appears only distantly, codifies in the dregs of the administered world what becomes of people under the total social spell more faithfully and powerfully than do any novels

> about corrupt industrial trusts ... Whereas his work must renounce any claim to transcending myth, it makes the social web of delusion knowable in myth through the *how*, through language ... In his writing, absurdity is as self-evident as it has actually become in society.[50]

In 'Metamorphosis,' for instance, the transformation of Gregor Samsa into an insect describes alienation and reification – the conversion of people into things – more powerfully than could the more conventional methods of social science, critical journalism, or committed art. The relative importance that Adorno assigns to form is driven primarily by the emphasis he places on mediation as a crucial element in critical thought. More realistic accounts of suffering under capitalism run the risk of giving meaning to a misery whose real significance is that it is utterly devoid of meaning; they pretend that human beings are still able to experience their world when that ability has long since disappeared: 'The case which is presented as the one which is still worth recounting becomes for all its desperate nature an excuse for the world which has produced something so worthy of being related; while the real desperation expresses itself mutely in the fact that there is nothing more to be recounted and that all we can do is recognize it for what it is.'[51] Instead, the true aspiration and rare achievement of modern art is to render an experience of the world that is constituted by the complete *absence* of experience.[52] Similar to Kafka's stories, Picasso's *Guernica* uses an 'inhumane construction'[53] to qualitatively express human suffering with a clarity that paradoxically eludes more conventional, realist depictions of those events: 'Cubism could be interpreted as a form of reaction to a stage of the rationalization of the social world that undertook its geometrical organization; in these terms, cubism was an attempt to bring within the bounds of experience what is otherwise contrary to it, just as impressionism had sought to do at an earlier and not yet fully planned stage of industrialization.'[54]

Cubism manipulates shape, depth, and perspective to bring to consciousness an experience of the world that the human sensorium cannot process through its traditional categories for making sense of spatial relations. Its reliance on the shock of non-representational forms short-circuits the comfortable absorption of the audience in mere contemplation: 'What is qualitatively new in cubism is that, whereas impressionism undertook to awaken and salvage a life that was becoming numb in the commodity world by the strength of its own dynamic, cubism despaired of any such possibility and accepted the heteronomous geometrization of the world as its new law, as its own order, and thus made itself the guarantor of the objectivity of aesthetic experience.'[55] Impressionism sought to compensate for the shortcomings of industrial life within the aesthetic sphere; in contrast, cubism returns the responsibility for its form to the social world from which it originated. In refusing conventional aesthetic and semiotic forms, works such as *Guernica* temporarily forestall the affirmative, ideological moment that attends most art. A coherent, 'conciliatory' aesthetic form unwittingly promotes an ambivalent response to human suffering by offering the mistaken impression that there are activities, such as art, which escape the logic of reification. However, if words and images themselves can no longer be relied on to communicate experience, the crisis will necessarily be understood in more severe, systemic terms.

Abstract forms of modern art seem about as far removed from everyday life as anything could possibly be, yet, for Adorno they actually represent the most effective, truthful, and accurate mode of recording contemporary human experience – or rather the lack thereof. As the 'self-unconscious historiography of their epoch,'[56] the *forms* of artworks 'record the history of mankind more impartially than do documents.'[57] In the case of the 'natural' world, 'oppressed nature expresses itself more purely in works criticized as artificial, which with regard to the level of the technical forces of production, go to the extreme, than it does in circumspect works whose *parti pris* for nature is as allied with the real domination of nature as is the nature lover with the hunt.'[58] When the commodification of art initially freed it from direct social control, art paradoxically acquired the monadological capacity to serve as a social cipher. In the very act of turning its back on society, art comes to reflect it most perfectly. The apparent freedom of artworks, then, is a ruse of aesthetic rationality: the forms with which art is able to escape the empirical world are, in fact, precisely those which tie it all the more firmly to that world: 'Each and every one of their elements binds them to that over which, for their happiness, they must soar and back into which at every moment they threaten once again to tumble.'[59] In large part, this seemingly magical power is derived from the necessary affinity that the sociality of labour guarantees between its productive and aesthetic variants: 'The aesthetic force of production is the same as that of productive labour and has the same teleology; and what may be called aesthetic relations of production – all that in which the productive force is embedded and in which it is active – are sedimentations or imprintings of social relations of production.'[60] Art not only keeps alive the dream of a different kind of world, but also acts as a most faithful historian of the current one: this proposition lies at the core of Adorno's voluminous work on music:

> Here and now, music can do nothing else but represent, in its own structure, the social antinomies which also bear the guilt of its isolation. It will be the better, the more deeply, it can make its forms lend shape to the power of those contradictions, and to the need to overcome them socially – the more purely the antinomies of its own formal language will express the calamities of the social condition and call for change in the cipher script of suffering. It does not behoove music to stare at society in helpless horror; its social function will be more exactly fulfilled if the social problems contained in it, in the inmost cells of its technique, are presented in its own material and according to its own formal laws. The task of music as an art comes thus to be a kind of analogue to that of social theory.[61]

Adorno is fond of noting, for example, that if one listens to Beethoven and does not hear echoes of the revolutionary bourgeoisie then one fails to understand his music:[62] 'Art perceived strictly aesthetically is art aesthetically misperceived.'[63] Conceiving of the aesthetic object, be it popular or critical, as a monad that expresses broader social processes is the central proposition that drives a cultural criticism that must become, in his own words, 'social physiognomy.'[64] This is no less true for jazz than for Schönberg. Some have claimed that Adorno does not believe that mass culture has a truth content compared to serious, modern art.[65] Insofar as mass culture sacrifices art's concern with immanent aesthetic problems for its effect on an audience, this is true. However, mass culture's 'truth' emerges as it reflects the social conditions in which it is produced: in this sense, jazz is a 'social cipher' for capitalism just as are Schönberg's atonal compositions. Indeed, one might say that the problem with mass culture, for Adorno, is its complicity with reality: unlike modern art, its lies are not strong enough to break the spell of the commodity form. Serious, modern art incorporates traditional forms but simultaneously 'works' on them: the traces of this struggle can then be read as both an indictment of social structures and an increasingly negative exploration of alternative futures. The culture industry, on the other hand, meekly reproduces the forms thrust upon it by capitalism, seeking only to disguise their ever-sameness with the trivial differences of pseudo-individuation.

In both cases, connections between the artwork as monad and the social structures and processes it expresses do not spring forth, fully formed, generated by the act of aesthetic contemplation alone. Rather, aesthetic experience requires conceptual mediation by critical commentary and aesthetic philosophy: 'What is mediated in art [i.e. society], that through which the artwork becomes something other than its mere factuality, must be mediated a second time by reflection: through the medium of the concept.'[66] In the case of serious art, as Albrecht Wellmer notes, philosophical interpretation is especially important in order to ensure that the aesthetic experience does not fall entirely captive to the semblance (*Schein*) generated by the artwork:

> That which aesthetic experience, which loses itself in an emphatic 'now,' *has*, is the intuition of the world in the light of redemption; however, caught in the illusory character of artistic beauty, aesthetic experience does not understand what it experiences: it does not understand the oblique reference of the artwork to something not present, to a nonbeing; in short, aesthetic experience does not understand the semblance to which it succumbs.[67]

Aesthetics and philosophy come to need each other, the one to mimetically liberate, generate, and express non-identity and sensuous particularity, the other to bring these elements to conscious reflection and thereby free the human imagination from its imprisonment in the binary logic of an instrumental rationality that gets the job done and the blissful charms of 'good-for-nothing' fantasy.

I hope I have provided in these last few pages a sense of Adorno's enormous philosophical investment in aesthetic practice grounded in his belief that culture is necessarily the lynchpin in any possible liberation of humanity from the 'dialectic of enlightenment.' As the final piece in the culture industry puzzle, it helps us better understand his bitter disappointment in a mass culture that so completely betrayed and sacrificed these hopes. More than this, though, it also points toward a dialectical *rapprochement* with Benjamin's speculative exploration of the emancipatory possibilities that lie at the heart of the commodity form. Both agree that the chances for an enlightenment that does not succumb to myth lie with an experience of alienation that makes visible the self-destructive effects of our current instrumental relationship with objects. Both locate the mimetic faculty at the core of any such experience. And both rely heavily on the monadological qualities of cultural objects in producing such an experience. This is not to say that significant differences do not remain. However, the basic homologies between their two approaches lend credibility to the idea that these differences represent the contradictory possibilities that inhere in the same object. Benjamin himself testifies to this dynamic: 'In my own essay ['The Work of Art'] I attempted to articulate the positive moments as clearly as you have articulated the negative ones.'[68] A commodified mass culture holds many dangers for humanity; but it simultaneously offers opportunities that arise out of these dangers. Benjamin begins to show how these opportunities need not wait on modernist aesthetics for their activation; rather, similar methods can be used in the production of a critical *popular* culture. This potential in no way detracts from the alarming thesis of the culture industry, but it may help 're-dialecticize' it in pointing toward its possible, though by no means necessary, supersession.

## Mimesis, Memory, and the Redemption of Experience

Following Freud, Benjamin believes that consciousness, insofar as it tries to protect itself against shocks, is not able to fully sterilize the human capacity for experience. The conscious faculties can insulate themselves against the permanent registering of external stimuli; however, they can perform no such service for the body itself. As shocks are deflected away from consciousness, they are often inscribed deeply on the unconscious. The transition from *Erfahrung* to *Erlebnis* means that memories are no longer consciously transferred through oral traditions and communal rituals; even so, these fragments of experience that are inscribed on the body and the unconscious occasionally break through the barriers erected against them by consciousness. As a consequence of their 'isolation,' they acquire a heightened intensity and presence whenever they appear once again. What Benjamin takes from psychoanalytic theory is the capacity of the unconscious to register elements of experience that are not fully 'experienced' at the time they occur. The presence of these subterranean memories offers the hope that they may be excavated and thereby 'actualized' at some future moment.

In fictional form, Marcel Proust furnishes a model of how this can occur. In a famous scene from *Remembrance of Things Past*, Proust describes his frustration at being unable to wilfully remember anything of the town in which he spent his childhood. Memories of this time are restored only through the taste of a *madeleine* biscuit soaked in tea, a sensory experience that opens the floodgates of what Proust terms *mémoire involuntaire* and that virtually transports the past into the present. *Mémoire voluntaire* provides details of our past, but 'the information it gives ... retains no trace of that past.'[69] It is limited to the recollection of isolated events and facts, mere data or information; it is not genuine experience itself that is remembered, but an abstract record of it: 'The *mémoire voluntaire* ... is a registry providing the object with a classificatory number behind which it disappears. "So now we've been there."'[70] Moreover, voluntary memory is often unable to retrieve the memories of those experiences which leave the most powerful impressions, because such experiences have not been recorded within its sphere. Rather, they have been inscribed elsewhere in the human organism, in the secret archives of involuntary memory. For Proust, the past often lies 'somewhere beyond the reach of the intellect.'[71] Traces of it lodge in objects or, more properly, in the sensations they can arouse in the human body itself. Certain tastes, smells, textures, and sounds, for example, have the capacity to release powerful memories that otherwise lie forgotten.

This approach is consistent with Freud's own work on memory: 'We should be able to say that the excitatory process becomes conscious in the system *Cs.* but leaves no permanent trace behind there; but that the excitation is transmitted to the systems lying next within and that it is in *them* that its traces are left.'[72] In this case, 'them' refers to psychic systems that bear a strong resemblance to Proust's *mémoire involuntaire.* In the absence of *Erfahrung,* the recall of experiences into memory is often routed through the unconscious and the body and is therefore not governed by rational processes. Individuals are unable to bring such memories wilfully to consciousness; not only that, but the harder they try using the intellect the less success they have. Benjamin likens the relation between voluntary and involuntary memory to Penelope's tapestry in *The Odyssey*:[73] 'Here the day unravels what the night has woven. When we awake each morning, we hold in our hands, usually weakly and loosely, but a few fringes of the carpet of lived existence, as woven into us by forgetting. However, with our purposeful activity and, even more, our purposive remembering, each day unravels the web, the ornaments of forgetting.'[74]

In the 'forgetting' sponsored by sleep and, above all, by dreaming – just as in the boredom which serves as the dream bird that hatches the 'egg of experience' – consciousness is temporarily displaced as the gatekeeper of internal and external stimulation; the barriers erected against the body and the unconscious are momentarily lowered, allowing repressed and deflected memories to break into consciousness, albeit often in distorted form. Elsewhere, in reference to surrealism, he defines this state as the 'ancient practice of *complete* relaxation.'[75] In other words, an 'absent-minded' disposition enables the accessing of memories that are otherwise inaccessible to consciousness. Benjamin's focus on distraction in this context bears many similarities to the 'suppression of the critical faculty' recommended to the patient by Freud during psychoanalytic therapy. Such a state of mind relaxes the censorship mechanisms imposed by consciousness and allows images from the unconscious to surface.[76]

For Proust as well as for surrealism – which similarly trades in unconscious memories and fantasies – it is up to chance whether or not one stumbles on the sensuous triggers that can unlock the memories and, consequently, the experience buried deeply within. While Benjamin agrees that this is often the case, he cites Proust's own writings as an example of how particular aesthetic practices can deliberately – though indirectly and with no guarantee of success – attempt to restore a full experience of the past.

> It is the world in a state of similarity, and in it the *correspondances* rule; the Romantics were the first to comprehend them and Baudelaire embraced them most fervently, but Proust was the only one who managed to reveal them in our lived life. This is the work of *la mémoire involuntaire*, the rejuvenating force which is a match for the inexorable process of aging. When that which has been is reflected in the dewy fresh 'instant,' a painful shock of rejuvenation pulls it together once more.'[77]

Proust's work not only reveals the presence of resemblances between the past and the present in everyday life, but also and more importantly demonstrates their power to trigger the process of recall so as to allow past experiences to flood back through one's mind and body. He shows, in other words, the pivotal role that mimesis plays in the practice of genuine remembrance. In the taste of a cookie, past and present can be suddenly brought together as the identification of a sensual element shared by both opens a pathway into memory.

The ignition of *mémoire involuntaire* is not sparked by the perception of sensual similarities alone: it can also be fired by the non-sensuous similitudes activated within and through language. Indeed, given that the (adult) human capacity to perceive resemblances is now so deeply intertwined with it, language holds tremendous potential to become the dominant medium through which resemblances manifest themselves. In its destructive moment, language has the power to shatter organic unities and networks that organize memories and experience into particular configurations. A non-sensuous mimetic logic can then be used to reconstruct these shards of experience into constellations that group them into patterns and make linkages between them that otherwise might not have occurred. Language can bring together seemingly irrelevant moments or ideas, which can then generate a flash of memory. While such flashes most commonly arise through tactile stimuli, Benjamin urges us to consider the possibility that language might exercise a similar effect: 'The expression "the book of nature" indicates that one can read the real like a text. And this is how the reality of the nineteenth century will be treated here. We open the book of what happened.'[78] Reality is not a text, but it can be read like one. Such readings enable a mimetic destruction/reconstruction of reality so that the experiential and mnemic resources lying hidden or frozen within it might be released. They bring into play the mimetic sensitivity of language to the hidden correspondences between different experiences, and thereby increase the chance that memories which lie buried deep within the body and the unconscious will be released.

In other words, the perception of non-sensuous similitudes is deeply connected to a fluid, non-linear sense of time and history. For Benjamin, the most important resemblances are not those within the present, but those which connect the present with the past. Following Freud, the pathways that lead back into the past are often marked only by distorted traces that must be 'read' or deciphered before particular memories can be triggered. Language can serve as an entry into the past *if* the mimetic faculty is open to interpreting the effect of words in this way – an effect that may have little or nothing to do with their meaning as signs. In other words, one 'reads' the world 'like a text' *not* to foreground the linguistic constitution of 'reality,' but rather to use language as a tool to illuminate the non-sensuous similitudes that bind things together. In recollecting his own childhood in Berlin, Benjamin observes that language often serves as an entry point into the subterranean memories of the unconscious: 'Just as when you awake, a certain kind of significant dream survives in the form of words though all the rest of the dream-content has vanished, here [in this memory] isolated words have remained in place as marks of catastrophic encounters.'[79] In the absence of a web of tradition to preserve, contextualize, and transmit individual and collective experience, these distorted traces are one of the few access points through which we gain (re)admission to our past. As Proust, Baudelaire and the surrealists confirm for Benjamin, it is only through mimesis that these mnemic tunnels can be opened.

As we pass through those tunnels, our conventional experience of time is shattered as the months and years that divide present from past are momentarily swept aside in the instant of *Jetztzeit* or 'now-time.' The past is experienced anew: 'Our life, it can be said, is a muscle strong enough to contract the whole of historical time.'[80] It is not the memories themselves that power this contraction, but the *images* contained within them:

> Language has unmistakably made plain that memory is not an instrument for exploring the past but its theater. It is the medium of past experience, just as the earth is the medium in which dead cities lie buried ... the matter itself is merely a deposit, a stratum, which yields only to the most meticulous examination what constitutes the real treasure hidden within the earth: the images, severed from all earlier associations, that stand – like precious fragments or torsos in a collector's gallery – in the sober rooms of our later insights.[81]

By image, then, Benjamin is referring not to a visual representation, but to the fusion of an individual's sensory and perceptual apparatuses, cognitive faculties, and mnemic field, including the unconscious, in the full experience of a particular moment in time: 'Only images in the mind vitalize the will. The mere word, by contrast, at most inflames it, to leave it smoldering, blasted. There is no intact will without pictorial imagination. No imagination without innervation.'[82] As Weigel explains, images are a 'heteronomous and heterogeneous similitude in which figures of thought correlate with those of history or of experience and reality.'[83] When they come together, it is as if experience finally receives its proper name.

In many cases, the significance of a particular event can only be understood – or more accurately, can only be truly experienced – long after it has actually transpired. Such is the real value of memory for Benjamin. It gives human beings the luxury of circumventing the seemingly inexorable march of history by enabling their literal return to the past to rescue the images that are stranded there. But unlike Proust, Baudelaire, and even the surrealists, Benjamin imagines that this process can occur not simply at the level of the individual, but also collectively for human society. In theological terms, it makes possible the redemption (*apocastasis*) of the hopes, dreams, and suffering – in short, of the experiences – of past generations. In a 1937 letter, Horkheimer criticizes Benjamin's open-ended conception of history as idealistic, noting that 'the murdered are really murdered.' The latter's response is highly instructive:

> The corrective to this line of thinking may be found in the consideration that history is not simply a science but also and not least a form of remembrance [*Eingedenken*]. What science has 'determined,' remembrance can modify. Such mindfulness can make the incomplete (happiness) into something complete, and the complete (suffering) into something incomplete. That is theology, but in remembrance we have an experience [*Erfahrung*] that forbids us to conceive of history as fundamentally atheological, little as it may be granted us to try to write it with immediately theological concepts.[84]

Conversely, in the absence of such memoration, '*even the dead*' will not be safe from the enemy if he wins.[85] In an early programmatic essay, Benjamin attacks Kant for basing his philosophy of human experience on a schema provided by the natural sciences.[86] Such a system, he argues, is unduly restrictive and fails to take into account the variety of experiences – including those of a metaphysical character – that constitute human existence. In this later fragment, one can see how important memory is as an experiential ingredient that can 'modify' the empty, linear time that science has apparently 'established.'[87] Memoration has the power to shatter this empty time by literally opening up history, allowing us to return to the past and rescue the possibilities that, once closed down by a certain course of events, can only now be redeemed in the current historical conjuncture.

The goal, however, is not a conservative resurrection of the past. Benjamin's loyalties lie firmly with the present insofar as he believes that its own latent potential can only be fully actualized by way of its immersion in the memories of the past. At one point, Benjamin compares his historical method with 'the process of splitting the atom [which] liberates the enormous energies of history that are bound up in the "once upon a time" of classical historiography.'[88] All historical moments contain an enormous range of possible futures that can only be activated insofar as they are infused with the images of the past.[89] These images have the power to charge a future that is otherwise shut down by dominant political, social, economic, and cultural structures. They often involve events, experience, or knowledge that could not be adequately or fully experienced, understood, or actualized at the time. Benjamin cites André Mongold: 'The past has left images of itself in literary texts, images comparable to those which are imprinted by light on a photosensitive plate. The future alone possesses developers active enough to scan such surfaces perfectly.'[90] Each image from the past is marked by a historical index that determines its moment of readability. In moments of danger and/or opportunity, these images flash up into consciousness, appearing only when the latent possibilities within the original experience can effectively charge and actualize their counterpart in the present:[91]

> It's not what is past casts its light on what is present, or what is present its light on what is past; rather, image is that wherein what has been comes together in a flash with the now to form a constellation. In other words, image is dialectics at a standstill. For while the relation of the present to the past is a purely temporal, continuous one, the relation of what-has-been to the now is dialectical: is not progression but image, suddenly emergent.[92]

The mimetic faculty makes it possible to read the similarities that exist between historical periods: as a form of perception, it is deeply embedded in temporality and acutely sensitive to the multiplicity of linkages between different historical periods that escape the restrictive chronological apparatus which dominates the production of official history. Inspired by Marx, his favourite example of such a juxtaposition of past and present is furnished by the French Revolution: 'To Robespierre ancient Rome was a past charged with now-time, a past which he blasted out of the continuum of history. The French Revolution viewed itself as Rome reincarnate.'[93] What Rome was unable to realize in its day, revolutionary France might accomplish by raising not only the memory of Rome, but by ripping its *image* out of history and using it to charge its own present with 'now-time.' Perhaps the most eloquent single example he provides of such juxtaposition is an excerpt from Pierre-Maxime Schuhl from the Arcades project: 'The bombers remind us of what Leonardo da Vinci expected of man in flight: that he was to ascend to the skies "in order to seek snow on the mountaintops and bring it back to the city to spread on the sweltering streets in summer."'[94] Juxtaposing this fragment with the actual use of the *Luftwaffe* in Spain shows how one might 'brush history against the grain'[95] by identifying and 'quoting' images from the past in order to deliver an emancipatory shock by radically destabilizing the 'necessity' of the present. Just as the past is torn from its context, so too is the present ripped out of conventional narratives. Thus is one able to catch a momentary glimpse of a different future which shows that things need not be as they are and prompts one to wonder why things did indeed turn out that way.[96]

This explosive arranging of memory and experience was not possible in the *Erfahrung* of old. Instead, the compulsory weaving of events into *Erfahrung* as mediated through the memories furnished and organized by tradition locked individuals into a world of meaning and experience that was historically predetermined. While events were connected with one another, they were always mediated by established webs of tradition that effectively dampened any volatile combination of experience and memory. The shocks of capitalist modernity burst this mnemic tapestry asunder, breaking up memory and experience into a serialized pattern according to the template furnished by homogenous, empty time. The isolated quality of these memories actually intensifies their presence when they arise in later configurations: they furnish 'images, severed from all earlier associations.' In reference to his own experience, Benjamin notes that 'there are memories that are especially well-preserved because, although not themselves affected, they are isolated by a shock from all that followed. They have not been worn away by contact with their successors and remain detached, self-sufficient.'[97] The discrete memories that slumber within *Erlebnis* harbour explosive possibilities unlike previous forms of experience: 'In order for a part of the past to be touched by the present instant [*Aktualität*], there must be no continuity between them.'[98] Destruction of the 'chains of memory' once held fast by tradition and culture opens up remarkable possibilities for an experimental reframing of the images within social life. Writing about the impoverishment of 'communicable experience' – that is, experience shared through traditional cultural forms – forced onto humanity by the First World War, Benjamin invokes a 'new, positive concept of barbarism' that is preparing to 'outlive culture': 'For what does poverty of experience do for the barbarian? It forces him to start from scratch; to make a new start ... [People] long to free themselves from experience; they long for a world in which they can make such pure and decided use of their outer poverty – their poverty, and ultimately also their inner poverty – that it will lead to something respectable.'[99] For Benjamin, future redemption is necessarily foreshadowed by the ruin of the present. Shattered into pieces, mnemic and experiential fragments have suddenly become available for assembly into constellations according to the possibilities and dangers faced by human beings.

Dangerously, however, serious impediments block the desire, will, and ability to seize this opportunity. In the first place, the transformation of *Erfahrung* into *Erlebnis* has rendered individuals incapable of perceiving these ruins *as ruins* because of how the present is disconnected from its past. For the most part, we are simply unaware of how we might access the past; we dismiss the images that occasionally do flash up as irrelevant or amusing fantasies. In broad terms, historicism participates in a similar dynamic insofar as it seals off historical experience from the present: its 'scientific method' deploys the schematic of cause and effect to bind past events into a fixed, orderly sequence – 'like the beads of a rosary'[100] – in much the same way that consciousness transforms modern experience into 'moments that have been lived' (*Erlebnis*). One can debate the interpretation of historical events and processes, and one can even argue about the lessons to be learned from specific incidents. But such inquiry freezes history into something that has happened and is now finished; we can wonder about its meaning or significance, but it may never be experienced again. The past becomes something that confirms rather than challenges the present. Benjamin is bitterly disappointed with how social democracy turns its back on 'generations of the downtrodden' in favour of a gaze firmly fixed on the progressive future that lies ahead. Adopting such a position means that the dreams of the past can never be juxtaposed with their utter ruin in the present to bring about the moment when, in the words of Marx, 'man is at last compelled to face with sober senses, his real conditions of life, and his relations with this kind.'[101]

Moreover, capitalism has woven a phantasmagoric veil over its own petrified landscape, promoting the investiture of desire and meaning into its lifeless products in order to animate them as modern fetishes. A new dream-sleep has fallen over Europe, writes Benjamin, and with it, 'a reactivation of mythic forces.'[102] Like the fantastic pictures within a dream, the commodity pretends to express and satisfy the wishes of a slumbering humanity in order that its sleep may continue unabated. Benjamin believes that humanity possesses the memories and experiences with which it might bring this sleep to an end. However, the increasing predominance of a defensive and adaptive posture on the part of the mimetic faculty has seriously damaged the capacity to mobilize these experiential resources in an emancipatory fashion. The 'flashing up' of images from the past in times of danger is not something that occurs automatically; rather, it requires not only an 'absent-minded' openness to experience and to the memories particular events might summon – 'to have presence of mind means to *let oneself go* at the moment of danger'[103] – but also a desire to use mimesis in generating and following the associative connections between experience and memory. Conversely, the evolution of mimesis under capitalism into a mimesis of death forestalls the production and recognition of the correspondences that provide access to the images of the past. As communication between the body/unconscious and consciousness is defensively shut down, the capacity to register and above all to *name* these correspondences is fatally damaged. Images that flash up must be seized on immediately by those who know their significance: 'The true image of the past flits by. The past can be seized only as an image that flashes up at the moment of its recognizability, and is never seen again ... For it is an irretrievable image of the past which threatens to disappear in any present that does not recognize itself as intended in that image.'[104] These images must be perceived *as opportunities* or *moments of danger*: insofar as they are enjoyed merely as objects of aesthetic contemplation, their irretrievable disappearance is assured. The capacity to view images as marking opportunities and/or dangers is intimately connected to their *collective* perception. While images present themselves to individuals for contemplation, they are seized on by a collective as a spur to action: 'Fashion has a nose for the topical, no matter where it stirs in the thickets of long ago; it is the tiger's leap into the past. Such a leap, however, takes place in an arena where the ruling class gives the commands.'[105] The cyclical plundering of the past in the interests of fashion serves as a perpetual marker of how easily the 'tiger's leap into the past' can be appropriated in the interests of capital. Finally, the displacement of use-value by exchange-value in the commodity form disrupts the mimetic faculty and the associated retrieval of experience from memory by increasingly binding objects and experiences into a vast web of artificial similarities. Adorno, for example, quotes Nietzsche to the effect that 'to perceive resemblances everywhere, making everything alike, is a sign of weak eyesight.'[106] This web acts as a distortion field, making it more and more difficult to perceive the 'true' similarities between different objects and experiences.

## Dialectical Images and the Renovation of Critique

To briefly take stock of our discussion of Benjamin thus far: commodity fetishism, the transformation of mimesis into a defensive rather than an innervating practice, and the decay of experience into *Erlebnis* prevent people from recognizing and acting on the transformative potential that lies frozen within the social totality. A mimetic faculty that could activate and deploy human memories, experiences, and images to emancipate both subject and object has been defensively shut down. The experiential resources for transformative social action exist, but the desire and the ability to access them have both been repressed. Benjamin speculates that within capitalist modernity, such desire and ability can be (re)activated only through a 'progressive' shock: 'The masses do not wish to be "instructed." They can absorb knowledge only if it is accompanied by the slight shock that nails down inwardly what has been experienced.'[107] The synthetic generation and delivery of such shocks is mediated by what he suggestively calls a 'dialectical image,' an interpretive device for critically arranging existing images, objects, and experiences so that the contradictions contained within them are compressed into a single, charged moment.[108] The explosive force thereby generated blasts both subject and object out of conventional social structures (e.g., narratives of bourgeois subjectivity, ideals of historical progress, relations of exchange and identity) that have so far appropriated, defused, and repressed their potentiality. The dialectical image occupies a key place in Benjamin's later writings as a revolutionary pedagogy that can tear apart – and ultimately redeem – the phantasmagoric veil woven by the commodity form. It can inspire, organize, and sustain a collective self-extrication from the mythic dream-sleep into which humanity has been seduced by the promises of industrial capitalism. Awakening from this sleep requires more than its methodical demystification as irrational, and more than simply clever propaganda: such anemic strategies will necessarily fail to break the deeper circuits that bind us libidinally, somatically, and cognitively to the commodity form. Rather, the energies that flow through these circuits must themselves be tapped and reorganized and then used to explode the system from within. Insofar as the kinetic charge of the dialectical image is itself generated by the extension of the commodity form, Benjamin's work in this area can begin to lay the groundwork for the redialecticization of the culture industry thesis.

Dialectical images begin with the objects, practices and spaces of industrial capitalism. For Benjamin, these things are always 'overdetermined':[109] as monads, they express the socioeconomic structures in which they have been created and consumed, but they also act as repositories for the desires, dreams, and hopes of humanity.[110] In the case of Paris, for example, the city streets bear witness to the destructive expansion of capitalism (e.g., the reorganization of the city by Haussmann) and the restrictive inscription of mythic forms onto new urban technologies such as the Arcades; but they also hold the memories of revolt and revolution. Indeed, it is precisely this dual identity that both enables and is required for their subsequent use in constructing dialectical images. In his 1935 treatment for *The Arcades Project*, Benjamin describes these latter impulses as emerging from a 'collective unconscious' animated by the memory of a classless society:

> In the dream in which each epoch entertains images of its successor, the latter appears wedded to elements of primal history [*Urgeschichte*] – that is, to elements of a classless society. And the experiences of such a society – as stored in the unconscious of the collective – engender, through interpenetration with what is new, the utopia that has left its trace in a thousand configurations of life, from enduring edifices to passing fashions.[111]

In responding to this intermediate framing of the *Passagenwerk*, Adorno is quite critical of Benjamin's use of the concept of the collective unconscious. In the first place, it needlessly summons up reactionary baggage insofar as it conceptually articulates his project with the ideas of Carl Jung and Ludwig Klages. More dangerously, however, it deploys the past as a 'Golden Age' that is undialectically contrasted with the commodified 'Hell' of modernity; in doing so it eclipses the key point that later propelled *Dialectic of Enlightenment*. These two seemingly opposed epochs are in fact dialectically intertwined. Conversely, Benjamin negates modernity 'in a way that actually causes the primal state to appear as truth,' and thus myth becomes the *de facto* solution.[112]

Yet the term 'classless society' refers not to some actually existing historical episode, but rather to a perennial, utopian impulse that Benjamin thinks can never be entirely expunged from suffering individuals. Moreover, it is a concept that looks to the future – to a time when the ever-present dream of a classless society might be realized – as much as to the past. As Wohlfarth argues (citing Benjamin), it is helpful to read it in the context of Benjamin's 'messianic Marxism':

> Marx's idea of a classless society secularized the idea of messianic time. And this was as it should be ... A classless society cannot be conceived as existing in the same time as the struggle for it. The concept of the present to which the historian is committed is, however, necessarily defined by both these temporal orders. The historian who does not in some way measure the past by the touchstone of a classless society cannot but falsify it. To that extent every concept of the present partakes in that of the Last Judgement.[113]

Benjamin claims the authority of no less than Marx for such a view: 'Our election cry must be: Reform of consciousness not through dogmas, but through the analysis of mystical consciousness that is unclear to itself, whether it appears in a religious or a political form. Then people will see that the world has long possessed the dream of a thing – and that it only needs to possess the consciousness of this thing in order to really possess it.'[114] Both the collective unconscious and images of the classless society are always historically specific and mediated through existing social relations, places, objects, and communal traditions (i.e., they are *not* timeless in a metaphysical, Jungian sense).[115] It is perhaps noteworthy that Adorno's own words – 'perspectives must be fashioned that displace and estrange the world, reveal it to be, with its rifts and crevices, as indigent and distorted as it will appear one day in the messianic light'[116] – partake of a similar logic. He also recognizes that the source of such a perspective may very well be images furnished by the past. Dissecting the significance of the episode with the Lotus-Eaters in *The Odyssey*, Horkheimer and Adorno propose that 'The eating of flowers, as is still customary during dessert in the East and is known to European children from baking with rosewater and from candied violets, bears the promise of a state in which the reproduction of life is independent of conscious self-preservation ... a memory of the remote and ancient joy which flashes up before the sense of smell.'[117] The archaic past furnishes many such images, which have a part to play in fanning the flames of human desires that might otherwise be forgotten.

Utopian impulses once took up residence in theology, high art, and the folktale. Today, however, the explosion of commodities that offer themselves as an accommodating surface on which desire can be inscribed in an urban social space, combined with the decay of traditional forms of collective memory, has led to the domicile of utopian impulses in everyday life. One of Benjamin's favourite locations for such 'overdetermination' is the sphere of technology: new technological developments consistently assume a form taken from history. 'In the beginning, railroad cars look like stagecoaches, autobuses like omnibuses, electric lights like gas chandeliers, and the last like petroleum lamps.'[118] Technology *as magic*, for example, can rekindle the desire for leisure time – a desire that can only now, with the advent of industrialized society, be fully realized. Witness, for example, Aristotle's fantasy that if 'every tool we had could perform its task, either at our bidding or itself perceiving the need, and if – like the statues made by Daedalus or the tripods of Hephaestus, of which the poet says that "self-moved they enter the assembly of the gods" – shuttles in a loom could fly to and fro and a plucker play a lyre of their own accord, then master-craftsmen would have no need of servants, nor masters of slaves.'[119]

Benjamin's exploration of the utopian imagery of Fourier fits into this schematic. These images represent the collective's hope 'both to overcome and to transfigure the immaturity of the social product and the inadequacies in the social organization of production.'[120] Yet to the extent that the hope that fuels these images remains unconscious, the presence of the images themselves forestalls the recognition of the real potential that lies within social and technological developments. Caught within the dream, these images risk being experienced as the realization of the collective wishes of humanity, rather than as a sign of (unsatisfied) desire. Insofar as wishes take take physical form in objects, buildings, and monuments, the danger of misrecognition is compounded: their materialization gives 'the illusion of being the realization of those wishes rather than merely their reified expression.'[121]

In short, the materialist turn of Benjamin's later work on the arcades is animated by the belief that the wishes of humanity for a better social existence now take shape largely in the objects and spaces of capitalist society. As Weigel points out, 'Benjamin follows Freud's lead in the way he focuses on bodies, things, commodities, monuments, topography, and so on, reading these wish-symbols as materializations of collective memory; and in so doing, he restores matter to its central significance for psychoanalysis and for the means of expression of a language of the unconscious.'[122] He insists on reading the object world of urban capitalism in psychoanalytic terms: just as dreams are, for Freud, the expression of wishes that cannot be consciously acknowledged, the material world can be similarly read as the petrified expression of desires for things such as material abundance, freedom, and self-development. As these wishes are taken up by capitalism, they are distorted in the same way that the censorship mechanisms of consciousness perform 'dream-work' in the distorted representation of wishes that cannot be allowed to enter consciousness in their original form. In capitalist society, dreams of a classless society can only attain expression in a reified, fetishized form. Commodities *as fetishes* are consumed and mimetically worshipped in the hope that human beings might partake of some of the independence, autonomy, and 'life' that these inanimate objects now seem to possess.

Thus the phantasmagoric dream-sleep of capitalism is neither simply an objective illusion that is woven before the eyes of passive, helpless human subjects, nor is it a case of subjective 'false consciousness' that can be rationally dispelled. Adorno, for example, criticizes Benjamin's use of dream rhetoric in exploring the effects of the commodity form, claiming that 'the fetish character of the commodity is not a fact of consciousness; it is rather dialectical in character, in the eminent sense that it produces consciousness.'[123] He seems to think that reliance on the language of dreams inevitably leads to the conclusion that commodity fetishism is somehow a product of the mind. Thus one risks the knowledge that the objective origins of this phenomenon lie in production, not human consciousness. Margaret Cohen suggests that the origins of Adorno's frustration can perhaps be attributed to an understanding of dream rhetoric that is rooted in a conventional Enlightenment discourse wherein the dream is counterposed to rational thought as a subjectively generated distortion of reality. However, Benjamin is actually drawing from a much different discursive context – one offered by Freud – in which the dream is a complex response to a variety of somatic, libidinal, cognitive, and social stimuli as mediated through the censorship mechanisms of the conscious faculties.[124] He does not wish to deny that commodity fetishism produces consciousness, but rather also to insist that this consciousness is simultaneously overdetermined by irrepressible human desires:

> To understand humanity's history in this way as its dream means, in effect, that although the true desires and longings of human beings, for fulfillment and happiness, do achieve expression, they only do so in a displaced, censored and repressed form. Such dream work keeps humanity from the awakening that would signal an end of history and the onset of the messianic kingdom. The 'doctrine of the historical dreams of the collective' thus restores to historical phenomena their ambivalent aspect, reveals them as forms expressing simultaneously the failures and the chances of history.[125]

Benjamin's later work, then, is preoccupied with psychoanalysing the places, objects, and things of contemporary society as traces that bear mute witness to the dialectical interpenetration of dream and ruin under capitalism.

Commodities are, of course, unable to fulfil the hopes, dreams, and desires that attend their purchase. This gap does not simply mark the space between the advertised virtues of a good or service and its actual qualities. Rather, it is a consequence of the limits imposed by commodification itself: the worship or consumption of a fetish can never be an adequate substitute for that which it represents. The phantasmagoric life that is attached to the (purchase of the) object will always fall short of the real, human social relations from which it has been abstracted and reified. Disappointment is inevitable. Objects too are degraded as they are enclosed in the hard shell of identity imposed by the exchange relation. The subjective projection of desire, as mediated through and solicited by commodification, is only the most recent and undoubtedly the most violent and extensive example of the post-lapsarian 'overnaming' described by Benjamin in his essays on language:

> Nature, which was once lifted from its muteness and anonymity by the divine immediacy of the Adamic name, is now caught up within the multiplicity of systems of instrumental name-giving, and is thereby overnamed ... [This] transforms the thing as expressivity of signification into an entirely new configuration, one in which 'signification' is relegated to the arbitrary imposition of subjective, and hence abstract and instrumental, mythical judgement over the sphere of the existing.[126]

The instrumental, sadistic imposition of identity on the object comes to its apotheosis through the market, in which objects as commodities solicit their buyer's fantasies.

Unfortunately, knowledge – or more importantly, an experience of disappointment *vis-à-vis* capitalism's massive restriction of possibilities for both subject and object – is largely foreclosed by the transformation of social life described above. The displacement of *Erfahrung* by *Erlebnis* means that consciousness is deployed against registering the disappointment that is inscribed on the body and unconscious as they mutely resist enslavement within the labour process. Moreover, those moments of sadness, disappointment, and anger which do break through this barrier are experientially and mnemically disconnected from one another and from the dreams whose ruin inspires such a reaction. To the extent that it is compartmentalized and forced into conventional narratives of bourgeois subjectivity, even the most bitter frustration takes on a pathological rather than an emancipatory turn. It may be internalized in the form of self-hatred, projected onto others who are then hated as the bearers of one's own faults, or even recommodified and sold as a kind of cathartic narcotic. But such frustration is only rarely directed against the system from which it is born. The 'facticity,' the apparent utility, of most commodities makes it difficult for people to understand how such objects – or more precisely, a system that satisfies needs by producing more and better commodities – might actually constitute a barrier to human self-development. The endless production of material objects helps foster the illusion that bourgeois society is actually delivering on its promises. As they are fetishized, these objects are worshipped as the realization of a wish, rather than simply its image. When displaced onto these fetish objects, the libidinal desire that accompanies the wish is effectively detached from the dreamer; just as happens when 'dead labour' is turned against living labour, desire is subsequently organized, condensed, and directed back at the dreamer.

The dialectical image aims to interrupt this cycle – to allow for a reading of wish-images as signs that dreams have not been fulfilled but in fact continue to be denied. Taking Proust at his word that contemporary experiences can only be generated synthetically, Benjamin hopes to foster a collective experience of how the hopes and desires nurtured by the 'modern age' (i.e., the promised realization of utopian impulses through technology) have been betrayed by capitalist forms of social organization: 'The dialectical image can be defined as the involuntary memory of redeemed humanity.'[127] As the autonomous operation of memory has been sabotaged by commodification and historicism, which are the twin agents of modern amnesia, the historical materialist must produce images that can bring together desire and disappointment in a visceral union. It is not a question, as Adorno thinks, of choosing between either a 'Golden Age' or 'Hell,' but rather of bringing these two crashing together. As these moments are experienced simultaneously, individuals are shocked out of the mythic dream-sleep of capitalism. In an instant, the phantasmagoric veil is ripped apart so that the *mis*investment of desire and hope in commodities can finally be recognized as such. The fetish is exposed and, more importantly, is experienced in its debased form *as a fetish*. Capitalism is stripped of its enchantment as it is exposed as myth.

This shock-like quality of the dialectical image is why Benjamin refuses the theoretical mediation so eagerly sought by Adorno. The mimetic faculty cannot be rationally or methodically activated; it must be jump-started with a visceral, lightning-like shock. The image must synthetically generate a situation where the reader or audience is forced to use mimesis to make sense of what it is experiencing. Theory cannot manage this; in fact, theory actually gets in the way – its mediation between the different elements of the dialectical image offers itself as a substitute for mimetic cognition. The moment of mediation in the dialectical image is not sacrificed in favour of some mythic immediacy: Benjamin is as critical of Heidegger as Adorno. But its mediation is constructed *imagistically*; images from the dream-world are deliberately arranged in order to transform them into dialectical images: 'As an immediate, quasi-mystical apprehension, the dialectical image was intuitive. As a philosophical "construction," it was not. Benjamin's labourious and detailed study of past texts, his careful inventory of the fragmentary parts he gleaned from them, and the planned use of these in deliberately constructed "constellations" were all sober, self-reflective procedures.'[128]

Freud notes with respect to dreams: 'It is like a firework, which takes hours to prepare but goes off in a moment.'[129] Adorno fears that the lack of theory effectively hides the broader social totality from view, leading to the production of archaic or dream images rather than those which are properly dialectical, images that can easily be taken up by the very system they purport to attack, perhaps even to be commodified and sold by the culture industry itself.[130] For him, only the combination of aesthetics and philosophy can shatter the false immediacy spread by the culture industry. The dialectical method is to deconstruct images into their scriptual components and thereby deprive them of their power.[131] Thus, it is 'methodologically inappropriate to give conspicuous individual features from the realm of the superstructure a "materialist" turn by relating them immediately, and perhaps even causally, to certain corresponding features of the substructure. The materialist determination of traits is only possible if it is mediated through the *total social process*.' Benjamin's method is criticized for being a 'wide-eyed presentation of mere facts ... located at the crossroads of magic and positivism. This spot is bewitched. Only theory could break this spell.'[132] Adorno wreathes his own analysis in a complex, exceedingly dense theory not only to 'break the spell' but also to insulate his own work from appropriation by mainstream, one-dimensional conceptual systems. Yet this is precisely the kind of interpretive approach that Benjamin disavows as anemic and ineffective because it neglects the bodily dimension of cognition.

Adorno's claim that one can only perform a materialist analysis of culture through theoretical mediation ignores one of the central components of the dialectical image. Benjamin and Adorno agree that certain objects and fragments reproduce within themselves the totality of the social process in monadological form: in effect, these objects and fragments *express* the socioeconomic structures in which they are produced. And like Adorno, Benjamin believes there are substantial shortcomings to Marxist forms of cultural criticism guided by a simplistic model of cause and effect. 'In almost every case' of such criticism, he writes, 'what we find is a thick-skinned tracing out of the lines in the works themselves ... [But] the Marxist's hope that he can look around inside the work with the gaze of the sociologist is doomed to disappointment.'[133] In explicit contrast to this approach, Benjamin seeks the 'expression' of the economy in culture, including the secret ways in which the contradictions of a capitalist economy manifest themselves in specific objects and practices. For Adorno, jazz is emblematic of capitalism; for Benjamin, the commodities of nineteenth-century Paris are emblematic of the same thing. Adorno, however, believes that a dense theoretical mediation – 'second reflection' – is required to transform such cultural objects into monads: they are never discovered 'pre-formed.' Benjamin agrees that the intervention of a theoretically informed historical materialist is needed for such a transformation, but he also contends that the nature of this intervention ought to be primarily imagistic: 'Thinking involves not only the movement of thoughts, but their arrest as well. Where thinking suddenly comes to a stop in a constellation saturated with tensions, it gives that constellation a shock, by which thinking is crystallized as a monad.'[134] It is the *interruption* of patterns of thought that have become routine – the temporary suspension of conceptual consciousness – that sponsors the transfiguration of a moment, object, or place into a monad. The interruption of thinking kick-starts mimetic cognition and forces us to reckon with events or things as expressive of much deeper and more expansive forms of historical experience.[135] Such monads occupy a critical place in dialectical images insofar as they magnify and extend the power of shock to indict the entire social system. These verdicts are not patiently assembled by tracing out cause (economic base) and effect (superstructure) in the production of commodities or cultural objects. Rather, in a lightning-like act of mimetic cognition, the object – more particularly, one's own relations with it – is (re)cognized as a microcosm of the broader network of social relations in which one is embedded. Aided by the synthetic web of similarities by which exchange-value binds together objects, experiences, and memories, awareness blazes through these phenomena like a brush fire, allowing us to understand and experience them as if for the first time. The skill of the historical materialist then lies in the ability to arrange and interpret fragments in such a way that their hidden monadological quality becomes visible in the dialectical image.

Dialectical images must not be fetishized into having an autonomous, objective power in and of themselves. Their purpose is to activate and organize the experiential resources of human beings. The dialectical compression of dream, ruin, and the commodity form into a single, shocking image ignites buried individual and collective memories that can somatically, libidinally, and cognitively confirm the oppressive, restrictive, and dominating nature of capitalism. Knowledge about social existence simply cannot be imparted to people except by attaching it to their own experiences and memories. More precisely, this knowledge will have no revolutionary effect unless it is so attached. Thus Benjamin asks, 'In what way is it possible to conjoin a heightened graphicness [*Anschaulichkeit*] to the realization of the Marxist method?'[136] How might the contradictions of capitalism be experienced in such a way that they activate the desire for change? How can psychic resources currently mobilized by capital in maintaining the dream-sleep of human beings be transformed into energies for awakening? The point is to enlist people's own dreams and frustrations in the critique of the commodity form: 'The realization of dream elements, in the course of waking up, is the paradigm of dialectical thinking.'[137] Being fully awake under capitalism sponsors the use of reason and consciousness as a buffer against a full experience of the social environment. We are left without access to the collective hopes of humanity. Conversely, slumbering in capitalism's dream-sleep, we are unaware of the mythic, repetitive cycle of desire and frustration in which we are caught. The function of the dream is, after all, to prolong sleep. Both sets of conditions are experienced at work, in everyday life, and in popular culture, but neither condition *on its own* gives humanity the creative, cognitive, or social resources necessary for transformative social action. The schizophrenic temperament of *Erlebnis* means that these moments are rarely if ever brought together. But, Benjamin argues, true, experiential knowledge of capitalism can occur only where these two worlds touch. We must live the dream *awake*: 'Is awakening perhaps the synthesis of dream consciousness (as thesis) and waking consciousness (as antithesis)?'[138] Awakening, then, is not the state of being awake but the simultaneous experience of consciousness and dreaming. While the function of the dream is to prolong sleep, the original impetus of the wish that is managed by the dream is to awake. The expressions of desire – both collective and individual – that energize the dream must be arrayed against the knowledge of their betrayal by the socioeconomic system. With the memory of past hopes fresh in mind and body and only the dream has the energy to return to these images with sufficient force – in a flash of visceral insight we are confronted by their betrayal and by our own psychic complicity in that betrayal through the commodity form: 'Such juxtapositions of past and present undercut the contemporary phantasmagoria, bringing to consciousness the rapid half-life of the utopian element in commodities and the relentless repetition of their form of betrayal: the same promise, the same disappointment.'[139] Only in such a moment, when knowledge and experience are fused into one, might the grip of bourgeois society over people's material, psychic, and cognitive existence be exploded.

Throughout his writings, Benjamin places a high value on the 'destructive character': 'where divine power enters into the secular world, it breathes destruction.'[140] The eradication of that which exists – especially the organic unities that bind subjects and objects in particular patterns – is a necessary step in clearing the way for a future that is not predetermined:

> The destructive character sees nothing permanent. But for this very reason he sees ways everywhere. Where others encounter walls or mountains, there, too, he sees a way. But because he sees a way everywhere, he has to clear things from it everywhere. Not always by brute force; sometimes by the most refined. Because he sees ways everywhere, he always stands at a crossroads. No moment can know what the next will bring. What exists he reduces to rubble – not for the sake of rubble, but for that of the way leading through it.[141]

This destructive impulse lies at the core of the dialectical image as it rips objects, images, and experiences out of dominant historical narratives and social structures. Yet this hermeneutic violence must not be conceptualized in an idealistic or nihilistic fashion. In many respects the dialectical image merely feeds off the radical restructuring presided over by capitalism itself. Capitalist social relations shred tradition and the 'chains of memory' for the subject; at the same time, they tear objects out of their conventional habitat, and displace their use-value with exchange-value. At one level, just as with the shift from *Erfahrung* to *Erlebnis*, this destructive effect is highly emancipatory in that it liberates objects from the confines of tradition and makes them available, as fragments, for a seemingly infinite range of configurations. As Adorno himself points out, Benjamin's discussion of the collector's dream 'in which things are freed from the drudgery of being useful'[142] is a 'brilliant turning point for the dialectical salvation of the commodity.'[143] Indeed, 'the devaluation of the world of things in allegory is surpassed within the world of things itself by the commodity.'[144] Yet what the commodity gives with one hand it immediately takes away with the other as the ruins created by capitalism are enchanted once again and a new myth is born. The dialectical image attacks the phantasms, myths, and historicist narratives that block a full experience of the destruction wrought by the commodity form. It strives to drain the world of its illusions: 'To cultivate fields where, until now, only madness has reigned. Forge ahead with the whetted axe of reason, looking neither right nor left so as not to succumb to the horror that beckons from deep in the primeval forest. Every ground must at some point have been made arable by reason, must have been cleared of the undergrowth of delusion and myth.'[145]

Paradoxically, however, the foundation for such a project is the very social process that is being criticized. It is capitalism itself that makes possible the dialectical image, that destroys the traditional structures of memory and experience so that these fragments can be arranged in new and explosive ways. This is not to read a teleological narrative into Benjamin, but rather to highlight how the dialectical image functions as a critical parasite, drawing its very lifeblood from that which it arrays itself against.[146] The growth of the commodity form brings not only massive dangers but also opportunities for its dialectical supersession.

To the extent that dialectical images succeed in using elements of the dream in a moment of awakening, individuals – and more importantly, society at large – come to share the historical perspective of Benjamin's angel of history. For an instant, the endless sections of empty time that stretch back into the past appear before us, with nothing in their wake but the broken lives and shattered dreams of the dead: 'Where a chain of events appears before *us, he* sees one single catastrophe, which keeps piling wreckage upon wreckage and hurls it at his feet.'[147] Amidst the ruins of history, surrounded by the now lifeless objects of capitalism, *Erlebnis* is finally experienced as such. The poetry of Baudelaire – the foremost esoteric prototype of the dialectical image – is praised so highly by Benjamin precisely because it mobilizes contemporary experience in providing just such an emancipatory glimpse of the world. In his descriptions of gambling, for example, 'the poet does not participate in the game. He stands in his corner, no happier than those who are playing. He too has been cheated out of his experience – a modern man. The only difference is that he rejects the narcotics the gamblers use to dull the consciousness that has forced them to march to the beat of the second hand.'[148] Impoverished experience does not unfold autonomously out of Baudelaire's poetry; rather, the poems *name* an already existing form of experience: 'Spleen ... *exposes* the isolated experience [*Erlebnis*] in all its nakedness. To his horror, the melancholy man sees the earth revert to a mere state of nature ... This is the nature of the immediate experience [*Erlebnis*] to which Baudelaire has given the weight of long experience [*Erfahrung*].'[149]

Baudelaire's favoured poetic device for achieving this effect is allegory. This poetic form first attracted Benjamin's attention in his analysis of *Trauerspiel* or 'mourning plays,' which were largely dismissed or ignored by most literary scholars. Baroque playwrights regularly used allegory to depict the utter degradation of a world dominated by 'natural-history.' In an allegory, 'any person, any object, any relationship can mean absolutely anything else': it constitutes the literal devaluation of the human, social, and natural landscape.[150] In the case of Baudelaire, allegory constituted a perfect literary expression of the rapid commodification of everyday life in nineteenth-century Paris. Just as Adorno praises serious modern art as the 'absolute commodity,' Benjamin champions Baudelaire's incorporation of the exchange relation into the very core of his poetry: 'The specific devaluation of the world of things, as manifested in the commodity, is the foundation of Baudelaire's allegorical intention.'[151] Just as the logic of exchange destroys the use-value of an object, allegory forcibly strips objects of their particularity, vitality, and meaning as they are embedded in an empty, barren semiotics: 'Baudelaire's poetic sensibility ... bears the mark of an experience of dehumanization, of reification or the transformation of the self into a dead object ... "Spleen" refers specifically to the mode of melancholia in which the subject can no longer mournfully "observe" the permanent catastrophe of natural history, but rather in a quite literal sense, *is* this catastrophe.'[152]

Remember here Benjamin's analysis of the revolutionary mimetic impulse of the surrealists: subject quite literally *becomes* the object in order to expand one's experience of it beyond the boundaries of formal reason. This is precisely what Baudelaire's use of the allegorical form does with the commodity. The prostitute figures so prominently in his poetry because her existence exemplifies the unification of use-value and exchange-value in a single moment, *in a single body*: 'The whore is the most precious booty in the triumph of allegory – the life which signifies death.'[153] And rather than gaze upon her as a discrete object of contemplation and fade into melancholic paralysis, Baudelaire uses this image to reflect on and express his own commodification as a writer. He 'knew the true situation of the man of letters: he goes to the marketplace as a flâneur, supposedly to take a look at it, but in reality to find a buyer.'[154] The shock of this realization tears apart the phantasmagoric veil with which capitalism seeks to enchant the market and its crowds. 'Allegory dissolves myth,' notes Max Pensky, 'by depicting the nakedness and degradation of the object for what it is and for exposing, however momentarily, the soul of the commodity as hell.'[155] A devaluation of the world of things both visible and visceral kills the fetish that energizes the phantasmagoria of commodity fetishism. As Benjamin argues, 'advertising seeks to disguise the commodity character of things. What resists the mendacious transfiguration of the commodity world is its distortion into allegory. The commodity wants to look itself in the face.'[156] Baudelaire's allegorical poetry brings nothing new to the table; instead, it tries to complete the destructive impulse presided over by capitalism itself and thereby pass a 'destructive, but just verdict'[157] upon it. It attacks the rebirth of myth sponsored by commodity fetishism and in doing so forces a true reckoning with a social legacy at once catastrophic and highly emancipatory. Using a second-order, aesthetically mediated and expressed mimesis of death, the allegorical form can bring the first-order, apotropaic mimesis in labour and everyday life to consciousness.

However, the moment of demystification is hardly sufficient. In the case of *Trauerspiele*, for example, their merciless exposition of human history as little more than a pile of corpses led into an idealistic *cul-de-sac* in which death in this world suddenly reverses into a negative allegory of redemption in the next.[158] Conversely but no less dangerously, an isolated confrontation with a world that has suddenly been rendered meaningless can lead to a paralyzing and privatized melancholy. The dreams that Benjamin finds at the heart of capitalist society do not simply fuel the destructive rage that attends the recognition of their betrayal. They must also be deployed to excite both the knowledge that things could be different and the collective desire to make it so. As he observes in his final thoughts on history:

> The past carries with it a secret index by which it is referred to redemption. Doesn't a breath of the air that pervaded earlier days caress us well? In the voices we hear, isn't there an echo of now silent ones? ... If so, then there is a secret agreement between past generations and the present one. Then our coming was expected on earth. Then, like every generation that preceded us, we have been endowed with a *weak* messianic power, a power on which the past has a claim.[159]

The current system is destroyed 'not for the sake of the rubble, but for that of the way leading through it.' Destruction for its own sake necessarily collapses into nihilism and the individualistic, arbitrary imposition of meaning on a mute natural world. We must not only adopt the same vantage point of the angel of history, but also come to share his desire: 'The angel would like to stay, awaken the dead, and make whole what has been smashed.'[160] An experience of the past *as loss* is therefore a vital component of the dialectical image. Benjamin valorizes the Baudelairean *correspondance* because of how it gives absence – the memory of something – the weight of an experience.[161] It transforms beauty, for example, into a memory. And while such memories can never be entirely resurrected even as they are redeemed, their absent presence dampens the hypertrophy of a subject otherwise drunk on its own power to narcissistically assign new meanings to the ruins that surround it.[162] Without such a presence, ruins are once again enchanted and the cycle begins anew. Conversely, the desire to redeem the past, accompanied by the knowledge that such redemption can only ever be incomplete, can arouse a subject that is otherwise cast into a paralyzing melancholy by the hopelessness of destruction. The invocation of loss Benjamin leaves to a theological impulse that has been secularized. The services of theology are requisite to the success of historical materialism because they furnish this redemptive impulse, this link with the dreams/suffering of the past that actually enables a future which is *not* entirely predetermined through its collapse into myth.

## Surreal Technologies: Film as Dialectical Image

Benjamin identifies new cultural technologies, especially film, as ideal media for producing dialectical images – that is, for bringing the images lodged within individual and collective memory into an explosive confrontation with the present. Insofar as they adopt the aesthetic techniques pioneered by surrealism, media such as film and photography use progressive forms of shock to initiate a new mode of cultural consumption – 'distraction' – in which mimesis is reactivated as a mnemic tool in the retrieval of buried memories, experiences and images. Such recall 'interrupts' conventional narratives of the bourgeois subject, historical progress, and capitalism as the source of material abundance and happiness. But simultaneously it provides the resources for the *innervation* of the masses in building a new social order.

Any discussion of the role of cultural technologies in the production of dialectical images must be prefaced with the caveat that such assessments are always historically specific. It is impossible to identify a particular aesthetic strategy as offering a timeless blueprint for historical materialist pedagogy. Dialectical images, notes Benjamin, always have a 'historical index': 'For the historical index of the images not only says that they belong to a particular time; it says, above all, that they attain to legibility only at a particular time. And, indeed, this acceding "to legibility" constitutes a specific critical point in the movement at their interior. Every present day is determined by the images that are synchronic with it: each "now" is the now of a particular recognizability.'[163]

That which delivers a progressive shock at one historical conjuncture may not necessarily have the same effect at another time. It is especially important to be aware of this given the culture industry's power to comodify, integrate, and defuse artistic endeavours that were once highly critical. Thus, one cannot read Benjamin's endorsement of surrealism or film as perennial; that said, neither can one dismiss his theoretical work in this area by resorting to evidence about the hegemonic effects of Hollywood. Hansen argues that read *counter*factually, 'the Artwork Essay only enhances the utopian modality of its statements, shifting the emphasis from a definition of what film *is* to its failed opportunities and unrealized promises.'[164] With this proviso in mind, I want to take a closer look at the qualities of surrealism and film that Benjamin speculates could be marshalled in dialecticizing the images that lie within contemporary experience.

For its raw material, surrealism looks to the world of the everyday. It is a form of art whose significance and effects depend on mobilizing a set of experiences shared, at one level or another, by all who live in an urban environment. Disavowing the hermetic practices of most art, it plunges into the very heart of capitalist society, exploiting its products and spaces as the source of a 'profane illumination' that all can share. Benjamin credits André Breton, a key figure in the surrealist movement, for perceiving 'the revolutionary energies that appear in the "outmoded" – in the first iron constructions, the first factory buildings, the earliest photos, objects that have begun to be extinct, grand pianos, the dresses of five years ago, fashionable restaurants when the vogue has begun to ebb from them. The relation of these things to revolution – no one can have a more exact concept of it than these authors.'[165]

These 'revolutionary energies' are a by-product of the ever-quickening cycles through which capitalism must circulate use-value in order to produce exchange: to stimulate insatiable cravings for novelty, what is fashionable today must be rendered obsolete tomorrow. This unceasing production of desire, however, nurtures a secret rage that, as it accumulates, threatens to explode into revolutionary mobilization. Disappointment follows ever closer on the heels of the consumptive act: commodities quickly lose their sparkle once they have been ejected from the circuits of exchange that gave them their life. Every generation, notes Benjamin, experiences 'the fashions of the one immediately preceding it as the most radical antiaphrodisiac imaginable.'[166] Consequently, strategic use of these fashions can reverse the polarity of libidinal energies that flow through practices of consumption, and in so doing momentarily transform attraction into repulsion. One can tap into the heightened anxiety and anger that attend the disappointment inherent in practices whereby greater and greater emotional investments are made and actively solicited by the culture industry. Of course mass culture remains extremely effective at reversing this rage once again, using it to increase its own strength and to attack those critical impulses which challenge its hegemony. Yet the rage that follows upon being disappointed or betrayed yet again by commodities remains the weak link in the chain, and thereby attracts Benjamin's attention.

'The trick by which this world of things is mastered,' he writes, 'consists in the substitution of a political for a historical view of the past.'[167] History divides events, separating them into discrete compartments: the dreams that once enveloped objects and spaces are isolated from the revulsion that is the by-product of their decay into waste and ruin. Politics, however, compresses these experiences into a singular space, thereby generating a dialectical confrontation between subjects and the world they inhabit: it brings 'the immense forces of "atmosphere" concealed in these things to the point of explosion.'[168] Surrealism foregrounds the emancipatory potential that lingers within the 'trash' of urban capitalism: the outmoded object preserves the memory of desire once invested in it, while its status as trash simultaneously demonstrates the betrayal of that desire. The Parisian arcades perfectly symbolize the political explosiveness of ruin: 'They had been destroyed by the dynamics of the very capitalist system, the origins of which they had been built to celebrate ... They were a monument, not to tradition, but to historical transiency.'[169] Moreover, the potential of the arcades to inaugurate radically new forms of social space and human interaction far exceeded their actual use as shopping malls: many of the most potent images in *The Arcades Project* are designed to bring this potential *and* its repression by capital to consciousness. Such consciousness might subsequently evolve into an awareness of the logic of creative destruction that dominates capitalist society: 'With the destabilizing of the market economy, we begin to recognize the monuments of the bourgeoisie as ruins even *before* they have crumbled.'[170] Capitalism stands indicted as a mythic machine that produces ruins instead of fulfilling dreams. Once the glow of exchange-value has subsided, it becomes easier to understand and experience commodities as merely the expression of a wish rather than its concrete realization. In perceiving the strategic possibilities for emancipatory experience that attend the production of obsolescence – a key moment in the circuit of exchange – surrealism helps Benjamin identify dialectical possibilities that lie at the core of the commodity form.

Without question, surrealism's most significant legacy for Benjamin is the method of montage: 'This project must raise the art of quoting without quotation marks to the very highest level. Its theory is intimately linked to that of montage.'[171] Wolin, for example, describes montage as 'the ontological basis of Benjamin's theory of knowledge.'[172] Aside from the empirical and theoretical melange in his unfinished work on the arcades, Benjamin's most striking use of this technique occurs in *One Way Street*, in which philosophical fragments take their place alongside seemingly unrelated scenes from everyday life, leaving – or rather, forcing – readers to try and make the connections themselves. The aesthetic juxtaposition of seemingly unrelated objects or ideas – be they represented visually or through language – reactiviates an *exoteric* mimetic cognition. The bringing together of extremes provides a progressive shock, jolting individuals out of a predetermined relationship with or form of understanding of an object. To the extent that a shock induces us to wonder why certain ideas or images have been synthetically assembled, we are forced beyond logic to draw from other cognitive resources in the extraction of meaning. Thus, 'inconceivable analogies and connections between events are the order of the day.'[173] Montage exercises the mimetic faculty in a manner that departs from the defensive, insular posture into which it has decayed under the barrage of shocks that attend modern existence.

Montage also has a salutary destructive effect as objects and experiences are ripped out of the conventional social, economic, and semiotic structures in which they are usually embedded. Benjamin finds the epic theatre of Bertolt Brecht especially compelling in this regard, as a 'retranslation of the methods of montage ... from a technological process to a human one.'[174] Conventional plays cultivate an empathy between audience and characters by reproducing the linear structure of experience that prevails in daily life; in contrast, Brecht intentionally disrupts narrative flow through the episodic intensification of dramatic artifice: 'The art of the epic theater consists in producing not empathy but astonishment. In a word: instead of identifying with the protagonist, the audience should learn to feel astonished at the circumstances under which he functions.'[175] This astonishment does not depend on dramatic contradictions internal to the plot; rather, it 'has to be of the sort that the audience can validate [*kontrollieren*] at crucial points on the basis of its own experience.'[176] In other words, the skilful juxtaposition of scenes produces an alienation or estrangement of conventional structures of meaning as our ability to adequately make sense of particular situations is radically called into question. Instead, the spectator is forced to confront these scenes – which are often taken from the everyday – with fresh eyes: 'The truly important thing is to discover the situations for the first time. (One might equally well say "defamiliarize" them.) This discovery (or defamiliarization) of situations is fostered through interruption of the action.'[177] In other words, the interruption of narrative illusion shocks people into drawing from their own experience to perceive reality in hitherto undeveloped ways: 'The songs, the captions, the gestic conventions set off one situation from another. This creates intervals which ... are provided so that the audience can respond critically to the player's actions and the way they are presented.'[178] Above all, epic theater fosters critical agency insofar as it strips the aura of inevitability from traditional patterns of organizing human behaviour and interaction, thereby sparking an awareness that these patterns represent merely one possibility in a vast field of potential human action.

As an aesthetic medium, film shares with allegory, surrealism, and epic theatre a capacity for destruction: 'The social significance of film, even – and especially – in its most positive form, is inconceivable without its destructive, cathartic side: the liquidation of the value of tradition in the cultural heritage.'[179] At one level, this liquidation proceeds via film's capacity to reproduce culture and thereby destroy its 'aura' – a sense of authenticity that attaches to unique cultural objects and fosters their imprisonment within the confines of tradition. Reproduction enables a popular engagement with and interrogation of the prized cultural treasures of humanity as their images appear independent of the many rituals that embedded them in bourgeois ideologies of progress, social order, and civilization. Besides emancipating specific aesthetic objects, film eradicates prevailing definitions of culture by creating a form of art that is based not on the creation of singular works, but rather on the production of images that are to be disseminated as widely as possible. As such, it takes as its subject that which most interests the masses: 'Namely: *the desire ... to "get closer" to things, and their equally passionate concern for overcoming each thing's uniqueness* [Überwindung des Einmaligen jeder Gegebenheit] *by assimilating it as a reproduction*. Every day the urge grows stronger to get hold of an object at close range in an image [*Bild*], or, better, in a facsimile [*Abbild*], a reproduction.'[180]

As noted in our earlier discussion of *Erfahrung* and *Erlebnis*, Benjamin regards the liquidation of tradition as a necessary step for social emancipation. Experiences that have been liberated from the 'chains of memory' can be deployed in explosive new ways; the same can be said of culture, once it has been freed of its subservience to tradition: '*Instead of being founded on ritual,* [artistic production] *is based on a different practice: politics.*'[181]

Capitalism produces vast collective forces, but they have little sense of themselves. In part, this can be attributed to remnants of the bourgeois subject, but it can also be explained by the sheer absence of cultural tools through which the collective can (re)present and thereby (re)cognize itself. Writing on the emerging mass media of radio, film, and newspapers, Benjamin consistently defines their importance as new cultural technologies in terms of their as yet unutilized capacity to provide people with avenues for self-expression. Of radio, for example, he argues:

> The crucial failing of this institution has been to perpetuate the fundamental separation between practitioners and the public, a separation that is at odds with its technological basis. A child can see that it is in the spirit of radio to put as many people as possible in front of a microphone on every possible occasion; the public has to be turned into the witnesses of interviews and conversations in which now this person and now that one has the opportunity to make himself heard.[182]

Benjamin disparages newspapers for communicating experience as information, but he also discerns a dialectical moment within the 'impatience' that characterizes the mind of the avid reader seeking political gossip or stock tips: 'Behind it smolders the impatience of people who are excluded and who think they have the right to see their own interests expressed.'[183] And in a capitalist society, the legitimate expression of these interests must take a class form. For example, he criticizes the capitalist film industry for 'stimulating the involvement of the masses through illusionary displays and ambiguous speculations' such as polls and beauty contests: 'All this in order to distort and corrupt the original and justified interest of the masses in film – an interest in understanding themselves and therefore their class.'[184] He credits precisely such a vision to Soviet filmmaker Sergei Eisenstein whose *Battleship Potemkin* Benjamin defends as representing the proletariat as a transformative mass movement: 'No other medium could reproduce this collective in motion. No other could convey such beauty or the currents of horror and panic it contains.'[185] Deeply moved by the experimental vigour of the Soviet media, which he observed during an extended stay in Moscow in the late 1920s, Benjamin regularly contrasts the failures of capitalist media with an idealized portrait of the U.S.S.R.'s apparent progress in erasing the distinction between those who produce culture and those who consume it.[186]

Like the dialectical image, the revolutionary potential of film does not reside so much in its specific content as in the mode of reception it imposes on an audience. As Howard Eiland observes, Benjamin uses the word 'distraction' (*Zerstreuung*) to express a variety of different and contradictory ideas.[187] For example, in two pieces from the early 1930s he contrasts the critical defamiliarization of Brecht's epic theatre with the distraction or 'complacent diversion' offered by more traditional forms of entertainment. This meaning of the term clearly prejudiced Adorno's initial encounter with Benjamin's work on film: 'I cannot find your theory of "distraction" at all convincing – if only for the simple reason that in a communist society, work would be organized in such a way that human beings would no longer be so exhausted or stupefied as to require such distraction.'[188] However, Benjamin's use of the term in the 'Work of Art' essay goes far beyond the pejorative meanings customarily associated with it; it invokes a far more complex mode of reception that fully emerges only when considered in the context of his evolving approach to memory, mimesis, and experience and his speculative work on how to disrupt bourgeois forms of subjectivity.

Benjamin repeatedly constellates film with epic theatre, suggesting that the emancipatory potential of each medium is rooted in their shared capacity to interrupt conventional patterns of spectatorship: '*Like the images in a film*, the epic theater moves in spurts. Its basic form is that of the shock with which the individual, well-defined situations of a play collide.'[189] Elsewhere, he notes how epic theatre proceeds 'jerkily, like the images of a film strip.'[190] When we invert the emphasis in these claims, it becomes clear that the type of film Benjamin is talking about does not include the smooth, linear narratives that for the most part dominate the offerings of the culture industry. Instead, like epic theatre, it is film's (underutilized) capacity to interrupt such narratives through discontinuity and fragmentation – above all through montage – that grounds his theoretical observations. In this context, one can make more sense of the differences between Benjamin and Adorno regarding the emancipatory effects of film. The former focuses mainly on film's capacity to produce shock in an audience – an effect that would have been especially noteworthy in early, silent cinema; the latter argues that the capitalist film industry develops the means to reduce the presence of shocks in favour of products that can be easily and comfortably consumed. Music, for example, 'attempts to interpose a human coating between the reeled-off pictures and the spectators. Its social function is that of a cement, which holds together elements that otherwise would oppose each other unrelated – the mechanical product and the spectators, and also the spectators themselves. It seeks to breathe into the pictures some of the life that photography has taken away from them.'[191]

Benjamin agrees with Adorno's worries in this regard: 'I see more and more clearly that the launching of the sound film must be regarded as an operation of the film industry designed to break the revolutionary primacy of the silent film, which had produced reactions that were difficult to control and hence dangerous politically.'[192] Nevertheless, he insists that the success of the culture industry's reactionary strategies does not dampen the utopian potential of certain types of film to inaugurate revolutionary new forms of perception and experience.

To the extent that film does take the form of montage, assembling images and sequences that astonish rather than satisfy the viewer, it can force the audience to apply the mimetic faculty in deciphering what appears on the screen. Recall Benjamin's basic definition of mimesis: it is the gift for seeing resemblances or perceiving similarities between things. When film disrupts linear, temporal narrative structures, alternative perceptual strategies must be applied in order to extract meaning from the otherwise meaningless juxtaposition of images. At its most destructive, film allegorizes everything it touches, thereby supercharging the mimetic faculty in offering a veritable playground for the construction of mimetic associations. At the very least, the function of mimesis is reversed: its use as a defensive tactic is displaced by a self-directed posture that actively engages in the mimetic processing of these images (i.e., the search for and reflection on similarities, associations, and linkages between them not captured by instrumental, identitarian rationality). As alternative rationalities are invoked, the body and the unconscious potentially become equal partners in systems of human cognition. Successful mimetic cognition coaches humanity to once again take note of messages and signs from the body and the unconscious that it has long been trained to ignore. And this has immense implications for human memory. Hansen explains:

> Introducing a 'tactile' element into the field of 'optical reception,' allegorical devices like framing and montage would thus have a therapeutic function similar to other procedures – the planned rituals of extraordinary physical and mental states, like drug experiments, flaneurist walking, Surrealist seances or psychoanalytic sessions – procedures designed to activate layers of unconscious memory buried in the reified structures of subjectivity.[193]

The construction of linkages is not limited to the material presented on the screen. Rather, it opens up a vast field of subterranean memories that might be triggered, retrieved, and consciously experienced as mediated through film. Consider, for example, the parallels between film and the dream. According to Freud, dreams represent the manifestation of wishes that cannot be acknowledged in waking consciousness. Within the dream, the tendency of the conscious faculties to anaesthetize the body and choke off repressed impulses from the unconscious is reduced. The suspension of formal logic within the dream plays a key role in this process: as images are condensed, displaced, and associated with one another in patterns that appear to rationality as random or senseless, repressed impulses and desires are permitted to express themselves in a distorted form. Films that adopt parallel tactics of disorganization can, Benjamin suggests, produce similar effects. Disarmed by equally potent mimetic logics, the defensive posture that the psyche assumes in *Erlebnis* is reduced, allowing for a greater 'openness' to experience and memory. The shock effects of film induce an 'intensified presence of mind [*Geistesgegenwart*]'[194]; the suspension of formal logic via montage then channels this heightened state of awareness into mimetic forms of perception and cognition. Triggered by resemblances between that which appears on the screen and that which lies within the *mémoire involuntaire,* a repressed past can suddenly flash into consciousness. Unlike the reception of dreams, however, films are perceived in a state of awakening, not sleep.

In this context, awakening is more than simply a literal reference to the fact that we are conscious when viewing a film. It also invokes the image of a collective awakening to its own social power and to the historical obligations which accompany that power. Writing about epic theatre, Benjamin suggests that the audience, 'being a collective, will usually feel impelled to take a stand promptly.'[195] In bourgeois modes of aesthetic consumption, the individual appears alone, unsure, and deferential before great works of art: 'contemplative immersion' becomes 'a breeding ground for asocial behaviour.'[196] Conversely, when individuals gather themselves into a group – and especially when that group has a sense of itself as a class – they find themselves inspired with the self-confidence that is an essential prerequisite for the kind of revolutionary use of culture that Benjamin has in mind. Initially, this desire manifests itself as a craving for entertainment, for distraction in the pejorative sense; but embedded in this craving is a far more radical objective. As the masses grow in strength, they gain the power to seize culture for their own purposes and in their own interests; ultimately, they wrest this power away from its customary placement in the ideologies of the ruling class: 'A person who concentrates before a work of art is absorbed by it; he enters into the work ... By contrast, the distracted masses absorb the work of art into themselves. Their waves lap around it; they encompass it with their tide.'[197] The parallel here with Benjamin's reflections on history and the dialectical image is striking. Like the isolated spectator, historicism stands in awe before history: as it empathizes with historical events, it is uncritically absorbed by them. Like the masses, the historical materialist 'blasts' the objects of history out of the historical continuum, bringing them to bear on the actuality of his or her present. In the cinema, the reactions of individuals are 'determined by the imminent concentration of reactions into a mass. No sooner are these reactions manifest than they regulate one another.'[198] The presence of the collective dissipates a reverential awe before culture in favour of a relaxed, self-interested disposition in which a film's images can be used to (re)experience one's own environment in new ways.

As a consequence, the '*extremely backward attitude toward a Picasso painting changes into a highly progressive reaction to a Chaplin film.* The progressive attitude is characterized by an immediate, intimate fusion of pleasure – pleasure in seeing and experiencing – with an attitude of expert appraisal.'[199] Both Chaplin and Picasso offer mimetic engagement with instrumental rationality. Yet irrespective of whether a Picasso painting inspires puzzlement, respectful adoration, or even rage, the reaction remains 'backward,' because at the level of the masses it does not invigorate a collective (re)engagement with the conditions of modern existence. On the other hand, the eager reception of Chaplin in the movie hall sponsors precisely this 'progressive attitude.' His stylized movements mime the worker's submission to the machine and, more broadly, the body's fragmentation under the disciplinary gaze of capital. As people laugh at his exaggerated gestures, the possibility opens up that they will recognize themselves in his movements. In the moment of shock this inspires, memories and images may be released through which a lifetime of exploitation and repression might finally be experienced as such. Benjamin approvingly quotes Philippe Soupault: 'The undeniable superiority of Chaplin's films ... is based on the fact that they are imbued with a poetry that everyone encounters in his life, admittedly without always being conscious of it.'[200] In this context, Chaplin represents a return to the storyteller insofar as he is 'communicating' experience that his audience can mimetically recognize as their own. The use of mimesis to transmit experience overcomes the barriers to intersubjectivity that have been heightened in capitalist modernity to protect individuals from externalized shocks. For the first time, that which rules daily life enters the perceptual field as a representation with which cognition can engage in a mediated, conscious relationship.

In short, Benjamin's essay on technologies of cultural reproduction makes three crucial assumptions that distinguish his conception of film from the very different products championed by the culture industry. First, film must take as its subject the social and material conditions lived by the masses – especially those lived by the working class. Second, in order to activate the audience's mimetic faculty, it must privilege montage as a means of creating representational tableaux riven with contradictions. Third, reception must be collectively organized to stimulate the popular appropriation of film as a tool through which people can wilfully conceptualize and experience their lives in entirely new ways. When all three conditions are present, members of the audience acquire the identity of 'experts': 'Anyone who has listened to a group of newspaper boys leaning on their bicycles and discussing the outcome of a bicycle race will have an inkling of this.'[201] The newspaper boys bring their own expertise as bicycle riders into play through the medium of the race; they take stock of it, 'testing' it against their own experience, and thereby use the race to mediate that experience, elevating it to an object of conscious attention. Film harbours the potential to similarly thrust humanity into a reflexive relationship of expertise with its own existence – especially those elements of existence which are systematically repressed by capitalism.

Film is especially well-suited for enabling people to perceive how the material environment defines and regulates patterns of human action and interaction in ways that do not reveal themselves to the naked eye: 'It is through the camera that we first discover the optical unconscious, just as we discover the instinctual unconscious.'[202] Freud's writings raised the unconscious to consciousness by transforming phenomena that had previously passed without notice into objects of scrutiny and analysis. As Benjamin notes, a slip of the tongue no longer escapes attention the way it once did.[203] Similarly, he heralds film as 'the first artistic medium which is able to show how matter plays havoc with human beings [*wie die Materie dem Menschen mitspielt*]': it can, therefore, 'be an excellent medium of materialist exposition.'[204] In the defensive posture that is characteristic of *Erlebnis*, the human organism minimizes exposure to the shocks of urban capitalism through apotropaic mimesis and/or the cultivation of attentiveness as a buffer against experience. Adorno suggests that modern art can 'deterrorize' mimesis; in the same vein, Benjamin speculates that film can deterrorize many forms of contemporary experience. Insofar as the reception of film is organized within a class-conscious collective, faculties of perception and apperception are oriented away from an unconditional submission to naturalized reality and toward a critical testing of that reality in light of the possibilities it holds for different modes of social life: 'Our bars and city streets, our offices and furnished rooms, our railroad stations and our factories seemed to close relentlessly around us. Then came film and exploded this prison-world with the dynamite of the split second, so that now we can set off calmly on journeys of adventure among its far-flung debris. With the close-up, space expands; with slow motion, movement is extended.'[205]

Film reveals diverse aspects of lived reality that touch body and mind but remain beyond the '*normal* spectrum of sense impressions.'[206] As these aspects are presented, the immense potential that lies coiled within any given moment, object, or situation is rehearsed and humanity is assured of 'a vast and unsuspected field of action [*Spielraum*].'[207] Such moments truly are 'dialectics at a standstill' – that is, the dialectical compression of time into space in such a way that the multiple futures of any given past or present overflow their enclosure within a fixed, causal, and linear temporality. Caygill explains: 'This suspension or "the damming of the stream of real life, the moment when its flow comes to a standstill" momentarily frees action from necessity, "making life spurt up high from the bed of time and, for an instant, hover iridescent in empty space."'[208] Like the dialectical image, film can destabilize the necessity of the present and simultaneously open up the future.

Film imagines technology as an instrument for the innervation of the senses, rather than as an instrument of their repression and forced atrophy (the processes that dominate most encounters with the reified technological apparatus of capital). Insofar as it rejects the desire for beautiful semblance that animates most forms of aesthetic practice, film inaugurates culture as a play-space [*Spielraum*] in which experimentation with the relations between technology, human beings, and nature becomes the order of the day.[209] The key to this transformation lies not in the meaning or content of any given sequence on the screen, but rather in how film as a cultural technology is able to model the playful (yet deadly serious) experimentation with images that Benjamin insists must become habit if the working class is ever to redeem the dreams of revolution frozen in its past and thereby become 'the avenger that completes the task of liberation in the name of generations of the downtrodden.'[210] As a cultural tool, film exemplifies an emancipatory practice of image making that has a more general field of application to all facets of human experience: 'The sort of distraction that is provided by art represents a covert measure of the extent to which it has become possible to perform new tasks of apperception ... *Reception in distraction – the sort of reception which is increasingly noticeable in all areas of art and is a symptom of profound changes in apperception – finds in film its true training ground.*'[211]

The shattering of experience into shards of isolated memory makes possible radical new forms of apperception: *Erlebnis* enables us to juxtapose past experience and present perception far more fluidly than we could within *Erfahrung*. Memories can now be stitched together just as a film maker splices together disparate scenes in a movie. However, this playful experimentation with memory only becomes possible in a state of distraction once the sterile posture of attentiveness has been displaced by an absent-minded openness to the deduction of resemblances between traces of otherwise dispersed experiences: 'The stripping of the veil from the object, the destruction of the aura, is the signature of a perception whose "sense for sameness in the world" has so increased that, by means of reproduction, it extracts sameness even from what is unique.'[212] Symbiotically, film educates and is educated by this prevailing 'sense for sameness' – to be understood, notes Benjamin figuratively in his writing on hashish, as a mode of seeing the stones in a sidewalk in Marseilles as precisely like those in Paris.[213] Film charges a patchwork of fluid mnemic connections between events, people, places, and things. In its most innovative form, it trains the mimetic faculty to survive and ultimately flourish in a world where the traditions that once sustained it lie in ruins. Film expands the space through which humanity can travel mimetically and thereby increases the chance that long-buried memories – especially those of forgotten utopian dreams, will be triggered and flood into mind and body in moments of revolutionary innervation.

However, there are dangers here as well. New cultural technologies can charge the mimetic faculty in the retrieval of (involuntary) memory and experience, but they also have the potential of shutting it down. Photography, for example, bestows on 'the moment' a shock-like quality, freezing it and thereby facilitating its serial integration into voluntary memory: 'The "snapping" by the photographer had the greatest consequences. Henceforth a touch of the finger sufficed to fix an event for an unlimited period of time. The camera gave the moment a posthumous shock, as it were.' Consequently, 'the perpetual readiness of voluntary, discursive memory, encouraged by the technology of reproduction, reduces the imagination's scope for play [*Spielraum*].'[214] Organizing the expansion of mimetic space through the culture industry has, after all, catastrophic effects. Benjamin links film together with epic theatre, and this leads him to emphasize the emancipatory possibilities that flow out of the identification between audience and actor: 'The majority of citydwellers, throughout the workday in offices and factories, have to relinquish their humanity in the face of an apparatus. In the evening, these same masses fill the cinemas, to witness the film actor taking revenge on their behalf not only by asserting *his* humanity (or what appears to them as such) against the apparatus, but by placing that apparatus in the service of his triumph.'[215]

Adorno counters that as long as such identification is filtered through the commodity form, the empathy is actually with capital, not with the struggle against it. Benjamin himself notes that 'photography has made more and more segments of the field of optical perception into saleable commodities. It has conquered for commodity circulation objects which up to then had been virtually excluded from it.'[216] Once the space opened up by new cultural technologies is colonized by the market, so that its *production* is governed by the commodity form, an entirely new set of 'similarities' is inscribed on its surface, obliterating the previous *correspondances* that lay there. Given capitalism's successful appropriation of 'trash' under the motif of 'retro' and its capacity to commodify the 'antiaphrodisiac' that is the recently outmoded, Adorno's critique (i.e., that in Benjamin's work 'the capitalist function of the ragpicker – namely, to subject even rubbish to exchange-value – is not articulated') remains germane.[217] As the circuits of exchange begin to feed on their own waste, the interstices in which the commodity *as ruin* (rather than ruin *as commodity*) can be perceived are shrinking. And so our remembrance of things past, as mediated through the culture industry, 'consigns [them] a second time to oblivion.'[218] To paraphrase Marx: while the inability of humanity to act on the potential fetishized by such objects in their first life is tragic, their resurrection as trash in the circuits of exchange has about it an aura of farce.

Indeed, Adorno's relentless critique of identitarian conceptual systems is irreplaceable when it comes to making sense of the harmonization of new cultural technologies within capitalism. Realism continues to be the dominant mode of cultural expression; this ensures that the aesthetics of new media are efficiently mapped over a framework of thought and experience in which the distinction between concept or image and object is progressively reduced. Whether the thing depicted is a dinosaur from the past, a spacecraft from the future, or a city street from today is irrelevant: all that matters is that the representation be understood and experienced as a perfect replica or simulation. However authentic (or not) the duplication, the culture industry lends its might to the systematic eradication of anything that might signify the flawed or partial quality of signs and concepts: 'Reality is always *constructed* with an infantile attachment to the mimetic and then "photographed."'[219] Jean Baudrillard and many others fixate on the tautological referentiality such cultural systems can imply; in contrast, Adorno's negative dialectics emphasize how erasing the distinction between concept and object leads to the repression of any sense that an object's materiality and potentiality always evade any and all attempts to give it positivistic expression. This sort of conceptual totalitarianism effectively purges traces of non-identity from the cultural landscape and thereby affirms the dangerous illusion of a perfect representational fidelity to reality. Benjamin does a superb job of ferreting out the traces of difference that stubbornly survive these illusions. Of early portrait photography, for example, he writes: 'No matter how artful the photographer, no matter how carefully posed the subject, the beholder feels an irresistible urge to search such a picture for the tiny spark of contingency, of the here and now, with which reality has (so to speak) seared the subject, to find the inconspicuous spot where in the immediacy of that long-forgotten moment the future nests so eloquently that we, looking back, may rediscover it.'[220]

Such a spark, he goes on to note, foreshadows the potential of visual technology to reveal the optical unconscious, thereby triggering an exoteric mimetic rationality which discerns mnemic pathways that would otherwise remain closed as a defensive response to the countless shocks that dominate life under capitalism. Yet the sense of wonder produced by revelations of the optical unconscious also enhances the belief that improvements in media technology will close (and even collapse) the gap between the real and our capacity to represent it. As all conceivable dimensions of the real flood into view, representations take on the allure of being experienced as flawless simulations. Adorno's account of how identity not only dominates human cognitive patterns, but also has been libidinized through commodified mass culture, theorizes the appeal of such images in terms of the hostile disposition of most people to real difference. It is much easier to process ideas and images as totally subsuming that which they represent; furthermore, it *feels* better because the imposition of such a schematic facilitates the smooth discharge of libidinal energy.

In a suggestive reading of 'cyberspace,' Julian Stallabrass argues that its primary intent and effect is to reproduce bourgeois dreams of total knowledge, 'to survey the world from one's livingroom, to grasp the totality of all data within a single frame, and to recapture a unified knowledge and experience.'[221] New cultural technologies participate fully in the Enlightenment's program of ridding itself of all things that cannot be quantified (or digitized): 'The transparency of meaning in cyberspace, the absolute match between concept and appearance, is a utopian feature that stands in marked contrast to the real world of meaningless detail and redundant matter.'[222] This dynamic emerges from the identitarian tendencies of modern reason; furthermore, it reproduces and affirms the logic of equivalence enforced by the commodity form. Benjamin's hope is that new media might reinvigorate the relations between body and consciousness; in fact, embodied experience is often one of the first casualties of such technology. The mythological appeal popularized by advocates of cyberspace to abandon the imperfections and limitations of embodied identity mimic capital's dream of eliminating the 'friction' of labour and nature as impediments to the production and circulation of value. The objectives of digital design and reproduction, notes Gary McCarron, often go beyond the exact duplication of an original toward its improvement by reducing or eliminating the 'noise' that makes an object less than perfect. This project, he argues, flows out of a capitalist political economy of technology driven by the 'subjugation of individual acts of labour and the elimination of all traces of the relations of production.'[223] Beyond this programmatic intensification of the commodity as fetish (i.e., completely displacing commodities from the social relations in which they were conceived and produced), one can simultaneously read this trend of digital production, reproduction, and enhancement as promoting the deliberate and systematic excision – at a microscopic level – of all traces of contingency, excess and 'otherness' from cultural texts.

Adorno's philosophical critique of identity, coupled with his account of how the culture industry forces identitarian logic onto modes of thinking, feeling, and being, thus provides an invaluable corrective to Benjamin in theorizing the developmental trajectory of new cultural technologies within capitalism. When positioned together, the critical implications of these two perspectives accentuate each other. On the one hand, the pessimism invoked by Adorno intensifies insofar as it is measured against the unrealized utopian potential of these new technologies to disrupt and reverse the one-dimensional patterns of experience they currently promote. On the other hand, the desire to theorize, understand, and emancipate this potential – expressed so eloquently by Benjamin – becomes more intense as the risk grows that such potential will be sacrificed to capital. Similarly, Adorno's dark portrait of mimesis within mass culture as a self-destructive form of adaptation to a world that is at once terrifying and inscrutable helps position Benjamin's similarly bleak analysis of fashion as a counterpoint to his more hopeful remarks on cultural technology. Reading Adorno alongside Benjamin makes it clear that the real horror that lurks within the new media is not the disappearance of the body *per se* and the blissful imprisonment of consciousness within a discrete world of signs. Rather, it lies in the diffusion of forms of experience in which the subordination of non-identity to identity becomes both routine and systematic. As Benjamin notes, the commodification of sex appeal in fashion foreshadows this relation by demanding the mortification of living bodies, the prostration of the organic before the inorganic. Yet mass culture possesses the horrifying power to magnify such an inversion seemingly without end as the culture industry's 'talking masks' are mimetically taken up as ideal forms of human subjectivity. Insofar as the digital reproduction and perfection of human life through mass culture is driven by an increasingly meticulous *abstraction* from lived experience (much like commodified labour power is abstracted from real labour), humanity is seduced into reproducing itself in mimetic tribute to an inert and ultimately lifeless abstraction, a 'mimesis: of death.'[224] Contemporary advertising leads the way in offering the dream of carefree vitality and autonomy on the condition that such a mimesis of death be Taylorized: we turn the fetishizing gaze onto ourselves, breaking our bodies and identities into constituent fragments that are then subjected to constant inspection and improvement through a never-ending supply of images and commodities.

My objective here is not to set up a choice between Benjamin and Adorno and then adjudicate between them, treating one as right and the other as wrong. Materialist cultural analysis must be extremely attentive to the ebb and flow of the pedagogic and political opportunities that accompany the evolution of new cultural technologies, seizing these fertile moments as they flash by. For if one fails to lay one's hands on them as they wait, anxiously, at the crossroads of sleep and awakening, their emancipatory potential will be lost until they are discharged from the circuits of exchange. Their invisible utopian charge will then only be read by a future generation, if at all.

## Toward a Redialecticization of the Culture Industry Thesis

Reading some of Adorno's later essays on cultural education, one cannot help being struck by the almost wilful naivete with which he proposes to respond to the culture industry's pervasive conditioning. On the one hand, he embraces the most conventional of solutions, perhaps inflected through psychoanalysis: one must bring to consciousness the subconscious mechanisms through which people are manipulated. In an interview broadcast seven days after his death in 1969, Adorno argued in favour of 'working energetically to make education an education for contradiction and resistance':

> I could envision one attending commercial films in high school (but in the grammar schools, too) and quite simply showing to the students what a fraud they are, how full of lies, etc., or in the same way immunizing them against certain Sunday morning radio programs that play happy and carefree music, as if we were still living in a 'healthy world' (a term that gives true cause for alarm); or reading a magazine with them and showing them how they are being taken for a ride by an exploitation of their own instinctual needs; or I can imagine a music teacher who does not happen to come from the youth music scene analyzing hit songs and showing why these hits are incomparably worse than a movement of a Mozart or Beethoven quartet, or a really genuine piece of modern music.[225]

In 'Education after Auschwitz,' he recommends that rural areas be 'educated' as to their susceptibility to cultural control. Groups of volunteers should go into the countryside, bringing the message of Kantian autonomy to the people; he even advocates the use of television programs to get out the message.[226] Writing about fascist propaganda, Adorno notes that 'the strongest hope for effectively countering this whole type of propaganda lies in *pointing out* its self-destructive implications.'[227] On the other hand, his infamous 'mandarinism' emerges in a call for a review committee of 'responsible and independent sociologists, psychologists and educators' to censor television programs that result in the 'stultification, psychological crippling and ideological disorientation of the public.'[228] It hardly needs to be said that both strategies appear shockingly incongruent with Adorno's broader philosophical project. It is almost as if he is deploying these feeble gestures toward an anemic rationalism not as signs of the desire to defuse the psychodynamics of mass culture, but rather as markers of his own growing sense of despair and as retroactive validations of his own biographical form of resistance.

In fact, Adorno himself offers many reasons why such a pedagogy is unlikely to succeed: 'Simply indicating unconscious conditions is fruitless unless those who are implicated in these conditions can illuminate them spontaneously with recourse to their own experience, unless the illumination occurs within their own consciousness.'[229] Given the denigration of experience presided over by the culture industry, it seems unlikely that conventional pedagogical techniques will break the barriers that stand between contemporary individuals and authentic experience: 'For reflection, which in the healthy subject breaks the power of immediacy, is never as compelling as the illusion it dispels.'[230] The popularity of mass culture is a trick, but its appeal is real. Its hold cannot be broken simply by exposing and describing how it works and the interests it serves. Moreover, such a model of enlightenment carries its own considerable baggage. We cannot forget why the project of negative dialectics insists on an alliance between philosophy and aesthetics. Only as the sensual and cognitive are reunited might one provisionally cheat the 'dialectic of enlightenment' and tentatively avoid the collapse into myth that follows from the triumph of one over the other. Adorno values art for how it provides an arena in which aesthetic and rational impulses can come together in a moment of mutual critique and affirmation:

> Art must ... struggle in effigy against that opposition with objective critique it in effect embodies; if art is banished to the sensuous pole alone, the opposition is thereby merely reconfirmed. That untruth which is the deeper critical object of all art is not rationality itself, but rather the latter's static opposition to the particular; if art extracts the moment of the particular as an object of mere contemplation, it ratifies precisely that reified rigidity and valorizes precisely the waste products that social rationality abandons and excludes in order to draw attention away from itself.[231]

To array rationality and sensuousness against each other, then, is the sin for which negative dialectics is the penance. It is the physical moment of suffering that makes such atonement possible: Auschwitz forces materialism upon metaphysics; it thrusts a mode of thinking upon us that might finally give expression to a suffering before which rational thought necessarily stands helpless.[232] Furthermore, Adorno agrees that both the body and the unconscious possess valuable resources that can – indeed, must – be drawn from in order to (re)invigorate the critical ideals of truth and freedom: 'He alone who could situate utopia in blind somatic pleasure, which, satisfying the ultimate intention, is intentionless, has a stable and valid idea of truth.'[233] And 'the dawning sense of freedom feeds upon the memory of the archaic impulse not yet steered by any solid I ... Without an anamnesis of the untamed impulse that precedes the ego – an impulse later banished to the zone of unfree bondage to nature – it would be impossible to derive the idea of freedom.'[234]

In other words, the sensual moment in thinking – the possibility of a cognition that is constantly and viscerally reminded of its own somatic genesis and existence – is critically important to Adorno. This is the objective of modern art's 'shudder.' In this context, the fusion of the sensual and the logical into a mimetic disposition takes on political significance. The works of Kafka, Beckett, Picasso, and Schönberg succeed as political acts insofar as their representations of a degraded world are mimetically rather than rationally organized. They enable a suspension of self-preservation, a displacement of the ego, and a reminder of the nature that lies within; they make possible a kind of experience that simply lies beyond the reach of cognition alone.

Why, then, does Adorno invoke such simplistic educational strategies when it comes to fighting the effects of the culture industry? At one level, he recognizes that the highly mediated pleasures of aesthetic mimesis *vis-à-vis* modern art are beyond the experiential capacity of most people. Physically and mentally exhausted by an impoverished working environment, they seek rest and relaxation in their 'free time' – qualities that are incompatible with serious aesthetic contemplation. The question remains, however, why he then turns to conventional education instead of speculating whether mimetic stimulation might be delivered outside the esoteric confines of modern art.[235] The answer, I believe, lies in his unparalleled fear of the unconscious as a source of images that can be manipulated by the culture industry and/or fascist politics. This fear explains why he refuses to countenance any attempts to mine the unconscious – instinctual *or* optical – for experiential residues that could overload the libidinal circuits of mass culture. Rather, in a conventional Freudian sense, the unconscious must be 'disarmed' by bringing it to consciousness: 'It seems to me rather that what is conscious could never prove so fateful as what remains unconscious, half-conscious, or preconscious.'[236] In the context of the culture industry, Adorno understands desire and instinct as themselves preformed: 'What takes place is that merger between id and superego that psychoanalytic theory already focused on, and it is precisely where the masses act instinctively that they have been preformed by censorship and enjoy the blessings of the powers that be.'[237] There is no point in scouring the unconscious for images and energies that might challenge capital, because what one finds there is only its reflection. Dream life and waking life have been seamlessly fused together according to a blueprint furnished entirely by the latter. As a form of image writing, mass culture is able to bypass critical cognition and colonize the restless energies of the unconscious, constructing the dreams and affective patterns that henceforth come to regulate the flow of desire.

Most terrifying for Adorno, this process is co-extensive with the rapid dissemination of the identitarian poison of the commodity form throughout all social relations. The peculiarly toxic combination of culture and capitalism in the culture industry hides the encroaching mediation of all things under a fog of false immediacy, thereby libidinizing the exchange-relation: 'Immediacy, the popular community concocted by films, amounts to mediation without residue, reducing men and everything human so perfectly to things, that their contrast to things, indeed the spell of reification itself, becomes imperceptible.'[238] In the face of such disaster, Adorno reluctantly returns to conventional pedagogy. The only hope lies in interrupting the circuits that bind culture, the commodity form, and the body and the unconscious into an amorphous union. The mediated quality of this false immediacy must be brought to consciousness: 'Dialectic discloses each image as script. It teaches us to read from its features the admission of falseness which cancels its power and hands it over to truth.'[239] As reified as it has become, language – especially of the bristling style favoured by Adorno – can offer a palpable disruption of images, denaturalize them, and foreground their arbitrary quality. Mediation is perhaps the ultimate critical tactic for him, in that it demonstrates how one thing (e.g., concept, value, universal) is never identical to any other (e.g., object, subject, particular). Defending the use of 'foreign words' in his writing, he claims that 'the discrepancy between the foreign word and the language can be made to serve the expression of truth. Language participates in reification, the separation of subject matter and thought.

The customary ring of naturalness deceives us about that. By acknowledging itself as a token, the foreign word reminds us bluntly that all real language has something of the token in it.'[240]

Similarly, the abstract techniques of modern art foreground the deliberate mediation, via aesthetic form, of the somatic and libidinal impulses that they arouse in their audience. That abstraction forcefully interrupts feelings of immediacy that have historically been the purview of art. Instead, it is only the *memory* of such immediacy that is now allowed; such mnemic copies allow access to an ideal that condemns existence without the consequent danger that the aesthetic expression of this ideal will be mistaken for its realization. For Adorno, the exile from the culture industry of abstraction as an aesthetic technique means that the only method of restoring a sense of mediation is through linguistic and conceptual deconstruction. In his writings on the culture industry, he deploys conceptual exaggeration in order to shock the reader into viewing the cultural apparatus in a new light. And – which cannot be said of the visual shocks of surrealism – there is no danger that these efforts will themselves be commodified and integrated into mass culture.

But what does such a perspective ultimately sacrifice? On this question, Benjamin's work poses a forceful challenge. Adorno largely perceives the culture industry as a closed system that can be attacked only from the outside; Benjamin searches for an immanent critique that might turn the very energies deployed by mass culture against itself. Adorno keeps rhetorical faith with the belief that there are limits to reification, and his acute sensitivity to the dangers of co-optation pulls him back from the admittedly more dangerous speculative theory practised by Benjamin. As dialectical images put into play the same imagistic tactics used by mass culture, they certainly open themselves up to being integrated by it. Yet Benjamin makes a strong argument that the terrain of the image is hardly one that can be forfeited to the culture industry: thinking-in-images as a practice of bodily cognition is absolutely vital in securing the revolutionary innervation of the masses – a collective innervation that is the prerequisite for any transformation of social relations. Adorno agrees that critical thought and physical innervation must necessarily coincide: 'Of the possibilities which exist for ... a truly progressive consciousness ... One is innervation, the nerval reactions of the artist, that which, that is, ought to be the reaction of the theoretician – at any rate, of the philosophic theoretician – nerval reactions to that for which the time has come.'[241] However, this innervation is inevitably couched in the individualistic, esoteric confines of aesthetic practice: no possibility for a collective innervation is allowed. Conversely, Benjamin insists that such innervation can and must touch the masses as a whole:

> In Germany, there have always been many people ... who believe that *what* they know, and the fact that *they* know it, are the key to situation and that from now on everything will have to change. But they have only the vaguest notion about how to give this knowledge any direction and how to bring it to the people. They imagine you just have to express it, stress it. They are miles away from the idea that knowledge which contains no indication of how it should be propagated is of little use, and that in truth it is no knowledge at all.[242]

Or, more succinctly, 'anyone who fails to pay tribute to the masses' collection of images must fail.'[243] Warnings such as this grow ever more important as dominant forms of cognition are increasingly structured according to the imagistic patterns of the dream. Logical intervention simply will not break the libidinal pathways that mass culture has imposed on psychic economies. Thus it would seem that strategies other than the anemic rationalism of conventional education are required. Benjamin's work explores how the affect and desire mobilized by the culture industry can be used to prevent their perversion by that same system. It restores a dialectical perspective to cultural criticism: What are the contradictions within the object, and how might they be activated?

Benjamin's different understanding of the relationship between the body, consciousness, and the unconscious is the key that unlocks the conceptual space in which one can think dialectically about the effect of commodified culture. At the same time as he criticizes changes to human experience under capitalism, he analyses the possibilities these changes have enabled. Most certainly the decay of critical faculties has eroded – and continues to erode – the capacity of human beings to reflect on their world. Yet for Benjamin this suspension also opens up the chance that repressed images and memories which reside in the unconscious and the body might be triggered and flood into consciousness. Adorno confines the application of his insights regarding mimesis and the cultural object as monad to modern art; Benjamin is much more willing to speculate that such practices can also – indeed, must – occur amidst the degraded products of the culture industry. Discussing the 'political significance of film,' Benjamin writes: 'At no point in time, no matter how utopian, will anyone win the masses over to a higher art; they can be won over only to one nearer to them ... This will never happen with most of what is propagated by the avant-garde of the bourgeoisie.'[244] The exaggerations of the culture industry thesis must be read negatively as signs of hope, and Benjamin takes this hope absolutely seriously, identifying and exploring the somatic and unconscious residues that suggest the lingering potential of resisting the commodity form. His explosive conception of memory furnishes an analytic apparatus which suggests that the seemingly inexorable expansion of the culture industry may contain the seeds of its own destruction. Clearly, Adorno rejects the optimistic tone that often attaches itself to Benjamin's writings; yet the underlying homology between his aesthetics (especially the centrality of mimesis) and the dialectical image – namely, the synthetic generation of an authentic experience of the alienation, reification, and poverty of capitalist social relations – enables us to constellate these two seemingly opposed approaches to mass culture. At the very least, this grouping begins to articulate a more promising response to the culture industry – certainly one that is more in line with Adorno's goal of a negative dialectics than is found in the rather conventional pedagogy of some of his later essays.

This constellation does not involve 'choosing' Benjamin over Adorno. Rather, the point is to suspend these perspectives in a dialectical 'force field': two seeming opposites are held together in a productive tension, each expressing different, contradictory tendencies that reside within the object itself. One cannot forget that the entire thrust of *Negative Dialectics* is the desire to avoid conceptually subsuming the object beneath the concept:

> The task of dialectical cognition is not, as its adversaries like to charge, to construe contradictions from above and to progress by resolving them ... Instead, it is up to dialectical cognition to pursue the inadequacy of thought and thing, to experience it in the thing. Dialectics need not fear the charge of being obsessed with the fixed idea of objective conflict in a thing already pacified; no single thing is at peace in the pacified whole. The aporetical concepts of philosophy are marks of what is objectively, not just cogitatively, unresolved.[245]

In this spirit, Benjamin's work delivers a needed shock to the culture industry thesis, jolting it out of a bitter but comfortable complacency that every song, every story, every film can be easily carved into so many constituent pieces and devoured by its voracious theoretical appetite. Adorno's exaggerations are undoubtedly true; but so are Benjamin's utopian speculations. Both are true. Both point to tendencies that exist within their objects. And out of this seeming paradox emerges the possibility of understanding both the dangers and the opportunities that attend the commodification of culture. In the essay 'On Jazz,' Adorno notes that 'jazz is not what it "is" ... Rather, it is what it is used for.'[246] At one level, this analytic focus reveals many qualities of jazz that might otherwise go unnoticed. But at another level, as Adorno himself reminds us, 'what is, is more than it is.'[247] In *Aesthetic Theory*, he similarly observes that 'aesthetic comportment is the capacity to perceive more in things than they are.'[248] This too must inform theorizing about culture and its effects, both real and possible. Arranged together in a constellation, the work of Adorno and Benjamin is invaluable in developing a theory of the intersection of mass culture and the commodity form that can successfully articulate its horrors together with its potential.

In this constellation, the goals shared by Adorno and Benjamin remain as important as their differences. They are united by their horror at the rapid growth of the commodity form, the subsequent (re)enchantment of the ruins of capitalism, and the return of humanity to a world of myth. Benjamin's optimistic investigation of film, for instance, is driven by the potential it holds to supersede cultural and social practices, not by its current existence in the suffocating embrace of capital: 'So long as moviemakers' capital sets the fashion, as a rule the only revolutionary merit that can be ascribed to today's cinema is the promotion of a revolutionary criticism of traditional concepts of art.'[249] The tracing out of the possibilities within a cultural object or practice must not be mistaken for a belief that such possibilities can be actualized within the contemporary social relations in which that object or practice is bound. The arcades, for instance, held immense social promise as a social space that might have shattered the bourgeois *intérieur* as an interpellative casing for bourgeois subjectivity, revealing the bankruptcy of conventional individuality. Instead, they were used as shopping malls by capital. The masses were thus constructed as a consumptive force rather than a revolutionary one. Proletarian self-consciousness as the true producer of the objects found in the arcades was thereby disguised. In other words, Adorno and Benjamin share an intense frustration with the means by which commodification restricts and confines the potential of the object and the subject and, most importantly, the relations between them. As easy and tempting as it is to think otherwise, the creative use of speculative theory to access this potential must never displace the equally important recognition that such potential has not been actualized. On this note, Adorno's stark warning about the real impoverishment of mass culture is a necessary antidote to the (mis)appropriation of Benjamin by those who want to suture his writings together with the belief that resistance is everywhere. The culture industry thesis inflects Benjamin's work in a more critical direction, allowing it to be read as an indictment of commodified social existence rather than as an apology for cultural rebellion. Adorno's work foregrounds mass culture's ability to fake a kind of spatial potentiality that is ultimately always denied, thereby acclimatizing humanity to a pattern of defeat that reinforces the limitations of contemporary existence as the only possible one. This highlights the considerable danger of co-optation that inevitably accompanies Benjamin's radical pedagogical strategies; it also magnifies their own critical tone.

Ultimately, both Adorno and Benjamin deploy the illusions that accompany the commodity form to energize an immanent critique of its fetishization. Paradoxically, the commodity stirs the dream of objects that have been liberated from the tyranny of instrumental rationality, the dream of something that is identical only to itself. As illusions, these visions disguise the real degradation of subject and object under capitalism. As semblances, however, they also invigorate the promise of a social existence that is not governed by the principles of identity: 'The utopia of the qualitative – the things which through their difference and uniqueness cannot be absorbed into the prevalent exchange relationships – takes refuge under capitalism in the traits of fetishism.'[250] The first moment of critique occurs as the search for meaning amidst the reified objects of contemporary existence is revealed as utterly bankrupt. The investment of cognitive, somatic, and libidinal energies in commodities is viscerally experienced as nothing but a betrayal. Mimetically, 'the reflective onlooker, meeting the laughing placard of a toothpaste beauty, discerns in her flashlight grin the grimace of torture.'[251] This is the *Erfahrung* of *Erlebnis* that Adorno and Benjamin both seek. But critique can hardly stop there. Instead, the visceral horror that is experienced provides the foundation for the *potential* redemption of all that has been denied. Coiled within the perception of the commodity as ruin is the possibility that things need not be this way: it is only against the possibility of transcending such a state, that its maintenance takes on such a deathly pallor: 'Grayness could not fill us with despair if our minds did not harbor the concept of different colors, scattered traces of which are not absent from the negative whole. The traces always come from the past, and our hopes come from their counterpart, from that which was or is doomed ... "For the sake of the hopeless only are we given hope."'[252]

Baudelaire's *correspondances* are valued so highly by Benjamin for their poetic instantiation of this last line (which Adorno takes from Benjamin's essay on Goethe). They represent hope for a past that has forever vanished. But, as he might have said, forever is measured in the linear 'scientific time' of *Erlebnis*, not the redemptive 'now-time' of revolution. Within the latter, the wishes and dreams of those without hope – the dead – are reborn in the lives of those to whom history grants the opportunity for their actualization.

With his theory of the culture industry, Adorno sketches the apocalyptic union of culture and the commodity form in sharp, bold strokes. His acute sensitivity to the horrors that lie beyond the banal faces on television and movie screens inspires their mimetic transformation into emblems of hell. Benjamin, in contrast, offers a glimpse of what it might mean for us to take such knowledge deeply into ourselves and have it penetrate to the core of our experience. His brilliant speculations spark the hope that such horror might be stirred by those very forces which now mask it. The more we try to buy life by surrounding ourselves with that which is dead, the higher grows the pile of bones that serve as the kindling on which the highly combustible spark of memory might one day fall. Held together in a dialectical antinomy, the work of Adorno and Benjamin stands as a nuanced, complex, and radical theory of mass culture.

# 4

# From Mass to Popular Culture: From Frankfurt to Birmingham

> A difficulty arises with the whole concept of masses ... There are in fact no masses; there are only ways of seeing people as masses.
>
> Raymond Williams, *Culture and Society*

The radical thrust of the British empirical tradition lies coiled within the above words of Raymond Williams – namely, the refusal to allow moribund concepts and categories to seal off theoretical inquiry from the heterogeneity of human experience. As far as cultural studies has perhaps travelled from the assumptions, methods, and goals of its 'founding fathers,'[1] it continues to proclaim allegiance to this basic desire and analytic project. In 1958, when *Culture and Society* was published, this declaration was directed mainly against a conservative cultural criticism that, allied with reactionary political ideology, transformed the masses into 'something to be hated or feared.'[2] In the hands of a fledgling cultural studies, however, this attack was just as easily turned against the bristling prose of Horkheimer and Adorno and their savage attack on mass culture. Assimilating their sweeping denunciations into the 'culture and civilization' tradition of Matthew Arnold and F.R. Leavis was not a difficult task. Indeed, they both were seen as sharing a common elitism, on the one hand hastily condemning mass culture as the total manipulation of a passive audience, and on the other nostalgically mourning the loss of high culture.

The Centre for Contemporary Cultural Studies (CCCS), established at Birmingham University in 1964, wanted no part of this sort of cultural criticism. Although its initial work under the direction of Richard Hoggart did engage in a critique of mass culture, and although it deployed many of the methods of Leavisite literary criticism,[3] the CCCS was deeply committed to defending the cultural creativity of subordinate groups. Inspired by the cultural Marxism of E.P. Thompson and by his meticulous excavation of the hidden agency that lay at the core of the making of the English working class, the scholars who gathered around Stuart Hall transplanted Thompson's recuperative project to the very heart of the culture industries, tracing the active and even oppositional means by which subordinate groups consumed mass culture. 'Ordinary people,' Hall asserted, 'are not cultural dopes.'[4] At one level, this phrase – echoed throughout cultural studies as a founding mantra – invokes a praiseworthy democratic sensibility and orientation. But it also has other effects. With respect to the Frankfurt School, it constructs a self-constitutive, disciplinary boundary, one that effectively trumps any desire or obligation to examine, discuss, or even adequately refute the culture industry thesis. Rhetorically, the assertion that 'ordinary people are *not* cultural dopes' takes the form of a counterclaim, one which raises the spectre of those who, it is implied, believe the opposite to be true. And in the field of Marxist cultural theory, the identity of those who hold such beliefs is an ill-kept secret. Once the judgment that 'people are dopes' has been firmly denied, it becomes easy to reject theses that seem to be predicated on precisely such a claim. Perhaps the most compelling evidence of this tendency lies in the CCCS's failure to engage with the Frankfurt School in any systematic way.[5] Irrespective of their distaste for the apparently elitist cultural politics of critical theory, this absence is remarkable. Hall himself admits that 'the rapid displacement of Lukacs, Goldmann and the 'Frankfurt School' by the French structuralists is one of the most intriguing episodes in recent English intellectual history.'[6] After all, both share an interest in the role of culture in advanced capitalism. Both claim allegiance to a Marxist problematic while admitting the need to move beyond its traditional forms. Both are alarmed at the ability of conservative social forces to mobilize the contradictions of capitalism in their own interests. At the very least, one would have thought that some kind of formal reckoning or debate with the culture industry thesis – even a systematic demolition of its arguments – would have been in order. Yet the rich theoretical reservoir of Adorno, Horkheimer, and Benjamin is almost untapped by the Birmingham School.

Hall recalls that during the formative years of the CCCS in the late 1960s and early 1970s, these thinkers were introduced to British scholars 'second hand' through the criticisms of mainstream American social science.[7] As suspicious as they were of the liberal pluralism emanating from conventional sociology, members of the CCCS must have had some sympathy for the American-led critique of Adorno and Horkheimer as vastly overstating the efficacy of the culture industries in controlling the behaviour of ordinary citizens. Only one article-length evaluation of the Frankfurt School by the CCCS was ever published (compared with many treatments of French theorists such as Barthes, Lacan, and Althusser). Written in 1974 by Phil Slater and appearing in the centre's journal, *Working Papers in Cultural Studies*, it contains a rather harsh dismissal of Adorno's work on culture in favour of that of Bertolt Brecht and Walter Benjamin.[8] Slater offers a passable account of the culture industry thesis but ultimately concludes that Adorno's pessimistic diagnosis of the masses as 'totally manipulable' and his 'repudiation of discursive communication' signals the irrelevance of his work for critical aesthetic practice. This assessment seems to have been largely accepted by others in British cultural studies. Discussing theories of the media, for example, James Curran, Michael Gurevitch, and Janet Woollacott note that 'the work of the Frankfurt School was relatively marginal in developing and generating research in mass communications, in providing a theoretical paradigm within which media studies could proceed.'[9] Steve Burniston and Chris Weedon fault Adorno for a crude, Marxist reductionism: 'With regard to form, Adorno accepts a simple, reflective model of the relationship between art and the economic level, without the Lukacsian mediation of the economically constituted, historically ascendant social class.'[10] In *Policing the Crisis*, Marcuse's work on the one-dimensional nature of advanced capitalism is identified as being only 'fitfully useful.'[11] Aside from Slater, the only substantive discussion of the culture industry thesis appears in two articles by Tony Bennett that survey the 'state of the field' in cultural theory.[12] Although his treatment is somewhat more sympathetic – he acknowledges the Frankfurt School's role in returning ideology to Marxism's agenda – he concludes that the school's failure to make 'positive suggestions' about how reality might be changed raises serious questions about its continuing relevance for the study of popular culture.[13] Once again, the culture industry thesis is dismissed not so much for its analytic shortcomings as for the 'monumental pessimism' with which it regards mass culture. In short, Adorno's cultural theory has received no sustained attention from British cultural studies. At best, it is accorded mere historical significance; at worst, it is caricatured or even ignored altogether. The reaction to Benjamin is somewhat more ambivalent. His work is occasionally cited as inspiring a more sympathetic treatment of mass culture, but his project as a whole receives almost no attention.[14]

A more complex explanation of why Birmingham refused to take Frankfurt very seriously emerges when we consider the former's much stronger engagement with other theoretical opponents. In three specific cases – the already mentioned elitist cultural criticism of Arnold (and the working class variant developed by Hoggart), the economic reductionism of traditional Marxism, and the textual, psychoanalytic film criticism of *Screen* – one can just make out the ghost of Adorno lingering in the shadows. When read symptomatically, these debates shed further light on how and why the culture industry thesis came to be 'repressed' so effectively during the evolution of British cultural studies.

Largely because of the influence of Williams, Thompson, and Hoggart, one of the early targets of British cultural studies was the definition of culture advanced by Matthew Arnold in *Culture and Anarchy*: 'Culture ... seeks to do away with classes; to make the best that has been thought and known in the world current everywhere.'[15] Williams's famous counter-claim that 'culture is ordinary,' combined with Thompson's exposition of culture as (class) struggle, provided theoretical resources for redefining culture as the heterogeneous practices through which people express and live their experience, rather than as a normative category in which those practices – or, more commonly, the textual artifacts they produce – are classified and judged. Without question, in the CCCS's terms, Adorno's caustic denunciations of mass culture place him squarely in the latter camp. His favourable references to serious art – especially in the context of the culture industry's shortcomings – are easy to construe as evidence of a sympathetic orientation toward bourgeois aesthetics and hence a commitment to Culture rather than culture(s). Describing the pitfalls of past approaches to popular culture, Bennett notes that 'to study popular culture has also meant to adopt a position against and opposed to it, to view it as in need of replacement by a culture of another kind, usually "high culture" – the view not only of reformist critics, such as F.R. Leavis, but, oddly enough, equally influential in Marxist circles too, especially in the work of Theodor Adorno, Herbert Marcuse and the other members of the Frankfurt School.'[16] Glossed over with the tragicomic details of Adorno's wartime exile to California, it is not difficult to assimilate Adorno's attack on commodified culture into the elitist cultural sensibilities of conservative critics of mass society. What the Birmingham School fails to grasp, however, is that for conservatives the commodification of mass culture generally stands as an *empty* signifier for a variety of other faults, such as standardization, banality, and lack of cultural tradition. For Adorno, on the other hand, it is the commodity form *itself* that is the root problem. Moreover, as we have seen, his objective is hardly to replace 'low' with 'high' culture, since he thinks that both have been corrupted by capitalism. He indicts the totality of capitalist society and culture, and his theoretical objectives are far more radical than a simple return to a bourgeois past.

But it is not simply the valuation of bourgeois over working class culture that troubles the centre; rather, it is the idea of using one cultural formation to compare and criticize another, especially when the process seems to be tainted with nostalgia. Notwithstanding his status as a 'founding father,' Hoggart's lamentation that traditional working-class culture is being displaced by the 'candy floss world' of commercial entertainment also attracts firm censure from the CCCS. In his discussion of *The Uses of Literacy*, Colin Sparks describes Hoggart's belief

> that there was, in the 1920's and 1930's, a clear and definite working-class culture which was more valuable, more authentic, more homogenous, more independent ... more working class, than any subsequent development. This vanished culture becomes the standard of judgement for later formations, and they are all found wanting ... [However] ... the culture of later decades was a response to a particular historical experience ... It was and is different, and if we are to judge either it is not by some nostalgic, inverted teleology of culture. If we accept the authenticity of one cultural formation, then we must accept the authenticity of another.[17]

No one would ever accuse Adorno of longing for working-class culture, but it is easy enough to read him in a nostalgic mode, as using an ideal of what art once was to spurn the degraded products of today. He certainly does use strategies of juxtaposition to generate critical distance from an existing cultural formation, but his intent in this is to blast open the present in the interests of the future, not to return to the past. For Adorno, culture acquires value not so much as an expressive practice, but because its *potential* for autonomy enables it to secure some distance from reality and thereby open up a space for critical reflection on one's experience of that reality. Not all cultural texts and formations are equally able to play this social role. Insofar as members of the CCCS reject this comparative approach, preferring instead to trace out the authenticity inscribed on *all* cultural practices, they likely feel justified in dismissing Adorno's work as merely another variant of the age-old practice whereby mass culture's evisceration is secured through its counter-factual juxtaposition against utopian idealizations of either high art or a romanticized working-class past.

At the opposite end of the political spectrum, the reductionist cultural Marxism of the Second International that emerged during the first half of the century – ostensibly as a radical reply to the idealist aesthetics of bourgeois culture – is another favoured target for the Birmingham School. Spawned from a few simple phrases of Marx, its basic analytic principle is derived from the base/superstructure metaphor: culture and politics are conceptualized as being part of a superstructure that arises from and 'reflects' the economic base. Within such a restrictive framework, cultural analysis is limited to the demystification of cultural texts and practices as bourgeois ideological devices. The class identity or ideological orientation of any particular cultural object, and therefore its political impact, is predetermined by the social origins of its production. Hall recalls that in the debate between Leavisite and Marxist literary criticism, the former won not because it was right, but rather because the Marxist alternatives were simply too crude and mechanical.[18] However, accusations of class reductionism are aimed not only at the 'vulgar' Marxism of the Second International, but also at the more theoretically sophisticated variant developed by Lukacs. Reading a direct line of descent from German Idealism to so-called 'Western Marxism,' Hall argues that Lukacs transposed the concept of *Weltanschauung* – the principle that all nations and/or historical periods have a unique and dominant world view – into a class problematic:[19]

> In many ways the earlier Marxist tradition – Lukacs and Goldmann are good exemplifications here – conducted the analysis of specific cultural formations largely by conceiving them as the products or expressions, at the cultural-ideological level, of the 'world outlooks' or *visions du monde* of particular classes. Class structures, class domination and class contradictions also constituted, at the level of cultures and ideologies, parallel formations – class ideologies.[20]

There is little evidence that the Birmingham School attends either to the significant differences between Lukacs and the Frankfurt School or to those elements of Lukacs's theoretical work that are not dominated by class. Instead, all previous Marxist traditions – with the obvious exceptions of Volosinov and Gramsci – are grouped together, and their work is collectively consigned to a paradigm of class reductionism. Insofar as one adopts a Marxist perspective that maintains a concept of economic determinacy, no alternative models are conceivable. Thus the CCCS accepts the base/superstructure model as the only theoretical framework in which questions of economic determinism can be discussed.

The CCCS has developed a critique that is directed not against economism *per se* (i.e., the claim that culture is determined by the economic structures in which it is produced and consumed) but rather against *class* reductionism (i.e., the claim that the ideas of the ruling class are imposed directly on the proletariat and that this displaces their own incipient cultural formations). In the case of youth or subcultures, for example, their autonomy from and determination by the economic is defined and measured according to their proximity to both parent and hegemonic class cultures.[21] While later formulations exchange an expressive relation between individual, class, and culture for a more complex understanding organized around concepts of hegemony and articulation, they too continue to operate according to a class-based model of economic determinism. For example, Bennett's discussion of the advantages of hegemony is expressed almost entirely in terms of how it escapes the errors of class reductionism.[22] Equations of class reductionism with economism sponsor the dismissal of very different theories of economic determinism on a single set of narrow and simplistic grounds. The culture industry thesis, for example, relies very little on class-based arguments, instead tracing the effects of the commodity form on cultural production and consumption. Yet it is discarded quickly because its economistic approach connotatively signifies, for cultural studies, a conceptual proximity (and susceptibility) to class reductionism. Critique of the base/superstructure metaphor, in other words, also serves as an ersatz critique of Adorno and Horkheimer's more complex thesis, and this effectively excuses the CCCS from conducting a more extensive debate with critical theory.

During its heyday in the 1970s, the journal *Screen* was seen as the most important British alternative to the cultural analysis pioneered by the CCCS. The film criticism organized around this journal drew heavily from the psychoanalytic structuralism of Jacques Lacan and – to a lesser extent – from the Marxist variant developed by Louis Althusser. *Screen*'s theorists conceptualize culture as an ideological machine that produces 'subject-positions,' into which individuals are placed or 'interpellated' through various textual strategies. The only way to break the hold of ideology is to use avant-garde film techniques that can disrupt the complacent and disempowered subjectivities installed by realist narratives. In most respects, this eminently idealist account of culture differs considerably from the views of Adorno and Horkheimer. Yet there are several similarities that raise an interesting parallel between the Birmingham School's critique of *Screen* and its dismissal of the Frankfurt School.[23] First, *Screen*'s basic claim is that a filmic text can fully and completely locate an individual in a subject-position, thereby defining his or her capacity for experience and limiting the possibility for critical thought and action irrespective of other social, material, or cultural influences. This bears a strong resemblance to the culture industry thesis *as understood* by the CCCS. For instance, in a paradigmatic account of Adorno's view of mass culture, Bennett notes that it 'produces "the people" in its own image – a totally homogeneous mass of individuals, alike even in their pseudo-individuality, and lacking any roots in any otherness, in any socially located vision of the world, which has not been tailored to suit the requirements of the culture industry.'[24] In some important ways, this description does not substantively depart from *Screen*'s own conceptualization of the passive, manipulated qualities of a conventional film audience. It is certainly probable, in other words, that in dismissing critical theory, CCCS scholars draw from their criticisms of *Screen* – especially those which counter the totality and singularity of textual positioning with notions of active, creative subjects and polysemic texts. Second, Adorno's valorization of modern art as the only possible cultural response to commodification bears some resemblance to *Screen*'s own advocacy of the avant-garde as a disruptive aesthetic strategy. Conversely, the Birmingham School is deeply unsympathetic to any advocacy of patronizing cultural tactics that presuppose the need to radically 'shock' the masses. Instead, progressive politics must begin with the masses themselves and work within cultural forms that have become popular. By raising the topical resemblance between *Screen* and critical theory, I do not mean to suggest that the CCCS believes that these two theoretical perspectives share the same approach to cultural analysis. Yet it is likely that the CCCS's extensive critical engagement with *Screen* combine with these similarities to reinforce the sense that Horkheimer and Adorno have little to offer a radical theory of culture.

I hope that I have just sketched some of the principal reasons why the Birmingham School never felt compelled to engage with the provocative arguments of the culture industry thesis in any serious manner. For the most part, however, these reasons are based on fundamental *misreadings* of the Frankfurt School. Consequently, we are not left with any real sense of the dialogue that ought to have been held. In the following pages, I want to reconstruct one aspect of such a dialogue – namely, how a critical cultural theory ought to deal with the commodification of culture. To what extent does the CCCS develop an analytic framework that adequately theorizes the effect of the commodity form on cultural activities and practices? I propose that it is this question, and not issues of elitism or reductionism, that ought to drive the comparative assessment of these two 'schools.' Broadly speaking, the answer emerges out of the Birmingham School's tactical choice to focus on the *specificity* of cultural and ideological formations, rather than the relation between culture and the economy.[25] Let us begin by exploring this choice in greater detail.

## From Totality to Specificity: The Althusserian Turn

Interrogating the origins of the base/superstructure metaphor used by Marx to describe the relations between different social practices and structures, Williams argues that its original intent was to assert the *connectivity* of culture, politics, ideology, and economic processes.[26] Yet ironically, its most important effect for Marxist cultural theory is to enforce the compartmentalization of different types of human activity, thereby restoring – albeit in an inverted form – the idealist distinction between thought and being that Marx so forcefully rejected. Culture, counters Williams, should be viewed as a material, social process inextricably intertwined with other elements of the social formation. Accordingly, the principal task of cultural critique should be to investigate and map the mutually constitutive relations between different planes of social life. For Williams, what makes culture an interesting area of inquiry is not the isolated qualities that inhere in any particular object, but rather how cultural forms are able to constitute the dominant 'structure of feeling' of certain historical periods and express how a specific social formation is actually lived and experienced. As it takes shape in Williams's early work, this approach to culture as a 'way of life' is strongly criticized by Thompson for effectively excluding the often fierce battles waged by subordinate groups against dominant cultural and ideological formations.[27] For Thompson, cultural processes are energized by the never-ending need of human beings to find new ways of expressing, giving meaning to, and thinking about their experiences; as long as capitalism determines that class exploitation will be the dominant experience for most, culture is necessarily a site of struggle. Despite initial differences in terms of focus – that is, on a 'common culture' versus class struggle within culture – both thinkers share an underlying assumption: cultural practices cannot be adequately theorized in isolation from their relations with the broader social formation. As Williams notes: 'A society is not fully available for analysis until each of its practices is included. But if we make that emphasis we must make a corresponding emphasis: that we cannot separate literature and art from other kinds of social practice, in such a way as to make them subject to quite special and distinct laws. They may have quite specific features as practices, but they cannot be separated from the general social process.'[28]

To put it somewhat differently, Thompson and Williams both believe that a concept of totality is an integral part of Marxist cultural theory. Reductionist accounts have failed to develop an adequate explanation of economic determinism; however, this does not release radical theorists from dealing with this issue. Rather, it intensifies the need to explore it in more complex and sensitive ways. In Thompson's words, 'the logic of capitalist process has found expression within all the activities of a society, and exerted a determining pressure upon its development and form: hence entitling us to speak of capitalism, or of capitalist societies.'[29] Therefore, tactical priority must be given to the question of how cultural objects and practices are shaped and influenced by economic relations and structures.

The critique and ultimate rejection of the Marxist humanism of Williams and Thompson – euphemistically known as 'culturalism' – is often identified as the defining moment for British cultural studies. Excited by the new territory opened up by the rapid appropriation of French structuralism in the 1970s, the CCCS developed a range of innovative theoretical and empirical projects to extend and apply these new ideas to the study of culture. Although the centre remains nominally committed to exploring how specific cultural practices express particular kinds of (class) experience, there is a new concentration on the specific structural dynamics through which cultural practices acquire meaning. As Hall puts it:

> If the weakness of [Williams and Thompson] was their tendency to *dissolve*

> the cultural back into society and history, structuralism's main emphasis was on the specificity, the irreducibility of the cultural. Culture ... was itself a practice – a *signifying practice* – and had its own determinate product: meaning. To think of the specificity of the cultural was to come to terms with what defined it ... as a practice: its internal forms and relations, its internal structuration.[30]

Questions about the relations between culture and other structures are largely displaced in favour of the systematic identification of the internal codes and structures that govern autonomous cultural practices. For it is these codes that actually make culture possible. Many continuities remain with the earlier tradition; for example, the materiality of cultural practices continues to serve as a cornerstone of the CCCS. Similarly, one might say that Thompson's insistence that culture be defined as struggle, stripped of its particular inflection through class, constitutes the driving imperative of cultural studies. In a seminal lecture, for example, Hall argues that the 'more or less continuous struggle over the culture of working people, the labouring classes and the poor must be the starting point for any study, both of the basis for, and of the transformations of, popular culture.'[31] However, these basic principles are transcribed within a structuralist problematic that (re)conceptualizes them as the unique qualities of cultural practices, rather than as means for linking culture back to a larger conception of society. Ironically perhaps, the move into structuralism has been driven by the perception that culturalism fails to adequately describe and account for these linkages. Both Williams and Thompson are faulted for collapsing the distinction between culture and other activities and thereby adopting an 'expressive' conception of the social totality in which all of its elements fuse into a single unity. If the economic and the cultural are not be defined as discrete entities, it is virtually impossible to isolate and theorize the particular lines of determination that connect them together. Although culturalist approaches produce very rich and suggestive work on specific historical events, texts, and processes, it appears either unable or unwilling to abstract from its investigations any theoretical principles or modes of analysis other than the vague, indeterminate proposition that everything is constitutive of everything else, and that the particular details in any one case can only be resolved by empirical investigation.[32]

Conversely, Althusserian structuralism offers the attraction of continuing to work within a Marxist framework that formally recognizes culture's dependence on the economic base, but at the same time provides a theoretically sophisticated legitimation of the study of culture as an independent and autonomous area of inquiry. In particular, Althusser's critique of the expressive totality resonates profoundly with the CCCS as it tries to navigate its own course through the pitfalls of economic reductionism, bourgeois idealism and the indeterminacy of its culturalist forefathers.[33] In *For Marx*, Althusser attacks the Hegelian dialectic for reducing the complexity of social formations to a single, defining principle or contradiction. All other elements are explained (away) as the mere manifestation or expression of this central dynamic: 'Every concrete difference featured in the Hegelian totality, including the "spheres" visible in this totality (civil society, the State, religion, philosophy, etc.), all these differences are negated as soon as they are affirmed: for they are no more than "moments" of the simple internal principle of the totality ... these differences are all equally "indifferent."'[34]

The potential for one societal process to 'determine' others is thereby conceptually liquidated because all such processes are nothing more than alienated expressions of the central idea. For Althusser, simply replacing the notion of a central idea with a social and material relation or contradiction does not fundamentally escape the idealist problematic, the essence of which remains as long as everything that is not directly part of such a relation is treated as either its expression (however mediated) or historically irrelevant. In philosophical terms, to the extent that differences ultimately fade into an architectonic identity, one remains trapped within the suffocating embrace of the Hegelian totality.

In its place, Althusser defines the Marxist totality as necessarily complex and uneven, composed of practices and structures whose differences from one another are real and must be taken seriously. In turn, this allows us to think through the domination of the social formation by a particular contradiction as a totality that is 'structured in dominance.' Crudely put, for one contradiction or social level to dominate all others, the thing or process that is being dominated must possess a 'relative autonomy' from the thing or process that is dominating. Otherwise, the determination of the one by the other is merely the determination of itself and therefore purely tautological. Borrowing a theoretical architecture from both psychoanalysis and structuralism, Althusser proposes a radically new way of conceptualizing the transformative energies that lie within all historical formations that are characterized by social contradiction. Citing the example of the October 1917 Revolution in Russia, he asserts that the possibility for class contradictions – present in all historically known societies – to become explosive does not depend exclusively on the tension within the economic sphere, but rather on the 'overdetermination' of other contradictions. Chance for revolution emerges when the energies coiled within the contradictions of all social levels are coordinated and condensed into a single, ruptural unity. In the absence of this coordination, the revolutionary potential generated by social contradictions effectively remains latent through displacement. Contradictions are rendered non-antagonistic because of a basic disjuncture between their individual tendencies to crisis. For any one to explode, all of the others must be similarly primed. In an analytic sense, this radically challenges Marxism's traditional focus on the economic base and its matching confidence that the superstructures will 'scatter before His Majesty the Economy as he strides along the royal road of the Dialectic.'[35] Instead, Marxists must look to how the disparate tensions present at all social levels are fused into a ruptural unity. And this, in turn, requires a much greater awareness of how each particular level operates: '*The theory of the specific effectivity of the superstructures and other "circumstances" largely remains to be elaborated*; and before the theory of their effectivity or simultaneously (for it is by formulating their effectivity that their *essence* can be attained) there must be elaboration of *the theory of the particular essence of the specific elements of the superstructure*.'[36]

Althusser insists that giving the specific effectivity of the superstructures analytic priority is only the first step in assembling a suitably complex model of the social whole that is ultimately determined 'in the last instance' by the economic. The determinacy of the economic is defined as its capacity to establish the decisive social level – economic, political, or ideological – in which the resolution or exacerbation of a particular crisis will be played out. Compared to the provocative analysis of crisis formation or the strenuous case for superstructural autonomy, this watered-down concept of determination is probably the weakest link in the Althusserian model. It stands as evidence that insisting on the specific effectivity of each structural level makes it difficult to sustain a meaningful notion of determination. In any case, the centrifugal inertia of structural Marxism exercises a considerable influence on the trajectory of cultural studies, pulling it away from looking to the relations between culture or politics and the social totality in favour of exploring the unique ways in which superstructures function.

The arc of this trajectory is inscribed in Hall's mobilization of the Althusserian problematic in developing the 'differentiated unity' model, which deeply influenced the CCCS in the 1970s. Based on a dense, complex reading of the '1857 Introduction' to the *Grundrisse*, Hall extracts from Marx's discussion of the different moments of production a set of methodological principles for understanding the unity of a particular social process:

> We must 'think' the relations between the different processes of material production as 'members of a totality, distinctions within a unity.' That is, as a complexly structured differentiated totality, in which distinctions are not obliterated but preserved – the unity of its 'necessary complexity' precisely *requiring* this differentiation ... In the examination of any phenomenon or relation, we must comprehend *both* its internal structure – what it is in its differentiatedness – as well as those other structures to which it is coupled and with which it forms some more inclusive totality.[37]

Hegel looks for the 'immediate identities' behind any set of differences; Marx, in contrast, emphasizes that their unity is in fact *complex*, formed by and based on these differences. In other words, the accurate representation of a particular totality requires that its unity be defined not through the identification of similarities between its various moments or elements (i.e., a shared, common essence), but rather through their differences. Discussing the practices that make up any given social totality, Hall explains that their 'relatedness must be "thought" *through* the dislocations between them, rather than through their similarity, correspondence or identity.'[38] Like Althusser, Hall grants material production a determining role insofar as it specifies the 'the system of similarities and differences, the points of conjuncture, between all the instances of the mode, including which level is, at any moment of a conjuncture, "in dominance."'[39] However, it has very little influence over the 'inner laws' that govern the operation of other social practices because it is these laws that generate the differences which are necessary for the ensemble of practices to function together as a complex totality. Accordingly, the internal logic that guarantees the specific effectivity of a particular practice is insulated from transformative external pressures. Effects may be condensed into a ruptural unity or serially dispersed and absorbed by the social formation, but the particular processes through which they are produced remain largely autonomous.

Although it was originally developed in reference to the circuit of production, this theoretical model quickly became ubiquitous within the Birmingham School and were used to ground the analysis of a wide variety of social phenomena.[40] For example, in an article that traces the evolution of Marx's conception of 'the political' and 'the economic,' Hall applies this conceptual framework to class struggle. In his early writings, Marx remains caught in a Hegelian problematic; consequently, he treats class struggle as a simple contradiction that is similarly expressed at both the economic and the political levels. However, following the collapse of the 1848 revolutions, he was obliged to rethink this simple relation in more complex terms in order to account for the differences between the economic and political forms of class struggle. Hall explains that the primacy of the economic thrusts class struggle into the political sphere, but the form it takes and the logic it obeys at this level will depend on a set of inner laws that are not defined by the economic. Once class struggle is 're-presented' in political terms, it acquires its own dynamic, which cannot subsequently be (re)translated into economic or even class forms: 'The level of the political class struggle, then, has its own efficacy, its own forms, its specific conditions of existence, its own momentum, tempo and direction, its own contradictions internal to it, its "peculiar" outcomes and results.'[41] This way of conceptualizing the social formation emphasizes the development of concepts and principles that can adequately represent and theorize the irreducibly unique qualities of any specific part or level of the social formation.

Notwithstanding the rich diversity of research programs this approach potentially implies (*vis-à-vis* the many social practices that each require the development of specialized theoretical vocabularies), it is the specificity of the ideological sphere that attracts most of Althusser's attention. His theory of ideology has three basic components. First, he argues that ideology has a material existence. Ideas neither arise nor exist autonomously; rather, they are '*material actions inserted into material practices governed by material rituals which are themselves defined by the material ideological apparatus from which derive the ideas of* [a particular] *subject.*'[42] They are the effects that are generated as 'raw' physical experiences are 'processed' by an apparatus such as family, schools, or trade unions. The materiality of these practices does not, however, suggest an affinity between ideology and other social processes given that they all share a common material basis as, for example, Williams and Thompson suggest. Rather, for Althusser, there are many different modalities of materiality, and his focus is on the effects and mechanisms of ideological apparatuses as distinguished from other kinds of practices. The essence of this specificity constitutes the second component of his theory of ideology:

> In ideology men do indeed express, not the relation between them and their conditions of existence, but *the way* they live the relation between them and their conditions of existence: this presupposes both a real relation and an *'imaginary,' 'lived'* relation. Ideology, then, is the expression of the relation between men and their 'world,' that is, the (overdetermined) unity of the real relation and the imaginary relation between them and their real conditions of existence.[43]

Just as class struggle is *re*presented as it passes through the political, so too is experience – the 'real' relation between people and their material conditions of existence – *re*presented as it passes into ideology. There it is subject to a discrete set of unconscious operations that give it meaning, that allow it to be 'lived' as *meaningful* experience. The meanings that particular experiences acquire are not logically determined by the material 'reality' of those experiences, nor do individuals produce them intentionally: 'The level of ideology, of consciousness and of experiencing must be thought in terms of this de-centering of material practice *through* ideological forms and relations.'[44] The disjuncture between 'raw' physical experience and ideology, rather than their expressive continuities, becomes the key moment of ideological analysis for Althusser. This disjuncture helps explain how the bourgeoisie and much of the proletariat can live their relation to capitalist economic relations, in their capacity as either exploiters or the exploited, as the instantiation of freedom. In more abstract terms, it demonstrates how social and material contradictions can be lived or experienced as non-contradictory. For Althusser, then, social and material structures and processes – or more properly, their effects – only enter human consciousness after they have passed into ideology and have been transformed according to its internal mechanisms.

The final component of Althusser's theory of ideology relates to the constitution of individuals as subjects through a process of interpellation. Individuals can access or understand their experiences *as meaningful* only insofar as they take up various 'subject-positions' created through ideological apparatuses. Conversely, these apparatuses can only have a material effect once individuals have been placed in these positions:

*'The category of the subject is only constitutive of all ideology insofar as all ideology has the function (which defines it) of "constituting" concrete individuals as subjects.* In the interaction of this double constitution exists the functioning of all ideology, all ideology being nothing but its functioning in the material forms of existence of that functioning.'[45]

Althusser explains the process of subject constitution through the metaphor of hailing: individuals are 'called' by ideological discourses, which establish specific kinds of subject positions that must be assumed by anyone who wishes to be an individual in order to 'respond' or participate in the activities that are governed by those discourses. Within a family, for example, patriarchy inscribes the subject-positions of son/brother, daughter/sister, and mother/wife under the authority of father/husband. To participate in that structure and experience the family as a meaningful set of social relations, real individuals must be positioned by (i.e., addressed as) *and* position themselves within (i.e., respond to) these identities. For Althusser, the most prominent albeit largely invisible effect of bourgeois subjectivity – traced out within the very ambiguity of the term itself – is that it allows individuals to experience themselves as the authors of their own actions and ideas: 'The individual *is interpellated as a (free) subject in order that he shall submit freely to the commandments of the Subject,* i.e. in order that he shall (freely) accept his subjection, i.e. in order that he shall make the gestures and actions of his subjection "all by himself."'[46] Althusser believes that social relations are impossible without ideological subject-positions because ideology *per se* always has been and always will be a necessary part of human existence. However, he does attribute emancipatory possibilities to the study and explanation of these hitherto unknown processes. Indeed, he praises Marx's 'anti-humanism' – the capacity to analyse social processes without relying on the concept of constituting subject – as his greatest contribution to revolutionary theory.

This brief excursus into Althusserian Marxism should not be read as indicating that the Birmingham School wholeheartedly adopts either its assumptions or its approach. Clearly, the CCCS is enthusiastic about many of Althusser's ideas; that said, it is equally sceptical of many others. For example, the CCCS raises important questions about the incipient functionalism of Althusser's description of ideology. Casual references to 'bad subjects' do not seem adequate for theorizing the active, creative agency of subordinate groups in resisting or subverting dominant ideologies, nor are they adequate for theorizing the contradictions that exist within popular culture. Also, the CCCS is deeply reluctant to use a theory of ideology to explain culture: in its view, there is something about the local, disorganized, and heterogeneous nature of cultural practices that seems to escape the disciplinary logic of an ideological formation.[47] Finally, the CCCS is not altogether comfortable with the pre-eminence that Althusser – influenced by the psychoanalytic structuralism of Lacan – accords to ideological and discursive processes in determining subjective experience. In an address to a conference of radical historians, for example, Hall claimed that 'in the end, [the study of popular culture] yields most when it is seen in relation to a more general, a wider history.'[48] Similarly, in response to an attack by one of *Screen*'s theorists, the CCCS noted that 'this is indeed the hub of the issue between us: the emphasis on the *absolute* autonomy of signifying practice. This stress seems to us to preclude the referencing of Language-in-general to any particular language, and to refuse any attempt to analyse signifying practices as part of the "material factors which determine the cultural formation."'[49]

Even so, Althusser's influence on the Birmingham School was profound. Hall explains, for instance, that 'my work is neither a refusal nor an apologia of Althusser's position. I refuse certain of those positions, but Althusser certainly has had an enormous influence on my thinking, in many positive ways that I continue to acknowledge, even after he has gone out of fashion.'[50] Althusser's most important influence was to shift the study of culture away from the expressive totality of culturalism toward the complex unity of differences in which each social practice is understood as having its own 'relatively autonomous' inner laws. As we shall see in the following section, even though the CCCS insists that broader 'material factors' are important, its application of Althusser to the study of culture unquestionably privileges the specificity of this social level at the expense of linking it to the totality of the social formation. The significance of the ideological level – and by association, the cultural level – in making human existence meaningful through the operation of a distinct set of practices has been highly influential in shaping how the CCCS approaches the study of culture and politics.

## Founding Cultural Studies I: The Politics of Signification

Althusserian Marxism furnished the dominant problematic used by the CCCS in the 1970s; that said, several other theoretical streams converged on the Birmingham School while it was laying the foundations for contemporary cultural studies. Two of these merit special examination. First, the semiotics of Roland Barthes show how the concepts of linguistic structuralism can be modified and applied to the analysis of specific cultural texts. Althusser's theories of the social formation and ideological apparatuses operate at a high level of abstraction; in contrast, Barthes's more concrete 'readings' illustrate how the inner workings of discourse can produce powerful social effects. Second, the CCCS uses the innovative Marxist philosophy of language pioneered by V.N. Volosinov to explain how and why culture is more than a transmission belt for dominant ideology (as Althusser's functionalism sometimes suggests); it is also a site of active struggle and resistance. Most notably, Volosinov theorizes the sign as fundamentally polysemic, capable of bearing a variety of meanings depending on the broader context in which it is deployed. In the next few pages I explore how the CCCS has selectively combined these two theoretical impulses with the general social theory borrowed from Althusser to generate a distinctive approach to the study of culture. Besides Barthes and Volosinov, I will consider three specific 'applications' of this approach by the CCCS: the analysis of news media, the investigation of subcultures, and the evolution of the well-known 'encoding/decoding' model. Throughout, I will focus on how the overarching commitment to the specificity or relative autonomy of signifying practices affects the possibility of theorizing the connections between culture and other social processes such as commodification.

Ferdinand Saussure founded linguistic structuralism in his *Course in General Linguistics*. Language, he famously argues in that book, needs to be conceptualized synchronically as organized systems of signifiers and signifieds; this has the effect of diverting attention from the study of individual words as well as from the relationship between language and reality. Focusing on the *internal* organization of language, he identifies two novel properties of linguistic systems. First, meaning does not inhere immanently in specific words, signs, or symbols themselves; rather, it is a function of the internal relations and, more specifically, the differences between signs. A sign can be positively identified only because it is negatively juxtaposed to all the other signs in a given network; it has no discrete, positive identity itself. The unity of a linguistic system is constituted by this set of differences. Second, and following from this first point, the relationship between a particular signifier (sound) and signified (concept) is entirely arbitrary. Thus, for example, there is no logical reason, other than the internal structure of the English language, why the sound 'tree' (or the letters t–r–e–e) should signify the concept *tree*. Besides laying the groundwork for the differentiated unity model, Saussure's claim that the production of meaning in language is both *internal* and *arbitrary* has had two lasting effects on cultural studies. First, it theoretically justifies assigning methodological priority to a single discrete structure in explaining why human beings think about and experience the world in a particular way. Second, and more relevant to a radical politics, it accentuates the possible emancipatory effects that might be generated at the level of culture itself, such as the raising of consciousness, as well as the necessary centrality of semiotic struggle to transformative social action.

In *Mythologies*, Barthes uses structuralist concepts to analyse a variety of popular cultural texts and activities. His objective is to deconstruct the '"naturalness" with which newspapers, art and common sense constantly dress up a reality which, even though it is the one we live in, is undoubtedly determined by history.'[51] Describing this as a bourgeois 'ideological abuse,' he tries to account for the widespread presence of myth in an ostensibly rational, disenchanted society. Of course, this objective bears a remarkable similarity to Horkheimer and Adorno's investigation into how 'enlightenment reverts to mythology.'[52] Yet the methods and conclusions of these two studies are very different. For Barthes, the creation of myth is a radically semiotic act: 'It is a mode of signification, a form.'[53] A myth is created when a complete sign – composed of a signifier (image/word) and a signified (concept) – is used as a signifier in a larger, meta-linguistic system. To illustrate this dynamic, Barthes describes a photograph of a black soldier saluting a French flag that appeared on the cover of a Parisian magazine. On the one hand, the photo is a signifier for the action that has taken place – namely, the saluting of the flag. This is its *denotative* function. On the other hand, it also signifies the inclusive vitality of French imperialism. This is its *connotative* function. In order for this latter semiotic operation to succeed, the historicity and specificity of the meaning produced by the denotative (linguistic) sign – that a certain black soldier once saluted a French flag – must be detached from its specific, historical referent, associatively transferred and subordinated to the already existent meaning of the connotative (mythic) sign. This gives imperialism a tangible, natural quality that it would never have possessed in the absence of such a transfer. In other words, the picture can only signify or connote imperialism because it also signifies or denotes a black soldier saluting a French flag.

However, these two semiotic moments are never simultaneous: as soon as both are thought at the same time and the instrumental connection between them becomes clear, the spell of myth is shattered. When read as myth, though, there is a rapid, imperceptible oscillation between these two moments. As the first sign is read as a signifier, the specificity of its signified – that a black soldier once saluted a French flag – is not eradicated; rather, it is momentarily stripped of its history and then used to fill the emptiness that would otherwise compromise the meaning of the second sign. The mythic signifier

> does not suppress the meaning [of a first-order sign], it only impoverishes it, it puts it at a distance, it holds it at one's disposal. One believes that the meaning is going to die, but it is a death with a reprieve; the meaning loses its value, but keeps its life, from which the form of the myth will draw nourishment. The meaning will be for the form like an instantaneous reserve of history, a tamed richness, which it is possible to call and dismiss in a sort of rapid alternation: the form must constantly be able to be rooted again in the meaning and to get there what nature it needs for its nutriment; above all, it must be able to hide there. It is this constant game of hide-and-seek ... which defines myth.[54]

Once a sign has been used in the construction of myth, it undergoes a fundamental change. As Barthes explains, the ultimate effect of a signifying system in which the connotative and denotative levels play 'hide-and-seek' with each other is the transformation of history into nature. Insofar as the picture of the black soldier constantly shifts between signifying a real event and a mythic concept, it functions to naturalize both: in circular fashion, the photo confirms the legitimacy of imperialism as natural even while imperialism reinforces the normality of the photo.

As a consequence of these signifying practices, the very historicity of social processes is frozen and enslaved to the production of a pristine, mythic nature. In these circumstances, history 'is a kind of ideal servant: it prepares all things, brings them, lays them out, the master arrives, it silently disappears: all that is left for one to do is to enjoy this beautiful object without wondering where it comes from.'[55] Myth 'is constituted by the loss of the historical quality of things: in it, things lose the memory that they once were made.'[56] As a description of how capitalism is lived and experienced, these words could come just as easily from Adorno or Benjamin. Yet Adorno and Benjamin firmly reject any suggestion that effects on the plane of meaning can be adequately explained without reference to an extra-discursive reality. Instead, Adorno and Benjamin draw from Marx's analysis of the fetishism of commodities in order to provide a convincing account of how an economic process can intervene in the generation of a specific kind of meaningful experience. Rooted in this framework, critical theory connects the dominance of the commodity form to a reified experience of capitalist social relations as a 'second nature' without history. Yet despite Barthes's obvious Marxist sympathies, the concept of commodity fetishism never appears in Barthes's text. Instead, he describes the emptying of reality by myth as *exclusively* an effect of semiotic processes. Signification may draw from the 'real' world for its raw material, but it is the internal laws of discursive structures that orchestrate the transformation of history into myth. Some may object that Barthes's mobilization of the body in later works such as *The Pleasure of the Text*[57] contradicts this position. It is certainly true that he comes to recognize the influence of the material body on processes of reading and writing. However, this influence most often appears in the form of a break or interruption of dominant signifying processes, especially in the case of *jouissance* as opposed to the more docile *plaisir*. The possibility that non-signifying material practices such as commodification might have a determining impact on signification goes largely unexplored.

As 'messages without codes,' photographs are especially useful objects for generating of myths. They are iconic signs: at the denotative level, we do not seem to need a semiotic code in order to decipher their meaning. A picture is what it is: it signifies the event or scene it depicts. At the connotative level, however, an image can easily signify things other than what it visually represents owing to its surreptitious placement in a broader structural code. For the most part, the linkages these codes generate between images, concepts, and desires are not governed by rational logic but rather by alternative frameworks of meaning. Yet these second-level codes often go unnoticed because the need for a code to decipher the image at the first level seems so clearly unnecessary. The appearance of a direct or natural correlation at the denotative level subsequently determines how the broader connotations of the image will be read, not as the consequence of a larger interpretive system, but as the obvious, natural effects of the image itself. Thus, 'the denoted message naturalizes the symbolic message, it innocents the semantic artifice of connotation ... the discontinuous connotators are connected, actualized, "spoken" through the syntagm of the denotation, the discontinuous world of symbols plunges into the story of the denoted scene as though into a lustral bath of innocence.'[58] The synthetic, deliberate, and motivated association of particular connotations with a specific image thus appears to the consumer of myths as completely normal and natural.

Barthes's discussion of the formation of myth and his analysis of the denotative and connotative attributes of signs played an important role in the CCCS's early work on the effects of the mass media. According to Hall, Barthes initiated a 'new problematic' at the CCCS.[59] His work accounts for the naturalization of social relations without falling back on the crude, class-reductionist explanation that the ideas of the ruling economic class inevitably become the ideas of everyone else. In particular, it is very useful for exploring the production of news, which is regarded by the Birmingham School as an especially potent site of myth making in contemporary society. Hall, for instance, brings the connotation/denotation model to bear on the process of choosing news photographs, thus connecting Barthes's semiotics to the production of ideology.[60] In addition to its myth-making properties (which are shared by all iconic signs), news has two additional properties that make its visual images especially potent in the production of ideology. First, it draws from notions of journalistic objectivity to intensify the seeming transparency between signifier and signified, thereby increasing the likelihood that connotative associations will be understood as natural. Second, it tends to focus on political issues and events, thereby clustering images, which generate an interlocking set of ideological connotations that may reinforce one another. At the denotative level, Hall notes, a particular story will have 'news value' that determines its worthiness to be covered: perhaps it depicts a violent, dramatic, or sensationalized act. This is the logic that openly dominates the institutional world of news production, which is governed by the need to sell newspapers and advertising. The broader ideological implications of news, however, are determined mainly at the connotative level of signification: 'It is via this double articulation that the institutional world of the newspaper, whose manifest function is the profitable exchange of news values, is harnessed to the latent function of reproducing "in dominance" the major ideological themes of society.'[61] Although the economic imperative dominates the denotative level insofar as certain images are more saleable than others, the ideological effect of those images is explained separately:

> The ideological function of the photographic sign is always hidden within

> its exchange value [i.e. it may appear that the paper is merely printing that which sells]. The news/ideological meaning is the *form* in which these sign-vehicles are exchanged. Though the economic dialectic, here as elsewhere, determines the production and appropriation of 'symbolic' values, it is 'never active in its pure state.' The exchange value of the photographic sign is thus, necessarily, over-determined.[62]

In essence, Hall wants to *distinguish* between what sells and what is ideological in order to investigate the discrete logics that govern these two separate imperatives. The fact that a particular image is used depends on the convergence of two distinct processes: one is dominated by commodification, the other – at the level of ideology – *is not*. And the strategic priority for cultural studies is the latter, not the former. Discussing the 'external' influences on television broadcasting, Hall explains:

> We say 'power and the dominant ideologies' rather than money and the profit motive because, although television has, since the ending of monopoly, provided a 'frontier province' for the crudest commercial calculations, the role of broadcasting in reproducing the power relations and ideological structure of society appears to me far more central an issue than its incidental financial kickbacks.[63]

Again, the distinction between 'crude commercial calculations' and the 'ideological structure of society' is noteworthy. It demonstrates either an inability or an unwillingness to consider the possible relations between these two social levels. That the commodity form itself might have a direct ideological impact or decisively influence the inner laws of a signifying system is not considered. Instead, 'crude commercial calculations' are to be filtered out of the mix so that one can examine the ideological system in its purest form. Needless to say, this approach is entirely consistent with both Althusser's emphasis on the specific effectivity of the superstructures and Barthes's exploration of how ideological effects are semiotically generated.

Perhaps the most influential legacy of the Birmingham School to cultural studies is its strong insistence on the polysemic character of cultural signs and texts: the same object can take on a wide range of meanings depending on how it is inserted into the different signifying practices of various social groups. The intellectual lineage of this concept can be traced to two basic sources. First, Barthes's use of the connotation/denotation model dramatically expands the possibilities for generating meaning beyond the rigid structuralism of Saussurean linguistics. Mythic signs function the way they do because they can bear more than a single meaning; they are able to connote multiple themes. While the early work on myth emphasizes the ideological closure imposed by dominant signifying systems on the ambiguities invoked by connotation (e.g., advertising's use of the caption), the later writings attribute considerably more autonomy to the reader in deciphering images and texts as she or he pleases. There is also a corresponding shift in the normative valuation of polysemy: from its original role as the semiotic sponsor of myth and bourgeois ideology, it is transformed into the guardian of hermeneutic freedom and agency. In his influential essay 'The Death of the Author,' Barthes explains that 'we know now that a text is not a line of words releasing a single, "theological" meaning (the "message" of the Author-God) but a multi-dimensional space in which a variety of writings, none of them original, blend and clash.'[64] Words such as these deliver a radical challenge to traditional conceptions of the masses as passive and as manipulated, in that they displace creative agency from the sphere of production to that of consumption. For the Birmingham School, raised on the stories and practices of an active working class that wrested its own cultural identity from a hostile elite, Barthes's account of textual polysemy rings true at a very basic level. It offers a way of countering Althusser's functionalist excesses *without* fundamentally altering the model of the complex totality. On the one hand, focus on the specific effectivity of ideological and cultural practices is retained; on the other, semiotic polysemy is grafted onto a notion of social struggle as an explanation of how it manifests itself *within* culture and ideology.

For the CCCS, the merits of this basic framework are confirmed and extended in V.N. Volosinov's *Marxism and the Philosophy of Language*. Signs, Volosinov argues, do not simply reflect the world; they also refract it because of the intersection 'of differently oriented social interests within one and the same sign community, i.e., *by the class struggle*.'[65] The semiotic capacity to register and express this social conflict is based on the 'social *multiaccentuality*' of individual signs: 'Each living ideological sign has two faces, like Janus. Any current curse word can become a word of praise, any current truth must inevitably sound to many other people as the greatest lie.'[66] Volosinov's text emphasizes the possibility that any given sign can be interpreted in a variety of ways depending on the context in which it is used. His use of everyday examples to illustrate these arguments suggests the pervasive role of semiotic polysemy in human societies. Indeed, he notes that it is the multiaccentual potential of signs that makes them so useful: '*What is important for the speaker about a linguistic form* [or sign] *is not that it is a stable and always self-equivalent signal, but that it is an always changeable and adaptable sign.*'[67] Given this emphasis, it is relatively easy to conclude that signs are *inherently* polysemic; and, I would argue, this is precisely what the Birmingham School does. Noting the text's 'decisive and far-reaching impact on our work,' Hall explains: 'Volosinov's account counterposed the exercise of cultural power through the imposition of the norm in an attempt to freeze and fix meaning in language to the constant eruption of new meanings, the fluidity of heteroglossia, and the way meaning's *inherent* instability and heterogeneity dislocated and displaced language's apparently "finished" character.'[68]

Elsewhere, he notes that 'the ideological sign is *always* multiaccentual and Janus-faced'[69] and that 'meaning is polysemic *in its intrinsic nature.*'[70] Beyond this specific point, Volosinov's work is also employed as evidence for 'the definitively discursive character of ideology.'[71] Hall argues, in other words, that *Marxism and the Philosophy of Language* provides a coherent theory of the specific effectivity of ideological processes. In a similar vein, Bennett writes that 'its more general theoretical and political significance ... is that, escaping the economic reductionism of Lukacs' position, it allows the signifying systems which constitute the sphere of the ideological to be granted their own specific role and effectivity within social life.'[72] Volosinov's speculative Marxist theory of language is assimilated by British cultural studies according to the principles of the broad problematic initially laid down by Althusser.

A comparison of the CCCS's appropriation of Volosinov with his actual text reveals just how deep the commitment to the autonomy of ideological and discursive practices runs in British cultural studies. First, let us look closer at the issue of multiaccentuality. Strictly speaking, Volosinov does not actually argue that signs are inherently polysemic. While they all bear within them the potential to be interpreted in various ways, there is certainly no guarantee that this potential will always be realized. It is also important to note that simply because words and phrases take on a variety of connotations during everyday use, it does not necessarily follow that ideological and political signs are equally malleable. When Volosinov describes ideological signs as 'Janus-faced,' he does so with an important caveat:

> This *inner dialectical quality* of the sign comes out fully in the open only in times of social crises or revolutionary changes. In the ordinary conditions of life, the contradiction embedded in every ideological sign cannot emerge fully because the ideological sign in an established, dominant ideology ... tries, as it were, to stabilize the preceding factor in the dialectical flux of the social generative process ... so accentuating yesterday's truth as to make it appear today's.[73]

Multiaccentuality is present in every ideological sign, but it is only enabled through social struggle. The relation between semiotic polysemy and social struggle is both symbiotic and dialectical. In the absence of such struggle, the range of meanings that will be generated through the consumption of ideological signs is substantially reduced.

Second, Volosinov categorically rejects the 'definitively discursive' character of ideology. It is remarkable that the Birmingham School could take the claim that ideology is 'definitely discursive' from his text, because its core idea is that meaning is *socially* produced. It is all the more astonishing given that early work at the centre had criticized Barthes on precisely this account.[74] And for Volosinov, the social refers to the totality of social and material relations, not to the specificity of any particular type of relation: 'The understanding of any sign, whether inner or outer, occurs inextricably tied in with the *situation in which the sign is implemented ... the sign and its social situation are inextricably fused together*.'[75] Contrary to Hall's claims, signifying systems *cannot* be conceptualized as separate or distinct entities. That Hall, Bennett, and others at the CCCS should interpret Volosinov this way illustrates how dominant the compartmentalizing thrust of structuralist Marxism remains in British cultural studies. Some may counter that the CCCS quite willingly admits the context-bound nature of meaning. True enough, but context is only ever defined in semiotic terms. In the case of class struggle, for example, the initial impetus for representing this struggle through language may be caused by other social processes and will ultimately have an effect on them, but the laws that govern how this conflict is played out at the cultural level remain internal and discrete. This rather stark structuralist inflection of Volosinov provides a clear illustration of how the Althusserian problematic shapes the CCCS's reading and appropriation of other theoretical traditions.

Trying to extract a theory of cultural commodification from the Birmingham School is a difficult task because its scholars never grapple seriously with the question of how the commodity form affects cultural processes. The commodification of cultural objects is not conceived as having a determinant effect on the range of meanings that might be generated in the act of cultural consumption. Neither is the penetration of commodified social relations and the profit imperative into the production of culture. This is not to say that people can take any meaning they like from any given text: dominant social groups inevitably try to 'prefer' certain kinds of readings while closing down others. But they can only do this through specific cultural and ideological techniques. The commodity form itself is *not* counted as one such technique; instead, its effects are confined to an economic level. Perhaps it governs the external production, circulation, and distribution of cultural objects, but it does not affect their internal meaning: 'Commodities are, also, cultural *signs*. They have already been invested, by the dominant culture, with meanings, associations, social connotations ... Objects and commodities do not mean any one thing. They "mean" only because they have already been arranged, according to social use, into cultural codes of meaning, which *assign meanings to them*.'[76]

Meaning is a discrete property attached to commodities that is realized and modified through a social act of consumption. Only representational practices can fix or define meaning: non-representational practices, such as commodification, do not have any power at this level. Given that one of the essential characteristics of meaning is its inherent polysemy, once an object, activity, or experience passes through a representational practice and thereby becomes meaningful, it will necessarily also become polysemic:

> Language is the medium *par excellence* through which things are 'represented' in thought and thus the medium in which ideology is generated and transformed. But in language, the same social relation can be *differently* represented and constructed ... because language by its nature is *not fixed* in a one-to-one relation with its referent but is 'multi-referential': it can construct different meanings around what is apparently the same social relation or phenomenon.[77]

In terms of culture, the lines of determination between signifying practices and the commodity form run in one direction only: from the former to the latter.

Adorno's work on mass culture opens up a rather different perspective on the effects of commodification. In the first place, the commodity form not only influences meaning but also, at its most dominant stage in the culture industry, itself becomes the very meaning or ideology that is consumed. As it defines the underlying structure of cultural forms, commodification constructs the patterns of understanding and desire through which the world is experienced in terms of both meaning and pleasure. The Birmingham School often tends to define or measure polysemy according to the explicit content of a particular culture object. How do individuals or groups interpret cultural texts in different ways? One of the centre's main criticisms of *Screen* and Lacanian psychoanalysis, for example, relates to their refusal to consider the ideological effectivity of specific formations and their generalized emphasis on the operations of 'language in general.' Benjamin and Adorno are similarly critical of ahistorical conceptions of cognitive processes (cf. Horkheimer and Adorno's critique of Kant); however, they believe that it is at this structural level, rather than with the particularity of any specific 'reading,' that critical social theory must operate. For them, genuine polysemy (note that neither ever uses this term) is only possible once human cognitive and libidinal structures are able to process and generate a diversity of types of experience, rather than variations on the same experience. More importantly, cultural activities must activate and express a desire for this diversity, conceptualized philosophically as a willingness to accommodate non-identity. 'The reconciled condition,' writes Adorno, 'would not be the philosophical imperialism of annexing the alien. Instead, its happiness would lie in the fact that the alien, in the proximity it is granted, remains what is distant and different, beyond the heterogeneous and beyond that which is one's own.'[78] For critical theory, in other words, polysemy does not involve a multiplicity of meanings so much as the possibility for entirely different kinds of meaning or even the temporary suspension of the need and desire for meaning itself. Insofar as mass culture generates variations on a single theme, it can hardly be called diverse. Furthermore, while Adorno agrees that language's capacity to function semiotically holds the key to thinking non-identity, he does not attribute an essentialist power to language to keep diversity alive. Instead, he warns of the danger that language and even thought itself may be colonized by the commodity form and its dominant principle of identity. Nothing in a capitalist society automatically possesses an inviolable immunity to commodification: its terrifying power lies precisely in how it has been able to expand beyond an economic relation, to infect and colonize all other social levels and practices.

During the 1970s the most influential studies to emerge from the

Birmingham School related to subcultures. In *Resistance through Rituals*, the CCCS explores how the various styles developed by youth in the postwar era were motivated by attempts to resolve the contradictions between their parents' class-based existence and the freedoms promised by new, mobile consumer identities. The CCCS adopts the argument of Phil Cohen that 'the latent function of subculture is ... to express and resolve, albeit "magically," the contradictions which remain hidden or unresolved in the parent culture.'[79] In the case of skinheads, for example, their distinctive style represents the symbolic reconstruction of a dense, working-class community as a defensive response to the decline of real urban working-class neighbourhoods.[80] Analyses of the 'Ted' and 'Mod' subcultures reveal similar dynamics. The key to a subculture, in terms of both its formation and its interpretation, lies in its style. The relative freedom of leisure – especially given the erosion of informal working-class regulation of social life – compared to the greater discipline of work and family life, ensures that semiotic action is often the easiest route available for expressing and 'magically' resolving contradictory social experiences. There is an obvious affinity between this framework and Althusser's contention that ideology constitutes the 'imaginary, lived' relation between human beings and their existence. Yet the subcultural framework opens up a space for agency that is absent within an ideological state apparatus. While the symbolic means through which subordinate groups resolve structural contradictions ultimately impose severe limits on the efficacy and transformative potential of this kind of resistance, those means do represent a form of collective social action through which individuals can exercise some control over how they live their 'imaginary' relation to their existence.

The key that unlocks this agency is the multiaccentuality of the sign. Early in the development of the subcultural framework, there was some question as to how important polysemy really was in the formation of a style. Paul Willis's early work on 'biker boys' and hippies downplayed this concept in favour of analysing the strong links between particular experiences and certain cultural practices.[81] Using a definition of culture that owes more to Williams than to Althusser, he traced out the objective homologies between groups and the signs they used to signify their experiences. Summarizing this approach, John Clarke explains that for an object to be integrated into the subcultural formation of a social group, it must 'have the "objective" possibility of reflecting the particular values and concerns of the group in question as one among the range of potential meanings that it could hold.'[82] Use of the term 'objective' suggests that certain properties of an object itself, rather than simply the characteristics 'attached' to it as it passes through a signifying structure, will exercise a fixed, determinate influence on how it acquires meaning in a particular social context. Comparing the hippies and the biker boys, Willis looked at the importance of drugs to the one and motorcycles to the other: each object or practice had certain material properties that made it especially amenable to integration within the specific value and belief systems of these subcultures. Reciprocally, the importance of a particular cultural practice for Willis lay in its corresponding effect on the experiential structures of the subordinate group. However, the adoption of a more structuralist perspective shifts the focus away from the expressive relations between culture and experience toward the internal relations between different cultural systems. Once this move is made, the polysemy of signs takes on a far more important role in theorizing cultural practices. Levi-Strauss's notion of *bricolage,* 'the re-ordering and re-contextualisation of objects to communicate fresh meanings, within a total system of significances attached to the objects used,' provides the dominant explanatory framework for how subcultures are made.[83] Styles are not formed out of thin air, nor are they the 'pure' expressions of working-class experience. Instead, their force is generated through the disjuncture between the meaning conventionally attached to an object and its placement within a radically different network of objects and practices.

Dick Hebdige's *Subcultures,* a highly influential book in cultural studies, exemplifies this approach. Distinguishing his own assumptions from those in *Resistance through Rituals,* he argues that the 'raw material' or experience that subcultures are supposed to process is, in fact, never 'raw' but always mediated through pre-existing ideological apparatuses. Thus the real work of subcultures is not so much expressive as transgressive: the power of style does not arise out of the objective similarities between signs and a way of life, but rather in the differences between how a sign is normally used and its relocation by a subcultural group to a different semiotic context. Subcultures wage an ideological battle against the appropriation of semiotic space by dominant codes that, as Barthes shows, aspire to naturalize themselves: 'By repositioning and recontextualizing commodities, by subverting their conventional uses and inventing new ones, the subcultural stylist gives the lie to what Althusser has called the "false obviousness of everyday practice."'[84] In other words, the primary defence of a subculture against mainstream cultural formations is a strategy of defamiliarization through *bricolage*. The punk rock subculture perfected this tactic, taking it to its logical conclusion: punk constituted itself negatively via a dislocation of signifiers so severe that the possibility for meaning itself was fatally damaged: 'Clothed in chaos, they produced Noise in the calmly orchestrated Crisis of everyday life in the late 1970s – a noise which made (no)sense in exactly the same way and to exactly the same extent as a piece of *avant-garde* music.'[85] For Hebdige, experience itself as anything other than the clustering of signs fades into the background. Homologies are confined to the level of signification; objects are taken up not because of their similarity to a way of life, but because of how they 'fit' within a certain semiotic formation. The commodity form plays a limited ideological role insofar as the commercialization of a subcultural style effectively 'freezes' it, thereby enabling its ideological incorporation. But its influence basically remains an external one. And its effects can easily be subverted by subcultural practices because of the polysemic qualities that even – or perhaps especially – the most commodified cultural object takes on when it enters the level of signification.

The theoretical architecture that emerged from the CCCS during this period is codified in Hall's encoding/decoding model of cultural analysis. Invoking the Althusserian conception of a totality as complex and differentiated, Hall proposes that any communicative exchange comprises a series of distinct but articulated moments. In order for something to be communicated, it must first pass through a set of signifying practices. The result is a message that exists in a discursive form. For this message to be subsequently 'received' by an individual or group, it must be 'translated' by way of a second set of signifying practices. The first is the process of 'encoding,' the second that of 'decoding': 'While each of the moments, in articulation, is necessary to the circuit as a whole, no one moment can fully guarantee the next moment with which it is articulated. Since each has its specific modality and conditions of existence, each can constitute its own break or interruption of the "passage of forms" on whose continuity the flow of effective production (that is, "reproduction") depends.'[86]

Encoding describes how an ideological apparatus such as the media tries to ensure that particular messages are interpreted in certain ways. For example, news coverage of a demonstration may be framed so that protesters are interpreted as dangerous fanatics. Similarly, the use of specific camera angles and production techniques can codify a particular kind of body as an object of sexual desire. However, these encodings never fully determine how a message will be received: this depends on the semiotic resources that an individual or group brings to bear on the decoding process. Encoding and decoding are 'determinate' moments in the communicative process as a whole. Insofar as anything takes on meaning, it does so according to the specific rules of signification:

> When a historical event passes under the sign of discourse, it is subject to all the complex formal 'rules' by which language signifies ... In that moment the formal sub-rules of discourse are "in dominance," without, of course, subordinating out of existence the historical event so signified, the social relations in which the rules are set to work or the social and political consequences of the event having been signified in this way.[87]

Non-discursive 'reality' is determined by linguistic structures when it passes through representative practices. One of the most important rules of language is that a re-presented object or practice – a sign – is always susceptible to multiple interpretations while it exists within the domain of meaning. The possibility for the actualization of multiple interpretations depends on a struggle that is waged entirely in the realm of signifying practices. In the case of subcultures, for example, the receiver(s) of a message may draw from an alternative semiotic code to extract an entirely different meaning than had originally been intended.

The overarching dominance of certain basic codes within a cultural formation does ensure that most messages will be decoded by most people in similar ways. At the denotative level, these codes have been naturalized so effectively that their arbitrary origin is no longer experienced as such; therefore, the receiver does not know or believe that the sign can be interpreted in any other way than is prescribed by that code. However, as one moves toward the connotative level, the possibilities for alternative or even oppositional decodings increase significantly. For the Birmingham School, this is the pre-eminent arena for ideological conflict and struggle. A multiplicity of technical processes can be mobilized to prefer certain readings over others. But these processes may be disrupted if an individual or group has access to an alternative framework for decoding that enables a polysemic reading of a particular text or image. Even the practice of cultural studies itself can have a radical popular effect by using deconstructive strategies to break apart the uniformity of encoded messages. In a retrospective on the encoding/decoding model, Hall confirms that one of the tasks of the critic is to pull apart the preferring process and thereby turn ideology back into language: 'That is why this kind of critical work on encoding/decoding is always a deconstructive practice. It opens up the text to the variety of meanings or appropriations which were not legislated for in the activity of its encoding.'[88] Once the arbitrary and often politically motivated character of the code that governs a message has been exposed, the polysemy of a sign or message can be activated. And such exposure is contingent on a form of semiotic activism, rather than being rooted within a more holistic notion of experience.

In short, the encoding/decoding model confirms the autonomy of signifying practices and their dominance over how the 'real world' is represented when it enters the sphere of meaning. Faithful to the Althusserian problematic, it predicates the study of culture on its fundamental isolation from other social practices. Marking this compartmentalized social theory is the slippage that often attends Hall's explanation of the relationship between 'reality' and language: 'Reality exists outside language, but it is constantly mediated by and through language: and what we can know and say has to be produced in and through discourse. Discursive "knowledge" is the product not of the transparent representations of the "real" in language but of the articulation of language on real relations and conditions.'[89] These two spheres are conceptualized as discrete and largely disconnected. Hall readily admits that 'in the end the position dodges or ducks the question of any fixed or verifiable distinction between the real and the discursive, or between the discursive and the extradiscursive. I don't know where that extradiscursive is. I regard the extradiscursive as a kind of wager. It's a kind of bet that the world exists, which cannot be proven in a philosophical sense.'[90]

However, such slippage does not really trouble him because no more precise definition of 'reality' is required. Once it has been assumed that extra-discursive processes do not have any determinant effect on the inner rules of signification, there is no longer any pressing reason for cultural studies to theorize the real. Indeed, even if one wanted to theorize this relation, the isolated quality of discourse would make it almost impossible. One cannot, for instance, trace the effect of extra-discursive processes on systems of thought in the manner of Adorno and Lukacs. Instead, only the discrete mechanisms of discursive systems can be assessed. Commodification will determine the production and distribution of cultural objects, but it cannot affect how these objects are made to *mean* within a cultural formation. Certainly, capitalist ideological institutions will try to construct semiotic codes that favourably represent capitalism and that try to naturalize it as a social system. But their success or failure will be governed by the same discursive rules under which all other ideologies operate: they cannot 'rig the table.' And the encoding/decoding model suggests that the deck is actually stacked against them from the start: the decentralized nature of decoding processes – be they idiosyncratic or collectively organized – means that a centralized culture industry can never fully eradicate alternative readings. Diversity becomes an essential quality of discursive systems that capitalism cannot eliminate.

Arguably, the methodology for studying culture that emerges from Birmingham, grounded in the polysemy of autonomous signifying practices and its social correlate of an active, creative interpretive community of consumers, serves as the dominant problematic for critical cultural studies. As such, the effects of this methodology are many and diverse. In concluding this section, I will focus on only one effect. This paradigm is often used to locate cultural studies as a democratic, non-elitist practice, in opposition to, for example, the Frankfurt School, which is said to view the masses as completely docile and as controlled by the culture industry. This founding act sponsors the clustering of analytic concepts with normative values. Activity, agency, polysemy, pleasure, and freedom are all associated with one end of a continuum; passivity, manipulation, uniformity, and domination occupy the other end. The use of any single term automatically invokes the others. Although cultural studies has started to break out of this conceptual straitjacket in the past few years,[91] the cumulative effect of this continuum has fundamentally compromised its ability to grapple with the effects of the commodity form on cultural processes. Concepts such as activity, agency, polysemy, and pleasure must themselves retain a multiplicity of normative valances if they are to be of any use in dealing with this issue. While there has been a general recognition that pleasure cannot be simplistically equated with empowerment, there has been less willingness to acknowledge that the effects of something like polysemy are equally complex and ambiguous. Instead, the prevailing assumption has been that it is *always* a good thing, that it *always* stands as evidence that subordinate groups are struggling against a dominant ideological system striving for closure. For the most part, criticisms of cultural studies also buy into this framework; attacking the tendency to exaggerate the interpretive freedom of consumers simply confirms the 'polysemy good, uniformity bad' continuum. With a few notable exceptions, too little consideration has been given to how, at some level, polysemic cultural practices actually fit very well with the commodity form. Adorno's theory of pseudo-individuation, which he developed in order to probe the complexities of this relation, receives almost no attention from cultural studies. Instead, polysemy is interpreted as a sign that a commodity has been effectively expropriated and separated from its commercial incarnation. Similarly, the identification of passivity with the diagnosis of manipulation at one end of the continuum entirely occludes how Adorno actually develops a very sophisticated theory of the active nature of cultural consumption. This aspect of the culture industry thesis is casually dismissed via the logic that if Adorno views the masses as dominated, it follows that he conceptualizes their relation to culture as passive.

Once culture has been theorized as an autonomous set of practices, it is very difficult to incorporate any other social levels, practices, or structures into one's analytic framework. Some may object that it would be difficult to find a social level, practice, or structure that does not have a cultural component; such objections restore a holistic perspective 'through the back door,' as it were. But this was definitely *not* the trajectory of cultural studies at Birmingham during its formative period. Except for Willis's fascinating study of the ambiguous effects of education on working-class youth in *Learning to Labour*, the CCCS concentrates on how groups and individuals construct their collective and self-identities by consuming cultural commodities. Culture is the venue through which ruling ideological institutions try to persuade the people to interpret their world in a very specific fashion; in this way, it plays a key role in securing the authority of capitalist social relations. But culture is also the place where one can most easily struggle *against* the domination experienced in so many other parts of social life, such as politics, economics, education, and the family, where protest is more tightly regulated. In large part, this is a consequence of how the CCCS has theorized culture as a uniquely autonomous set of practices. Linguistic polysemy means that culture opens up a space for agency that is simply unmatched in any other social sphere:

> The 'masses' Stuart [Hall] refers to have become individual historical subjects, at least in western capitalist societies, not so much through the representative organs of parliamentary democracy (a fairly limited institution, especially in Britain), but through the diverse modalities of urban

> popular culture. It is there that the greatest exercise in the powers of individual and local choice and taste has been realized, effectively remaking the field of culture in a far more extensive fashion than the presence of the 'masses' in the more restricted field of politics has so far achieved.[92]

Similarly, the very real domination of commodification can be countered effectively, if only temporarily, if only 'magically,' at the cultural level. The unique properties of language – most notably its multiaccentuality – guarantee that the essence of culture as a second dimension of human existence will never be endangered by the commodity form.

**Founding Cultural Studies II: The Moment of Hegemony**

The primary analytic logic that drove the early work on subcultures and that attained formal expression in the encoding/decoding model was the isolation and separation of the moments of cultural production and consumption. Both were viewed as distinct processes with their own specific modalities, whese differences outweighed their similarities. The assimilation of Gramsci's theory of hegemony into British cultural studies has reversed this emphasis by asserting the need to think through the unity of a cultural formation based on the negotiated integration of dominant and subordinate cultures. This theoretical shift offers a number of benefits over the earlier approach. Some of the celebratory excesses that accompany the analysis of decoding as a self-contained process are tempered. A more sophisticated and inclusive theory of collective cultural agency is constructed by tracing how *all* cultural practices take shape rather than concentrating on the spectacular resistance of a few marginalized groups. Yet the continuities with the earlier paradigm are strong in a number of key areas. Detailed consideration of articulation – the basic theoretical principle through which Gramsci's theory is applied to the study of culture – must await the next chapter. For now, I want to highlight some of the effects that arise when hegemony is inflected through a structuralist problematic. Although the use of Gramsci weakens culture's stranglehold over signifying practices, the elevation of the political as the determinant moment in the formation of hegemony does little to enable reconsideration of how the commodity form affects culture.

For British cultural studies, hegemony is conceptualized mainly as the domination of one social group over another that emerges out of a co-ordinated and often self-conscious campaign to impose a particular set of goals and objectives on an entire society:

> In essence, it refers to all those processes whereby a fundamental social group (Gramsci speaks of alliances of class strata, not of a unitary and unproblematic 'ruling class'), which has achieved direction over the 'decisive economic nucleus,' is able to expand this into a moment of social, political and cultural leadership and authority throughout civil society and the state, attempting to unify and reconstruct the social formation around an organic tendency through a series of 'national tasks.'[93]

This expansion is not secured through coercion alone; consent and negotiation also play a part. In some respects, the adoption of terms such as *consent* and *negotiation* to describe the exercise of power raises as many problems as it solves. It restores a measure of agency to subordinate groups, but it also favours a kind of rational-choice Marxism whereby self-interested, exploited subjects negotiate the best possible deal they can in exchange for their willing participation in social structures. For example, Graeme Turner in his survey of British cultural studies argues that hegemony does not arise out of the manipulation of the masses; rather, 'the dominant group has to engage in negotiations with opposing groups, classes and values – and ... these negotiations must result in some *genuine* accommodation.'[94] A word like consent sets into motion an entire theoretical problematic oriented around the liberal subject. Such rationalist accounts of hegemony fail to capture the sense in which subordinate groups are persuaded to accept the hegemonic order not through logic but rather through the more fluid process of articulation. Connotative codes – *not* the logic of self-interest – arrange concepts and values into clusters, which are then accepted as a package: democracy, for example, invokes capitalism. Integration of a Freudian reading of mass culture might have helped counteract the creeping invasion of rationality into the hegemonic paradigm. Unfortunately, perhaps worried that any accommodation with Freud would signal an acceptance of Lacan, the Birmingham School largely fails to incorporate the psychodynamics of the Freudian paradigm into its work. A slightly better definition of hegemony relies on Williams's notion of determination, whereby hegemony is explained in spatial terms as the imposition of boundaries on social thought and action: 'A hegemonic order prescribes, not the specific content of ideas, but the *limits* within which ideas and conflicts move and are resolved.'[95] Yet once again we are left with an image of a static, fixed enclosure within which there is a considerable degree of real freedom.

The most sophisticated and interesting accounts of hegemony shift the focus away from the actions of rational agents towards the role of culture in establishing the very foundations of what is considered rational. They revolve around the idea that a dominant group will appropriate certain elements of subordinate social, cultural and political practices and articulate or connect them with its own objectives: 'Dominant culture gains a purchase ... not in being imposed, as an alien and external force, on to the cultures of subordinate groups, but by reaching into those cultures, reshaping them, hooking them, and, with them, the people whose consciousness and experience is defined in their terms, into an association with the values and ideologies of the ruling groups in society.'[96]

Within a hegemonic cultural formation, the individual elements of subordinate culture retain a distinct identity and presence; however, their political valences change as they are linked up with a very different set of values, beliefs, and objectives. In turn, these beliefs and objectives themselves join the ranks of common sense as they are associatively legitimized. The differentiated unity model is often invoked to describe a hegemonic cultural formation. Bourgeois culture, for example, is no longer conceived of as exclusively or purely bourgeois; instead, it is constituted out of a fluid set of practices that have been temporarily attached to a set of bourgeois social objectives. The goal and practice of politics is reconceived as the construction of (discursive) pathways between an explicit political project and popular cultural practices, rather than as the displacement of one set of ideas by another. These are 'organic' ideologies, and Hall argues that their essence lies in a network of connotative circuits. An organic ideology 'articulates into a configuration different subjects, different identities, different projects, different aspirations. It does not reflect, it constructs a "unity" out of difference.'[97] At one level, this returns us to the terrain of Barthes and his discussion of myth making: one of the primary effects of hegemony is to ensure that a particular set of ideological beliefs will be experienced as natural, normal, and inevitable. At another level, however, this dynamic is not unlike the one first diagnosed by Marx as operating through the processes of capitalist production: individuals are oppressed and tyrannized by their own social products, which return to them in an alien form. In terms of hegemony, the energies and values invested in popular cultural activities are harnessed to ideological formations that are often entirely unrelated and even opposed to the initial activity.

Notwithstanding the later appropriation of hegemony by American cultural studies, the construction and maintenance of a hegemonic formation does *not* occur through culture itself; this constitutes an important rejoinder to simplistic attacks on British cultural studies for endorsing a retreat from politics to culture. Culture furnishes the building blocks of hegemony, but the co-ordination of these blocks and their assembly into a coherent structure takes place elsewhere. Similarly, hegemony is not without an economic component but the possession of raw economic power is not automatically translated into social authority. Instead, hegemony is constituted through *political* activity. Only via the political moment can the economic dominance of a class be translated into a broad social and cultural leadership that is truly hegemonic: 'It is through politics that the "relation between common sense and the upper level of philosophy is assured."'[98] Consequently, the role of the state takes on a heightened importance. The state is the only entity through which a ruling group can organize and co-ordinate diverse social and cultural practices into a tightly woven hegemonic formation. 'Class interests,' notes Hall, 'are generalized in their passage through the mediation of the state: Gramsci refers to this process as "the decisive passage from the structure to the superstructure."'[99] In other words, the state translates economic power into cultural or ideological power, which in turn transforms the 'dull compulsion' of economic relations into the spontaneous consent of hegemony. Again, the mechanisms of this translation are governed by disjuncture, not by identity. Paradoxically, the only way for economic power to dominate other social processes is if its own force is sufficiently dislocated through politics as it passes from the 'structure to the superstructure.' Though the Birmingham School fervently rejects the class reductionism of traditional Marxism, it is interesting to observe the lingering influence of class on this model. Drawing from the (Althusserian) Marxist theory of the state pioneered by Nicos Poulantzas, Hall conceptualizes political power as propelled by the imperative of preserving the rule of the capitalist class, but needing a 'relative autonomy' from capitalism *per se* in order to do this effectively. The state is where the unity of the dominant ideology is constructed.[100] To put it another way, the dominance of capitalism is conceptualized through the rule of the capitalist class (or class alliance) rather than through the tyranny of the specific logic of capitalist social relations. A 'logic' cannot become hegemonic –

more accurately, it can only rule insofar as it is championed by a particular set of social interests.

This framework achieves prominence in the Birmingham School's analysis of the decline of social democratic hegemony in *Policing the Crisis* and, most notably, in Hall's work on the rise of Thatcherism in the 1980s. In many respects, *Policing the Crisis* champions an approach to social theory that is very different from earlier work on subcultures and the encoding/decoding model. It focuses mainly on how the state and its agents are able to use the media to impose a particular understanding of an event or process – in this case, 'mugging' – on the general public. In a period of social crisis, 'the mutual articulation of these two "relatively independent" agencies [state and media] is ... so overdetermined that it cannot work in any way other than to create *an effective ideological and control closure* around the issue. In this moment, the media – albeit unwittingly, and through their own "autonomous" routes – have become effectively an apparatus of the control process itself – an "ideological state apparatus."'[101]

Note the emphasis on closure. Unlike earlier texts, there is little investigation of how subordinate groups are able to resist or reinterpret conventional media accounts of an issue. Instead, attention is paid to how elements of working-class experience and culture (e.g., the value of work and self-discipline) are effectively hooked into the dominant ideology and then used to legitimate a law-and-order campaign. An increase in state coercion is both represented and perceived as the natural extension of individual morality and a perfectly acceptable means of controlling the rise of violent crime. The campaign, however, is not only deployed against marginal groups, but also mobilized by the *capitalist* state to discipline an increasingly militant working class. As such it is a perfect illustration of how an ideological campaign conducted through the media around one specific issue can be appropriated and used to justify a much broader range of state intervention. The analytic success of *Policing the Crisis* has convinced the CCCS that the key to unlocking the ideological impact of the media lies in the political sphere as *broadly* defined. Politics is not limited to debates about public policy or sporadic election battles. Rather, it is the place where state institutions – and most importantly, political organizations and campaigns, given their structural influence in the media – can intentionally appropriate popular cultural practices and values to cloak their own class-specific objectives in the language of general social interest.

The explanatory power of hegemony reaches its height in Hall's discussion of 'authoritarian populism' as a means of accounting for Thatcherism's apparent success in rewriting not only the rules of ideological and political discourse, but also the very terms of common sense.[102] As opposed to the narrow, economistic political vision attributed to the Labour Party and many others on the Left, Thatcher's Conservatives fully understand the significance of a broadly based cultural and ideological campaign that lays the foundations for hegemony in the colonization of civil society. For Hall, such a campaign constitutes further evidence of the polysemy of cultural and ideological fragments: the same basic element can be made to mean very different things depending on its articulation into a historically specific hegemonic formation. For example, the *connotative* linking of state and household budgets, between which there is no substantive logical basis for comparison, sponsors the dubious but widely accepted claim that it is simply good common sense for governments not to rely on deficit financing. Using tactics like this, Thatcherism constituted itself as an organic phenomenon by actively and deliberately rooting itself in popular culture, rather than simply trying to impose itself as an 'alien and external' set of ideas.

> It is possible for the right to construct a politics which does speak to people's experiences, which does insert itself into what Gramsci called the necessarily fragmentary, contradictory nature of common sense, which does resonate with some of their ordinary aspirations, and which, in certain circumstances can recoup them as subordinate subjects into a historical project which 'hegemonises' what we used – erroneously – to think of as their 'necessary class interests.'[103]

Accordingly, Hall asserts that 'the first thing to ask about an "organic" ideology that, however unexpectedly, succeeds in organizing substantial sections of the masses and mobilizing them for political action, is not what is *false* about it but what about it is *true*.'[104] The essays of this period accentuate the role of organized political action in the construction of hegemony: Thatcherism is not the effect of economic relations, but the deliberate product of an intentional, collective strategy. Although economic power is necessary for hegemonic rule, it is not a sufficient condition and certainly does little to help explain it. Only at the political level can such power be transformed into the broad leadership necessary to secure popular consent for radical social restructuring. This is the specificity of the political. Politics really does matter. Therefore, Hall insists that progressive social forces can and must learn from the experience of Thatcherism that the only way to build a counter-hegemonic opposition to capital is by conducting a similarly far-ranging 'war of position' within civil society.

So what does any of this have to do with culture and commodification? At one level, very little. It is notable that the commodification of culture virtually drops out of sight in *Policing the Crisis* before making a partial return in the work on Thatcherism. In the former case, this absence is entirely consistent with Hall's earlier claim that the commercial and ideological dynamics in the news media are two distinct processes that ought to be analysed separately. Sensationalized images of 'mugging,' for instance, may sell newspapers, but this fact hardly explains their ideological significance. Similarly, Hall acknowledges that a major component of Thatcher's hegemonic project was the connection of popular aspirations to a market economy, but the initiative for building this linkage is largely attributed to skilful ideological manoeuvring on the part of the New Right. The role of commodification in laying the *cultural* foundations for the construction of Thatcher's peculiar blend of neoliberal and neoconservative principles is never discussed.[105]

The commodity form finally (re)appears on the agenda of the Birmingham School in its exploration of the cultural and ideological implications that accompany the socioeconomic shift from Fordism to post-Fordism, euphemistically referred to as 'New Times.' As one commentator has noted, this paradigm does restore the role of economic developments in determining cultural phenomena.[106] However, it is a conception of economic processes that has itself already been thoroughly determined by structuralist semiotic principles. In other words, this restoration is little more than a tautology: semiotics in the guise of the economic returns to determine semiotics. While earlier work by the CCCS had generally been careful to distinguish between commodities and the meanings attached to them, the later paradigm tends to collapse the former into the latter. Consequently, cultural commodities *as commodities* are often defined as enabling a more diverse set of consumptive practices.[107] The emancipatory practices of the market itself are highlighted: 'If "people's capitalism" did not liberate the people, it nevertheless "loosed" many individuals into a life somewhat less constrained, less puritanically regulated, less strictly imposed than it had been three or four decades before.'[108] Although nominal recognition inevitably is given to the market's 'restrictive logic,' it is the capacity of the post-Fordist cultural industries to open up a wide variety of different cultural spaces that gets the most attention:

> These already allow those individuals who have some access to them some space in which to reassert a measure of choice and control over everyday life, and to 'play' with its more expressive dimensions. This 'pluralization' of social life expands the positionalities and identities available to ordinary people (at least in the industrialized world) in their everyday working, social, familial and sexual lives. Such opportunities need to be more, not less, widely available across the globe, and in ways not limited by private appropriation.[109]

Moreover, as the final sentence suggests, the limits of the cultural marketplace are conceptualized in terms of either access or direct control over the media. On the latter point, note Hall's rejoinder to the criticisms of New Times by a more orthodox Marxism: 'Have we become bewitched by *who*, in the short run, reaps the profit from these transactions (there are vast amounts of it being made), and missed the democratization of culture which is *also* potentially part of *their* hidden agenda?'[110] In a direct reversal of Adorno, the effect of commodification on the *form* of cultural products and consequently on the structures of experience of those who consume them is largely conceptualized in positive terms. Indeed, the Left itself is urged to adapt its own thought and practice so that it can compete effectively against the New Right on the cultural and ideological landscape that has been opened up by market forces.[111] Admittedly, the optimistic tone of many of the pieces written under the rubric of 'New Times' does not reflect the broader critical objectives of British cultural studies and should not be interpreted as representing it. Yet the intellectual flirtation of the Birmingham School with this celebratory mode – however brief or fleeting – speaks volumes about its failure to think critically about the commodification of culture.

In some respects, the hegemony paradigm represents an advance over the earlier subcultures model because it restores attention to the hermeneutic limitations imposed on cultural activity by its location within structures of power. Works such as *Policing the Crisis* explore culture's constitutive role in constructing and maintaining ideological domination in ways that simply were not available under the earlier theoretical paradigms. For example, it tempers an overoptimistic and celebratory conception of the freedom of decoding processes by asserting the need for organized and articulate counter-hegemonic forces to resist the ideological mechanisms of the state and the media. Furthermore, a focus on the molecular processes by which specific cultural practices can be 'hooked' into hegemonic formations is immensely suggestive as a way of thinking about the cooptive capacities of the culture industry. Yet the distinctive fashion in which the concept of hegemony is developed and applied by British cultural studies tends to prevent the use of this framework to study culture as commodity. Instead, the work on Thatcher and the rise of the New Right, coupled with passionate exhortations for the Left to learn from their successes, accents the collective intentionality with which a hegemonic formation is constructed. It is formed through the strategic actions – consciously hegemonic or otherwise – of a particular ruling alliance. It is not the result of a social process. Thus capitalism is said to be hegemonic only to the extent that dominant social interests are able to harness popular culture to it and thereby integrate it into the terms of common sense. In other words, culture and commodity are still defined separately and only come together as discrete processes through the mediation of the political. The principles that govern this (always tentative) union remain fundamentally unaffected by it: the extension of commodification to culture does not change in any significant way the rules according to which hegemony is constructed and secured. Above all, the polysemy of ideological and cultural elements remains the transcendent assumption of this model. Specific elements may be temporarily fixed into tendential articulations that make their recombination a more difficult task. But only the speed and/or effort required to erect or destroy a hegemonic formation is affected. The basic regime that governs this process does not change. Thus the inner laws of culture remain conceptually immunized against the predatory logic of the commodity form.

# 5
# Articulation and the Commodity Form: Rethinking Contemporary Cultural Studies

All reification is a forgetting.

Theodor Adorno to Walter Benjamin, *The Complete Correspondence*

In the past two decades, cultural studies has exploded out of Birmingham and taken up residence in a wide variety of disciplines and theoretical perspectives; each of these draws selectively from aspects of the CCCS legacy to invigorate its own intellectual practices. Simply 'defining' cultural studies has become a veritable industry unto itself; this labour has produced countless books and articles, each of which offers slightly different sets of principles for the study of culture. However, it is fair to say that at the core of this exercise in self-definition one finds most often the Birmingham School, in particular the work of Stuart Hall. Semiotic polysemy and the active, creative nature of cultural consumption – ideas to which the CCCS has long been committed – now serve as the central principles and values of contemporary cultural studies. Similarly, Gramscian hegemony, which is almost always read *through* Hall, has become the favoured theoretical framework, as it offers a means of balancing the freedom of subjects to take what they wish from culture against the constraints imposed on this process by dominant social forces.

The key concept that animates this framework is articulation.[1] Simply put, this refers to the organization of seemingly unrelated elements into a coherent formation by culture as well as by other social processes. Serving as a very loose theoretical problematic, it shifts analytic attention away from the essence or origin of cultural objects and practices toward their specific effects within historically contingent articulations. Besides marking the continuity between the CCCS and contemporary cultural studies, articulation also marks the site of key attempts to modify the earlier framework. One of the most significant of these attempts is Lawrence Grossberg's reorientation of cultural studies away from an exclusive concentration on culture toward the lines of effectivity that run between *all* social and material practices. Combining articulation with an emphasis on 'affect' grounds an investigation of the *asignifying* relations between people and cultural practices; this has the effect of decentring the semiotic template that plays such a dominant role in Birmingham. Clearly, Grossberg's theoretical framework has immense potential to (re)consider the question of culture as commodity in a way that had been effectively foreclosed by the earlier attention to the autonomy of cultural practices. Yet as much as Grossberg is willing to break with the Birmingham School in some areas, he remains well within its normative terrain in others, especially when he considers the relation between the commodity form and signification. Unfortunately, his reluctance to consider the economic in anything other than discursive terms tends to short-circuit his intriguing theoretical model when it comes to exploring the relation between culture and commodification. In the first half of this chapter I trace the genesis of articulation in Grossberg's work and sketch how it might be usefully developed as a means of theorizing cultural commodities. In the second half I look more directly at why this potential is not taken up; I do so through a more general discussion of how and why cultural studies marginalizes commodification as largely irrelevant for the analysis of contemporary culture. The respective positions of critical theory and cultural studies on semiotic polysemy and active cultural consumption frame an encounter between these two traditions – one that attends to their principal theoretical differences and to those issues on which a more co-operative intellectual exchange remains possible.

One brief observation before we begin. The debate between cultural studies and political economy has pushed critical theory even deeper into obscurity and irrelevance than it had been for the Birmingham scholars.[2] One might expect that attempts by cultural studies to define itself in the context of its emergence as a field of specialization would have sponsored a more systematic re-examination of the theoretical antecedents *and* antagonists of British cultural studies. Yet, following the lead set by the CCCS, the culture industry thesis is for the most part nowhere to be found. Paraphrasing Williams's earlier words, John Fiske notes in exemplary fashion that 'there is no mass culture, there are only alarmist and pessimistic theories of mass culture that, at their best, can shed light only on the industrial and ideological imperatives of the power-bloc, but none at all on the cultural processes by which the people cope with them and either reject them or turn them into popular culture.'[3] While Fiske's work is more exaggerated than most regarding the cultural autonomy of audiences, most within cultural studies would probably agree with the sentiment behind these words. Since the criticisms that cultural studies directs against the Frankfurt School simply recycle those of the CCCS, we need not revisit them again here. That said, one approach worthy of a brief mention is the occasional attempt to read Adorno in a postmodern vein as a kind of Jean Baudrillard *avant la lettre*. For example, a one-time member of the Birmingham School who has gradually moved into a postmodern orbit writes that

> it is possible to discern in the sheen of Baudrillard's breathless prose the unmistakable echoes of a critical configuration that resonates with Lukacs, the Frankfurt School, the Situationists and the vocabulary of alienated consciousness. Pushed to its logical limit, the commodification of the world – the 'hyper-reality' of a totally alienated social existence – comes to its final steady-state in the simulacrum: use values are obliterated in an incessant exchange of signs that bear 'no relation to reality whatsoever.'[4]

Similarly, Robert Miklitsch counsels a reading of Adorno's references to 'pure exchange-value' as sign value – another obvious reference to Baudrillard's simulacrum.[5] However, this smooth transpositioning of exchange-value into semiotics is symptomatic of the lingering dominance of the specificity framework. For Adorno, the triumph of exchange-value does not mark a complete disjuncture from 'reality,' but rather its utter triumph. Far from enabling an 'incessant exchange of signs,' the commodity form actually shuts down such an exchange. It cripples the capacity of the sign (culture) to *mediate* reality – or, more properly, to bring the mediated nature of reality to a consciousness that now only experiences such mediations as pure immediacy and thereby secures enough critical distance for semiotic and cultural systems to function. In short, attempts to 'save' Adorno by reading him through Baudrillard do a gross injustice to his work on mass culture by conjuring away its central thrust – namely, culture *as commodity*.

## Decentring Signification: Articulation and the Reframing of Cultural Studies

Ernesto Laclau's *Politics and Ideology in Marxist Theory* represents the first explicit attempt to develop a theory of articulation. In the course of trying to explain the social dynamic behind both fascism and populism, Laclau argues that ideological formations must be understood, not in their totality as inherently bourgeois or proletarian, but rather as comprising various elements from the national-popular culture that have been brought together, or articulated, with particular interests. To use one of his favourite examples, nationalism can be articulated just as easily with working-class ideologies as with those of the bourgeoisie. One must, he argues, '*accept that ideological "elements" taken in isolation have no necessary class connotation, and that this connotation is only the result of the articulation of those elements in a concrete ideological discourse. This means that the precondition for analyzing the class nature of an ideology is to conduct the inquiry through that which constitutes the distinctive unity of an ideological discourse.*'[6] To claim otherwise is to fall into the pit of class reductionism – that is, to attribute an inevitable class 'belonging' or essence to particular concepts or practices. He diagnoses the rise of Italian and German fascism as a consequence of working-class organizations making just such a mistake; the refusal of the latter to adopt a more nationalist focus allowed the fascists to successfully articulate nationalism – an ideological 'element' that played a key role in the 'constitution' of the German and Italian people – together with the interests of monopoly capital.

Borrowing heavily from Althusser, Laclau explains that the assembly of disparate fragments into a coherent ideological formation is governed by interpellative processes. A unified ideology is constructed by clustering certain subject-positions into an associative chain in such a way that the adoption of any one position evokes all of the others. In the case of Nazi Germany, for example, these different positions were fused together in the production of a singular fascist subjectivity: to be a father, a husband, a worker, a patriot, a soldier, was simultaneously to be a national socialist, or at the very least to be strongly pulled in that direction. The Nazi regime, by embedding itself and its cultural symbols in the social and material practices that interpellated real individuals as fathers, husbands, workers, patriots, and soldiers, succeeded in co-ordinating the cognitive and emotional investments solicited by these practices and linking them back to itself. Drawing from psychoanalysis, Laclau describes this process as a form of condensation: 'a single operation represents itself in many associative chains at the intersection of which it is situated. From the economic point of view it is then invested with energies which, attached to those different chains, add to it.'[7] In terms of ideology, certain practices are bound together insofar as the energies from each can be associatively transferred along a chain of signifiers to cumulatively build and condense into one element. There is no logical connection between these signifiers; instead, synthetic codes are generated through cultural and ideological strategies that connotatively suture otherwise unconnected elements together into a specific ideological formation. For Laclau, it is this molecular process, rather than the clash of preformed class or other perspectives, that constitutes the essence of ideological struggle. Still working within a Marxist paradigm at this point, he conceptualizes such struggle as the attempt by different classes to 'charge' their own political projects by discursively connecting them to various elements, values, and subject-positions within civil society.

The potential to create new ideological formations varies with the stability of a social formation. Under normal or stable circumstances, one of the main functions of dominant ideologies is to *dis*organize the relations between the different subject-positions inhabited by subordinate groups. This enables concrete individuals to 'live' a wide variety of social practices without actually 'experiencing' the contradictions within and between them:

> The ideology of dominant classes not only interpellates dominant subjects but also dominated classes, with the effect of neutralising their potential antagonism ... The basic method of this neutralisation lies in a transformation of all antagonism into simple difference. The articulation of popular-democratic ideologies within the dominant discourse consists in an absorption of everything in it which is a simple differential particularity and a repression of those elements which tend to transform the particularity into a symbol of antagonism.[8]

Accordingly, the psychoanalytic principle that governs this process is displacement rather than condensation. In other words, the authority of a dominant ideology is secured in part through its transformation of contradiction into serialized difference. This makes it unlikely that subordinate subject-positions will fuse together into a ruptural or oppositional unity. However, such displacements are vulnerable to the tendency of social crises to exacerbate cultural, political, and economic contradictions, making it more and more difficult to slide unproblematically from position to position. As displacement mechanisms are weakened, the possibility grows that the contradictions between these different positions will actually be recognized and lived, breaking apart the ideological formation in which they had previously been contained. In such cases, conditions are ripe for the construction of a new formation that can, once again, offer subjective coherence by binding different subject-positions and their associated values and practices together into a stable network or chain. Living social and material contradictions *as contradictions* produces an experience that is both displeasurable and dysfunctional; consequently, people are eager for ideological strategies that, either through an 'active' condensation or a 'passive' displacement, allow them to manage these contradictions more effectively.

Laclau's work on articulation is adopted enthusiastically by Hall and by other members of the Birmingham School as adding theoretical depth and complexity to Gramsci's account of hegemony. It sponsors the selective assembly of elements from Barthes (connotation), Althusser (interpellation; differential unity) and Volosinov (polysemy) into a more or less coherent retheorization of how hegemonic formations are constructed, maintained, and destroyed. It directs attention to the molecular practices through which discrete and diverse ideological elements are assembled into an operational unity. As defined by Hall, 'a theory of articulation is both a way of understanding how ideological elements come, under certain conditions, to cohere together within a discourse, and a way of asking how they do or do not become articulated, at specific conjunctures, to certain political subjects.'[9] Despite the expansive and often nebulous terms often used by Hall – practices, structures, relations, and so on – *discursive* principles such as polysemy and connotation clearly have the upper hand in this process. Cultural strategies bind ideological elements into a connotative network, establishing the coherence of the formation, enabling the condensation of interpellative investments, and channelling them into support for a ruling alliance. Just as Laclau describes the connections between subject positions in a fascist identity, Hall similarly explains Thatcher's appeal:

> The whole discourse of Thatcherism combines ideological elements into a discursive chain in such a way that the logic or unity of the discourse depends on the subject addressed assuming a number of specific subject positions. The discourse can only be read or spoken unproblematically if it is enunciated from the imaginary position of knowledge of the self-reliant, self-interested, self-sufficient taxpayer; ... or the subject passionately attached to individual liberty and passionately opposed to the incursion of liberty that occurs through the state; or the respectable housewife; or the native Briton.[10]

Hall makes extensive use of articulation to chart the transition in the United Kingdom from social democratic hegemony to the triumph of the Conservative Party in the 1980s. Thatcherism did not impose a preconstituted neoliberal ideology on the British people. Instead, it capitalized on the economic crises of the 1970s to disarticulate social democratic discourse, pulling elements out of their previous associative paths within that discourse and then reconnecting them to its own transformative political project. For Hall, the unique characteristics of Thatcher's rise to power confirm the conjunctural bias of cultural studies: ideologies do not 'reflect' a broader social logic, as Marxist class reductionism claims; rather, they are produced through the arrangement of distinct elements into a singular formation that must be analysed in terms of its specificity.

Hall is always quite careful to distinguish his use of articulation from that of scholars who exaggerate the ease with which ideological formations can be discursively deconstructed and reconstructed. For example, he distances himself from Laclau's decidedly post-structuralist collaboration with Chantal Mouffe in *Hegemony and Socialist Strategy*.[11] Ideological elements cannot be freely arranged and rearranged in an infinite plurality of ways; instead, they have a 'tendential alignment' depending on how they have been historically articulated with certain classes or groups: 'Traditional couplings, or "traces" as Gramsci called them, exert a powerful traditional force over the ways in which subsequent discourses, employing the same elements can be developed. They give such terms, not an absolutely determined class character, but a tendential class articulation.'[12] Such alignments make it even more necessary to analyse every articulation in its historical specificity, and not as an abstract, isolated phenomenon. Ideological elements are *always* articulated in particular ways that frame the extent to which they can be disarticulated and integrated with other elements in new ways. In the case of British patriotism, 'ideas of "national identity" and "national greatness" are intimately bound up with imperial supremacy, tinged with racist connotations, and underpinned by a four-century-long history of colonization, world market supremacy, imperial expansion and global destiny over native peoples. It is therefore much more difficult to give the notion of "Britain" a socially radical or democratic reference.'[13]

Once again, however, such claims tend to remain at the level of signification. Admittedly, hegemony is framed quite broadly as the combination of ideological elements, cultural practices, institutional structures, political forces, and economic relations. Yet the linkages that bind these different things together are conceptualized discursively. As an analytic device, articulation is largely confined to exploring how the semiotic aspects of various practices are networked together to form the differentiated unity of an ideological formation. Even when their effects are dispersed through the entire social formation, the articulatory circuits that bind disparate elements together are formed, 'energized,' and regulated by systems of signification. The broader relations of these networks to other kinds of practices remain relatively undertheorized. Culture, ideology, and language do not constitute the entirety of hegemony; that said, they do monopolize the venue through which political, economic, or social power is transformed into a hegemonic formation.

Grossberg identifies this lingering obsession with signifying practices as one of the greatest problems facing a postmodern cultural studies. Instead of fingering Althusserian structuralism as the main culprit for this tendency, he traces its genealogy through the adoption of a communicative model that surreptitiously locates cultural studies within a Kantian philosophical paradigm. Replacing ontology with epistemology, this paradigm elevates culture into something that inevitably *stands between* and therefore *determines* the relationship between human beings and reality: 'Following the idealist tradition of modern philosophy and social thought, "the real" – the material conditions of possibility and of effectivity, the material organization and consequences of life – disappears into culture, and social life is reduced to experience. All cultural studies has to worry about is culture!'[14] On the one hand, this confines cultural analysis to the production of meaning through structures and processes of signification. The mapping of the effects of culture on the social formation is limited to describing how culture enables people to interpret and understand their social and material existence in meaningful and, occasionally, pleasurable ways. Isolated to this hermeneutic plane, cultural studies tends to collapse the world into a series of texts, or – at the very least – it argues that the world only registers on experience as it is transformed into a text or passes through language. At the same time, an immense efficacy is attributed to signifying practices, which are given a monopoly over the generation of experience; as a result, power and subjectivity are theorized as the products of these practices, governed by their own discrete laws. This theoretical move 'installs the primacy of signification (with its logic of identity and difference) over power (with its logic of determination). It reduces the entire project of cultural studies to the admittedly important political and contextual struggle to put questions of ideology (signification, representation, and identity) on the agenda.'[15] The role of other structures and relations in directly generating these kinds of social effects is either ignored or subordinated via the architectonic mediating function of culture. This valorization of cultural practices, argues Grossberg, can inspire not only celebratory excess, but also the belief that semiotic action – often romanticized in the terms of guerrilla warfare – constitutes a sufficient, emancipatory, and/or transformative form of politics.

In its place, he proposes a 'postmodern materialism' that locates signification within a much broader theoretical framework, treating it as only one of a broad range of social practices that produce the 'real.' Drawing from the work of Michel Foucault, Gilles Deleuze, and Felix Guattari, Grossberg argues that these thinkers displace the Kantian paradigm by dissolving the distinction between ontology and epistemology, preferring instead to conceptualize reality as an interlocking series of events that are themselves the effects of a radically heterogeneous and fluid array of apparatuses and practices. According to Foucault:

> It is not a question of putting everything on a certain plane, that of the event, but of seeing clearly that there exists a whole series of levels of different types of events, which do not have the same range, nor the same chronological breadth, nor the same capacity to produce effects. The problem is to both distinguish the events, differentiate the networks and levels to which they belong, and to reconstitute the threads which connect them and make them give rise to one another.[16]

From Deleuze and Guattari, Grossberg takes 'rhizomatics,' 'a strategy of drawing lines or connections' that fixes events and practices in hierarchical structures and at the same time constructs avenues that temporarily enable subjects to escape them:

> What these lines represent are the productive links between points within a multidimensional and multidirectional field ... 'Lines of intensity' map out reality in terms of the productive relations between the points linked. Productivity is synonymous with effects or, more accurately, 'effectivities.' That is, something exists as an object related to other objects only in its multifarious effects at other points and their effects at the point of its apparent locus ... But the description of any point cannot be confined to a particular 'regime' or domain of effects, such as the signifying. Lines must always be drawn between disparate regimes of effects.[17]

Cartographic metaphors abound as the emphasis of cultural studies moves away from interpreting events or processes as they pass through language and culture, becoming meaningful, toward the mapping of their effectivity – that is, the tracing of their intersection with all other parts of the social formation on which they have effects and/or that exert effects on them. Most importantly for Grossberg, these effects are not predefined in semiotic terms. Rather, the specificity of the cultural 'is shattered into the plurality of regimes of effects traversing it and its place within an organization of power.'[18] In this way the polarity of cultural studies is quite literally reversed; it switches from the inner laws of signifying systems to the multiplicity of relations – conceptualized in terms of reciprocal effects – that culture has with/upon other structures and practices. According to this analytic logic, the most innovative and useful studies of culture may not actually end up describing culture at all; instead, they may chart its effects on and constitution by other aspects of the social formation.

Notwithstanding the value of materialist postmodernism as a means for breaking out of the semiotic restrictions imposed by the specificity/communications paradigm, Grossberg is wary of its tendency to emphasize the heterogeneity of micropolitical practices and the irreducible specificity of individual events, thereby exaggerating the differences between and isolation of different social processes. Consequently, he mobilizes articulation as a form of constructive logic, expanding its conceptual reach beyond ideology to describe how practices and events are always fixed within much broader structures: 'Articulation is the production of identity on top of difference, of unities out of fragments, of structures across practices. Articulation links this practice to that effect, this text to that meaning, this meaning to that reality, this experience to those politics. And these links are themselves articulated into larger structures, etc.'[19]

In the words of Jameson, articulation serves as 'a punctual and sometimes even ephemeral totalization.'[20] Given his sympathies with postmodernism, Grossberg is highly suspicious of any association between articulation and totality, claiming at one point with formulaic modesty that cultural studies 'has no pretensions to totality or universality.'[21] Perhaps it is more accurate to say that the conceptual totalities or unities constructed through articulation are predominantly spatial rather than temporal, historically contingent rather than teleologically determined, and constructed from the bottom up rather than from the top down. Grossberg argues that the effects of cultural objects and practices are never determined by their origins – the mistaken assumption of both classical Marxism and traditional communications studies – but can only be adduced by looking to the specific contexts in which they are embedded from moment to historical moment.

Context no longer merely introduces the analysis of a specific object or process, fading into the background as more substantive attention is focused on the phenomenon itself. Instead, an alternative analytic sequence is prescribed: one starts by investigating a phenomenon as a radical singularity; then, using this as a base, one methodically traces all of its lines of connection with other phenomena in ever-expanding concentric circles. Thus, framing the context of an issue in the broadest possible terms constitutes the final objective or endpoint of a critical investigation. As compared with the framework handed down by the Birmingham School, this analytic mode involves switching from a principally horizontal or temporal focus on the logic of a single social process – signification – over a period of time to a vertical or spatio-social orientation in which the reciprocal effects of different kinds of social processes on one another within a historical conjuncture are described. To take a very simple example, instead of following the fate of a message over time as it is encoded and decoded, it is conceptualized as an effect of a constellation of structures and practices, both signifying *and* asignifying, which in turn have effects on other structures and practices. As they radiate outwards from single points of origin, these conceptual articulations may grow to touch on all aspects of a social formation. Yet like Foucault, Grossberg believes that the multiplicity of these points, their bottom-up orientation, and the reciprocity of the determinations they describe, all serve to protect these kinds of contingent totalities from the dangers of a conceptual and identitarian totalitarianism that reifies a complex reality and in doing so transforms it into a singular, functional theoretical system.

In expanding the definition of culture beyond the boundaries of signifying systems, Grossberg invokes the concept of affect to highlight the fact that culture does more than simply give meaning to lived experience. It also determines how and why certain beliefs or practices come to matter or to feel important to an individual or a particular group. Although affect is never defined with any taxonomic precision in Grossberg's work, it is loosely visualized in Freudian terms as a kind of non-libidinal psychic energy. Essentially, it regulates the relations between somatic, libidinal, and cognitive structures, thus establishing the extent to which one is able to 'invest' oneself in and therefore care about a particular experience, practice, meaning, or pleasure. Grossberg refers to these patterns as 'mattering maps' that '"tell" people how to use and how to generate energy, how to navigate their way into and through various moods and passions, and how to live within emotional and ideological histories.'[22] For example, ideologies do not become effective simply through the dispersal of concepts, ideas, and signs that logically express the interests of certain segments of the population; rather, people must actively connect themselves to an ideological formation through the plane of affect. In other words, the effectivity of signification and discourse is located within a broader social matrix in which signs and concepts must be actively and continuously made to matter: 'Affect has a real power over difference, a power to invest difference and to make certain differences matter in different ways. If ideology and even pleasure constitute structures of difference, these structures are unrealized without their inflection through an affective economy.'[23] Popular culture is the pre-eminent domain for generating affective energies. In part, this is because of how it 'often inscribes its effects directly upon the body: tears, laughter, hair-tingling, screams, spine-chilling, eye-closing, erections, etc. These visceral responses, which often seem beyond our conscious control, are the first mark of a work of popular culture: it is sentimental, emotional, moody, exciting, prurient, carnivalesque, etc.'[24] The endless mobilization of expectations that bypass cognitive processes and their mechanisms of reality testing and/or rational evaluation sponsors an experiential framework in which the dominant sensation, emotion, or mood corporealizes possibility itself. As Hollywood never stops reminding us in a well-worn but uncannily apt cliché, it is the place where dreams are made. In this sense, affect is perhaps best understood as a quantity of 'potentializing' energy that activates a willingness and desire to become emotionally involved in a particular process or connected to a certain object because of the possibilities it represents.[25]

Affective energies are generated largely through culture but are not confined to culture. Instead, articulatory networks enable their associative transfer and condensation at various sites throughout the social formation. As connections are formed among local cultural practices, 'affective alliances' are formed: 'an organization of concrete material practices and events, cultural forms, and social experience that both opens up and structures the space of our affective investments in the world.'[26] In turn, paths may be cleared between such alliances and more explicit political projects, as was the case in the 1960s with the 'rock formation' and social protest. Such linkages energize political activity, renewing it as a space of collective possibility in which individuals can invest at a visceral and emotional level; this substantially increases the scale of commitment that accompanies the motivation beyond that inspired only by rational self-interest. These investments may temporarily move ideological structures and beliefs beyond the sphere of signification, beyond discourse, and, it follows, beyond rational assessment or logical debate. In fact, articulation helps explain why – despite the frequent absence of direct, rational, self-interested connections between people and ideological formations – powerful bonds may exist between certain individuals and particular political positions. To describe how individuals are connected to, and connect *themselves* to, affective flows, Grossberg draws from the framework of interpellation used by Althusser, Laclau, and Hall. Subject-positions do not function simply as entry points into discursive structures that regulate intelligible or meaningful participation in social practices; they also mark nodal positions in networks of affect. Thus, taking up one of these positions allows individuals to hook themselves into affective flows; this in turn enables certain activities or beliefs to matter to them, thereby establishing the basis not only for individual and collective identity but also for inspired, passionate, and self-directed action (i.e., will). However, the articulated nature of these flows means that they may carry an individual to a variety of other 'sites,' irrespective of the political valence or lack thereof implied in the initial subject-position or those practices immediately or directly associated with it.

Articulations, however, can do more than construct pathways that enable the flow of affective energies; they may also have the reverse effect of blocking the passage of affect from culture to the political or economic sphere. Grossberg describes the essence of neoconservative hegemony in the United States in precisely these terms. He agrees with Hall that the political and cultural leadership of Thatcherism was secured by reconstructing common sense via its articulation to conservative social ideology on the one hand, and neoliberal economic doctrine on the other; however, he locates the rise of the American New Right in a somewhat different cultural logic. As discussed earlier, the power of popular culture to produce affect is rooted in its capacity to deliver an experience of kinetic potentiality that offers people an alternative to the boredom of the everyday. For example, in rhizomatic terms, rock music

> draws or produces 'lines of flight' which transform the boredom of the repetition of everyday life into the energizing possibilities of fun. It creates temporary and local places and spaces of mobility and deterritorialization. It challenges the particular stabilities or territorializations of the everyday life within which it exists by producing and celebrating mobilities ... Although it cannot break out of everyday life, the trajectory of its mobilities at least points to (even if it cannot define) a world beyond, an alternative to, everyday life.[27]

In the past two decades, however, neoconservative attacks on contemporary culture, and their success in framing it in certain ways, have effectively bent these 'lines of flight' back on themselves, surreptitiously channelling affective energies into a closed, tautological circuit from which there is no exit. Grossberg calls this 'disciplined mobilization' or 'structured mobility': 'The result is the construction and celebration of an apparently unconstrained mobility that is nothing but a principle of constraint.'[28] As flows of affect double back on themselves, other sites in the social formation – most notably the state and the economy – are effectively insulated against and even erased from the mattering maps of many people.

This isolation of affect from conventional political activity is part of a broader social logic that Grossberg identifies as the central characteristic of postmodernity:

> The postmodern condition manifests the increasingly distant and precarious relations between affect on the one hand and ideology and desire on the other. It reflects the historical appearance of an expanding series of

> ruptures or gaps between these planes, between the available meanings, values and objects of desire which socially organize our existence and identity, and the possibilities for affectively investing in them.[29]

In other words, the differences constructed through ideological structures and libidinal economies (i.e., the pleasures that attend the discharge of libido onto *this* rather than *that* object or process) are no longer co-ordinated with flows of affect. It is not so much that nothing matters, but that it is increasingly difficult to use these other systems to define what matters. Affect as an anaclitic energy that depends on a coupling with ideological or libidinal structures is replaced by affect as free-floating. Yet just as libidinal energy must be sporadically discharged, so too must affect. People still have to find places, things, and practices that matter. In the absence of fixed circuits and stable sites of investment that enable affective flows to charge complex forms of thought and action, popular habits of cultural and political consumption become significantly more mobile, as driven by the endless need to find places where affect can be released before those places too collapse under waves of indifference. Reagan's popularity, argues Grossberg, serves as striking evidence of the pervasiveness of this dynamic. The former president's appeal lay mainly in his ability to reconstitute the nation as a site of affective, *and only affective,* investment: 'America must have a center to which we are absolutely committed, but that center must remain empty. This is a nationalism with no content.'[30] Even though most Americans explicitly disagreed with his policies, they were drawn to him because his exemplary dedication to the United States reconstituted the nation *through* him as an idea that could once again matter to them.

As a speculative theoretical framework, Grossberg's work on articulation makes it possible for us to investigate the relations between commodification and culture by breaking with the hegemony of signification installed by British cultural studies. According to the logic of articulation, the rapid expansion of capitalist relations and practices into all areas of social life – including, increasingly, cultural production – should place them high on the analytic agenda of an intellectual practice whose aim is to map all of the lines of connection between particular phenomena and external structures and practices. The assumption that these lines of connection may cross the boundaries that mark off one type of practice from another (e.g., economic from affective, ideological, or libidinal) opens up the possibility that the commodity form may exercise a *direct* influence over the structures of meaning, pleasure, and desire that ground how people experience and think about their social and material existence: 'Cultural practices must be located not only in a context within which social facts determine interpretations and vice versa, but in other regimes in which texts have asignifying effects and are determined through asignifying practices. The result is that, rather than locating power in the context of signification, signification is to be located in the context of relations of power.'[31] In particular, the vaunted commitment of cultural studies to semiotic polysemy and to the active, creative nature of cultural consumption can no longer form the (unexamined) basis of that discipline's investigative practices. More importantly, locating the presence of these in a certain cultural event or practice can no longer automatically invoke a normative code that describes them as markers for human agency and/or resistance to hegemony. The actual effects of polysemy and cultural agency must be mapped out in order to be evaluated; not only that, but their own constitution must be assessed in terms of other social practices. In particular, this ought to produce a much more direct and systematic reckoning with commodification – the 'context' in which practically all contemporary cultural activity is located – than has tended to appear in cultural studies.

Articulation also provides a useful framework for both expressing and exploring the ambiguities of popular culture as it is located within the totality of the social formation. If a cultural activity is analysed on a single plane, that of signification, the evaluation of its effects will also tend to be charted out in a single dimension. For example, it may enable semiotic polysemy for an individual or group or, alternatively, it may effectively enforce a preferred reading/decoding. Even those analyses which are highly attuned to the potential of semiotic resistance to be integrated into a hegemonic formation tend to conceptualize these moments in serial or temporal sequence. Punk, for instance, was oppositional for a brief time but was then co-opted by commercial processes. Articulation, on the other hand, enables us to think through these moments simultaneously: that which enables resistance at one level may, in fact, feed into and reinforce the larger structures of domination against which such resistance is actually directed:

> Popular culture can be an important source of empowerment in a number of different ways. So can struggles over the politics of everyday life. But this 'empowerment' (even when it involves struggles) is caught up within the disciplined mobilization of everyday life, so that the very activities

> which empower us – in fact, the very forms of empowerment – become partly responsible for the disciplined mobilization itself. Empowerment becomes politically disabling, a weapon to be used against people. The very practices which empower people in everyday life also disempower them by rendering them unable to get out of everyday life itself.[32]

Unfortunately, this conception of cultural practices as overdetermined can sometimes collapse into the banal caveat that culture will always contain equal proportions of resistance and domination, never constituting either total control or total freedom. However, to the extent that articulation connects the pleasures and meanings of popular culture to the structures of capitalism, it enables us to begin exploring how they may be directly grafted onto the commodity form. More radically, it opens up theoretical space to speculate on how such pleasures and meanings may actually be caused or facilitated by commodification itself as it exercises a molecular control over the techniques and aesthetic values of cultural production that establish certain pleasures and meanings (e.g., those of identification) as socially dominant. The potential affinities with the culture industry thesis are, I think, obvious. This is not to suggest that articulation necessarily leads cultural studies in this direction: if Grossberg's work is any indication, it certainly does *not*, and he would doubtless oppose strongly any attempt to situate his own theoretical models in proximity with Adorno. My point, rather, is that the theoretical boundaries of articulation as a mode of social theorizing do not close off cultural studies to critical theory – and its concern with commodification – in the same fashion as the problematic developed by Birmingham.

Symptomatic of this potential compatibility is a similarity between Grossberg's exploration of the 'rock formation' and Adorno and Benjamin's more general comments on the relationship between work, leisure, and culture. Grossberg persuasively argues that one of the key attractions of rock music for youth is its capacity to reconstitute negative experiences of everyday life into opportunities for celebration and affective investment. Thus, in place of emphasizing the differences between culture and more repressive social structures – which the Birmingham School tends to do – Grossberg highlights their similarities:

> Rock and roll does not turn anger, boredom, despair, and so on into pleasure. Rather it turns the material basis of such experiences (repetition, noise, anonymity, etc.) into the occasion for pleasure. It is this reversal that

> is the source of the empowerment, that enables one to find power in, for example, one's anonymity, or pleasure in the repetitiveness constitutive of rock and roll. This process echoes Freud's repetition compulsion: 'the traumatic event is repeated not in spite of the unpleasure that is attached to it, but on account of this very unpleasure.'[33]

Contemporary cultural practices increasingly do not represent an 'escape' from the drudgery of everyday life in any substantive, structural sense; instead, they reproduce its boredom and repetition within a different affective economy that enables these dominant patterns to serve as 'the occasion for pleasure.' According to Freud, one of the primary motives for the repetition compulsion is the desire, always frustrated, to master stimuli retroactively that are initially experienced without an adequate form of psychic protection.[34] Placing popular culture in this context invokes some strong parallels with critical theory's conception of commodified culture as involving a mimetic response and adaptation to a reified social world. It also replicates the tone of Adorno's argument that 'the only escape from the work process in factory and office is through adaptation to it in leisure time.'[35] Obviously, many differences remain between Grossberg and critical theory: where the former often marvels at the ability of culture to achieve such an effect, the latter are unabashedly horrified. These differential normative inflections register very different theoretical assumptions and objectives. Nevertheless, the similarities remain highly suggestive and indicate the possibility of using articulation to explore some of the same themes highlighted by the culture industry thesis.

In fact, articulation could be used to investigate commodification itself as one of the pre-eminent 'territorializing machines' of the postmodern social formation: 'A territorializing machine produces lines of specific vectors, intensities, and densities that differentially enable and enact specific forms of mobility and stability, specific lines of investment (or anchoring) and flight. It maps the ways in which people live the always limited freedom to stop in and move through a field of force.'[36] Earlier I discussed how rhizomatics is primarily a strategy for drawing or illuminating the lines of connection between different events and practices. While such linkages are often viewed through a semiotic lens, expanding analytic possibilities beyond the territory of the sign drops into bold relief the articulatory networks that capitalism constructs to regulate the circulation of and relations between objects, people, practices, and structures. The systematic eradication of use-value by exchange-value brings together unlike objects and activities into a web of equivalence on a truly massive, world-historical scale. First, this creates very specific conditions that govern the formation of affective alliances – namely, profit and the need to realize exchange-value (or to use Adorno's philosophical term, identity). Given the growing dominance of the commodity form, there is little chance that any objects or practices which are fundamentally incompatible with it will be given the space or resources to become a coherent formation. Second, the subsumption of specificities beneath the predatory logic of identity means that it becomes much easier to form connective links along these pathways. Commodification dramatically expands the possibilities for articulation by maximizing the chances for a smooth interface between different kinds of objects and practices. As culture is increasingly designed and created with an eye to convergence and 'synergistic' combination, a particular kind of articulation subtended by the commodity form becomes almost impossible to avoid. Third, the cognitive processes and affective/libidinal energies that flow through these circuits are engaged in a reciprocal exchange with them. On the one hand, a condition of smooth passage is that they adjust themselves to the particular demands and restrictions imposed by the commodity form and its identitarian logic. On the other hand, commodification and identity extract a 'toll' for this passage and are themselves surreptitiously charged with affective/libidinal energies, as well as being cognitively valorized.

The most obvious manifestation of this form of articulation is contemporary advertising. A multibillion dollar industry, advertising is dedicated to one basic objective: fusing commodities to culture that connotes a wide variety of desirable themes such as happiness, freedom, pleasure, and power. It constitutes the most systematic, far-reaching, and energetic attempt ever mounted to manufacture articulated unities on a global, industrial scale. Advertisers hope to (literally) capitalize on culture's ability to generate, in affective terms, an experience of potentiality and empowerment. Sounds, images, and (more rarely) texts that signify these experiences are creatively juxtaposed with particular commodities or brands, which are thereby represented as the requisite catalysts for energizing possibility itself. The expectation is that the affective, libidinal, and/or cognitive significance marked by the original experience can be associatively attached to the advertised good or service:

> It's worth remembering that the branding process begins with a group of people sitting around a table trying to conjure up an ideal image; they toss around words like 'free,' 'independent,' 'rugged,' 'comfortable,' 'intelligent,' 'hip.' They then set out to find real-world ways to embody those ideas and attributes, first through marketing, then through retail environments like superstores and coffee chains, then – if they are really cutting edge – through total lifestyle experiences like theme parks, lodges, cruiseships and towns.[37]

This form of commercialized montage proceeds at an ever accelerating rate, given the increasing pace at which cultural signifiers are being harvested and depleted.[38] However, advertising not only scavenges among the meanings and pleasures of other cultural activities, but also influences them. Most obviously, it erodes their authenticity as the cynicism directed toward the culture industry rebounds back onto that which it devours. More ominously, though, it also performs an articulation on these activities. Co-ordinated campaigns, for example, organize individual ads into 'lifestyle' formations in which the purchase of a single commodity necessarily activates an entire chain of activities – directly consumptive or otherwise – that are advertised as the requisite complement to that purchase. These activities attain their unity through the creation of subject-positions that position individuals as the authors of their own actions that enable meaningful and pleasurable forms of experience or social interaction. Yet this unity is, in fact, orchestrated by the commodity form itself as it harmonizes each of these activities through its passage into exchange-value.

In this respect, articulation constitutes the *raison d'être* of advertising. Linking a broad range of images, practices, and feelings with specific objects and activities is precisely what advertising tries to achieve. And the reach of these articulatory networks does not stop with the ads themselves – indeed, they represent only the proverbial tip of the iceberg. Marketing as a process has now penetrated to the very core of production and stands as a dominant influence in the conception and design of any new product.[39] Its tyranny is especially pronounced in the cultural industries, in which there are no physical functions that a cultural object must simultaneously perform. Andrew Wernick explains that 'when a piece of music, or a newspaper article, or even an academically written book about promotional culture, is fashioned with an eye to how it will promote itself – and, indeed, how it will promote its author and distributor, together with all the other products these named agencies may be identified with – such goods are affected by this circumstance in every detail of their production.'[40]

Advertising's effective colonization of practically every visible space in advanced capitalist countries means that these marketing cues embedded in objects are not discretely offered to the consumer, who can do with them as he or she likes after the moment of purchase. Instead, they constitute a dense set of pedagogic cultural strategies that systematically educate consumers as to how an object should be used, what pleasures it can provide, and what needs it ought to satisfy, thus exercising a powerful influence over how an object is integrated into the lived experience of an individual. A seemingly infinite range of ads for an equally infinite number of products that mobilize a vast array of seemingly different cultural strategies tends to disguise the basic shared logic that underlies all forms of advertising: two or more things that are dissimilar are identified as sharing a common essence. Each image or practice in an advertisement is skewered together with the others, in a more or less subtle fashion, by the demand that something be sold or promoted. For Adorno the terror lying behind this imperative is not so much the specific nature of the objective (i.e., sale or promotion), but rather lies in the fact that all forms of cultural production and consumption increasingly force cognitive, affective, and libidinal processes into a single register: identity.

Despite the theoretical potential of articulation to explore the relations between culture and commodification, relatively little effort has been directed this way. Part of this reluctance is a consequence of the general hostility between cultural studies and political economy. Insofar as articulation is a conceptual tool of cultural studies, political economy refuses to use it; and cultural studies avoids attributing any special significance to commodification because such recognition might resurrect a primitive form of economic and/or class reductionism. For cultural studies, however, a more substantive theoretical barrier looms. Articulation breaks with the specificity/autonomy of culture advocated by Birmingham, but it also reinstalls a form of spatialized specificity that refuses to countenance the presence of totalizing social processes – and this is *especially* true for economic processes – that generate equivalent effects across different social, cultural and historical conjunctures. Instead, these effects must be mapped out anew in every case, for one can never specify with an adequate level of precision how a certain practice will be articulated together with others at any particular moment: 'The commodity is an abstract concept with an enormous purchase: it is a necessary aspect of the description of the economic conditions of many countries, over at least four centuries. But for just that reason it does not tell us much about the articulation of the commodity in any particular conjuncture and it does not, by itself, provide a particularly powerful political intervention.'[41]

Or, more bluntly, cultural studies 'rejects the notion that because a cultural text is produced as a commodity by capitalism you know ahead of time what its politics are.'[42] Thus the sacred gap between cultural production and consumption is recanonized. While, strictly speaking, we are well advised to reject 'productivism' in its most extreme formulation (which not many would advocate in any case), statements such as these also suggest that commodification does not have any appreciable standardized impact on the meanings, pleasures, and desires that a text may satisfy and/or activate.

The politics such a stance favours is benign neutrality with respect to capitalism: one cannot indict the effects of commodification on culture because one never really knows the nature of these effects until after they have happened. Most importantly, the cumulative impact of capitalist social relations – the growing intensity of the profit motive as it is hammered ever deeper into the molecular processes of cultural activity – is denied by way of a theoretical model that insists on the *essentialized* radical diversity of reality itself. The postmodernism of Foucault, Deleuze, and Guattari, notes Grossberg enthusiastically, 'describes a reality that is *always* pluralizing itself. The real is like crabgrass (not just metaphorically, either), constantly extending itself by producing effects at some place other than itself; its existence is only in the tangled web of often inseparable lines ("rhizomatic flows"). Reality is its own production – "a monism of plurality."'[43] The possibility that certain social processes might have a totalizing, unifying, or flattening effect over time is conceptually exorcised as a defence against (Hegelian) Marxist teleology. Such theoretical assumptions are not inherent in the concept of articulation itself; rather, they are rooted in the desire to confine the concept to a local and temporally specific form of analysis. Unfortunately, these safeguards make it difficult to apply the concept effectively to the relations between culture and the commodity form in terms of investigating the basic social logic by which the latter imposes itself upon the former.

## 'Unfinished Business': Cultural Studies and the Commodity Form

Given the dramatic expansion of the culture industry over the past several decades and its extensive integration with other sectors of the economy, the objects and practices that constitute contemporary culture almost always take the form of commodities in capitalist societies. Although few in cultural studies would deny this basic fact, it plays only a minor role in how most in the discipline conceptualize the effects of culture on daily life. The commodity form is nestled in all aspects of cultural experience, where it has acquired a curious sort of immunity from critical reflection. Its influence on culture is growing, yet paradoxically it has faded into the background of the one field of intellectual inquiry that places culture at the centre of its analytic gaze. At one level, it is tempting to attribute this absence to the naturalization that follows the molecular colonization of every social process in modern life by the commodity form: everywhere, it is also nowhere to be seen. It is no use, so the saying goes, asking a fish about the water. Yet this is not an entirely satisfactory explanation. After all, the 'water' that is language has experienced precisely the opposite fate in recent decades. Critical resources have been poured into the study of discourse and signs, deconstructing that which humanity once took for granted as merely reflective of its world. The rewards of this new attentiveness to language have been remarkable. As the constitutive function of discourse comes into view, awareness blooms that the representation of the world is a fundamentally historical, social, and political act. The innocence of language disappears in favour of a conscious reckoning with it; we look not only to how it shapes our patterns of experience, but also to how we can exercise some control over that process, changing the way we use language to help change the world in which we live.

In a similar vein, Benjamin and Adorno reconstruct the commodification of culture as a threshold experience; they call on us to witness both the possibilities and the dangers that attend this historical, social, and political process. Critical theory positions us on an analytic razor's edge that demands an immediate confrontation with how the commodity form mobilizes and at the same time represses the potential it calls into being as culture is freed from the suffocating bonds of tradition and ritual. Benjamin's return to the dreams of nineteenth-century Paris and Adorno's obsessive readings of the death throes of serious art represent two different albeit complementary strategies for generating a sense of contingency about a type of cultural life that most human beings accept as normal and natural. Above all, each struggles against what Benjamin once called 'left-wing melancholy,' in which critical analysis metamorphosizes 'from a compulsory decision into an object of pleasure, from a means of production into an article of consumption.'[44] In the remainder of this chapter, I want to bring critical theory and cultural studies into contact with each other by comparing their views on the commodification of culture. Marshalling Grossberg and Hall as key representatives, I will begin by reviewing the core strategies that cultural studies uses to discount the relevance of commodification in the study of contemporary culture. Then, drawing from the framework developed in the first three chapters, I will interrogate these strategies from the alternative perspectives offered by critical theory. I will conclude the chapter by identifying the commodification of difference as a subject of mutual interest through which we might initiate a dialogue between critical theory and cultural studies.

Althusser's structuralism long ago fell out of favour with many in cultural studies, yet his argument that culture constitutes a set of relatively autonomous practices continues to ground the dismissal of commodification – and by extension political economy and critical theory – as largely irrelevant to the study of culture. Cultural studies admits that mass culture is commodified in character, but then it immediately tames this concession by erecting a series of conceptual barriers that divide the economic function of a cultural object from its ideological effects as defined at a cognitive, affective, and/or libidinal level. Grossberg, for instance, notes that he is not unsympathetic to the claim that cultural practices – including the production of meaning and consciousness – have been 'incorporated into capitalist commodity relations.'[45] However, he quickly adds that such a claim is not especially helpful in understanding the significance of cultural practices, for two important reasons. First, he argues, given that art and culture have existed as commodities throughout human history, the commodity form as an analytic concept is too general and abstract to explain the unique effects of culture within particular historical articulations. Second, the existence of culture as a commodity 'does not deny that it still may be other things as well ... The concrete complexity of the practices of consumption suggests that ... artistic practices, even if they situate the audience as consumer, may also situate them in other contradictory subject-positions.'[46] A cultural object or practice may be commodified or even produced first and foremost as a commodity, but this does not preclude its adoption and use for a wide variety of other purposes that are not determined or limited by its existence as a commodity.

These surplus or excess effects can be distinguished from the object as commodity in a variety of ways. Arjun Appadurai's work was initially developed within an anthropological frame of reference; even so, it offers a clear example of how commodification is theorized as a temporally limited process. An object, he argues, does not exist as a commodity for all time; rather, commodification is a set of relations within which an object acquires significance at particular moments of its existence. Analysing the 'social life' of things involves tracking their movement in *and out* of what he calls 'the commodity phase.' An object can only be properly described as a commodity when '*its exchangeability (past, present, or future) for some other thing is its socially relevant feature*: ... In this processual view, the commodity phase of the life history of an object does not exhaust its biography; it is culturally regulated; and its interpretation is open to individual manipulation to some degree.'[47] Miklitsch adapts this 'resolutely temporal approach' to cultural studies, praising it in terms of how it accounts for not only the commodification of an object, but also its 'de-commodification.'[48] As a way of organizing cultural analysis, it fits well into a theory of articulation that emphasizes the fluid effects of different events, practices, and objects as they fit together in different ways over time. As an object is removed from exchange-relations and embedded in a different context of use, its existence as a commodity recedes into the background, effectively displaced by a new and often unrelated set of properties. Conversely, an analytic structure that theorizes culture *only* as a commodity offers limited explanatory value because of how it effaces the many phases through which cultural objects and practices move.

Given the pervasive nature of commodification, however, culture is more commonly distinguished from commodity by considering the effects it may simultaneously have independent of and unrelated to its economic function. Grossberg explains, for example, that cultural objects take on different properties as they are positioned within what he calls modernist or postmodernist practices. The former define objects in terms of their relation to a totality; the latter resist all forms of totalization. 'In what sense,' he asks, 'is the postmodernist fragment, even when it accepts the inevitability of its existence as a commodity, something other than a commodity?' As commodities, objects are subject to a totalizing impulse that 'gives meaning, not only to the particular object (e.g., as status, fashion, or exchange value) but also to the general process of commodification.'[49] Modernist practices connect objects to broader structures of value, meaning, and desire; they acquire significance only insofar as they are exemplary of these structures. Yet objects can also be located within 'postmodern' practices that deny this totalizing impulse by treating them in their irreducible specificity as fragments 'without context or significance.'[50] The status and use of the object, then, depends on which set of practices it is articulated with at any particular moment.

Hebdige uses punk to argue that different styles can temporarily displace the dominant meaning of signs and inflect them in alternative ways; Grossberg attributes a similar power to the affective alliances of rock, in order to disarticulate the commodity from practices that define it solely in terms of its exchange-value. As they are located within these alliances, commodified objects or experiences acquire a significance that is independent of their economic identity. He calls this process 'excorporation':

> Rock and roll removes signs, objects, sounds, styles, and so forth from their apparently meaningful existence within the dominant culture and relocates them within an affective alliance of differentiation and resistance. The resultant shock – of both recognition and an undermining of meaning – produces a temporarily impassable boundary within the dominant culture, an encapsulation of the affective possibilities of the rock and roll culture.[51]

As a postmodern cultural practice, rock reconstitutes commodities as fragments that acquire affective significance as avenues of escape from general social processes such as commodification. They acquire a discrete affective significance that elevates their irreducible particularity and momentarily destroys their capacity to serve as signs or representatives for something else within a larger system of meaning. For Grossberg, the extent to which an object is commodified ultimately has little to do with whether or not it performs a totalizing or a disjunctive role. Instead, this depends on how it is embedded in particular cultural practices and how those practices, in turn, are organized into an affective alliance. The incorporation or co-optation of rock music into hegemonic cultural structures occurs when it no longer energizes these pathways out of everyday life – when its power to 'excorporate' is lost: 'Co-optation is a decathexis of the boundary, a de-encapsulation of the music and its culture and an incorporation of its affective alliance into the hegemonic organizations of desire. Co-optation indicates an affective realliance of the music rather than an alteration of the aesthetic or ideological constitution of the text.'[52] Rock music that excorporates and rock music that incorporates are both commodities; thus, one cannot say that commodification plays a constitutive role in determining how a cultural object affectively positions a consumer. 'Selling out' is a euphemism for affective processes, not economic ones. When all culture exists in the form of commodities, critical cultural analysis must attend to the differences *between* commodities and to the processes that allow one kind of commodity or commodified practice to have different effects from others. Conceptual instruments that are not sensitive to these distinctions – that tar every object, insofar as it is a commodity, with the same brush – are of limited help in explaining how culture works. As the decisive effects of culture are determined by non-economic processes, commodification drops down or even off the analytic agenda.

Grossberg conceptualizes excorporation in affective rather than semiotic terms; that said, his model is clearly indebted to the Birmingham School's assertion that within the cultural sphere, the semiotic qualities of an object necessarily trump its identity as a commodity. Hall and others distinguish culture from commodity in three important ways. First, while commodification may determine the path of a cultural object through the circuits of exchange and thereby regulate access to it, its simultaneous existence as a sign allows it to play a variety of additional roles – roles that are fundamentally unrelated to the vagaries of its economic history. The essential complexity of cultural processes means that objects have certain dimensions that always elude the grasp of commodification. Second, the centre's work underscores how specific consumptive practices can deliberately displace certain object-signifiers from their initial position within more conventional patterns of use, meaning, and enjoyment. In particular, meanings and pleasures inscribed on a cultural text at the point of production and often intended to exercise hegemonic influence over their consumers may be resisted and/or transfigured. This dynamic, which is influenced by Mikhail Bakhtin's notion of carnival, is often expressed in terms of the frequent *reversals* that are engineered within a certain context of consumption. For instance, the same object can play either a hegemonic (stabilizing) or counter-hegemonic (disruptive) role depending on how it is actually used. Third, the active nature of cultural consumption guarantees that the effect of a cultural practice in a given context can never be adequately predicted in advance. As the ethnographic investigations pioneered by Birmingham show, consumptive practices play a key role in how culture is lived and experienced. Even if one does grant commodification a structural influence in determining how a particular cultural object is designed, made, and distributed, this influence does not have any lasting permanence, given the contextual variance that defines how it is used and that shapes its effects on everyday life. In other words, the diversity of consumptive environments guarantees a multiplicity of effects that necessarily escape the point of production.

It is fair to say that most who work in cultural studies would be comfortable accepting some combination of these basic premises. Cultural studies is founded on the understanding that cultural consumption is, at its core, an active process whereby a multiplicity of meanings, pleasures, and uses are taken from the objects and activities of popular culture *irrespective* of how they were originally produced. With respect to this cultural polysemy, John Clarke observes:

> It is this 'field of possibilities' that constitutes cultural consumption as a social and cultural practice – as opposed to seeing it collapsed into the economic and ideological domination of the exchange relationship. It is also the idea of active cultural practice which cultural studies in its varied forms has sought to stress: the bending of received cultures to a role in a 'lived' cultural project; the making sense of the social relations which people inhabit, and the construction of cultural strategies for surviving those processes.[53]

In a more polemic tone, Paul Gilroy warns that 'consumption is a vague word that trips far too easily off the dismissive tongue.' Writing about the appropriation of mass culture by black audiences, he explains that 'however trivial the black music record sleeve may seem to the outsider, it points to a fund of aesthetic and philosophical knowledge which the record as a commodity has been made to contain *in addition* to its reified pleasures.'[54] Culture necessarily overflows the commodity containers into which it has been poured by the culture industries. In his discussion of the active, productive reception needed to make sense of the dissociated fragments that now dominate postmodern culture, Hebdige argues that

> 'consumption' with its connotations of passivity, of waste, digestion, disappearance, needs to be replaced by some other term capable of convey-

> ing the *multi-accentuality* and *duration* over time and in different cultural-geographical contexts of commodified objects and forms as they move from one dislocated point to the next, from design, through production, packaging, mediation, and distribution/retail into use where they are appropriated, transformed, adapted, treated differently by different individuals, classes, genders, ethnic groupings, invested with different degrees and types of intensity.[55]

Insofar as these types of claims make the point that there will always be more to culture than commodification, they are impossible to dispute. A problem arises, however, when these objections have the intellectual effect of displacing commodification altogether as an economic process that is fundamentally irrelevant to the study of culture.

How might the critical theory developed by Adorno and Benjamin address some of these assumptions? Let us begin with the claim that culture's perennial existence as something to be bought and sold disqualifies the commodity form as a concept that can tell us anything about the specificity of contemporary cultural formations. In the first place, such a charge betrays a surprising lack of familiarity not only with Marxist cultural criticism, but also with Marx's conception of capitalism. The simple buying and selling of goods, including cultural objects, does not constitute capitalist social relations. Rather, these relations are formed through the gradual subordination of all forms of social production – most importantly, the organization of labour – to the logic of commodification. As generations of Marxists have observed, the expansionary logic of capital produces an *increasing* scale and intensity of effects as it penetrates more and more areas of social life.[56] Lukacs, for instance, claims that 'the commodity can only be understood in its undistorted essence when it becomes the universal category of society as a whole. Only in this context does the reification produced by commodity relations assume decisive importance.'[57] To make the claim, for example, that the commodification of culture had the same effects one hundred years ago as it does today is absurd. Likewise, it is spurious to use the fact that culture has always, to some extent, been commodified to condemn the concept itself as excessively abstract. As an analytic framework, the culture industry thesis argues that the commodification of culture brings with it certain growing structural pressures – pressures that shape how culture is produced and its social effects within societies in which capitalist social relations have become the dominant form of organizing human interaction. Similarly, Benjamin identifies nineteenth-century Paris as a privileged object of inquiry because of how a dramatic increase in the production and marketing of commodities at that time inaugurated new forms of experience that remain dominant today.

Critical theory (like political economy) is regularly attacked for its 'productivism' – that is, for the sin of giving far too much explanatory power to how culture is *produced* in determining the effects it will have when it is *consumed*. After all, the design, production, and marketing of a commodity is only one moment in a much longer history or 'social life' of an object. Along these lines, critical theory is commonly derided for a 'hypodermic needle' approach to cultural analysis the vulnerable masses are effortlessly 'injected' with the dominant ideology by way of hyper-effective media.[58] Ironically perhaps, the attribution of fantastic powers of manipulation to the media actually makes more sense within a structuralist problematic in which culture exercises powerful effects on human experience independent of the grounding of that experience in other social spheres. Critical theory faults the culture industry not for being too strong, but rather for being too weak. Horkheimer and Adorno note that compared to the most powerful sectors of industry, 'the culture monopolies are weak and dependent.'[59] Under the rule of capital, culture renounces its traditional function of creating and protecting a space for critical reflection and utopian imagination in favour of a slavish reproduction of everyday life. For Adorno, the characteristics and effects of mass culture are a consequence of the totality of capitalist social relations and in particular the organization of the labour process: people 'want standardized goods and pseudo-individuation, *because* their leisure is an escape from work and at the same time is molded after those psychological attitudes to which their workaday world exclusively habituates them.'[60] Mass culture serves the degraded subjects produced by work; it does not create them entirely on its own. It organizes, reinforces, and intensifies patterns of thought, action, feeling, and pleasure that have become socially dominant because of their simultaneous embodiment in a wide range of similarly commodified structures and practices. Similarly, Benjamin explains *Erlebnis* as a type of experience that evolves out of the need to adapt to the growth of capitalist urbanization. He too identifies the capitalist organization of labour, not any autonomous cultural dynamic, as the leading edge of this transformation: 'The process of the atrophy of experience [*Erfahrung*] is already underway within manufacturing. In other words, it coincides, in its beginnings, with the beginnings of commodity production.'[61] For both Benjamin and Adorno, the culture industry's greatest crime lies in what it *fails* to do rather than in what it actually does. As it turns its back on serious aesthetics and experimental cultural practice, it abandons the promise of culture – borne of the separation between mental and manual labour – to energize critical engagement with the real by cultivating new patterns of thought, desire and experience. For critical theory, this betrayal is at least as significant as the role the culture industry plays as an ideological advocate for capitalism.

At its most extreme, Adorno's claim that cultural commodities serve no other function but to libidinize the exchange-relation is justly criticized as neglecting other dimensions of cultural experience. Yet cultural studies serves up little more than a mirrored inversion of this claim when it suggests that there are discrete moments in the cycle of cultural consumption that are entirely independent of the commodity form. One of the highest priorities for critical cultural studies in an age of capital must be how to theorize the *relation* between these competing forces. Culture is never entirely the instrument of capital, but it is also never entirely free from it; and just as the linguistic turn in social theory teaches us to be most suspicious of language when it appears most 'natural' (i.e., a simple 'reflection' of the real), critical theory counsels an equally cautious stance when culture appears most independent of the commodity form. Consider, for example, Grossberg's claim that we can distinguish postmodern practices from capitalist social processes by their ability to constitute objects as fragments, removing them from semiotic, economic, and other organizing structures. Such practices, in other words, are notable for their *de*signifying and *de*contextualizing functions. Yet the prototype for these practices is surely the commodity form. 'All that is solid melts into air,' Marx famously writes, 'all that is holy is profaned.'[62] Capital systematically rips objects out of their social relations of production in order to facilitate their easy passage through circuits of exchange as well as their 'resignification' by the semiotic crafts of various promotional industries. As objects are commodified, their extraction from organic totalities is as important as their subsequent integration into different totalizing structures. This is an essential prerequisite in the creation of the commodity as fetish, an object that is subsequently misperceived as having unique properties or powers unto itself. Instead of conceptualizing totalizing and particularizing practices as completely separate processes – the one associated with commodification, the other not – Benjamin's theory of the dialectical image investigates their simultaneous presence within the commodity form. On the one hand, dialectical images partake of the explosive transformative energies released by the 'destructive character' of capitalism; but on the other hand, those same images directly challenge the dissipation of these energies as cultural objects are subsequently 're-enchanted' within capitalist phantasmagoria. Like Grossberg's postmodern cultural practices, these images produce fragments by blasting historical objects and experiences out of the narratives and structures in which they are embedded. For Benjamin, however, this process must include an explicit confrontation with commodification: 'The commodity tries to look itself in the face.' In the absence of any such direct reckoning with the commodity form, the valorization of fragments as detached and autonomous risks the illusionary exorcism of real totalities – exchange relations, for example – that pose an ever-present threat to the radical possibilities that inhere in those fragments. Bringing these two moments together, however, primes the contradictions between particularizing and totalizing impulses, and allows us to hold the commodity form to account for its systematic repression of the potential that it has itself released.

The most damning charge that cultural studies lays before critical theory – especially the culture industry thesis – is that it fails to make sense of a postmodern cultural environment characterized by semiotic diversity on the one hand and active practices of cultural consumption on the other. Rigid characterizations of mass culture as dominated by an inescapable sameness do a profound injustice to the creativity and heterogeneity of contemporary culture. In responding to these claims, the first thing to point out is that they often rest on misreadings of critical theory – misreadings that are especially common when certain pieces of work are read in isolation from their broader theoretical commitments. As our exploration of Adorno and Benjamin's work in the first three chapters has shown, critical theory's position on mass culture rests on a far more supple and complex theoretical basis than it is generally credited with by cultural studies. However, just as important as the debunking of these exegetical mistakes is a measured closing of the theoretical divide that is perceived between these two schools of thought. There is little question that substantive differences separate critical theory from cultural studies; that said, there are also intriguing parallels – or, better stated, points of contact – which suggest that something other than outright dismissal could characterize a dialogue between them. In the final pages of this chapter, I discuss the twin themes of cultural polysemy and creative consumption both to defend critical theory from its detractors and to highlight some of the places where the differences between them are not as great as many believe.

Inspired by works such as Hebdige's optimistic reading of punk *bricolage* in *Subcultures,* Michel de Certeau's reflections on the art of 'making do' in *The Practices of Everyday Life,* and (most egregiously) Fiske's brash celebration of consumptive agency in *Reading the Popular* and *Understanding Popular Culture,* certain strains within cultural studies define cultural consumption as an active process that resists, subverts, and transforms the meanings and pleasures of cultural commodities.[63] As objects pass into discourse, they are subject to the specific rules of discursive systems, including the assumption that as object becomes sign it necessarily becomes polysemic, acquiring a variety of meanings. No matter how hard the capitalist culture industries try to dictate how their products will be used and consumed, their purchase and relocation to a wide variety of social contexts inevitably generates an equally wide range of cognitive, libidinal, and somatic effects. Insofar as cultural studies commits itself to the structuralism or poststructuralism of the linguistic turn, the presence of cultural difference is essentialized. Irrespective of whether the creation of meaning is viewed as stable or unstable, it remains an exclusive function of the differences between signs within an autonomous signifying system. Difference is the basic building block of all discrete semiotic structures; it is the essential prerequisite that binds signs together into a more or less coherent totality and that allows them to take on meaning as signs. For the most part, studying culture in this way obviates the need to look at the effects of economic and other social processes on culture, because the internal rules of discursive systems always trump those effects. Besides foreclosing any substantive investigation into the relations between culture and commodity, such approaches also tend to valorize all forms of semiotic diversity as expressive of an active consumer in opposition to a hegemonic apparatus that seeks to minimize difference. Polysemy is conceptualized as inherently emancipatory, as denoting a subversion of the totalitarian imposition of approved meaning and licensed pleasures. In ideological terms, it seems that capitalism is always striving in vain to limit difference; it follows that the affirmation or multiplication of difference represents a challenge to its power.

Fortunately, Grossberg's innovative rethinking of cultural studies reflects the tendencies of many who have moved away from the one-dimensional semiotics that often dominated early work in the field.

Signifying and asignifying processes come together in the production of meaning, experience, pleasure, and affect; recognition of this suggests a greater openness to considering the effects of commodification on culture. Especially noteworthy, for instance, is a growing sensitivity to how the production and marketing of difference has become a core strategy of a post-Fordist culture industry. 'Capital has fallen in love with difference,' remarks Jonathan Rutherford, 'advertising thrives on selling us things that will enhance our uniqueness and individuality ... From World Music to exotic holidays in Third-World locations, ethnic tv dinners to Peruvian knitted hats, cultural difference *sells*.'[64] Describing the relation between ethnicity and capitalism, Hall similarly observes that commodified culture operates according to a differentiating logic that accommodates a measure of diversity in order to secure its ongoing expansion: 'Alongside that drive to commodify everything, which is certainly one part of its logic, is another critical part of its logic that works in and through specificity ... In order to maintain its global position, capital has had to negotiate and by negotiate I mean it had to incorporate and partly reflect the differences it was trying to overcome.'[65]

At one level, these words betray a lingering normative commitment to polysemy insofar as capitalism and difference are portrayed as warring combatants, with the former trying to 'overcome' the latter's struggle to preserve a measure of autonomy from the system. Yet they also suggest that where it cannot erase particularities, capitalism installs them as differences within a complex totality over which it ultimately presides: 'It stage-manages independence within it, so to speak.'[66] In other words, the relationship between difference and capitalism acquires a complexity that it lacks in much of the Birmingham School's work, in which polysemy is almost always conceptualized as a sign of cultural emancipation. Instead, difference is conceptualized as compatible with and even functional for capitalism.

From this conceptual territory, it is not far to the recognition that postmodern capitalism itself functions through the organized seeding of vast fields of cultural difference to maximize the volume and rate at which cultural commodities are harvested and exchanged. Semiotic polysemy has become, in so many ways, both functional for *and* a function of capitalism itself. This leads Antonio Negri and Michael Hardt to caution that 'the affirmation of hybridities and the free play of differences across boundaries ... is liberatory only in a context where power poses hierarchy exclusively through essential identities, binary divisions, and stable oppositions. The structures and logics of power in the contemporary world are entirely immune to the 'liberatory' weapons of the postmodernist politics of difference.'[67] This is not to say that all forms of difference are equally the product of power or that they have become irrelevant to human emancipation. It does mean that the immunity from critical reflection and judgment that concepts such as difference and polysemy have traditionally enjoyed in cultural studies must come to an end. After all, the ironic effect of portraying consumers as cultural *bricoleurs* who take from cultural commodities what they wish 'is to replicate the view of capitalism which capitalism would most like us to see: the richness of the marketplace and the freely choosing consumer. The other side – the structures of production and the inequalities of access to the marketplace – are missing, and these absences emphasize the "free-floating" quality of the sign, making it available for any use or meaning that may be attached to it.'[68] Attending to this 'other side' requires a more critical assessment of cultural difference. How, for example, does one assess the merits, substance, and even 'reality' of difference? How does one describe difference, understand it, experience it? Most importantly, are there different types of difference, each playing a different role and having a different kind of effect? Questions like these place us back on the terrain of critical theory.

As a Marxist, Adorno is fully aware that one of the results of capitalist expansion has been an explosive increase in the number and variety of commodities available through the market. The culture industry leads the way in such offerings: 'Something is provided for everyone so that no one can escape; differences are hammered home and propagated.'[69] He clearly recognizes that capitalism works by expanding rather than reducing diversity. However, he argues that this diversity carries no broader emancipatory significance unless it enables critical reflection on the conditions of human experience, both in terms of how it is socially organized and at a much deeper level in terms of the relation between subject and object. True difference is redefined in an experiential context as awareness of non-identity that is simultaneously cognitive and somatic – as a visceral sense of the materiality, potentiality, and 'otherness' of the world that inevitably escapes all attempts to direct conceptual or aesthetic representation. It arises out of a complex dialectic between culture and the real, never from within culture alone. Only culture has the capacity to cultivate, protect, and impose this sense of non-identity on human subjects, yet this capacity is under constant threat from prevailing forms of instrumental rationality. Far from constituting inevitable guarantors of difference, language and culture are subject to the same logic of identity as other social processes under capitalism. On the one hand they represent privileged locations where humanity can acquire an awareness of this logic and its dangers; on the other hand, the penetration of identitarian logic to their core – as sponsored in large part by the commodification of culture – means that they can also excise human receptivity to forms of difference as defined by the relation between subject and object.

Adorno is fairly criticized for refusing to acknowledge many forms of semiotic diversity within culture. Yet compiling an inventory of cultural difference is hardly his main intention. Rather, he wants to recalibrate our sensitivity to forms of alterity that are not necessarily reflected in semiotic difference. Indeed, he fears that the well-publicized presence of such differences provides little more than ideological assurance that all forms of difference continue to survive and flourish. Juxtaposing Adorno's criterion for true difference – that subject engage with object through a range of experiential modes – with what normally passes for diversity within the culture industry delivers a destabilizing shock to the way in which cultural difference is normally defined. In other words, the assessment of difference is displaced from the level of meaning, pleasure, and affect to a rigorous philosophical investigation into the conscious and unconscious patterns through which human beings engage with their environment. Culture, for Adorno, can sponsor a temporary suspension of the paralyzing rigidity, spawned from terror, that characterizes the relation between subject and object within the 'dialectic of enlightenment,' thereby enabling an experience of ourselves, others, and the broader material world that is not subtended by identity. Likewise, Benjamin speculates that culture can disrupt the insular, defensive nature of psychic mechanisms and activate an exoteric mimetic cognition that reconceives memory and experience as a *Spielraum* in which we can both reinvent ourselves and redeem the world in which we live. While the latter foregrounds the explosive potential that lies within capitalism to generate these kinds of experiential ruptures – that is, the *possibility* of difference – the former's polemics warn against the dangers of reading the signs of that potential prematurely as markers of its realization. Critical theory does not reject the possibility of difference within mass culture as much as it provides a theoretical model in which such differences can be explored *and critically assessed*.

Adorno's description of the diversity of mass culture as 'pseudo-individualization' follows from this critical stance. While this term has acquired considerable notoriety within cultural studies – where it is viewed as evidence of Adorno's elitist, patronizing disposition – it is certainly in hailing distance of Hall's assertion that capital 'stage-manages independence.' A cultural object may retain – indeed, for promotional purposes it *must* appear to have – a distinctive identity compared to the rest of the products in the marketplace, but its properties cannot stray far from standardized patterns of thought and action, given capital's demand that commodities be consumed as quickly, easily, and extensively as possible: 'By pseudo-individualization we mean endowing cultural mass production with the halo of free choice or open market on the basis of standardization itself. Standardization of song hits keeps customers in line by doing their listening for them, as it were. Pseudo-individualization, for its part, keeps them in line by making them forget that what they listen to is already listened to for them, or "pre-digested."'[70]

Conceptually, Adorno uses this concept to distinguish between those forms of cultural difference which challenge dominant patterns of experience, thought, and feeling and those which do not. As pseudo-differences are more and more aggressively constructed and promoted by capital, it is critical not only to identify them as such but also to explore their consequences for deeper or more radical forms of difference. For as the culture industry thesis describes at length, difference that is produced within or integrated into commodified mass culture reinforces one-dimensional cognitive, somatic, and libidinal structures that make it almost impossible for individuals to experience genuine difference. Pseudo-differences are not merely incidental, harmless distractions; they play a central role in the constitution of a subjective disposition that is unreceptive to real diversity and often hostile to it as well. These two forms of difference do not simply exist side by side: they cannot be realized or expressed simultaneously. Although the potential for real difference can never be eradicated and – as Benjamin argues – actually overdetermines the production of commodities, the mistaken identification of this potential as realized is the single biggest obstacle to its actualization. The semiotic polysemy often trumpeted in mass culture as a sign of liberal plurality and consumer freedom depends on the eradication of particularity enforced by the commodity form. Critical theory insists that we recognize a dialectic between real and *ersatz* difference – that we move beyond a timid relativism which at best refuses to judge between them and at worst celebrates the latter as evidence of the former.

Cultural studies often distinguishes itself from critical theory by defending the active nature of cultural consumption – that is, the consumer's ability to adapt culture to his or her own social and material context. The multiple readings given hegemonic texts are expressive of mass culture's accommodation of individual and collective agency. These democratic sentiments are often used to separate cultural studies from the elitist proclivities of critical theory. Benjamin is usually excluded from these ritual condemnations because he is so often (mis)identified as a progenitor of cultural studies, one who was presciently able to discern the glimmer of radical democratic potential within new media. These appropriations rarely acknowledge his insistence that such potential can only be realized after these technologies have been emancipated from the commodity form. Adorno, in contrast, is routinely scorned for viewing the consumption of commodified culture as an entirely *passive* activity. This is probably the most common and certainly the most egregious misreading of the culture industry thesis – a fertile indicator of the extent to which the invocation of cliché has replaced an attentive reading of his work. Again and again Adorno makes it perfectly clear that the most horrifying aspect of the culture industry is how it facilitates the *active* self-integration of individuals with the system. For him, our relation with the culture industry is anything *but* passive. The basic psychological dynamic at the core of commodified consumption is the projection of desire onto objects that have been stripped of their specificity. As an endless sequence of images, cultural commodities seduce the consumer by offering up an infinity of surfaces that invite the effortless inscription and consumption of fantasy. Culture becomes just what we want it to be; we take from it what we wish. The consumer actively supplies the meaning and pleasure that are reflected – not reflected *on* him or her but rather *back* to him or her – or more accurately, that are refracted back to him or her. Mass culture could not work without this participatory dynamic. However, such participation cannot be taken at face value as expressive of an active, creative, or autonomous agency. Standardization, repetition, and pseudo-individuation confine interaction with mass culture to an extremely narrow cognitive and libidinal range, one that is essentially defined by the pleasures of recognition that are produced by slight variations on a single dominant pattern. Any dissonant meanings and desires that depart from this basic framework are either ignored or hated for summoning a fragmentary image of an unrealized potential. Furthermore, Adorno insists that these desires must be contextualized within a broader theory of subject formation that traces out their genealogy in the context of a collective social regression to primary psychological and cognitive processes. The attempt to satisfy these desires does involve a form of self-directed activity, but it is a self or ego that has become thoroughly subjugated as a result of the repressive fusion of superego and id. These psychic developments ultimately ensure a cognitive and libidinal complicity with exploitative and oppressive social structures enacted at an almost molecular level. Such forms of agency reproduce the sadomasochistic logic that lies at the core of the 'dialectic of enlightenment,' in which both subject and object engage in endless cycles of reciprocal domination.

As I argued in Chapter Three, Benjamin's work supplies an essential complexity to the question of cultural agency that Adorno's own writings lack. In particular, he recognizes the authenticity of the utopian desires and wishes that are dispersed through the social and cultural dreamscapes of urban capitalism, as well as the essential role these fragments may play in generating revolutionary consciousness. But insofar as they remain frozen within the distortions imposed on them by capitalist social relations, these desires and wishes – precisely because of their 'genuine' origins and the repressed agency they represent – testify all the more convincingly to the power of the commodity form. Though a system that draws from our dreams for its sustenance may be more fragile than one that must manufacture its own, it is simultaneously more terrifying because of this very fact. To represent the one quality without the other is to bear false witness to a hope that remains unrealized. Many in cultural studies preface discussions of cultural agency with the caveat that its broader social and political implications are quite limited. However, the dialectic between agency and its repression is often conceptualized in hydraulic or spatial terms as a pressure or barrier that restricts the authentic expression of agency to a limited area. Cultural agency thereby takes the form of a 'beachhead' from which more ambitious emancipatory missions can be launched in order to extend and multiply that which already exists. Conversely, critical theory shows how these forms of agency or pseudo-participation actually mobilize a psychosocial logic that binds individuals ever tighter to the commodified social relations that make genuine autonomy impossible to attain. The twisted and broken forms of social action that currently pass for autonomy in mass culture can only stand *negatively* as augurs of an emancipated future, nothing more. For Benjamin, their revolutionary significance depends on the generation of dialectical images that represent the dream of human autonomy as literally inconceivable within contemporary forms of social organization.[71] The collective desire to redeem such images is the only force that can dissolve a capitalist phantasmagoria in which the systematic perversion of social agency is experienced as anything and everything but betrayal. Dialectically compressed, the agency solicited by the culture industry contains a breathtaking explosive potential; but its mere quantitative expansion does little more than secure the continuing dominance of the commodity form.

Benjamin's work on allegory offers a new perspective on assessing the emancipatory significance of the semiotic polysemy of postmodern culture. As a good example of how Benjamin is often misread by cultural studies, McRobbie positions him as sympathetic to forms of cultural resistance enabled by the diverse meanings that commodities can accommodate. Long before cultural studies, she argues, he recognized the '"multi-accentuality" of the sign, the instability of meaning, its capacity for change and the extent to which historical change itself was condensed and encapsulated in the forms and the meanings of the consumer goods which filled the display shelves of the shops and arcades.'[72] In the context of his discussion of Baudelaire, however, Benjamin reads an excess of meaning as an index of cultural and linguistic impoverishment. Baudelaire's commitment to an allegorical poetics looms large in *The Arcades Project* precisely because of how it enables a literal embodiment of the hellish social logic that is found at the core of the commodity form. 'Any person, any object, any relationship can mean absolutely anything else'[73]: the subject is utterly unencumbered in its tyrannical dispensation of meaning to a landscape of otherwise inert and lifeless objects. Just as exchange-value presides over the eradication of use-value, 'hollowing out' objects so that they may serve as empty vessels for the consumer's desires (and fears), allegory allows – rather, *forces* – experience to surrender itself to the needs of the poet. Hardly an ideal form of cultural consumption. Even so, Benjamin praises it as a brave attempt to sear the ruin of capitalist social relations deeply into human experience. Like Adorno, he believes that excessive semiotic malleability of an object at the hands of a subject testifies not to an expansive creative agency, but rather to the mythic reproduction of a highly restrictive mode of action, thought, and experience. As a violent 'overnaming' of things, allegory inscribes the tyranny of exchange value onto language itself. Benjamin hopes that the shock of such cultural violence will homeopathically inspire a momentary awareness of the much broader network of destructive social relations in which all of us are embedded. In other words, excessive polysemy may negatively point the way toward agency, but it hardly counts as its fulfilment.

Developments in contemporary advertising again furnish an excellent illustration of the 'active' patterns of consumption promoted by the culture industry. Consumers are constantly encouraged to play an active role in extracting the appropriate meaning from a series of decontextualized images that, at first glance, may bear little resemblance to the product being advertised. Such strategies are designed to counteract the instinctive revulsion and boredom with which media-savvy audiences have come to respond to more simplistic commercial messages. Note an advertising executive's description of the industry's creative objectives:

> I am out to have more kids memorize my commercials scene by scene and play them back to one another, singing them as if it's a puzzle they've solved. I am working on a Kraft commercial, right now, that has so many layers that I know it cannot be understood the first time. It's a puzzle. It's like a Super Mario world. If you've never played it, and it's all been designed for people who grew up playing Mario, old Mario World, whatever ... you're baffled by it. So most people will be baffled by this Kraft singles commercial, and upon repeated viewing there will be one-upmanship for being able to follow it.[74]

The ad solicits the active participation of the audience to solve the 'puzzle' and make the appropriate linkages between product and scene themselves.[75] Probably the best-known example of this kind of advertising is found in a campaign for Benetton apparel that featured a series of provocative political images that had no logical connection to clothing at all.[76] More commonly, advertising aspires to have individuals themselves appropriate the images it provides as signs of their own wishes and desires, thereby transforming the advertised commodity into a required catalyst and gatekeeper for their realization. In fact, without potential consumers actively 'charging' the sounds, images, and texts of advertising with their own fantasy energy, most ads would collapse into an irritating banality. Marketing through cultural objects succeeds not because the audience is a passive receptacle that can be 'programmed' to buy things, but precisely because of how its active interaction with culture can be attached or 'articulated' to other social processes such as commodification. With respect to advertising, Wernick explains how such articulations generate patterns of thought, action, and being that are organized around the commodity form itself, and not simply its particular manifestations: 'The consumerist address imprisons the subjectivity it projects in a totally commodified ontology. Being is reduced to having, desire to lack. No needs or desires are speakable without a commodity to satisfy them; no commodity without at least an imagined place for it in our affections. Satisfaction is always mediated by an object or programmed experience which inevitably ... has a price.'[77]

The efficacy of the culture industry depends on a psychosocial environment in which people have little choice but to accept and demand trivial forms of entertainment because that is the only avenue for affective and libidinal discharge that is possible within the reified social relations of capitalism. This is a kind of agency, but to confuse it with autonomy or even dismiss it as harmless fun is to legitimize an economic and cultural logic that freezes human potential into a hideous caricature of what it might have been and still might become.

Adorno suggests that as people actively write themselves into the puerile scripts furnished by the culture industry, their participation is more often than not accompanied by a half-conscious awareness of the ultimately pointless and even degrading character of the activity: 'The assent to hit songs and debased cultural goods belongs to the same complex of symptoms as do those faces of which one no longer knows whether the film has alienated them from reality or reality has alienated them from the film, as they wrench open a great formless mouth with shining teeth in a voracious smile, while the tired eyes are wretched and lost above.'[78] This agnostic disposition reaches its most acute form with regard to advertising. The creeping spread of promotional culture spawns a far-reaching scepticism about the tactics of advertisers – a scepticism borne of the knowledge that the images of difference which surround us are often intentionally manufactured and deployed so as to tap into and manipulate people's hopes and fears. That advertised associations between commodities and experiences are manipulative, deceitful, and false is an open secret. Most people know that the path to good friends, exciting experiences, and a happy life probably doesn't run through a beer can or a perfume bottle. Indeed, the mocking of such claims has become *de rigeur* for many and is now often included in the ads themselves. Yet the repeated invocation of cynicism as a defensive shield has substantial implications for how people engage with systems of cultural difference. The desire and willingness to invest oneself, not so much in the ads or the commodities they promote, but more importantly in the signifiers of difference appropriated by the ads, is often compromised. Differences remain, but the ability to care about them beyond an instant or two begins to fade. The initial colonization of 'sacred' cultural territory may initially excite outrage and condemnation: How *dare* they use Martin Luther King to flog cellular phones or Gandhi to sell computers? Yet as these episodes pile up one onto the next, bursts of anger collapse into more generalized waves of resignation and indifference as people come to accept – if not always embrace – that liberal capitalism ensures that any and all points of cultural reference are open to commercial appropriation by the highest bidder.

This suspicion of difference is aroused by the practices of contemporary advertising; it then acquires a more general validity in mass culture as a whole. Obviously the homogeneous cultural offerings of the early culture industry have been replaced by a much broader array of objects and practices, but this expansion of variety is driven and regulated by the need to maximize the rapid circulation of culture as a commodity. The 'distinctive' qualities and attributes of many contemporary cultural practices are explicitly (and often openly) designed as signposts to facilitate the efficient pairing of demographic segments with particular advertisers.[79] While this does not make these differences any less real, it does reduce the chance that they will be regarded as having autonomous significance as opposed to being the by-product of targeted marketing strategies. Beyond culture *per se*, this pattern is replicated in the vast array of goods and services that capitalism offers for consumption, in which the most trivial and superficial characteristics are often all that physically distinguish one product from another. For decades, marketing theorists and practitioners have advised that competition based on functional differentiation and/or price should be avoided at all costs.[80] Instead, semiotic differences or brand identities increasingly bear the burden of differentiating objects that are virtually the same. Admittedly, these differences continue to inform relationships with products beyond the moment of purchase: wearing a particular brand of sneakers, for instance, is as much about associating oneself with this brand's 'image' as it is with using sneakers that are superior to the competition. Yet insofar as semiotic difference is called on to vouch for functional differences that do not exist, there is a 'blowback' effect onto the concept of difference itself. In such an environment, many grow increasingly unwilling (and unable) to maintain long-term patterns of cognitive and emotional investment in differences that have been produced, appropriated, and infiltrated by a marketing machine that has become ubiquitous. When thought, language, and especially images become just another way of selling something, why should the differences constructed through them 'matter'? Indeed, as the attachment–detachment–reattachment of signifiers to an endless parade of commodity signifieds becomes ever more rapid and pervasive, a contemptuous and apathetic attitude toward *all* practices of signifying difference grows more widespread.

Adorno and Grossberg offer remarkably similar accounts of the defensive scepticism that masquerades as agency in the face of thoroughly commodified cultural experiences. Grossberg has coined the term 'authentic inauthenticity,' in explaining a strategy for living within the postmodern:

> It is a logic that allows one to seek satisfactions knowing that one can never be satisfied, and that any particular pleasure is likely, in the end, to be disappointing. For even if all images are equally artificial and all satisfactions equally unsatisfying, one still needs some images, one still seeks some satisfactions. Although no particular pose can make a claim to some intrinsic status, any pose can gain a status by virtue of one's commitment to it.[81]

These words recall almost exactly the terrifying finale of the mass culture chapter in *Dialectic of Enlightenment*: 'That is the triumph of advertising in the culture industry: the compulsive imitation by consumers of cultural commodities which, at the same time, they recognize as false.'[82] Adorno is never under any illusion that people are genuinely deceived by the pleasures of mass culture: the culture industry thesis does not offer a simplistic theory of false consciousness and never describes people as 'mere cultural dupes.' In fact, Adorno grounds the system's supple hegemony in the very cynicism that Grossberg describes: 'What is destroyed as truth outside its sphere can be reproduced indefinitely within it as lies.'[83] Grossberg's explanation of the appeal of 'authentic inauthenticity' uncannily echoes Adorno's rendering of the attractions of jazz. Where the former writes that 'feeling something, anything, is better than feeling nothing,'[84] the latter notes that 'merely to be carried away by anything at all, to have something of their own, compensates for their impoverished and barren existence.'[85] Given the fleeting quality of affective investments, Grossberg suggests that they are often experienced in surprisingly intense bursts that shatter an otherwise omnipresent cynicism: 'Current TV's most powerful annunciation is its emotionalism, the fact that it is structured by a series of movements between extreme highs and extreme lows. In fact it presents an image of an affective economy marked on the one side by an extreme (postmodern) cynicism ("Life is hard and then you die") and on the other by an almost irrational celebration of the possibilities of winning against all odds.'[86] This juxtaposition of seemingly opposed emotional states accords almost perfectly with Benjamin's discussion of capitalist experience as *Erlebnis*: individuals cycle through a series of disconnected events whose intensity is exaggerated by the absence of any broader narrative frame of reference in which to contextualize the experience. Sentiments that appear logically opposed – cynicism versus sentimentalism – are in fact intimately connected because the 'emotional highs' of mass culture sponsor a purging of emotion and acceptance of misery as a never-ending feature of a cruel and tragic world.

Notwithstanding his overt suspicion of critical theory, Grossberg's discussion of the relation between affect and difference offers a brilliant accompaniment to the basic concept of pseudo-individualization. Adorno is oriented toward the excavation of the logic of identity in mass culture, and he admittedly spares little time for theorizing how pseudo-differences are actually produced. Furthermore, these strategies have grown far more complex in recent decades, during which the creation and incorporation of semiotic difference has become a cornerstone of the culture industry. Grossberg's highly innovative account of the emergence of novel forms of postmodern difference neatly addresses this gap. Departing from the conventional characterization of postmodernity as an era of diversity, Grossberg argues that it actually marks 'the collapse of difference as an effective historical structure.'[87] The increasing separation of affect from signifying practices means that the differences constructed by those practices are no longer able to attract affective investment as differences that matter.[88] This gap signals a crisis in which the basic human need and desire to invest affective energies in objects and practices is thwarted by the absence of stable pathways for such investments. People have grown indifferent to traditional systems of creating difference: they simply don't matter anymore. Grossberg explains certain contemporary cultural practices as both an expression of and a response to this situation. Television, for example, 'is indifferent to differences even as it constructs differences out of the absence of difference.'[89] In other words, genuine difference does not exist in the world of television; rather, 'it locates identity in the absence of any difference by affectively investing in the difference of the same.'[90] Difference is constituted out of sameness through the mobilization of an endless parade of ridiculous minutiae – often self-identified as such – that enable mobile and ephemeral forms of affective investment.

*Seinfeld*, the most popular sitcom of the 1990s, serves as an excellent example of this dynamic. Each episode involved the use of well-crafted humour to enable an investment in social differences that had absolutely no broader significance. For example, a mainstray of the show was the construction of elaborate taxonomic schemes for classifying everyday forms of behaviour to the point of ridiculousness. Humour, of course, is the perfect avenue for such investment because of its temporary and self-deprecatory qualities. It discourages us from taking seriously what is actually involved in this form of cultural experience. As the show's creator and star proudly proclaimed, 'It's a show about *nothing*.' More accurately, perhaps, it created something (differences) out of nothing (the excruciating sameness of everyday life). Such 'differences' attract affect because of their irrelevance *vis-à-vis* broader ideological and signifying structures. Paradoxically, precisely because they don't mean anything, and because they don't have any broader significance, we can care about them – for an instant or two – until something else catches our attention. The ephemeral quality of these differences is a function of the tautological circle in which they are embedded. They initially matter because we choose to care about them, but the narcissistic origins of their status as meaningful or pleasurable quickly condemn them to insignificance. This expresses a cultural dynamic that fits very well with the commodity form. A culture industry that systematically erases specificity must still sell new products every day: the generation of its own set of differences out of the very sameness that it has itself produced is an ideal response to this situation. 'Making difference out of sameness': a more succinct definition of pseudo-individualization would be hard to find. According to critical theory, cultural commodities depend on generating forms of difference that, first, do not compromise the overall logic of identity that governs their production; second, can be easily and rapidly consumed; and third, possess sufficient novelty to justify their purchase. A postmodern alchemy through which something unfolds out of nothing, difference out of indifference, provides an almost perfect cultural expression of this economic logic.

Substantive differences obviously remain between Grossberg and Adorno and, more broadly, between critical theory and cultural studies. However, there are also significant points of contact that harbour the possibility of a dialogue between the two – a dialogue that can transcend the indifference and even hostility that currently defines their relationship. As I've suggested, a key theme through which such a dialogue might unfold is the effect of commodified culture on the production of different types of experience. As developed by Grossberg, the conceptual model of articulation invites such a dialogue precisely because of how it deconstructs the structuralist model of culture as an inviolable realm with its own laws and logic, instead fostering a critical investigation into the molecular interpenetration of cultural with other social processes. In its most radical, expansive form, articulation moves beyond a static conception of cultural processes that arrange/rearrange preformed entities in a broader structural field toward an exploration of how those entities, at their core, are themselves shaped and defined by social pressures and logics that lie beyond the cultural sphere. As the dividing line between culture and economy becomes blurred, it becomes possible to trace the effects of culture *as* commodity in a manner that bears a considerable theoretical affinity with the techniques deployed by Adorno and Benjamin. This is not to say that cultural studies must reproduce the analytic framework and priorities of critical theory, or that it has to unconditionally recognize the dominance of the commodity form as a precondition for any fruitful exchange. Rather, it is to insist that culture does not have any preconstituted conceptual immunity – semiotically or otherwise guaranteed – from the invasive reach of capitalist social relations. It is to reject any attempt to distil the commodity form out of cultural processes, explaining it away as a 'crude commercial calculation' that ultimately carries little significance for the real 'ideological structure of society.' Above all, it is to assert that foregrounding culture as commodity need not impoverish cultural critique: constellated together in a state of dialectical tension, Adorno and Benjamin point the way toward an analytic mode that clearly avoids the clumsy generalizations of vulgar economism so often caricatured by cultural studies. Benjamin's magnificent study of the arcades and Adorno's intricate readings of all forms of culture aptly demonstrate a dialectical mode of critique in which the latent potential of culture is arrayed against its repression by capital. What energizes their work is an insistence that the specificity of a particular cultural object, activity, or experience must be linked to the broader social and economic processes in which it has been produced and consumed, and which it thereby expresses in some way. Given the extent to which capitalist social relations have permeated all areas of social life, such a model does demand that the effect of the commodity form on the 'internal' forms and 'external' structuring of culture be explicitly theorized. As the similarities between Grossberg and Adorno regarding the effects of contemporary culture on human experience suggest, cultural studies can easily mobilize its considerable theoretical and empirical resources to investigate the relation between commodity and culture. And as the work of Adorno and Benjamin demonstrates, any attempt to understand the characteristics and effects of mass culture that does not allot to the commodity form a place of central importance remains dangerously incomplete.

# Concluding Thoughts

My attempt to restore the culture industry thesis to a position of contemporary relevance in the burgeoning field of cultural studies is not entirely without precedent. While their numbers are comparatively few, others have also noted how the systematic refusal by cultural studies to engage with critical theory has impoverished the conceptual tools with which it can study and theorize cultural processes. In *Cultural Studies as Critical Theory*, for instance, Ben Agger describes the culture industry thesis as the 'single most important theoretical development' to innoculate cultural studies against its 'cult-like' tendency to engage in 'an endlessly self-reproducing series of ungrounded readings not anchored in the framework of an overarching social theory and political practice.'[1] Keith Tester in *Media, Culture and Morality* passionately argues for the 'moral' supremacy of critical theory in preserving a critical conception of culture against the bankruptcy of (British) cultural studies, which simply mimics the normative values of liberal capitalist mass culture.[2] Ian Angus and Sut Jhally explain the ongoing importance of Horkheimer and Adorno's work in terms of 'attributing general significance to the commodity *form* as analytically distinct from questions of ownership,' thereby returning it to the agenda of critical cultural analysis.[3] More recently, Robert Miklitsch has explored the possibility of juxtaposing Adorno's relentless negativity with Gilles Deleuze's concept of affirmation in theorizing the dialectical tension that accompanies all forms of commodity fetishism.[4] Douglas Kellner, probably the most consistent American exponent of a potential *rapprochement* between critical theory and cultural studies, has argued for a selective merger of the two traditions, claiming that they actually complement each other by overcoming many of the weaknesses from which each suffers in isolation.[5]

While I remain sympathetic to the intentions of these assorted projects, I believe that they all suffer from a similar flaw. To a greater or lesser extent, each takes the work of Adorno in its starkest and most uncompromising form and positions it against the celebratory excesses of a postmodern cultural studies. In the first place, such an arrangement may end up minimizing the possibilities for a productive dialogue by maximizing the differences between these two traditions. Insofar as this disjuncture is treated heuristically and used to sharpen the intellectual distinctions between cultural studies and critical theory for analytic purposes, it can be a useful exercise. A clear understanding of the different theoretical assumptions of these two approaches is an important precondition for any further discussion; indeed, my own project partakes of this basic logic. However, major problems can accompany the formation of such a divide. First, the severe contrast between pessimism and optimism can inspire a banal form of pluralism: each 'side' has valuable insights into mass culture, but also suffers from a one-dimensional analytic model that limits a comprehensive understanding of cultural phenomena. The solution, therefore, lies in a 'balancing' of these two perspectives, since things are neither as bad nor as good as either side believes. The relentless critical edge of Adorno's work can help defray some of the unfounded optimism of cultural studies; conversely, the latter's (often ethnographic) investigations into the creative ways that people both resist and transform hegemonic culture can temper the totalizing readings offered by critical theory. Unfortunately, calls of this sort rarely explore either the real differences that might make these two approaches simply incompatible or the possible themes around which a common research agenda might be organized. In other words, we are left with the sense that since each has useful things to say, we ought to keep using both, but little indication is given as to how this might actually be done. Second, the heavy reliance on Adorno – in particular, the culture industry essay from *Dialectic of Enlightenment* – can also generate the opposite reaction, namely, that there is absolutely no common ground between critical theory and cultural studies and, therefore, no point in either side bothering with the other. Adorno's 'exaggerations,' we must not forget, have a tactical as well as a theoretical significance. To the extent that they can help reveal tendencies in capitalist culture and shock us into thinking about our experience of this culture in different ways, they can be extremely valuable. However, when mobilized as a kind of analytic ultimatum – that is, as a set of assumptions and principles that one must unconditionally accept in order to derive any benefit from Adorno's work – they can and have served to alienate many potential 'critical theorists' from critical theory.

My own project develops an alternative strategy that I believe avoids these problems. Quite simply, we must deploy Adorno's work on mass culture together with Benjamin's writings on culture, commodification, and experience *before* entering into an exchange with cultural studies. This 'redialecticization' of critical theory lays the foundations for a complex and substantive exchange that falls into neither hostile invective nor an insipid call for balance and mutual toleration. Scholars of critical theory have long acknowledged the importance of reading Benjamin and Adorno together; however, there has never been any systematic effort to mobilize these readings explicitly in countering the tendency of cultural studies to dismiss the value of critical theory. Bringing together Benjamin and Adorno for this specific objective holds a number of distinct advantages over erecting the more traditional opposition between a 'pure' Adorno and cultural studies. First and perhaps most importantly, it presents a critical theory of culture that is capable of theorizing the utopian potential that are find scattered throughout all social formations. At one level, this forestalls the usual objection that critical theory's critique of mass culture fails to recognize the possibility that people may engage with cultural objects and in cultural activities in ways that are not entirely determined by capital. Instead, Benjamin's work installs a new framework that recognizes this potential but at the same time insists that it must never be theorized outside of its complex relationship with the commodity form. In more positive terms, the addition of this framework to the culture industry thesis elevates the possible engagement between critical theory and cultural studies to a new level. Instead of tossing barbs back and forth regarding the ideological efficacy of mass culture (i.e. the infamous 'cultural dupe' question), we could develop a more substantive discussion with respect to culture's role in cultivating and managing forms of potentiality and constraint, fear and desire, hope and frustration, and to the effects of these in all spheres of social life. Benjamin's writings offer a wealth of resources that treat these themes with considerable sophistication and that could easily be used to sustain a rich dialogue with those in cultural studies.

Second, the use of Benjamin links the culture industry thesis to a theory of experience that locates the effects of mass culture in a much broader social and historical context. Benjamin's exploration of the transition from *Erfahrung* to *Erlebnis* describes a series of transformations in the mode of experience that constitute a framework through which people engage with the culture industry. This framework helps critical theory rebut the simplistic criticism that it attributes far too much autonomous power to mass culture when it comes to programming forms of thought and action. Instead, we must understand the culture industry thesis as only one piece of a large puzzle. The ubiquitous visibility of mass culture makes it an excellent cipher with which to explore the changes to social life in contemporary capitalist societies, yet as Benjamin and Adorno remind us, such ciphers, as monads, can most productively be read as *expressive* of the basic material conditions and relations of social existence. Culture acquires its logic, forms, and structural influence in a symbiotic relation with these broader conditions; thus it is this relation – in all its complexity – that constitutes the focus of critical theory. In other words, the *Erfahrung/Erlebnis* model helps us connect discussions of mass culture to much broader attempts to theorize the transformation of human experience brought about by the fusion of technology and capital in a modern urban environment. Furthermore, Benjamin's speculations about the explosive emancipatory potential that arises through the shift from *Erfahrung* to *Erlebnis* demonstrate a sensitivity to the immense opportunities enabled by the (post)modern fragmentation of traditional forms of subjectivity. This recognition helps counter the charge that critical theory is dominated by a nostalgia for a ('high') bourgeois cultural past and captivated by the (Freudian) ideal of a conventional subject in which the ego rules both the body and the unconscious with a firm grip. It also sketches another venue in which an engagement with postmodern cultural theory can be joined. The erosion of the unified subject in favour of the schizophrenic 'performance' of different subject-positions has long been heralded by cultural studies and many of its theoretical progenitors for liberating human beings from the restrictions of monocultural or one-dimensional identities. Benjamin's work provides critical theory with a framework for engaging with this position; it does so by admitting the possibilities that accompany these developments while simultaneously registering the barriers to their actualization imposed by capitalist social relations.

Third, Benjamin's concept of the dialectical image offers an innovative strategy for cultural critique – one which moves beyond the paralysis that Adorno's drastic prose can often inspire. A common objection that one often hears voiced about the culture industry thesis is that it leaves the reader (sympathetic or not) in an intellectual stasis; that is, it leaves little room for the possibility of change, even on a collective scale. It rails against the evils of the system in a language which that very system has cunningly condemned to oblivion; beyond that, it often seems to leave us little else to do except alternately curse and praise the 'accident of biography' that allows us to see and experience a world and its absence that remains invisible to others. The dialectical image, however, constitutes a speculative critical strategy that enables the social and psychological dynamic harnessed by the culture industry and the commodity form to turn against itself. In other words, it reconstitutes – at a specifically cultural level – the hope that has consistently energized Marxism as critical theory and an emancipatory social practice, namely, a conviction that what capitalism 'produces, above all, is its own grave-diggers'.[6] On a similar theme, Terry Eagleton has recently observed: 'Authentic utopian thought concerns itself with that which is encoded within the logic of a system which, extrapolated in a certain direction, has the power to undo it. By installing itself in those contradictions or equivocations in a system and where it ceases to be identical with itself, it allows that non-identity to reveal itself as the negative image of some future positivity.'[7]

The dialectical image provides a means of recognizing and accessing this utopian potential without misreading the traces that mark it as evidence of its realization. Moreover – as Benjamin's own keen interest in surrealism and film signifies – this intellectual strategy is well equipped to investigate the potential of new cultural technologies. The original culture industry thesis at times veers dangerously close to an antitechnological polemic *vis-à-vis* film, radio, and television and thereby raises doubts about its utility in critically analysing new developments in culture; Benjamin's work is not similarly vulnerable. Instead, the dialectical image lets us explore the possibilities for individual and collective self-expression, reflection and (re)creation through culture (i.e., film as a new 'play-space' in which human beings can reflexively 'master' their relations with first and second nature) while at the same time we are looking to the systematic denial of these possibilities in capitalist social relations. Given the sporadic flirtation of cultural studies with the ideas of Benjamin – which are often invoked as a foil to Adorno's pessimism – the dialectical image serves as an excellent bridging point in fostering a more substantial dialogue between critical theory and cultural studies.

Fourth, Benjamin's work on the interrelated themes of experience, memory, mimesis, and utopia can be used to construct a bridging network between Adorno's work on mass culture and the more 'dialectical' critical positions that Adorno advances in his aesthetic writings. With respect to mass culture, the face that Adorno turns to the world is severe and uncompromising: whether delivering a stern lecture about the evil banality of the culture industry's products or attacking the totalizing manner in which the administered society has colonized all aspects of social existence, he is generally understood in a single dimension. As this project has demonstrated, there are many signs of hope scattered throughout Adorno's work – gathered most coherently in *Aesthetic Theory* – that do point to the possibilities for critical thought, experience, and action which remain in contemporary societies. Yet the pathways linking these relatively esoteric strategies to the critique of mass culture are often tortuous and difficult to navigate. Consequently, the popular understanding of the culture industry thesis has a tendency to remain rather narrow, uninformed by the more complex social theory of which it is only one part. For instance, approaches to Adorno's work on mass culture that do not take into account his normative speculations on the differential experiential mode that aesthetic practices could foster are bound to misinterpret his anger at mass culture as a form of elitism and/or nostalgia. Benjamin helps mediate between these two moments through, for example, the discussion of mimesis; he also sketches out provocative new ways of reading Adorno against himself, of mobilizing his philosophical aesthetics to power a dialectical renovation of the culture industry thesis. Although these two are often placed on opposing sides of the culture debate, they can more fruitfully be read as illuminating the hidden dimensions of each other's work. Thus, Benjamin can help reveal in Adorno's work a sensitivity to utopian fragments and to the emancipatory potential of mimetic forms of experience – a sensitivity that often goes unnoticed, especially in the mass culture writings. To put it somewhat differently, Benjamin restores a vigour, motion, and reflexivity to Adorno's ideas that has arguably been lost to the present because of the compartmentalization that so often accompanies the uneven appropriation of the work of major intellectual figures. In turn, this makes for an Adorno who can defend himself far more effectively against the criticisms levelled against the culture industry thesis by those outside critical theory. Aside from this benefit, it also establishes a much deeper foundation on which to begin a discussion with cultural studies. For example, Adorno's 'praise' of modern art as 'the absolute commodity' opens up an intriguing set of affinities with many postmodern scholars, who suggest that homeopathic immersion in contemporary cultural logics that have been synthetically accelerated might hold the key to breaking the stranglehold of these very logics.[8] At the very least, the selective entry of some of Adorno's other work cannot help but improve the tone and substance of the debate over the culture industry.

Finally – and closely related to the last point – a tracing out of the conceptual and normative framework shared by Adorno and Benjamin stands against the latter's facile appropriation by those working in a more celebratory mode. Like that of other Marxists whose work has come has to us in fragments – the most notable example is probably Gramsci – Benjamin's work is easily subject to selective interpretation: one can make it fit an almost infinite variety of projects. Furthermore, his writings are often characterized by a deceptive simplicity that only obliquely points toward the rich meaning to be found beneath the surface. For example, the 'Work of Art' essay – perhaps his best-known piece – can be read easily enough as a celebration of the virtues of new cultural technologies with a few cautionary notes regarding their susceptibility to fascist colonization. This interpretation obviously misses entire dimensions of the essay, such as the psychoanalytic dimensions of experience embedded in the term 'distraction' and the evolving relations between subject and object signalled by the word 'aura'; yet there is a surface logic to the text that licenses such readings. Drawing linkages between Benjamin and Adorno, beyond their simplistic positioning as opponents in the mass culture debate, helps construct the broader philosophical structure in which Benjamin's work can be most fruitfully understood. Benjamin refused the conceptual mediation so aggressively urged on him by Adorno; even so, the careful reader can judiciously apply the latter's dense, abstract theory to nourish the growth of exotic insights out of the richness of Benjamin's texts. In my own project, Adorno's work has been especially important when it comes to thinking through the role of the commodity form in freezing the emancipatory potential, traces of which Benjamin locates in the detritus of capitalist society. In other words, it helps prevent the hermeneutic elevation of the contemplative moments in his texts to a dominant role whereby Benjamin's famed 'micrological' skill in deciphering social fragments[9] becomes – to paraphrase his own words – a means of continuing dream-sleep rather than an impetus for revolutionary awakening. One might say that Adorno's stern and consistent invocations of the present as Hell, and his identification of capitalist social relations at its centre exercises a weak gravitational force on Benjamin's speculative texts, preventing them from being pulled into the constellation of postmodern cultural studies. In short, the juxtaposition of Benjamin and Adorno in a state of constant dialectical tension offers an extremely potent intellectual forcefield in which the insights of one acquire their critical charge as they are positioned in close proximity with those of the other.

Obviously, the sympathies of this project lie with critical theory. I have not tried to achieve a synthesis of critical theory and cultural studies, in large part because I do not believe that any such effort could succeed. There are simply too many substantive differences that lie in the way of a genuine reconciliation between these two theoretical approaches. Moreover, I also remain sceptical of a toolbox approach to the study of culture in which one simply selects a random series of elements from different theoretical systems as required for the analysis of a particular cultural phenomenon. Consequently, my own efforts have been directed toward reconstructing critical theory's work on mass culture and a thorough, reasoned defence of how and why I believe this work is better equipped to explore the issues surrounding the commodification of culture than the conceptual tools and framework provided by cultural studies. For the most part, the developmental trajectory of cultural studies has marked the intersection of the commodity form and cultural practices as unworthy of serious consideration. Yet there are also clear indications that as cultural studies moves away from an insular commitment to the specificity of cultural practices, new points of contact will emerge between these two disciplines. To the extent that cultural studies acquires an interest in exploring the relations between economy, culture, and society, a fruitful theoretical partnership with critical theory may yet become possible. At the very least, a dialogue between critical theory and cultural studies that takes commodified culture as its object can reveal gaps or failures in their respective analytic frameworks, which may then force an internal reassessment and even reconstruction of the principles and assumptions that ground these frameworks. In my case, I hope that even those within cultural studies who remain unconvinced of the merits of Adorno and Benjamin have been given pause to (re)consider the effectiveness with which their own discipline deals with this important question as well as the legitimacy with which critical theory has until now been dismissed.

And the lines of communication and debate certainly ought to flow both ways. I believe critical theory does a much better job of theorizing culture *as* commodity than cultural studies, but this does not mean that the former has nothing to learn from the latter. Many scholars in cultural studies have done exemplary work in describing the characteristics and effects of specific cultural practices; furthermore, local ethnographic investigations into the reception of mass culture can provide valuable information about how these practices are actually taken up and used. When read as a universal indictment that unequivocally condemns *all* contemporary culture, the culture industry thesis necessarily fails to adequately engage with and reflect the differences that exist between various cultural objects and practices. Adorno's work is especially flawed in terms of its inability to theorize processes of cultural change and evolution as dynamic – in particular, its inability to theorize the endless emergence of incipient subcultures at the margins or interstices of society, subcultures that often evolve in conscious opposition to commodified mass culture. The culture industry relies heavily on appropriating the authentic creative impulses at work in these formations in order to stamp its own products with the illusion of novelty, development, and autonomy. 'Vestiges of the aesthetic claim to be something autonomous, a world unto itself,' Adorno himself admits, 'remain even within the most trivial product of mass culture.'[10] However, once the totalizing rhetoric of the culture industry thesis is set to one side, that is, once it is recognized to be as much a tactical manoeuver as a profound theoretical commitment – 'As a positive statement, the thesis that life is senseless would be as foolish as it is false to avow the contrary; the thesis is true *only* as a blow at the highflown avowal'[11] – the continuing relevance of this thesis as a mode of theorizing the relentless inertia of culture under capitalism becomes clear. It is easy enough to gather evidence that contradicts the monolithic totality of the culture industry thesis: alternative forms of culture and cultural practice do exist and sometimes even burst into mainstream venues. Yet the often shocking disjuncture between occasional flares of brilliance and the turgid monotony and crass opportunism of most mass culture drives home Adorno's basic point: when the pervasiveness of capitalist social relations demands that culture be produced first and foremost as a commodity – irrespective of whether the application of this principle is exercised centrally through hierarchical bureaucratic structures or internalized by producers loosely coordinated into flexible and decentralized subcontracting networks – culture is inevitably pressured, more or less successfully, to take on certain characteristics that can be abstractly theorized and that demand (and reinforce) certain cognitive and experiential patterns on the part of its consumers.

Those who insist that contemporary critical theory must reckon with the considerable differences between Fordist and post-Fordist cultural formations raise a valid point. Without question, a form of diversity has taken root as a result of the increased targeting of cultural products and advertisements to smaller and smaller demographic subsets and the subsequent erosion of the traditional 'mass audience.' Yet the influence of commodification over all forms of cultural production and reception has never been more powerful and all-encompassing. Hence critical cultural theory can best respond to these new developments not by abandoning the commodity form as a conceptual tool, but rather by theorizing how the consumptive agency and semiotic polysemy of new cultural formations fit into the broader logic of the commodified mass culture. For example, while the concept of pseudo-individuation provides an excellent framework for contextualizing the type of diversity favoured by the culture industry, one could argue that in Adorno's work this concept is both empirically and theoretically underdeveloped. In this context, Grossberg's characterization of postmodern culture as the formation of (affective) difference out of indifference (or sameness) offers intriguing new possibilities for extending and recasting Adorno's original concept. Similarly, the culture industry thesis lacks adequate tools for analysing the development of new forms of 'agency' with which mass culture tries to solicit the active participation of consumers. For example, the 'interactive' entertainment facilitated by the spread of personal computers and the Internet has novel characteristics that differ from (primitive) film, radio, and television, which so arouse the ire of Adorno. The integration of this technology into capitalist social relations may very well involve strategies that move beyond those outlined in the culture industry thesis. As marketing invades individual homes, the role of consumers in actively integrating themselves into the structures of the culture industry will probably expand beyond anything that Adorno or Benjamin could have envisaged. To the extent that contemporary cultural studies describes and theorizes these kinds of developments, it offers valuable resources to critical theory.

However, such an exchange must not – and, I think, need not – come at the expense of the powerful theme that lies at the core of critical theory's approach to mass culture – namely, that the critical investigation of cultural practices in a capitalist society *must* attend to the unique effects that arise out of the production and consumption of culture *as* commodity. The pleasures, desires, and dreams, the dangers, fears, and frustrations that it inspires – none of these experiences can be adequately understood in terms of either their effects on individual cognitive, libidinal, somatic, or affective structures or their broader social impact unless we explicitly consider the role of commodification. This does not mean that mass culture is to be only ever analysed as a species of capitalist ideology whose 'fake' pleasures merely reinforce the social power of the dominant system. Just as commodification imposes cognitive and libidinal patterns of identity on culture, culture allows people to experience a material and mental sense of *both* the horrors *and* the pleasures of the commodity form. Unquestionably, Adorno and Benjamin are critical of the effects of commodification on cultural practices. But their critique is not based on a simplistic conservatism that advocates a literal return to the idealized joys of a precapitalist past. Rather, the bitterness and frustration that characterize their work – especially that of Adorno – arise out of society's failure to realize the dreams spawned at least in part by the commodity form itself. For example, the triumph of exchange-value harbours the utopian possibility that human relations with an object may be emancipated from a utilitarian mode in which its 'use-value' – its 'being for us' – overwhelms all other aspects of its existence. By the same token, Benjamin's valuation of Fourier's fantasies suggests that commodity fetishism need not be destroyed so much as dialectically redeemed.

A common interpretive fallacy in readings of critical theory relates to the extrapolation of a generalized rejection of hedonism from its specific hatred of the pleasures of mass culture. For example, Miklitsch counters Adorno's claim that 'in a communist society work will be organized in such a way that people will no longer be so tired and so stultified that they need distraction' with the smug reminder that 'whatever social arrangements prevail in the future, "people" will always need to be distracted (i.e., "People [will] want to have fun").'[12] Admittedly, Adorno's own words sometimes suggest as much: 'Ascetic ideals constitute today a more solid bulwark against the madness of the profit-economy than did the hedonistic life sixty years ago against liberal repression.'[13] Yet the basic thrust of this critique is not that mass culture provides too much pleasure, but rather that it does not provide enough to demonstrate the impoverishment of contemporary experience. The problem with the culture industry is not that it deceives people by distracting them from 'reality,' but that it does not provide a sufficiently powerful distraction to stimulate the collective imagination to dream about new forms of thought and being. Remember Adorno's diagnosis of film: 'It is not because they turn their back on washed-out existence that escape films are so repugnant, but because they do not do so energetically enough, because they are themselves just as washed-out, because the satisfactions they fake coincide with the ignominy of reality, of denial. The dreams have no dream.'[14] But if the dreams of Hollywood have no dream, they are at the very least haunted by its absence. Benjamin's work on the Arcades shows how the eruption of utopian impulses in everyday life is not constituted out of a 'pure' opposition to capital, but precisely through the emancipatory potential that capital creates yet subsequently only allows expression in mute, petrified forms. Similarly, Adorno recognizes that the energies required to charge a messianic leap into the realm of history can only come from the very system that must itself be transcended: 'To become transformed into an insect, man needs that energy which might possibly achieve his transformation into a man.'[15]

Such a dialectical analysis of the pleasures of the culture industry is eminently more promising as a form of critical cultural analysis than the calls for 'balance' that increasingly issue from cultural studies as a means of tempering some of its earlier excesses. Grossberg, for example, writes: 'Echoing Hall, if reality was never as real as we have constructed it, it's not quite as unreal as we imagine it; if subjectivity was never as coherent as we imagine it, it's not quite as incoherent as we fantasize it; and if power was never as simple or monolithic as we fantasize it (reproducing itself, requiring giants and magical subjects to change it), it's not quite as dispersed and unchallengeable as we fear.'[16]

At one level, such balanced accounts of cultural processes can operate as useful empirical descriptions of the never-ending struggles between hegemonic cultural institutions on the one hand, and individuals and groups on the other. It is a truism to note that people are neither the helpless victims nor the cunning masters of the culture industry: at certain times we enjoy its sanctioned pleasures, at others we may be unaffected by them or even reject them with contempt. Yet such a 'reasonable' position disguises as much about contemporary culture as it reveals. Concordant with this dynamic of 'give and take,' there is an equally powerful logic boiling away beneath the surface of conscious experience. While the 'realistic disposition' of the former demands a diagnosis of balance, the latter dimension is characterized by a heightened sensitivity to the speculative moment, to the *potentiality* that lingers in all things. Its comprehension requires a truly dialectical form of thought that registers not only what a subject or an object is, but also what it might be, for it draws its energy from the gap between them. To recall Jameson's eloquent invocation, we must do

> the impossible, namely, to think [the development of capitalism] positively *and* negatively all at once; to achieve, in other words, a type of thinking that would be capable of grasping the demonstrably baleful features of capitalism along with its extraordinary and liberating dynamism simultaneously within a single thought, and without attenuating any of the force of either judgement. We are somehow to lift our minds to a point at which it is possible to understand that capitalism is at one and the same time the best thing that has ever happened to the human race, and the worst.[17]

Held together in a state of dialectical tension, Benjamin and Adorno provide the conceptual tools to do just that with contemporary culture, to think it as the expression (and embodiment) of an immense range of possibilities that are withdrawn at the same moment they are offered. Such a form of critical thought promises a depth and complexity to the study of culture beyond that which is offered by most forms of contemporary cultural studies.

The utopian moments in mass culture can only be accessed through a relentless form of negative critique that frees them, however fleetingly, from the suffocating embrace of the culture industry's false pleasures. This is no easy task. The commodity draws life from the exchange relation and thereby solicits the projected fantasies of the consumer, yet its utopian energies lie buried deep within. Benjamin studied the Parisian Arcades in the 1930s in large part because the phantasmagoria that had bathed these passages and their products in a lustral glow a century before had long since been extinguished by the passage of time. As ruins and only as ruins could they give up their secrets. From our stance just beyond the far edge of the twentieth century, it is difficult to imagine what it might be to reproduce Benjamin's method as something other than an exegetical academic exercise. If Benjamin looked to nineteenth-century Paris, what might constitute our own '*ur*-history'? Where might we excavate images of an exiled past to reveal the hellish course of historical progress inscribed in the social and material landscape of the twenty-first century? How might we charge a future-present in which such images can be redeemed?[18] As a minimum requirement, the capacity of the culture industry to recycle its own garbage, to commodify even its own ruins, presses the need for a destructive intellectual practice that is not as dependent on time to erode the false hopes sponsored by capital. 'To the process of rescue,' wrote Benjamin in the last years of his life, 'belongs the firm, seemingly brutal grasp.'[19] Few cultivated such a grasp better then Adorno. And that is why his mode of uncompromising critique is as important now as it has ever been. The culture industry has never been more powerful, never been more invasive, and certainly never been more dominated by the commodity form than it is today. While this may have intensified the utopian possibilities embedded in mass culture, it has also fortified the barriers that prevent their collective appropriation. Adorno's visceral attack on the facile pleasures of the culture industry is essential in forming, shaping, and energizing the 'destructive character' that alone holds any hope of redeeming these possibilities.

# Notes

### Introduction

1 Raymond Williams, *Keywords: A Vocabulary of culture and Society* (London: Fontana Press, 1988), 89.

2 For a thorough and insightful analysis of the contradictions that characterize the relationship between capitalism and new information technologies, see Nicholas Dyer-Witherford, *Cyber-Marx: Cycles and Circuits of Struggle in High Technology Capitalism* (Chicago: University of Illinois Press, 1999). A more focused discussion of the political economy of the Internet and World Wide Web is found in Dan Schiller, *Digital Capitalism: Networking the Global Market System* (Cambridge: MIT Press, 1999).

3 Julian Stallabrass, *Gargantua: Manufactured Mass Culture* (New York: Verso, 1996), 3.

4 In many respects, the term 'cultural studies' has become impossibly nebulous and vague in recent years, referring to an enormously diverse and often eclectic body of work spanning several academic disciplines. As I note later in this introduction, my own use of the term refers to the study of culture pioneered at the Centre for Contemporary Cultural Studies in Birmingham and to those who continue to be guided by the basic tenets of that approach. The work of Stuart Hall is exemplary in the former case; Lawrence Grossberg is a prominent representative of the latter.

5 Lawrence Grossberg, 'Cultural Studies vs Political Economy: Is Anybody Else Bored with this Debate?' *Critical Studies in Mass Communication* 12.1 (1995): 76. Grossberg is replying to an essay by Nicholas Garnham, 'Political Economy and Cultural Studies: Reconciliation or Divorce?' in the same issue.

6 Grossberg, 'Cultural Studies vs Political Economy,' 75.

7 For a useful survey of the political economy of communication, see Vincent Mosco, *The Political Economy of Communication: Rethinking and Renewal* (Thousand Oaks, CA: Sage, 1996). Recent exemplary works in the field include Noam Chomsky and Edward Herman, *Manufacturing Consent: The Political Economy of the Mass Media*, 2nd ed. (New York: Pantheon Books, 2002); Ben Bagdikian, *The Media Monopoly*, 6th ed. (Boston: Beacon Press, 2000); Robert McChesney, *Rich Media, Poor Democracy: Communication Politics in Dubious Times* (Chicago: University of Illinois Press, 1999); and Schiller, *Digital Capitalism*. A useful collection of key texts can be found in Peter Golding and Graham Murdock, eds., *The Political Economy of the Media*, 2 vols (Northampton: Edward Elgar, 1997).

8 Grossberg, 'Cultural Studies vs Political Economy,' 75.

9 Nicholas Garnham, 'Reply to Grossberg and Carey,' *Critical Studies in Mass Communication* 12.1 (1995): 96–7.

10 In his comprehensive introduction to the field of media political economy, Vincent Mosco identifies the relative failure to focus on commodification as a major gap in the field. See 'Commodification' in *The Political Economy of Communication.*

11 Garnham, 'Political Economy and Cultural Studies,' 65.

12 See 'The Culture Industry: Enlightenment as Mass Deception,' in *Dialectic of Enlightenment: Philosophical Fragments*, ed. Gunzelin Schmid Noerr, trans. Edmund Jephcott (Stanford: Stanford University Press, 2002). My direct incorporation of material from the *Dialectic of Enlightenment* into discussions of Adorno's work on mass culture should not be taken to indicate an implicit claim that the chapter on the culture industry properly belongs to him and not to Horkheimer. Archival research suggests that Adorno drafted the chapter, which was then intensively discussed and revised by the two authors together: see the discussion in Gunzelin Schmid Noerr, 'Editor's Afterword,' *Dialectic of Enlightenment*, 222–4.

13 'Culture Industry Reconsidered,' trans. Anson G. Rabinbach, in *The Culture Industry: Selected Essays on Mass Culture*, ed. J.M. Bernstein (London: Routledge, 1991), 85.

14 *Dialectic of Enlightenment*, 95.

15 'Culture Industry Reconsidered,' 86.

16 See, for example, Fredric Jameson, *Late Marxism: Adorno, or, the Persistence of the Dialectic* (New York: Verso, 1990), 141–4, and Peter Uwe Hohendahl, *Prismatic Thought: Theodor W. Adorno* (Lincoln: University of Nebraska Press, 1995), 127 and 145–7.

17 Deborah Cook's *The Culture Industry Revisited* (London: Rowman and Littlefield, 1996) constitutes a welcome exception to this trend. Calling for

a revaluation of Adorno's arguments on mass culture, she argues that both are more balanced and sophisticated than they seem at first glance. She offers a concise and highly accessible reading of the culture industry thesis as well as a reasoned defence of Adorno against many of his contemporary critics. However, her revisitation of the culture industry thesis is tilted heavily in favour of its psychological devices and mechanisms, and she does not devote much attention to the specificity of the commodity form *vis-à-vis* mass culture. Moreover, her renovation of the culture industry thesis fails to make use of the work of Walter Benjamin – a strategy that I believe can add an essential complexity and depth that Adorno's work taken on its own tends to lack.

18 In a recent issue of *New German Critique* entitled *Dialectic of Enlightenment*, for example, not a single essay treats the chapter on the culture industry at any length. See *New German Critique* 81 (Fall 2000).

19 See, for example, Nick Nesbitt, 'Sounding Autonomy: Adorno, Coltrane and Jazz,' *Telos* 116 (Summer 1999); Evelyn Wilcock, 'Adorno, Jazz and Racism: "Uber Jazz" and the 1934–7 British Jazz Debate,' *Telos* 107 (Spring 1996); Harry Cooper, 'On *Uber Jazz*: Replaying Adorno with the Grain,' *October* 75 (Winter 1996); James Harding, 'Adorno, Ellison and the Critique of Jazz,' *Cultural Critique* (Fall 1995); J. Bradford Robinson, 'The Jazz Essays of Theodor Adorno: Some Thoughts on Jazz Reception in Weimar Germany,' *Popular Music* 13.1 (1994); and Ulrich Schönherr, 'Adorno and Jazz: Reflections on a Failed Encounter,' *Telos* 87 (Spring 1991).

20 Adorno's difficulties in working with Paul Lazarsfeld in research into commercial radio testify to this fact. For an account of this episode, see Rolf Wiggershaus, 'Adorno, Lazarsfeld and the Princeton Radio Project,' in *The Frankfurt School: Its History, Theories and Political Significance*, trans. Michael Robertson (Cambridge: MIT Press, 1995), 237–45.

21 See, for example, 'Free Time,' trans. Gordon Williamson and Nicholas Walker, in *The Culture Industry*, 169; 'The Stars Down to Earth: The *Los Angeles Times* Astrology Column,' in *The Stars Down to Earth and Other Essays on the Irrational in Culture*, ed. Stephen Crook (New York: Routledge, 1994), 40; 'Analytical Study of the NBC Music Appreciation Hour,' *Musical Quarterly* 78 (Summer 1994): 370; and *Introduction to the Sociology of Music*, trans. E.B. Ashton (New York: Seabury Press, 1976), 2.

22 Adorno, *Minima Moralia: Reflections from a Damaged Life*, trans. E.F.N. Jephcott (London: New Left Books, 1974), 126–7.

23 Cited in Shierry Weber Nicholsen, 'Adorno, Benjamin and the Aura: An Aesthetics for Photography,' in *Adorno, Culture and Feminism*, ed. Maggie O'Neill (Thousand Oaks, CA: Sage, 1999), 60–1.

24 Theodor Adorno, 'Letter to Walter Benjamin, December 17, 1934,' in Theodor Adorno and Walter Benjamin, *The Complete Correspondence, 1928–1940*, ed. Henri Lonitz, trans. Nicholas Walker (Cambridge: Harvard University Press, 1999), 66.

25 Adorno, *Minima Moralia*, 247.

26 Richard Johnson, 'What Is Cultural Studies Anyway?' *Social Text* 16 (Winter 1986–7): 55–8.

27 See Douglas Kellner, 'Critical Theory and Cultural Studies: The Missed Articulation,' *Cultural Methodologies*, ed. Jim McGuigan (Thousand Oaks, CA: Sage, 1997). For a more extensive discussion, theorization, and application of a 'multi-perspectival cultural studies,' see Douglas Kellner, *Media Culture: Cultural Studies, Identity and Politics between the Modern and the Postmodern* (New York: Routledge, 1995), and Steven Best and Douglas Kellner, *The Postmodern Adventure: Science, Technology and Cultural Studies at the Third Millennium* (New York: Guilford Press, 2001), especially chapter 5.

28 Jane Bennett, 'Commodity Fetishism and Commodity Enchantment,' *Theory and Event* 5.1 (2001); also see this essay's placement in a broader theoretical framework in her *The Enchantment of Modern Life: Attachments, Crossings, and Ethics* (Princeton: Princeton University Press, 2001). Bennett's reading of the culture industry thesis is especially instructive as to the problems that arise when selective aspects of Adorno's work are taken in isolation from his broader theoretical project. Her insistence, for example, that Horkheimer and Adorno unequivocally endorse 'disenchantment' as a response to the charms of the culture industry stands in notable contrast to the basic critique of instrumental reason – i.e., the 'disenchantment' of the world – that constitutes the basic thesis of *Dialectic of Enlightenment* (as well as other key texts such as Adorno's *Negative Dialectics* and *Aesthetic Theory*, and Horkheimer's *The Eclipse of Reason*).

29 Robert Miklitsch, *From Hegel to Madonna: Towards a General Economy of 'Commodity Fetishism'* (Albany: State University of New York Press, 1998).

30 Walter Benjamin, 'O (Prostitution, Gambling) [2a,1],' *The Arcades Project*, Prepared on basis of German volume edited by Rolf Tiedemann, trans. Howard Eiland and Kevin McLaughlin (Cambridge: Belknap Press of Harvard University Press, 1999), 494.

31 The most thorough discussion of this relationship remains Susan Buck-Morss's classic study *The Origin of Negative Dialectics: Theodor W. Adorno, Walter Benjamin and the Frankfurt Institute* (Sussex: Harvester Press, 1977). Other good treatments include Miriam Hansen, 'Of Mice and Ducks:

Benjamin and Adorno on Disney,' *South Atlantic Quarterly* 92.1 (1993); Shierry Weber Nicholsen, *Exact Imagination, Late Work: On Adorno's Aesthetics* (Cambridge: MIT Press, 1997); chs. 4 and 5; Richard Wolin, 'Benjamin, Adorno, Surrealism,' *The Semblance of Subjectivity: Essays in Adorno's Aesthetic Theory* (Cambridge: MIT Press, 1997); and *Walter Benjamin: An Aesthetic of Redemption* (New York: Columbia University Press, 1982), ch. 6.

32 Benjamin, 'Letter to Adorno, June 30, 1936,' *The Complete Correspondence*, 144.

33 Adorno, 'Letter to Benjamin, March 18, 1936,' *The Complete Correspondence*, 131.

34 Fredric Jameson, *Postmodernism, Or, The Cultural Logic of Late Capitalism* (Durham: Duke University Press, 1991), 47.

35 Antonio Gramsci, *Selections from the Prison Notebooks*, ed. and trans. Quintin Hoare and Geoffrey Nowell Smith (New York: International Publishers, 1971), 276.

36 Philip Rosen, 'Introduction to Special Issue on *The Arcades Project*,' *Boundary 2* 30.1 (2003): 2.

37 Michael Jennings, 'On the Banks of a New Lethe: Commodification and Experience in Benjamin's Baudelaire Book,' *Boundary 2* 30.1 (2003): 96. An extremely fertile theoretical fragment that alludes to many of Benjamin's intentions with regard to this book is 'The Study Begins with Some Reflections on the Influence of *Les Fleurs du Mal*,' *Selected Writings*, Volume 4, 1938–1940, ed. Howard Eiland and Michael Jennings, trans. Edmund Jephcott and others (Cambridge: Belknap Press of Harvard University Press, 2003).

38 Angela McRobbie, *Postmodernism and Popular Culture* (New York: Routledge, 1994), 113; and Susan Willis, *A Primer for Everyday Life* (New York: Routledge, 1991), 11.

39 Don Slater and Fran Tonkiss, *Market Society: Markets and Modern Social Theory* (Malden, MA: Polity Press, 2001), 171.

40 Marcuse, *One Dimensional Man: Studies in the Ideology of Advanced Industrial Society* (Boston: Beacon Press, 1966).

41 On the problems that often attend such critiques, see Gilbert Rodman, 'Subject to Debate: (Mis)Reading Cultural Studies,' *Journal of Communication Inquiry* 21.2 (1997).

42 See, for example, Joel Pfister, 'The Americanization of Cultural Studies,' *Yale Journal of Criticism* 4.2 (1991) and Mike Budd, Robert Entman, and Clay Steinman, 'The Affirmative Character of U.S. Cultural Studies,' *Critical Studies in Mass Communication* 7 (1990). Hall himself contributed to

this perspective when he warned that the institutionalization of cultural studies within universities constituted a 'moment of profound danger.' See 'Cultural Studies and Its Theoretical Legacies,' *Cultural Studies*, ed. Lawrence Grossberg, Cary Nelson, and Paula Treichler (New York: Routledge, 1992), 285.

43 A selection of recent book-length histories and reflections on cultural studies over the past decade include Michael Peters, ed., *After the Disciplines: The Emergence of Cultural Studies* (Westport, CT: Bergin and Garvey, 1999); Lawrence Grossberg, *Bringing It All Back Home: Essays on Cultural Studies* (Durham: Duke University Press, 1997); Amitava Kumar, ed., *Class Issues: Pedagogy, Cultural Studies and the Public Sphere* (New York: New York University Press, 1997); Dennis Dworkin, *Cultural Marxism in Postwar Britain: History, the New Left and the Origins of Cultural Studies* (Durham: Duke University Press, 1997); Angela McRobbie, ed., *Back to Reality: Social Experience and Cultural Studies* (New York: Manchester University Press, 1997); Cary Nelson and Dilip Parameshwar Gaonkar, eds., *Disciplinarity and Dissent in Cultural Studies* (New York: Routledge, 1996); Ioan Davies, *Cultural Studies and Beyond: Fragments of Empire* (New York: Routledge, 1995); Douglas Kellner, *Media Culture;* John Clarke, *New Times and Old Enemies: Essays on Cultural Studies and America* (London: HarperCollins Academic, 1991); and Patrick Brantlinger, *Crusoe's Footprints: Cultural Studies in Britain and America* (New York: Routledge, 1990). Not surprisingly perhaps, a growing number of critiques of cultural studies have also emerged in recent years. The most comprehensive is Jim McGuigan, *Cultural Populism* (New York: Routledge, 1992), but other notables include Marjorie Ferguson and Peter Golding, eds., *Cultural Studies in Question* (Thousand Oaks, CA: Sage, 1997); Michael Pickering, *History, Experience and Cultural Studies* (New York: St Martin's Press, 1997); Keith Tester, *Media, Culture and Morality* (New York: Routledge, 1994); Ben Agger, *Cultural Studies as Critical Theory* (Washington: Falmer Press, 1992), and David Harris, *From Class Struggle to the Politics of Pleasure: The Effects of Gramscianism on Cultural Studies* (New York: Routledge, 1992). In a more popular vein, critics such as Thomas Frank and Russell Jacoby highlight the contradiction between the self-styled radicalism of cultural studies and what they see as its complicity with neoliberalism. See Thomas Frank, 'New Consensus for Old: Cultural Studies from Left to Right,' in *One Market Under God: Extreme Capitalism, Market Populism, and the End of Economic Democracy* (New York: Anchor Books, 2001), and Russell Jacoby, 'Mass Culture and Anarchy,' in *The End of Utopia: Politics and Culture in an Age of Apathy* (New York: Basic Books, 1999).

**1: Mass Culture and the Commodity Form**

1 Adorno, 'Freudian Theory and the Pattern of Fascist Propaganda,' *The Essential Frankfurt School Reader*, ed. Andrew Arato and Eike Gebhardt (New York: Continuum, 1982), 121.

2 Most obviously, the field of cultural studies has often grounded itself by repudiating the cultural elitism of the Frankfurt School in favour of a more democratic understanding of how people actively participate in cultural practices. While this may be a laudable goal, the claims of critical theory are often dismissed by referring exclusively to their diagnostic shortcomings (i.e., people are not *that* stupid) without actually addressing the arguments made about how the culture industry functions. I discuss the mutual critique of cultural studies and critical theory at greater length in Chapters Four and Five. Also, see the discussion in Hohendahl, *Prismatic Thought*, 9–14, 119–24.

3 Adorno (with the assistance of Simpson), 'On Popular Music,' *Studies in Philosophy and Social Science* 9 (1941).

4 Ibid., 19.

5 Ibid., 27.

6 'Interview with David Kendall, Warner Bros. Television,' *Making and Selling Culture*, ed. Richard Ohmann (Hanover: Wesleyan University Press, 1996), 62.

7 Horkheimer and Adorno, *Dialectic of Enlightenment*, 106.

8 See Bernard Gendron, 'Adorno Meets the Cadillacs,' *Studies in Entertainment: Critical Approaches to Mass Culture*, ed. Tania Modleski (Bloomington: Indiana University Press, 1986), for a discussion of the many difficulties of using the concept of industrial production to understand how culture is created.

9 Wiggershaus notes, for example, that between 1921 and 1932, Adorno published one hundred articles on music criticism and aesthetics, while his first publication on philosophy did not appear until 1933. See *The Frankfurt School*, 70. For an excellent discussion of Adorno's work on music, see Max Paddison, *Adorno's Aesthetics of Music* (New York: Cambridge University Press, 1993).

10 Adorno, 'On Jazz,' trans. Jamie Owen Daniel, *Discourse* 12.1 (1989): 47.

11 Adorno, 'The Radio Symphony: An Experiment in Theory,' *Radio Research 1941*, ed. Paul Lazarsfeld and Frank Stanton (New York: Duell, Sloan and Pearce, 1941), 116.

12 Adorno and Horkheimer, *Dialectic of Enlightenment*, 99.

13 Martin Jay, *Adorno* (London: Fontana, 1984), 123.

14 Huyssen, 'Adorno in Reverse: From Hollywood to Richard Wagner,' *New German Critique* 29 (Spring/Summer 1983): 31–2.
15 Horkheimer and Adorno, 'The Schema of Mass Culture,' trans. Nicholas Walker, in *The Culture Industry*, 75–6.
16 Adorno, 'On the Fetish Character of Music and the Regression in Listening,' trans. Maurice Goldbloom, in *The Essential Frankfurt School Reader*, 282–3.
17 Adorno, 'On Popular Music,' 21.
18 Adorno cited in Paddison, *Adorno's Aesthetics of Music*, 178. The original is from *Gesammelte Schriften*, 7: 156.
19 Adorno, 'Perennial Fashion: Jazz,' *Prisms*, trans. Samuel Weber and Shierry Weber (Cambridge: MIT Press, 1982), 121.
20 Adorno, *Introduction to the Sociology of Music*, 13.
21 In the case of early German jazz, two- and four-bar improvisations were actually highly codified and learned by rote from 'break manuals' published at the time. Robinson, 'The Jazz Essays of Theodor Adorno,' 10.
22 Adorno argues that a similar response to reification and commodity fetishism can be found in Heidegger's philosophy of being, the pseudo-metaphysical culture industry of intellectuals: 'The more reified the world becomes, the thicker the veil cast upon nature, the more the thinking weaving that veil in turn claims ideologically to be nature, primordial experience.' Adorno, 'Why Still Philosophy,' in *Critical Models: Interventions and Catchwords*, trans. Henry W. Pickford (New York: Columbia University Press, 1998), 7. For an extended critique of Heideggerian ontology *vis-à-vis* its attempt to reach directly for being, see Adorno, *Negative Dialectics*, trans. E.B. Ashton (New York: Continuum, 1995), 61–131. In the Dedication to *Minima Moralia*, Adorno sets out in precisely the opposite direction: namely, if one wishes 'to know the truth about life in its immediacy [one] must scrutinize its estranged form, the objective powers that determine individual existence even in its most hidden recesses,' 15.
23 Adorno, *Introduction to the Sociology of Music*, 46.
24 Adorno, 'The Essay as Form,' trans. Robert Hullot-Kentor and Frederic Will, *New German Critique* 32 (Spring/Summer 1984): 167.
25 Horkheimer and Adorno, *Dialectic of Enlightenment*, 97–8.
26 Ibid., *Dialectic of Enlightenment*, 99.
27 Horkheimer and Adorno, 'The Schema of Mass Culture,' 53.
28 Adorno, 'Letter to Benjamin, March 18, 1936,' *The Complete Correspondence*, 131.
29 See the discussion in Philip Rosen, 'Adorno and Film Music: Theoretical Notes on *Composing for the Films*,' *Yale French Studies* 60 (1980), especially 171–4. On the psychological significance of the iconic disposition of film

for Adorno, see Miriam Hansen's excellent discussion in 'Mass Culture as Hieroglyphic Writing: Adorno, Derrida, Kracauer,' *New German Critique* 56 (Spring/Summer 1992). Conversely, Adorno endorses the *non-iconic* (but *non-arbitrary*) form of script that is produced by the physical inscription of sound waves on the surface of a record. See the very interesting analysis by Thomas Levin, 'For the Record: Adorno on Music in the Age of Its Technological Reproducibility,' *October* 55 (Winter 1990).

30 Adorno, *Minima Moralia*, 202.

31 Adorno, 'Perennial Fashion – Jazz,' 131.

32 Horkheimer and Adorno, *Dialectic of Enlightenment*, 95.

33 Ibid., 103.

34 Ibid., 103–4.

35 Ibid., 127.

36 Benjamin, 'On the Concept of History,' *Selected Writings*, 4: 392.

37 Horkheimer and Adorno, *Dialectic of Enlightenment*, 111. For a more detailed discussion of the dialectic between failure and success in bourgeois art, see Adorno, 'Alienated Masterpiece: The *Missa Solemnis*,' *Telos* 28 (1976).

38 Adorno, *Negative Dialectics*, 320.

39 Horkheimer and Adorno, *Dialectic of Enlightenment*, xviii.

40 Ibid., 11.

41 Jameson, *Late Marxism*, 23.

42 See Pollock, 'State Capitalism: Its Possibilities and Limitations,' *The Essential Frankfurt School Reader*, 71–94. On the influence of Pollock's theory of state capitalism upon Horkheimer and Adorno, see the discussion in Douglas Kellner, *Critical Theory, Marxism and Modernity* (Baltimore: Johns Hopkins University Press, 1989), 57–63 and Rolf Wiggershaus, *The Frankfurt School*, 280–91.

43 Adorno, 'Culture Industry Reconsidered,' 85.

44 Bill Ryan, *Making Capital from Culture: The Corporate Form of Capitalist Cultural Production* (New York: Walter de Gruyter, 1992), 127.

45 Adorno, *Aesthetic Theory*, ed. Gretel Adorno and Rolf Tiedemann, trans. Robert Hullot-Kentor (Minneapolis: University of Minnesota Press, 1997), 109.

46 Horkheimer and Adorno, *Dialectic of Enlightenment*, 98.

47 In 'The Paris of the Second Empire in Baudelaire,' Benjamin traces the origins of such application of the division of labour to cultural production in the literary practices of the nineteenth century: 'It was said that Dumas employed a whole army of poor writers in his cellars.' See 'The Paris of the Second Empire in Baudelaire,' *Selected Writings*, 4: 15.

48 See the discussion in McChesney, *Rich Media, Poor Democracy*, 23.
49 Adorno, 'Perennial Fashion: Jazz,' 125.
50 Adorno, 'Letter to Benjamin, February 29, 1940,' *The Complete Correspondence*, 321.
51 Adorno, 'Television as Ideology,' *Critical Models*, 62.
52 In this context, one must not forget that Adorno is using a very particular definition of aesthetic 'use-value' that is hardly contained in the phrase itself. The true purpose of aesthetic practice is to create objects that are entirely *useless* in an instrumental sense: true aesthetic 'use-value' is, in fact, utter uselessness in the conventional sense of the word.
53 Horkheimer and Adorno, *Dialectic of Enlightenment*, 97.
54 Adorno, 'On the Fetish Character of Music,' 278.
55 Adorno, *Minima Moralia*, 231.
56 Adorno, 'On the Fetish Character of Music,' 279.
57 Horkheimer and Adorno, *Dialectic of Enlightenment*, 12.
58 Ibid., 131.
59 Adorno, 'On the Fetish Character of Music,' 279.
60 Horkheimer and Adorno, *Dialectic of Enlightenment*, 131.
61 Huyssen, 'Adorno in Reverse,' 14.
62 The classic though still relevant account of this subordination remains Harry Braverman, *Labor and Monopoly Capital* (New York: Monthly Review Press, 1974).
63 Adorno, 'On Popular Music,' 38.
64 Horkheimer and Adorno, *Dialectic of Enlightenment*, 109.
65 Adorno, *Minima Moralia*, 130.
66 Along these lines it is interesting to note that the only advanced capitalist country that averages longer working hours than the United States is Japan and it is also the only nation to spend more time per capita watching television. Juliet Schor cited in Mike Budd, Steve Craig, and Clay Steinman, *Consuming Environments: Television and Commercial Culture* (New Brunswick, NJ: Rutgers University Press, 1999), 94.
67 Horkheimer and Adorno, *Dialectic of Enlightenment*, 65.
68 Ibid., 98.
69 Ibid., 97.
70 Adorno, 'On Popular Music,' 22.
71 Horkheimer and Adorno, *Dialectic of Enlightenment*, 100.
72 Adorno, *Aesthetic Theory*, 300.
73 Adorno, 'On the Fetish Character of Music,' 280–1.
74 Horkheimer and Adorno, 'The schema of mass culture,' trans. Nicholas Walker, in *The Culture Industry: Selected Essays*, 62.
75 Kant cited in Horkheimer and Adorno, *Dialectic of Enlightenment*, 64.

76 Adorno, 'Culture Industry Reconsidered,' 91.

77 Adorno, 'The Stars Down to Earth,' 65–71.

78 Ibid., 78.

79 Symptomatic of the damaged cognitive apparatus is the ability of fascist propaganda to cast aside discursive logic in favour of an 'organized flight of ideas': 'The relation between premisses and inferences is replaced by a linking-up of ideas resting on mere similarity, often through association by employing the same characteristic word in two propositions which are logically quite unrelated. This method not only evades the control mechanisms of rational examination, but also makes it psychologically easier for the listener to "follow." He has no exacting thinking to do, but can give himself up passively to a stream of words in which he swims.' Theodor Adorno, Leo Lowenthal, and Paul W. Massing, 'Anti-Semitism and Fascist Propaganda,' in *Anti-Semitism: A Social Disease*, ed. Ernst Simmel (New York: International Universities Press, 1946), 129–30. Purposefully casting aside cognitive mediation, the fascist deploys the logic of the dream to tap directly into the unconscious of his audience. This dynamic is hardly different from that used by the culture industry.

80 Horkheimer and Adorno, *Dialectic of Enlightenment*, 20.

81 Ibid., 11.

82 Adorno, *Minima Moralia*, 80.

83 Adorno, *Introduction to the Sociology of Music*, 52.

84 Adorno, 'On the Fetish Character of Music,' 271.

85 Adorno, 'Analytical Study of the NBC Music Appreciation Hour,' 352.

86 Adorno, 'On Popular Music,' 35.

87 Horkheimer and Adorno, 'The Schema of Mass Culture,' 72.

88 Adorno, 'On Popular Music,' 22.

89 Adorno, 'On the Fetish Character of Music,' 289.

90 Among the most useful treatments of Freud's importance for critical theory are Gad Horowitz, *Repression* (Toronto: University of Toronto Press, 1977), and Joel Whitebook, *Perversion and Utopia: A Study in Psychoanalysis and Critical Theory* (Cambridge: MIT Press, 1995).

91 Adorno, 'Marginalia to Theory and Praxis,' *Critical Models*, 271.

92 Milner, cited in Horowitz, *Repression*, 167.

93 For a far-ranging critique of this gendered model of psychological evolution, see Jessica Benjamin, 'The End of Internalization? Adorno's Social Psychology,' *Telos* 32 (1977). More specifically, a critical discussion of Horkheimer and Adorno's reading of Odysseus *vis-à-vis* its gender exclusions can be found in Helga Geyer-Ryan, *Fables of Desire: Studies in the Ethics of Art and Gender* (Cambridge: Polity Press, 1994).

94 Horkheimer and Adorno, *Dialectic of Enlightenment*, 26.

95 This account should not be taken as evidence of a simplistic endorsement of Freudian ego psychology on the part of Adorno. Rather, *Dialectic of Enlightenment* constitutes a sophisticated critique of the catastrophic effects that attend the one-dimensional drive to secure the rule of the ego over the body and the id. Similarly, *Aesthetic Theory* is in large part animated by the hope that serious art can foster a very different relationship between ego and id. This dynamic will be explored at greater length in chapter 3.
96 See the discussion in Wiggershaus, *The Frankfurt School*, 150–4.
97 Horkheimer, 'Art and Mass Culture,' *Critical Theory: Selected Essays*, trans. Matthew J. O'Connell et al. (New York: Continuum, 1992), 276.
98 Cited in Adorno, 'Freudian Theory and the Pattern of Fascist Propaganda,' 122.
99 Ibid., 124.
100 Ibid., 126.
101 Adorno, 'Resignation,' trans. Wes Blomster, in *The Culture Industry*, 174.
102 Adorno, 'Perennial Fashion: Jazz,' 128.
103 Horkheimer and Adorno, *Dialectic of Enlightenment*, 168.
104 Walter Benjamin, 'The Paris of the Second Empire in Baudelaire,' 31.
105 Adorno cited in Walter Benjamin, 'N [On the Theory of Knowledge, Theory of Progress] [5,2],' *The Arcades Project*, 466.
106 Horkheimer and Adorno, 'The Schema of Mass Culture,' 56.
107 Adorno, 'On Jazz,' 54.
108 Adorno, 'On the Fetish Character of Music,' 279.
109 Horkheimer and Adorno, *Dialectic of Enlightenment*, 12.
110 Ibid., 82.
111 Adorno, 'On the Fetish Character of Music,' 290.
112 Adorno, 'Free Time,' 168. For a fascinating reading of the ambiguities of Adorno's views on sports – including the possibility that they might serve as a sort of physical variant of Kant's 'purposive purposelessness' – see William J. Morgan, 'Adorno on sport: The Case of the Fractured Dialectic,' *Theory and Society* 17 (1988).
113 Horkheimer and Adorno, *Dialectic of Enlightenment*, 111.
114 Adorno, 'Prologue to Television,' *Critical Models*, 50.
115 See, for example, the interesting discussion of television as a form of addiction in Sut Jhally, *The Codes of Advertising: Fetishism and the Political Economy of Meaning in the Consumer Society* (New York: Routledge, 1990). Note the opinion of a teacher whose words echoed many others surveyed by Jhally: 'I'd look forward to watching whenever I could, but it didn't give back a real feeling of pleasure. It was like no orgasm, no catharsis,

very frustrating. Television just wasn't giving me the promised satisfaction, and yet I kept on watching. It filled some sort of need, or had to do with an inability to get something started.' Cited on 180.

116 Horkheimer and Adorno, *Dialectic of Enlightenment*, 165.

117 Ibid., 159.

118 Benjamin, 'Commentary on Poems by Brecht,' *Selected Writings*, 4: 235.

119 Horkheimer and Adorno, *Dialectic of Enlightenment*, 107.

120 Adorno, 'Culture Industry reconsidered,' 89.

121 Adorno, *Aesthetic Theory*, 312.

122 Horkheimer and Adorno, 'The Schema of Mass Culture,' 80.

123 Horkheimer and Adorno, *Dialectic of Enlightenment*, 136.

124 Ibid., 112.

125 Adorno, 'On Popular Music,' 36–7.

126 Ibid., 46.

127 Benjamin, 'The Work of Art in the Age of Its Technological Reproducibility [Second Version],' *Selected Writings*, Volume 3, 1935–1938, ed. Howard Eiland and Michael Jennings, trans. Edmund Jephcott, Howard Eiland et al. (Cambridge: Belknap Press of Harvard University Press, 2002), 122.

128 Horkheimer and Adorno, *Dialectic of Enlightenment*, 115.

129 Adorno, *Minima Moralia*, 44.

130 Horkheimer and Adorno, *Dialectic of Enlightenment*, 104.

131 Ibid., 122.

132 Adorno, 'On Popular Music,' 42.

133 Horkheimer and Adorno, *Dialectic of Enlightenment*, 118. Expressing the hellish paradox of those who refuse the illusions of consumer society in the interests of a better world, Adorno notes (in an obviously personal vein) that 'he who is not malign does not live serenely but with a peculiarly chaste hardness and intolerance. Lacking appropriate objects, his love can scarcely express itself except by hatred for the inappropriate, in which admittedly he comes to resemble what he hates.' *Minima Moralia*, 25. Compare Benjamin's distillation of a less tortured though arguably more naive personal ethics from Brecht's lyric poetry: 'Anyone who wishes to see hardness yield should not let slip any opportunity for displaying friendliness.' 'Commentary on Poems by Brecht,' 249.

134 Horkheimer and Adorno, *Dialectic of Enlightenment*, 99.

135 Ibid., 118.

136 Horkheimer and Adorno, 'The Schema of Mass Culture,' 55.

137 Horkheimer and Adorno, *Dialectic of Enlightenment*, 8.

138 Horkheimer and Adorno, 'The Schema of Mass Culture,' 78.

139 Horkheimer and Adorno, *Dialectic of Enlightenment*, 11.

140 Adorno, 'On the Fetish Character of Music,' 292.
141 Cited in Horkheimer and Adorno, *Dialectic of Enlightenment*, 105–6.

**2: Capitalism, Mimesis, Experience**

1 Adorno, 'Letter to Benjamin, March 18, 1936,' *The Complete Correspondence*, 128.
2 Wohlfarth, 'Hibernation: On the Tenth Anniversary of Adorno's Death,' *Modern Language Notes* 94 (1979): 972, 979.
3 For a programmatic account of these differences, see Horkheimer, 'Traditional and Critical Theory.'
4 Wohlfarth, 'Hibernation, 965–6.
5 Benjamin, 'Blanqui,' *Selected Writings*, 4: 93.
6 An impressive array of scholarship provides an excellent introduction to Benjamin's writings. Among the most helpful book-length projects that have influenced my own work are Norbert Bolz and Willem Van Reijen, *Walter Benjamin*, trans. Laimdota Mazzarins (Atlantic Highlands, N.J.: Humanities Press, 1996); Susan Buck-Morss, *The Dialectics of Seeing: Walter Benjamin and the Arcades Project* (Cambridge: MIT Press, 1989); Howard Caygill, *Walter Benjamin: The Color of Experience* (New York: Routledge, 1998); Michael Jennings, *Dialectical Images: Walter Benjamin's Theory of Literary Criticism* (Ithaca, NY: Cornell University Press, 1987); John McCole, *Walter Benjamin and the Antinomies of Tradition* (Ithaca: Cornell University Press, 1993); Max Pensky, *Melancholy Dialectics: Walter Benjamin and the Play of Mourning* (Amherst: University of Massachusetts Press, 1993); Sigrid Weigel, *Body- and Image-Space: Rereading Walter Benjamin*, trans. Georgina Paul with Rachel McNicholl and Jeremy Gaines (New York: Routledge, 1996); and Wolin, *Walter Benjamin*.
7 Benjamin, 'N [1a,6],' 460.
8 Cited in Benjamin, 'The Paris of the Second Empire in Baudelaire,' 21.
9 Cited in Benjamin, 'The Paris of the Second Empire in Baudelaire,' 22.
10 Cited in Benjamin, 'L (Dream House, Museum, Spa) [5,4],' *The Arcades Project*, 415.
11 See Theodor Adorno, *Kierkegaard: Construction of the Aesthetic*, trans. Robert Hullot-Kentor (Minneapolis: University of Minnesota Press, 1989). Also see Benjamin's review, 'Kierkegaard: The End of Philosophical Idealism,' *Selected Writings*, Volume 2, *1927–1934*, ed. Michael Jennings, Howard Eiland, and Gary Smith, trans. Rodney Livingstone et al. (Cambridge: Belknap Press of Harvard University Press, 1999), 703–5.
12 Tom Gunning, 'The Exterior as *Intérieur*: Benjamin's Optical Detective,' *Boundary* 2 30.1 (2003): 106.

13 Benjamin, 'Short Shadows (II),' *Selected Writings*, 2: 701.
14 See Benjamin, 'Central Park,' *Selected Writings*, 4: 173.
15 Benjamin, 'I (The Interior; The Trace) [4,4],' *The Arcades Project*, 220.
16 Horkheimer and Adorno, *Dialectic of Enlightenment*, 89.
17 Adorno, 'The Stars Down to Earth,' 42.
18 Horkheimer and Adorno, *Dialectic of Enlightenment*, 5.
19 Adorno, 'The Stars Down to Earth,' 44.
20 Adorno, 'The Idea of Natural History,' trans. Robert Hullot-Kentor, *Telos* 60 (1984): 117. Adorno recognizes Benjamin's writings as accomplishing this objective most effectively: 'The peculiar imagistic quality of Benjamin's speculation, what might be called his mythicizing trait, has its origin in his melancholy gaze, under which the historical is transformed into nature by the strength of its own fragility and everything natural is transformed into a fragment of the history of creation.' Cited in Pensky, *Melancholy Dialectics*, 17.
21 See Adorno's critique of 'natural beauty' in *Aesthetic Theory*, 61–78.
22 Karl Marx, 'Alienated Labour,' *Karl Marx: Early Writings*, ed. and trans. T.B. Bottomore (Toronto: McGraw-Hill, 1964), 122–3.
23 Benjamin, cited by Michael Jennings, *Dialectical Images*, 75. The original is from *Gesammelte Schriften*, 1: 444. It was Lukacs who originally coined the term 'second nature' to describe this effective 'naturalization' of historical structures, institutions, and processes.
24 Benjamin, 'D (Boredom, Eternal Return) [10a,4],' *The Arcades Project*, 119.
25 Horkheimer and Adorno, *Dialectic of Enlightenment*, 39.
26 Ibid., 35.
27 Benjamin, S (Painting, Jugendstil, Novelty) [1,5],' *The Arcades Project*, 544.
28 Buck-Morss, 'Benjamin's Passagen-Werk: Redeeming Mass Culture for the Revolution,' *New German Critique* 29 (Spring/Summer 1983): 221.
29 Adorno, 'Progress,' trans. Eric Krakauer, in *Benjamin: Philosophy, Aesthetics, History*, ed. Gary Smith (Chicago: University of Chicago Press, 1989), 99.
30 Benjamin, 'Paris, the Capital of the Nineteenth Century [Exposé of 1935],' *The Arcades Project*, 8.
31 Buck-Morss, *The Dialectics of Seeing*, 98.
32 Adorno, 'The Idea of Natural-History,' 123.
33 Benjamin, *The Origin of German Tragic Drama*, trans. John Osborne (New York: Verso, 1985), 232.
34 Benjamin, 'K (Dream City and Dream House, Dreams of the Future, Anthropological Nihilism, Jung) [1a,8],' *The Arcades Project*, 391.
35 Ibid.
36 See James Rolleston, 'The Uses of the Frankfurt School: New Stories on the Left,' *Diacritics* 21.4 (1991): 91.

37 Benjamin, 'The Author as Producer,' *Selected Writings*, 2:774.
38 Rudolf Borchardt, cited in Benjamin, 'N [1,8],' 458.
39 Benjamin, 'On the Mimetic Faculty,' *Selected Writings*, 2: 720.
40 Buck-Morss notes that 'Benjamin was fully aware of the limitations of the consciousness of the child, who "lives in its world as a dictator."' *The Dialectics of Seeing*, 265.
41 Benjamin, 'Surrealism,' *Selected Writings*, 2: 217–18.
42 Weigel, *Body- and Image-Space*, 21.
43 For an excellent treatment of this theme see David McNally, *Bodies of Meaning: Studies on Language, Labor, and Liberation* (Albany: State University of New York Press, 2001), 186–8.
44 Benjamin, 'On the Mimetic Faculty,' 722.
45 Benjamin, 'On Language as Such and on the Language of Men,' *Reflections: Essays, Aphorisms, Autobiographical Writings*, ed. Peter Demetz, trans. Edmund Jephcott (New York: Schocken Books, 1978), 324.
46 Benjamin, 'On the Mimetic Faculty,' 722.
47 Weigel, *Body- and Image-Space*, 115.
48 Ibid., 126–7.
49 Horkheimer and Adorno, *Dialectic of Enlightenment*, 44.
50 Ibid., 149.
51 Ibid., 7.
52 Ibid., 19.
53 Benjamin, 'Some Motifs in Baudelaire,' *Selected Writings*, 4: 328.
54 The term comes from Weigel, *Body- and Image-Space*, 27.
55 Benjamin, 'Some Motifs in Baudelaire,' 329.
56 Ibid., 328.
57 Benjamin, 'Paris, the Capital of the Nineteenth Century [Exposé of 1935],' 8.
58 Benjamin, *The Origin of German Tragic Drama*, 216–17. Also note: 'The detailing of feminine beauties so dear to the poetry of the Baroque, a process in which each single part is exalted through a trope, secretly links up with the image of the corpse. This parceling out of feminine beauty into its noteworthy constituency resembles a dissection, and the popular comparisons of bodily parts to alabaster, snow, precious stones or other (mostly inorganic) formations makes the same point.' See 'B (Fashion) [9,3],' *The Arcades Project*, 79–80.
59 Benjamin, 'B [1,4],' 62.
60 Buck-Morss, 'The Flaneur, the Sandwichman and the Whore: The Politics of Loitering,' *New German Critique* 39 (Fall 1986): 121.
61 Benjamin, 'J (Baudelaire) [61a,1],' *The Arcades Project*, 339. The word 'girls' is in English in the original.

62 Benjamin, 'Some Motifs in Baudelaire,' 330.
63 Adorno, *Introduction to the Sociology of Music*, 203.
64 Horkheimer and Adorno, *Dialectic of Enlightenment*, 41.
65 Benjamin describes betting as 'a device for giving events the character of a shock, detaching them from the contexts of experience.' See note 54, 'Some Motifs in Baudelaire,' 351.
66 Benjamin, 'Letter to Adorno, December 9, 1938,' *The Complete Correspondence*, 296.
67 Ibid., 295–6.
68 Adorno, *Introduction to the Sociology of Music*, 170.
69 Adorno, *Minima Moralia*, 154.
70 Adorno, 'Transparencies on Film,' trans. Thomas Levin, *The Culture Industry*, 158–9.
71 Adorno takes this phrase from Leo Lowenthal: 'The implication is that somehow the psychoanalytic concept of multilayered personality has been taken up by cultural industry, and that the concept is used in order to ensnare the consumer as completely as possible and in order to engage him psychodynamically in the service of premeditated effects. A clear-cut division into allowed gratifications, forbidden gratifications, and recurrence of the forbidden gratifications in a somewhat modified and deflected form is carried through.' 'How to Look at Television,' 143.
72 Adorno, *Minima Moralia*, 231.
73 Hansen, 'Mass Culture as Hieroglyphic Writing,' 50.
74 Adorno, *Minima Moralia*, emphasis added, 25.
75 Horkheimer and Adorno, 'The Schema of Mass Culture,' 84.
76 Ibid., 82.
77 Ibid.
78 Ibid.
79 Adorno, 'On the Fetish Character of Music,' 292.
80 Horkheimer and Adorno, 'The Schema of Mass Culture,' 82.
81 Adorno, 'Freudian Theory and the Pattern of Fascist Propaganda,' 137.
82 Benjamin, 'The Storyteller: Observations on the Works of Nikolai Leskov,' *Selected Writings*, 3: 154.
83 Benjamin, 'Some Motifs in Baudelaire,' 316.
84 Benjamin, 'The Storyteller,' 149.
85 Ibid.
86 Ibid. 146.
87 Benjamin, 'The Crisis of the Novel,' *Selected Writings*, 2:299.
88 Benjamin, 'The Storyteller,' 148.
89 Benjamin, 'On the Image of Proust,' *Selected Writings*, 2:238.

90 Benjamin, 'Some Motifs in Baudelaire,' 315–16.
91 See Benjamin, 'The Paris of the Second Empire in Baudelaire,' 31.
92 Benjamin, 'Some Motifs in Baudelaire,' 328.
93 Ibid., 317.
94 Buck-Morss, 'Aesthetics and Anaesthetics: Walter Benjamin's Artwork Essay Reconsidered,' *October* 62 (Fall 1992): 18.
95 Benjamin, 'The Work of Art in the Age of Its Technological Reproducibility [Second Version],' *Selected Writings*, 3: 122.
96 Benjamin, 'Franz Kafka: On the Tenth Anniversary of His Death,' *Selected Writings*, 2: 806.
97 Adorno, 'Education after Auschwitz,' *Critical Models*, 198.
98 Freud notes, for example, that 'our abstract idea of time seems to be wholly derived from the method of working of the system *Pcpt.-Cs.* and to correspond to a perception on its own part of that method of working. This mode of functioning may perhaps constitute another way of providing a shield against stimuli.' Freud, 'Beyond the Pleasure Principle,' *On Metapsychology: The Theory of Psychoanalysis*, ed. Angela Richards, trans. James Strachey (Markham, ON: Penguin Books Canada, 1984), 300.
99 Benjamin, 'Some Motifs in Baudelaire,' 319.
100 Ibid. 330.
101 Benjamin, 'S [2,1],' 546.
102 Benjamin, 'J [92,4],' 386.
103 Benjamin, 'Some Motifs in Baudelaire,' 351n54.
104 Cited by Benjamin in 'O [4a],' 498.
105 Though in a letter to Benjamin describing his reaction to the second essay on Baudelaire, he notes his fundamental agreement with 'the contrast you draw between reflex behaviour and experience [*Erfahrung*].' Adorno, 'Letter to Benjamin, February 29, 1940,' *The Complete Correspondence*, 320.
106 Adorno, 'Theory of Pseudo-Culture (1959),' trans. Deborah Cook, *Telos* 95 (Spring 1993): 33.
107 Horkheimer and Adorno, 'The Schema of Mass Culture,' 60.
108 Calvin Thomas, 'A Knowledge That Would Not Be Power: Adorno, Nostalgia, and the Historicity of the Musical Subject,' *New German Critique* 48 (Fall 1989): 171. Thomas is particularly good at analyzing Adorno's critique of the spatialization of time in the culture industry.
109 Goethe cited in Adorno, 'The Meaning of Working Through the Past,' *Critical Models*, 91.
110 Adorno, 'Free Time,' 168.
111 Adorno, *Introduction to the Sociology of Music*, 48.
112 Adorno, 'On the Fetish Character of Music,' 278.

**3: Dreams of Redemption?**

1 Horkheimer and Adorno, 'The Schema of Mass Culture,' 80.
2 Adorno, 'On Popular Music,' 48.
3 See Theodor Adorno, Else Frenkel Brunswick, Daniel J. Levinson, and R. Nevitt Sanford, *The Authoritarian Personality* (New York: W.W. Norton, 1969).
4 Adorno, 'How to Look at Television,' 137.
5 Jameson, *Late Marxism*, 132.
6 Deploying Homer *against* Adorno, Cooper notes: 'Odysseus with a twist: Adorno heard the siren song, *then* tied himself to the mast.' Cooper argues that the crystallization of an analytic schematic of jazz in the 1920s and 1930s came to (rather undialectically) predetermine Adorno's experience of popular music for the rest of his life. See his 'On *Uber Jazz*,' 104.
7 Adorno, 'Letter to Benjamin, March 18, 1936,' *The Complete Correspondence*, 130.
8 I do not mean to suggest that Adorno's aesthetics are derivative of Kant. Although he favours the idea of 'purposeless purposiveness,' Adorno is sharply critical of Kant's valuation of aesthetics based only on their effect. Instead, following Hegel, he argues that aesthetic analysis ought to be directed toward a work's truth content, irrespective of its effect on an audience.
9 'Why Still Philosophy,' *Critical Models*, 15.
10 Horkheimer and Adorno, *Dialectic of Enlightenment*, 8.
11 Adorno, *Minima Moralia*, 224–5.
12 Adorno, *Aesthetic Theory*, 138.
13 Ibid., 288.
14 Adorno, cited in Nicholsen, *Exact Imagination, Late Work*, 18. The original is from *Aesthetische Theorie*, 249.
15 Wolin, 'The De-Aestheticization of Art: On Adorno's *Aesthetische Theorie*,' *Telos* 41 (Fall 1979): 119.
16 Adorno, *Negative Dialectics*, 5.
17 Ibid.
18 Ibid., 19.
19 Ibid., 362.
20 Adorno, *Aesthetic Theory*, 4.
21 Benjamin, 'On Language as Such,' 330.
22 Adorno, *Aesthetic Theory*, 76.
23 Adorno, *Negative Dialectics*, 135.
24 Adorno, *Aesthetic Theory*, 244–5.

25 Ibid., 266.
26 Cited in Horowitz, *Repression*, 165. Such 'dialectical regression' also bears a strong similarity to Marcuse's description of the temporary reactivation of primary narcissism in *Eros and Civilization* (Boston: Beacon Press, 1966). See the discussion in *Repression*, 202–11.
27 Adorno, *Aesthetic Theory*, 245.
28 Ibid., 275.
29 Fredric Jameson, *Marxism and Form: Twentieth Century Dialectical Theories of Literature* (Princeton, NJ: Princeton University Press, 1971), 24.
30 See Adorno, 'On the Question: "What Is German?"' *Critical Models*, 210–11.
31 *Repression*, 167.
32 Adorno, *Aesthetic Theory*, 169.
33 Adorno, *Negative Dialectics*, 203.
34 Adorno, *Aesthetic Theory*, 41–2, 323.
35 See the discussion in ibid., 9.
36 Adorno, 'On Lyric Poetry and Society,' *Notes to Literature*, Volume 1, ed. Rolf Tiedemann, trans. Shierry Weber Nicholsen (New York: Columbia University Press, 1991), 43.
37 Adorno, *Negative Dialectics*, 191.
38 Adorno, 'Subject/Object,' *Critical Models*, 254.
39 *Minima Moralia*, 52.
40 For a critique of this dynamic (and its broader effect on critical theory), see Benjamin, 'The End of Internalization.'
41 Jarvis, *Adorno*, 122.
42 Adorno, *Aesthetic Theory*, 119.
43 Ibid., 250.
44 Ibid., 31.
45 Ibid., 298–9.
46 Ibid., 236.
47 Ibid.
48 Horkheimer and Adorno, *Dialectic of Enlightenment*, 93.
49 Wolin, 'The De-Aestheticization of Art,' 112. Wolin's essay is particularly good at exploring the significance of de-aestheticization for Adorno's aesthetic theory.
50 Adorno, *Aesthetic Theory*, 230–1.
51 Horkheimer and Adorno, 'The Schema of Mass Culture,' 57.
52 J.M. Bernstein, 'Why Rescue Semblance? Metaphysical Experience and the Possibility of Ethics,' *The Semblance of Subjectivity: Essays in Adorno's Aesthetic Theory*, ed. Lambert Zuidervaart and Tom Huhn (Cambridge: MIT Press, 1997), 201.

53 Adorno, *Aesthetic Theory*, 237.
54 Ibid., 301.
55 Ibid.
56 Ibid., 182.
57 Adorno, cited in Paddison, *Adorno's Aesthetics of Music*, 218. The original is from *Philosophie der neuen Musik*, 44.
58 Adorno, *Aesthetic Theory*, 208–9.
59 Ibid., 6.
60 Ibid., 5.
61 Adorno, *Introduction to the Sociology of Music*, 70.
62 See ibid., 62.
63 Adorno, *Aesthetic Theory*, 6.
64 Adorno, 'Cultural Criticism and Society,' *Prisms*, 30.
65 See, for example, Simon Jarvis, *Adorno: A Critical Introduction* (New York: Routledge, 1998), 79, and Lambert Zuidervaart, *Adorno's Aesthetic Theory: The Redemption of Illusion* (Cambridge: MIT Press, 1991), 227.
66 Adorno, *Aesthetic Theory*, 358.
67 Albrecht Wellmer, 'Adorno, Modernity and the Sublime,' *The Actuality of Adorno: Critical Essays on Adorno and the Postmodern*, ed. Max Pensky (Albany: State University of New York Press, 1997), 113.
68 Benjamin, 'Letter to Adorno, December 9, 1938,' *The Complete Correspondence*, 295.
69 Benjamin, 'Some Motifs in Baudelaire,' 315.
70 Benjamin, 'H (The Collector) [5,1],' *The Arcades Project*, 211.
71 Marcel Proust, as cited by Benjamin, 'Some Motifs in Baudelaire,' 315.
72 Freud, 'Beyond the Pleasure Principle,' 296.
73 Under pressure to remarry in light of Odysseus' presumed death, Penelope agreed to choose a suitor when she had completed weaving a tapestry. Each night, under cover of darkness, she undid what she had woven during the day.
74 Benjamin, 'On the Image of Proust,' 238.
75 Benjamin, 'Review of Soupault's *Le coeur d'or*,' *Selected Writings*, 2: 66, emphasis added.
76 See Freud, *The Interpretation of Dreams*, ed. and trans. James Strachey (New York: Avon Books, 1965), 132–6.
77 Benjamin, 'On the Image of Proust,' 244.
78 Benjamin, 'N [4,2],' 464.
79 Benjamin, 'A Berlin Chronicle,' *Selected Writings*, 2: 602.
80 Benjamin, 'N [13a,1],' 479.
81 Benjamin, 'A Berlin Chronicle,' 611.

82 Benjamin cited in Susan Buck-Morss, *The Dialectics of Seeing*, 290. The original is from *One-Way Street*, 75.

83 Weigel, *Body- and Image-Space*, ix. Weigel's text offers a fascinating exploration of the significance of thinking in images to Benjamin's thought.

84 Benjamin, 'N [8,1],' 471.

85 Benjamin, 'On the Concept of History,' 391.

86 Benjamin, 'On the Program of the Coming Philosophy,' *Selected Writings*, Volume 1, *1913–1926*, ed. Marcus Bullock and Michael Jennings, trans. Mark Ritter (Cambridge: Belknap Press of Harvard University Press, 1996).

87 This rejection of linear time has led some commentators to suggest that Benjamin prefers space to time. For example, in the introductions to *Reflections* and *One-Way Street and Other Writings* (trans. Edmund Jephcott and Kingsley Shorter, London: New Left Books, 1979), Peter Demetz (p. xvii) and Susan Sontag (p. 13) respectively make this point. I would briefly offer the counter-claim that what Benjamin pursues is the *dialectical* spatialization or 'freezing' of time so as to escape the restrictive model of a linear temporality – 'the beads of a rosary' – in favour of the multiplicity of correspondances, associations, and linkages that might thereby be drawn. Yet this is hardly a rejection of time *per se* but only of one form of it – a form that has been imposed by 'scientific' models of experience. Indeed, we must remind ourselves that space is the pattern of *mythic* time, a return to which is hardly Benjamin's goal. In other words, although he values the shock-like effects that can accompany the radical juxtapositioning of space and time, it is not accurate to suggest that he prefers one over the other.

88 Benjamin, 'N [3,4],' 463.

89 For an excellent account of this aspect of Benjamin's work, see Caygill, *The Color of Experience*.

90 Cited in Benjamin, 'N [15a,1],' 482.

91 Incidentally, this conception of the relation between past and present enables a dialectical redemption of the gambler. In a fragment on gambling, Benjamin notes that the most successful gamblers place their bets at the last possible moment: 'It is only at the last moment, when everything is pressing toward a conclusion, at the critical moment of danger (of missing his chance), that a gambler discovers the trick of finding his way around the table ... gambling generates by way of experiment the lightning-quick process of stimulation at the moment of danger, the marginal case in which presence of mind becomes divination – that is to say, one of the highest, rarest moments of life.' See 'Notes on a Theory of Gambling,' *Selected Writings*, 2: 297, 298.

92 Benjamin, 'N [2a,3],' 462.
93 Benjamin, 'On the Concept of History,' 395.
94 Cited by Benjamin, 'N [18a,2],' 486.
95 Benjamin, 'On the Concept of History,' 392.
96 Wolin raises an interesting caution regarding Benjamin's approach to historical memory insofar as Benjamin largely fails to articulate the criteria by which one can distinguish a progressive from a reactionary reading of history. 'Aestheticism and Social Theory: The Case of Walter Benjamin's *Passagenwerk*,' *Theory, Culture and Society* 10 (1993): 174–5. Jennifer Todd makes a similar point in 'Production, Reception, Criticism: Walter Benjamin and the Problem of Meaning in Art,' *Benjamin: Philosophy, Aesthetics, History*, 107. While I think Benjamin does go some way toward answering this question in a variety of places (cf. the difference between communism and fascism in the 'Work of Art' essay; the comments about fashion representing a leap into the past that occurs in the arena of the ruling class, etc.), I do think it is important to avoid a simplistic endorsement of history as a 'rummage sale' (Todd, 107). In this regard, it is worth noting that those of Benjamin's time who were the most effective at 'quoting' ancient Rome were, in fact, Mussolini's fascists.
97 Benjamin, 'A Berlin Chronicle,' 630.
98 Benjamin, 'N [7,7],' 470.
99 Benjamin, 'Experience and Poverty,' *Selected Writings*, 2: 732, 734.
100 Benjamin, 'On the Concept of History,' 397.
101 Marx, 'Manifesto of the Communist Party,' in *The Marx-Engels Reader*, ed. Robert C. Tucker, 2nd ed. (New York: W.W. Norton, 1978), 476.
102 Benjamin, 'K [1a,8],' 391.
103 Benjamin, 'Notes (IV),' *Selected Writings*, 2: 687, emphasis added.
104 Benjamin, 'On the Concept of History,' 390–1.
105 Ibid., 395.
106 Adorno, *Minima Moralia*, 74.
107 Benjamin, 'Food Fair: Epilogue to the Berlin Food Exhibition,' *Selected Writings*, 2:136.
108 Both Jennings, *Dialectical Images*, and Buck-Morss, *The Dialectics of Seeing*, offer extended treatments of the significance of the dialectical image in Benjamin's work.
109 This term is, of course, drawn from Freud's theory of dreams. However, it has also been used by Louis Althusser in his application of psychoanalytic theory to Marxism. On the parallels and differences between Benjamin and Althusser *vis-à-vis* overdetermination, see the interesting discussion in Margaret Cohen, *Profane Illumination: Walter Benjamin and*

*the Paris of Surrealist Revolution* (Berkeley: University of California Press, 1993), 30–46.

110 One of the most prominent contemporary advocates of this approach to cultural interpretation is Fredric Jameson. See Jameson, *The Political Unconscious: Narrative as a Socially Symbolic Act* (Ithaca, NY: Cornell University Press, 1981), especially the conclusion, 281–300.

111 Benjamin, 'Paris, the Capital of the Nineteenth Century [Exposé of 1935],' 4–5. Note that Benjamin later eliminated this section in a second draft of the exposé that he prepared for Horkheimer in 1939.

112 Adorno, 'Letter to Benjamin, August 2, 1935,' *The Complete Correspondence*, 107.

113 Benjamin cited in Wohlfarth, 'On the Messianic Structure of Walter Benjamin's Last Reflections,' *Glyph* 3 (1978): 178. The original quotes are from *Gesammelte Schriften*, 1: 1231, 1245.

114 Marx cited in 'N [5a,1],' 467.

115 Winfried Meninghaus, 'Walter Benjamin's Theory of Myth,' trans. Gary Smith, in *On Walter Benjamin: Critical Essays and Recollections*, ed. Gary Smith (Cambridge: MIT Press, 1988), 302.

116 Adorno, *Minima Moralia*, 247.

117 Horkheimer and Adorno, *Dialectic of Enlightenment*, 50.

118 Léon Pierre-Quint cited by Benjamin, 'F (Iron Construction) [7,3],' *The Arcades Project*, 167.

119 Aristotle, *The Politics*, trans. T.A. Sinclair (Toronto: Penguin Books, 1981), 65. Benjamin notes Marx's use of this passage in 'Z (The Doll, The Automaton) [3],' *The Arcades Project*, 697.

120 Benjamin, 'Paris, the Capital of the Nineteenth Century [Exposé of 1935],' 4.

121 Buck-Morss, 'Benjamin's *Passagen-Werk*,' 214.

122 Weigel, *Body- and Image-Space*, 11.

123 Adorno, 'Letter to Benjamin, August 2, 1935,' *The Complete Correspondence*, 105.

124 See Cohen, *Profane Illumination*, 53.

125 Bernd Witte, *Walter Benjamin: An Intellectual Biography*, trans. James Rolleston (Detroit: Wayne State University Press, 1991), 179.

126 Max Pensky, *Melancholy Dialectics*, 51, 54.

127 Benjamin, 'Paralipomena to "On the Concept of History,"' *Selected Writings*, 4:403.

128 Buck-Morss, *Dialectics of Seeing*, 220.

129 Freud, *The Interpretation of Dreams*, 615.

130 See, for example, Adorno's critique of surrealism: 'Looking back on Surrealism,' *Notes to Literature*, vol. 1.

131 Horkheimer and Adorno, *Dialectic of Enlightenment*, 18.
132 Adorno, 'Letter to Benjamin, November 10, 1938,' *The Complete Correspondence*, 283.
133 Benjamin, 'False Criticism,' *Selected Writings*, 2:408.
134 Benjamin, 'On the Concept of History,' 396.
135 In this context, Benjamin's engagement with the work of Soviet linguist Lev Vygotsky is of interest. In a review of contemporary theories of language for the *Zeitschrift für Sozialforschung*, he quotes the following from Vygotsky: 'Whenever they [children] encountered a difficulty, our children exhibited an increase in egocentric language ... We therefore believe it justifiable to conclude that impedance or interruption of a smooth-running occupation is an important factor in generating egocentric language ... Thinking is brought into action only when an activity which has run unhindered up to then is interrupted.' See 'Problems in the Sociology of Language,' *Selected Writings*, 3: 82. In similar fashion, the dialecticization of images – i.e., tearing them out of conventional frameworks of meaning and pleasure – kick-starts the mimetic faculty in developing new strategies of coping with these images. It synthetically generates hermeneutic problems in order to stimulate the use of modes of perception and apperception that have been systematically repressed.
136 Benjamin, 'N [2,6],' 461.
137 Benjamin, 'Paris, the Capital of the Nineteenth Century [Exposé of 1935],' 13.
138 Benjamin, 'N [3a,3],' 463.
139 Buck-Morss, *The Dialectics of Seeing*, 293.
140 Benjamin, 'World and Time,' *Selected Writings*, 1: 226.
141 Benjamin, 'The Destructive Character,' *Selected Writings*, 2: 542.
142 Benjamin, 'Paris, the Capital of the Nineteenth Century [Exposé of 1935],' 9.
143 Adorno, 'Letter to Benjamin, August 2, 1935,' *The Complete Correspondence*, 113.
144 Benjamin, 'Central Park,' 164.
145 Benjamin, 'N [1,4],' 456–7.
146 Failure to appreciate this dimension of Benjamin's work can, unfortunately, align him with the more conservative project of disavowing capitalism in favour of a romanticized past. Harry Harootunian, for example, argues that Benjamin holds much in common with Japanese 'modernists' who sought to revive ancient customs and practices to 'interrupt' capitalist modernization. Both, he suggests, were 'driven by a desire to find a concrete experience outside of capitalism resistant to the conception of change and social abstraction it introduced.' See Harootun-

ian, 'The Benjamin Effect: Modernism, Repetition, and the Path to Different Cultural Imaginaries,' *Walter Benjamin and the Demands of History*, ed. Michael Steinberg (Ithaca, NY: Cornell University Press, 1996), 86. On the contrary, I would argue that Benjamin believes that the only means of 'interrupting' capitalism is by collectively passing through it with much greater somatic, affective, and cognitive intensity than has previously been the case.

147 Benjamin, 'On the Concept of History,' 392.

148 Benjamin, 'Some Motifs in Baudelaire,' 332.

149 Ibid., 336, 343, emphasis added.

150 Benjamin, *The Origin of German Tragic Drama*, 175. As Horkheimer and Adorno later note, the mythic prototype for the allegory (and the commodity form) is Odysseus' cunning juxtaposition of his own name with that of 'Udeis' to fool the Cyclops. See the discussion in *Dialectic of Enlightenment*, 50–4.

151 Benjamin, 'The Study Begins with Some Reflections on the Influence of *Les Fleurs du mal*,' 96.

152 Pensky, *Melancholy Dialectics*, 159, 170.

153 Benjamin, 'J [60,5],' 336.

154 Benjamin, 'The Paris of the Second Empire in Baudelaire,' 17.

155 Pensky, *Melancholy Dialectics*, 168.

156 Benjamin, 'Central Park,' 173.

157 Benjamin, *The Origin of German Tragic Drama*, 175.

158 For a discussion of this reversal, see Pensky, *Melancholy Dialectics*, 108–50 and Buck-Morss, *The Dialectics of Seeing*, 170–7.

159 Benjamin, 'On the Concept of History,' 390.

160 Ibid., 392.

161 See Benjamin, 'On Some Motifs in Baudelaire,' 335.

162 See Pensky, *Melancholy Dialectics*, 224–5.

163 Benjamin, 'N [3,1],' 462–3.

164 Hansen, 'Benjamin, Cinema and Experience: "The Blue Flower in the Land of Technology,"' *New German Critique* 40 (Winter 1987): 182.

165 Benjamin, 'Surrealism,' 210.

166 Benjamin, 'B [9,1],' 79.

167 Benjamin, 'Surrealism,' 210.

168 Ibid.

169 Buck-Morss, 'Review: *Walter Benjamin: An Aesthetics of Redemption*,' *Theory and Society* 13.5 (1984): 748.

170 Benjamin, 'Paris, the Capital of the Nineteenth Century [Exposé of 1935],' 13, emphasis added.

171 Benjamin, 'N [1,10],' 45.

172 See Wolin, 'Benjamin, Adorno, Surrealism,' 97. On the significance of montage in Benjamin's textual style, see Hans-Jost Frey, 'On Presentation in Benjamin,' *Walter Benjamin: Theoretical Questions*, ed. David S. Ferris (Stanford: Stanford University Press, 1996).
173 Benjamin, 'Surrealism,' 211.
174 Benjamin, 'Theater and Radio: The Mutual Control of Their Educational Program,' *Selected Writings*, 2: 584.
175 Benjamin, 'What Is the Epic Theater? (II),' *Selected Writings*, 4: 304.
176 Ibid., 302.
177 Ibid., 304.
178 Ibid., 306.
179 Benjamin, 'The Work of Art in the Age of Its Technological Reproducibility [Second Version],' 104. Three versions of this famous essay exist: the initial composition written in Paris in 1935; a revision and expansion completed in February 1936 and published in the same year in French translation in an abbreviated form in the *Zeitschrift für Sozialforschung;* and a final set of revisions completed in 1939, later published in Benjamin's *Schriften* in 1955 and translated as 'The Work of Art in the Age of Mechanical Reproduction,' *Illuminations*. Tracing the differences between these versions adds little of value to my project at this time (though see the excellent work on this question in Hansen, 'Benjamin, Cinema, Experience'). Instead, I will focus on the second version, which according to the editors of his selected writings, was the form in which he originally wished to see the work published.
180 Benjamin, 'The Work of Art [Second Version],' 105.
181 Ibid., 106.
182 Benjamin, 'Reflections on Radio,' *Selected Writings*, 2: 543.
183 Benjamin, 'The Newspaper,' *Selected Writings*, 2: 741.
184 Benjamin, 'The Work of Art [Second Version],' 114, 115.
185 Benjamin, 'Reply to Oscar A. H. Schmitz,' *Selected Writings*, 2: 18.
186 See, for example, the discussion in 'The Author as Producer.'
187 Howard Eiland, 'Reception in Distraction,' *Boundary 2* 30.1 (2003): 52.
188 Adorno, 'Letter to Benjamin, March 18, 1936,' *The Complete Correspondence*, 130.
189 Benjamin, 'What Is the Epic Theater? (II),' 306, emphasis added.
190 Benjamin, 'The Land Where the Proletariat May Not Be Mentioned: The Premier of Eight One-Act Plays by Brecht,' *Selected Writings*, 3: 331.
191 Adorno and Eisler cited in Rosen, 'Adorno and Film Music,' 171.
192 Benjamin, 'Letter to Adorno, December 9, 1938,' *The Complete Correspondence*, 295.
193 Hansen, 'Benjamin, Cinema, Experience,' 211.

194 Benjamin, 'The Work of Art [Second Version],' 132n33.
195 Benjamin, 'What Is the Epic Theater? (II),' 302.
196 Benjamin, 'The Work of Art [Second Version],' 119.
197 Ibid.
198 Ibid., 116.
199 Ibid.
200 Cited in Benjamin, 'Chaplin in Retrospect,' *Selected Writings*, 2: 222.
201 Benjamin, 'The Work of Art [Second Version],' 114.
202 Ibid., 117.
203 Benjamin, 'The Work of Art in the Age of Its Technological Reproducibility [Third Version],' *Selected Writings*, 4: 265.
204 Benjamin, 'The Work of Art' [Second Version], 126n21.
205 Ibid., 117.
206 Ibid., 118.
207 Ibid., 117.
208 Caygill, *Walter Benjamin*, 75–6.
209 See the discussion in Benjamin, 'The Work of Art,' 127–8n22.
210 Benjamin, 'On the Concept of History,' 394.
211 Benjamin, 'The Work of Art,' [Second Version],' 120.
212 Ibid., 105.
213 Benjamin, 'Hashish in Marseilles,' *Selected Writings*, 2: 677.
214 Benjamin, 'Some Motifs in Baudelaire,' 328, 337.
215 Benjamin, 'The Work of Art [Second Version],' 111.
216 Benjamin, 'Letter from Paris (2): Photography and Painting,' 240.
217 Adorno, 'Letter to Benjamin, November 10, 1938,' *The Complete Correspondence*, 284.
218 Adorno, *Minima Moralia*, 47.
219 Adorno, 'Letter to Walter Benjamin, March 18, 1936,' *The Complete Correspondence*, 131.
220 Walter Benjamin, 'Little History of Photography,' *Selected Writings*, 2: 510.
221 Julian Stallabrass, *Gargantua*, 41.
222 Ibid., 42.
223 Gary McCarron, 'Pixel Perfect: Towards a Political Economy of Digital Fidelity,' *Canadian Journal of Communication* 24 (1999): 235. Also see Andrew Herman and John H. Sloop, '"Red Alert!" Rhetorics of the World Wide Web and "Friction Free" Capitalism,' *The World Wide Web and Contemporary Cultural Theory*, ed. Andrew Herman and Thomas Swiss (New York: Routledge, 2000).
224 Horkheimer and Adorno, *Dialectic of Enlightenment*, 44.

225 Adorno, interviewed by Hellmut Becker, 'Education for Autonomy,' *Telos* 55–6 (1983): 109.
226 Adorno, 'Education after Auschwitz,' *Critical Models*, 196.
227 Adorno et al., 'Anti-Semitism and Fascist Propaganda,' 137, emphasis added.
228 Adorno, 'Television as Ideology,' 69.
229 Adorno, 'Taboos on the Teaching Vocation,' *Critical Models*, 188.
230 Horkheimer and Adorno, *Dialectic of Enlightenment*, 161.
231 Adorno, cited in Jameson, *Late Marxism*, 213. The original is from *Aesthetische Theorie*, 151.
232 See the discussion by J.M. Bernstein, 'Why Rescue Semblance?' 183–6.
233 Adorno, *Minima Moralia*, 61.
234 Adorno, *Negative Dialectics*, 221–2.
235 The one notable exception to this is found in his essay 'Transparencies on Film,' in which he admits the possibility that experimental cinema may foster a critical consciousness. See 'Transparencies on Film.' Also of interest is Hansen's introduction to the initial publication of the essay in English in *New German Critique* 24–5 (Winter 1981–2).
236 Adorno, 'The Meaning of Working through the Past,' *Critical Models*, 100.
237 Adorno, 'Sociology and Psychology I,' trans. Irving Wohlfarth, *New Left Review* 46 (1967): 80.
238 Adorno, *Minima Moralia*, 206.
239 Horkheimer and Adorno, *Dialectic of Enlightenment*, 18.
240 Adorno, 'Words from Abroad,' *Notes to Literature*, 1: 189.
241 Adorno, 'On the Historical Adequacy of Consciousness (with Peter von Haselberg),' *Telos* 56 (1983): 100.
242 Benjamin, 'Privileged Thinking: On Theodor Haecker's *Virgil*,' *Selected Writings*, 2: 572.
243 Benjamin, 'The Path to Success, in Thirteen Theses,' *Selected Writings*, 2: 144. Writing about a 1934 visit to Brecht in Denmark, Benjamin noted: 'On a window ledge [in Brecht's study] stands a little wooden donkey that can nod its head. Brecht has hung a little notice round its neck with the words: "I, too, must understand it."' See 'Notes from Svendborg,' *Selected Writings*, 2: 785.
244 Benjamin, 'K [3a,1],' 395.
245 Adorno, *Negative Dialectics*, 153.
246 Adorno, 'On Jazz,' 47.
247 Adorno, *Negative Dialectics*, 161.

248 Adorno, *Aesthetic Theory*, 330.
249 Benjamin, 'The Work of Art [Third Version],' 261.
250 Adorno, *Minima Moralia*, 120.
251 Ibid., 21.
252 Adorno, *Negative Dialectics*, 377–8.

**4: From Mass to Popular Culture**

1 In addition to Williams, E.P. Thompson and Richard Hoggart are usually included in this designation.
2 Williams, *Culture and Society, 1780–1950* (Harmondsworth: Penguin, 1961), 290.
3 For a survey of the initial influence of Leavis on the Birmingham School, see Grant Farred, 'Leavisite Cool: The Organic Links between Cultural Studies and *Scrutiny*,' *Dispositio/n* 21.48 (1996 [1999]). In *The Uses of Literacy* (Harmondsworth: Penguin, 1957), for instance, Hoggart famously took a very dim view of the effect of mass culture on working-class life. Similarly, according to Dan Schiller, Hall's early work on mass culture in the 1950s constituted 'a direct reprise of the mass culture thesis,' which criticized the deadening effects of the culture industry upon class consciousness. See the discussion in *Theorizing Communication: A History* (New York: Oxford University Press, 1996), 137–9. Later, in *The Popular Arts* (Toronto: Hutchinson Educational, 1964), Hall and Paddy Whannel develop a critical analytic practice with which to judge specific cultural texts, thereby distinguishing between 'good' popular culture (authentic products that express the experience of the people) and 'bad' mass culture (formulaic trash produced for easy consumption). Many of the criticisms of the latter continue to be reminiscent of the culture industry thesis. Yet Hall and Whannel do not ultimately connect these tendencies to the commodity form itself. For example, their contention that one can have 'good' advertising suggests that they do not share Adorno's fears about the use of culture to bind people into the exchange relation. Moreover, this dualistic framework with its evaluative objectives was abandoned by Hall as the CCCS evolved.
4 Hall, 'Notes on Deconstructing the Popular,' in *People's History and Socialist Theory*, ed. Raphael Samuel (Boston: Routledge, 1981), 232.
5 My own systematic review of the relevant literature by the Birmingham School did not reveal any substantive treatment of critical theory other than what is briefly discussed below. Douglas Kellner similarly confirms this absence in 'Critical Theory and Cultural Studies,' 37n.

6 Hall, 'Cultural Studies and the Center: Some Problematics and Problems,' *Culture, Media, Language: Working Papers in Cultural Studies, 1972–1979*, ed. Stuart Hall, Dorothy Hobson, Andrew Lowe, and Paul Willis (New York: Routledge, 1992), 284n.
7 Hall, 'Cultural Studies and the Centre,' 25.
8 Slater, 'The Aesthetic Theory of the Frankfurt School,' *Working Papers in Cultural Studies* 6 (Autumn 1974).
9 James Curran, Michael Gurevitch, and Janet Woollacott, 'The study of the Media: Theoretical Approaches,' in *Culture, Society and the Media*, ed. Michael Gurevitch, Tony Bennett, James Curran, and Janet Woollacott (New York: Methuen, 1982), 23.
10 Steve Burniston and Chris Weedon, 'Ideology, Subjectivity and the Artistic Text,' in *On Ideology*, ed. Centre for Contemporary Cultural Studies (London: Hutchinson, 1978), 207.
11 Stuart Hall, Chas Critcher, Tony Jefferson, John Clarke, and Brian Roberts, *Policing the Crisis: Mugging, the State, and Law and Order* (London: Macmillan Education, 1978), 95.
12 Bennett, 'Theories of Media, Theories of Society,' in *Culture, Society and the Media*, and Bennett, 'The Politics of "the Popular" and Popular Culture,' in *Popular Culture and Social Relations*, ed. Tony Bennett, Colin Mercer, and Janet Woollacott (Philadelphia: Open University Press, 1986).
13 It is interesting to note that Bennett's analysis in 'Theories of Society, Theories of the Media' (the more substantive of the two articles) relies predominantly on quotations from Marcuse's work. Only two quotes from Adorno are included, one from *Minima Moralia* and the other from the Slater article noted above. The paucity of original references to Adorno certainly raises questions about the extent to which Adorno's texts were directly reviewed by the Birmingham School. Also suggestive of a basic lack of familiarity with critical theory are references to 'negative dialectic' that betray a basic failure to understand the term as theorized by Adorno. See John Clarke, Stuart Hall, Tony Jefferson, and Brian Roberts, 'Subcultures, Cultures and Class,' in *Resistance through Rituals: Youth Subcultures in Post-War Britain*, ed. Stuart Hall and Tony Jefferson (London: Routledge, 1993), 63, and Stuart Hall, 'The Meaning of New Times,' in *Stuart Hall: Critical Dialogues in Cultural Studies*, ed. David Morley and Kuan-Hsing Chen (New York: Routledge, 1996), 229.
14 The only exception is a very interesting application of the 'Work of Art' essay to an early piece on television by Hall. See *Television as a Medium and Its Relation to Culture* (Birmingham: Centre for Contemporary Cultural Studies, 1975).

15 Arnold cited in Farred, 'Leavisite Cool,' 1.
16 Bennett, 'Introduction: Popular Culture and "the turn to Gramsci,"' in *Popular Culture and Social Relations*, xi.
17 Colin Sparks, 'The Abuses of Literacy,' *Working Papers in Cultural Studies* 6 (Autumn 1974): 9. Adorno, of course, completely rejected the claim that mass culture was an authentic 'response' or 'expression' of human experience in a particular historical moment.
18 Hall, 'The "First" New Left: Life and Times,' in *Out of Apathy: Voices of the New Left Thirty Years On*, ed. Robin Archer et al. (New York: Verso, 1989), 16.
19 Hall, 'The Hinterland of Science: Ideology and the "Sociology of Knowledge,"' in *On Ideology*, 13–14. Also see the similar discussion in Richard Johnson, 'Three Problematics: Elements of a Theory of Working-Class Culture,' in *Working Class Culture: Studies in History and Theory*, ed. John Clarke, Chas Critcher, and Richard Johnson (New York: St Martin's Press, 1979), 210–11.
20 Hall, 'Cultural Studies and the Centre,' 33–4.
21 See Hall et al., *Resistance to Rituals*, and Dick Hebdige, *Subculture: The Meaning of Style* (New York: Routledge, 1994). Throughout its history, the CCCS has had a very ambiguous relationship to the concept of class. On the one hand, its origins in the New Left and the lingering intellectual authority of figures such as Williams and Thompson ensured the importance of class during its formative years. The initial work on subcultures in particular leaned heavily on a class problematic and was explicitly directed against those who claimed that the new youth cultures represented confirmation of the 'embourgeoisiement' of the postwar working class. On the other hand, the centre's focus on the increasing importance and autonomy of consumptive practices in the formation of social identity gradually eroded the centrality of class experience. The explosion of race and gender issues in the late 1970s further challenged the primacy of class as an explanatory paradigm. For our purposes, the important point is how class was tightly bound together with the issue of economic determination: the two were either accepted or rejected as a conceptual package.
22 See Bennett's 'Introduction: Popular Culture and the "Turn to Gramsci"' and 'The Politics of "the Popular" and popular culture.'
23 For two short, critical accounts of *Screen* by the CCCS, see Hall, 'Recent Developments in Theories of Language and Ideology: A Critical Note,' in *Culture, Media, Language*, and Morley, 'Texts, Readers, Subjects,' in ibid. Also useful is an exchange between Rosalind Coward and members of the CCCS in *Screen* on the merits of their respective approaches to culture. See

Rosalind Coward, 'Class, "Culture" and the Social Formation,' *Screen* 18.1 (Spring 1977); the reply by Iain Chambers, John Clarke, Ian Connell, Lidia Curti, Stuart Hall, and Tony Jefferson, 'Marxism and Culture,' *Screen* 18.4 (Winter 1977–8); and Coward's 'Response,' *Screen* 18.4 (Winter 1977–8).

24 Bennett, 'The Politics of 'the Popular' and Popular Culture,' 17.

25 In *Theorizing Communication*, Dan Schiller uses the concept of labour to similarly criticize the limitations of an approach to culture that unduly concentrates on the specificity of cultural practices. See 'The Contraction of Theory.'

26 See Williams, 'Base and Superstructure in Marxist Cultural Theory,' *Problems in Materialism and Culture* (London: Verso, 1980), 32–47; as well as its expansion into a book-length thesis in *Marxism and Literature* (New York: Oxford University Press, 1977).

27 See Thompson's review of 'The Long Revolution,' *New Left Review* 9 and 10 (May/June and July/Aug 1961).

28 Williams, 'Base and Superstructure in Marxist Cultural Theory,' 44.

29 Thompson cited in Wood, 'Rethinking base and superstructure,' *Democracy against Capitalism* (Cambridge: Cambridge University Press, 1995), 58. The original is from *The Poverty of Theory*.

30 Hall, 'Cultural Studies and the Centre,' 30.

31 Hall, 'Notes on Deconstructing "The Popular,"' 227.

32 For a full explanation of this argument, see Johnson, 'Three Problematics: Elements of a Theory of Working-Class Culture,' 212–24 and Sparks, 'The Abuses of Literacy.'

33 Looking back on his own involvement in British cultural studies, for example, John Clarke recalls the 'emancipatory effect' generated by Althusserian structuralism. See Clarke, *New Times and Old Enemies*, 12.

34 Althusser, 'On the Materialist Dialectic,' *For Marx*, trans. Ben Brewster (London: Penguin, 1969), 203.

35 Althusser, 'Contradiction and Overdetermination,' *For Marx*, 113.

36 Ibid., 113–14.

37 Hall, 'Marx's Notes on Method: A "Reading" of the 1857 Introduction,' *Working Papers in Cultural Studies* 6 (Autumn 1974): 146–7.

38 Hall, 'Culture, the Media and the "Ideological Effect,"' *Mass Communication and Society*, ed. James Curran, Michael Gurevitch, and Janet Woollacott (Beverly Hills: Sage, 1979), 326.

39 Hall, 'Marx's Notes on Method,' 147–8.

40 These run from the style of a subcultural formation in Clarke et al., 'Subcultures, Cultures and Class,' to globalization itself in Hall, 'The Local and the Global: Globalization and Ethnicity,' in *Culture, Globalization and the*

*World-System: Contemporary Conditions for the Representation of Identity*, ed. Anthony King (Minneapolis: University of Minnesota Press, 1997).

41 Hall, 'The "Political" and the "Economic" in Marx's Theory of Classes,' *Class and Class Structure*, ed. Alan Hunt (London: Lawrence and Wishart, 1977), 46.

42 Althusser, 'Ideology and Ideological State Apparatuses,' *Lenin and Philosophy and Other Essays*, trans. Ben Brewster (New York: Monthly Review Press, 1971), 69.

43 Althusser, 'Marxism and Humanism,' *For Marx*, 233–4.

44 Hall, 'Culture, the Media and the "Ideological Effect,"' 324.

45 Althusser, 'Ideology and Ideological State Apparatuses,' 171.

46 Ibid., 182.

47 It should be said that Althusser himself did not think culture and ideology were the same. In his discussion of literature, for example, he located it midway between science and ideology in terms of its capacity to reveal the existence and operation of ideological mechanisms.

48 Hall, 'Notes on Deconstructing the Popular,' 230.

49 Iain Chambers et al., 'Marxism and Culture,' 109.

50 See 'On Postmodernism and Articulation: An Interview with Stuart Hall,' ed. Lawrence Grossberg, in *Stuart Hall: Critical Dialogues*, 148–9.

51 Roland Barthes, *Mythologies*, trans. Annette Lavers (Toronto: Grafton, 1987), 11.

52 Horkheimer and Adorno, *Dialectic of Enlightenment*, xviii.

53 Barthes, *Mythologies*, 109.

54 Ibid., 118.

55 Ibid., 151.

56 Ibid., 142.

57 Barthes, *The Pleasure of the Text*, trans. Richard Miller (New York: Hill and Wang, 1975).

58 Barthes, 'Rhetoric of the Image,' *Image-Music-Text*, trans. Stephen Heath (New York: Noonday Press, 1977), 45, 51.

59 Hall, 'Introduction to Media Studies at the Centre,' *Culture, Media, Language*, 119.

60 Hall, 'The Determination of News Photographs,' *The Manufacture of News*, ed. Stanley Cohen and Jock Young (London: Constable, 1973).

61 Hall, 'The Determination of News Photographs,' 180–1.

62 Ibid., 181.

63 Hall, *External Influences on Broadcasting: 'The External-Internal Dialectic in Broadcasting: Television's Double Bind,'* Stencilled Occasional Paper No. 4 (Birmingham: Centre for Contemporary Cultural Studies, 1972), 6.

64 Barthes, 'The Death of the Author,' *Image-Music-Text*, 146.
65 V.N. Volosinov, *Marxism and the Philosophy of Language*, trans. Ladislav Matejka and I.R. Titunik (Cambridge: Harvard University Press, 1973), 23.
66 Ibid.
67 Ibid., 68.
68 Hall, 'For Allon White: Metaphors of Transformation,' *Stuart Hall: Critical Dialogues*, 297, emphasis added.
69 Hall, *The Hard Road to Renewal: Thatcherism and the Crisis of the Left* (New York: Verso, 1988), 9, emphasis added. The reference is to the Volosinov quote cited above.
70 Hall, 'Ideology and Communication Theory,' *Rethinking Communication*, Volume 1, *Paradigm Issues*, ed. Brenda Darvin, Lawrence Grossberg, Barbara J. O'Keefe, and Ellen Warteila (Newbury Park, CA: Sage, 1989), 47, emphasis added.
71 Hall, 'For Allon White,' 295.
72 Bennett, 'Theories of the Media, Theories of Society,' 51.
73 Volosinov, *Marxism and the Philosophy of Language*, 23–4.
74 See Iain Chambers, 'Roland Barthes: Structuralism/Semiotics,' *Working Papers in Cultural Studies* 6 (Autumn 1974): 52–3.
75 Volosinov, *Marxism and the Philosophy of Language*, 37.
76 John Clarke et al., 'Subcultures, Cultures and Class,' 55.
77 Hall, 'The Problem of Ideology: Marxism without Guarantees,' *Stuart Hall: Critical Dialogues*, 36.
78 Adorno, *Negative Dialectics*, 191.
79 Cohen, 'Subcultural Conflict and Working-Class Community,' *Culture, Media, Language*, 82.
80 See John Clarke, 'The Skinheads and the Magical Recovery of Community,' in *Resistance through Rituals*.
81 See Willis, *Profane Culture* (London: Routledge, 1978).
82 Clarke, 'Style,' in *Resistance through Rituals*, 179.
83 Ibid., 177.
84 Hebdige, *Subculture*, 102.
85 Ibid., 114–15.
86 Hall, 'Encoding/decoding,' *Culture, Media, Language*, 129.
87 Ibid., 129.
88 Hall, 'Reflections upon the Encoding/Decoding Model: An Interview with Stuart Hall,' in *Viewing, Reading, Listening: Audiences and Cultural Reception* (Boulder, CO: Westview Press, 1994), 264.
89 Hall, 'Encoding/decoding,' 131.
90 Hall, 'Reflections upon the Encoding/Decoding Model,' 267.

91 In the next chapter, for example, I take up the work of Larry Grossberg, whose work problematizes the use of this conceptual framework from within cultural studies. For similar 're-evaluations' of some of the earlier excesses of the field, see the essays by Morley and McRobbie in *Cultural Studies in Question*. Also notable in this context is an essay by Meaghan Morris, one of the more astute, self-reflexive critics of cultural studies: 'Banality in Cultural Studies,' *Discourse* 10.2 (Spring/Summer 1988).

92 Iain Chambers, 'Waiting on the End of the World?' *Stuart Hall: Critical Dialogues*, 205.

93 Hall, 'Cultural Studies and the Centre,' 35.

94 Turner, *British Cultural Studies: An Introduction* 2nd ed. (New York: Routledge, 1996), 195.

95 Clarke et al., 'Subcultures, Cultures and Class,' 39.

96 Bennett, 'The Politics of 'the Popular' and Popular Culture,' 19. Also see Bennett's fascinating exploration of the concrete processes of hegemony formation in 'Hegemony, Ideology, Pleasure: Blackpool,' *Popular Culture and Social Relations*.

97 Hall, 'Gramsci and Us,' in *The Hard Road to Renewal*, 166.

98 Stuart Hall, Bob Lumley, and Gregor McLennan, 'Politics and Ideology: Gramsci,' in *On Ideology*, 52. The quote is from Gramsci, *Selections from the Prison Notebooks*, 331.

99 Hall, 'Culture, Media and the Ideological Effect,' 338.

100 See Hall, 'Culture, the Media and the "Ideological Effect"' for a discussion of the importance of Poulantzas.

101 Hall et al., *Policing the Crisis*, 76.

102 See the collection of essays in Hall, *The Hard Road to Renewal*, and the more theoretical discussion in Hall, 'The Toad in the Garden: Thatcherism amongst the Theorists,' *Marxism and the Interpretation of Culture*, ed. Larry Grossberg and Cary Nelson (Chicago: University of Illinois Press, 1988).

103 Hall, 'Gramsci and Us,' 167.

104 Hall, 'The Toad in the Garden,' 46. For a critique of this position on ideology see Jorge Lorrain, 'Stuart Hall and the Marxist Concept of Ideology,' in *Stuart Hall: Critical Dialogues*, and Colin Sparks, 'Stuart Hall, Cultural Studies and Marxism,' in ibid.

105 In emphasizing the term 'cultural,' I want to distinguish my argument from the more conventional objection levied by Bob Jessop (and others) against Hall that he fails to adequately take into account the role of economic factors in Thatcher's rise. See Jessop et al., 'Authoritarian Populism, Two Nations and Thatcherism,' *New Left Review* 147 (Septem-

ber–October 1984) and Hall's reply in 'Authoritarian Populism: A Reply to Jessop et al.,' in *The Hard Road to Renewal*. My own point is that commodification not only lays the foundations for a particular kind of conservative ideological articulation, but helps establish the dominance of articulation itself as a social logic.

106 McGuigan, *Cultural Populism*, 40.

107 Surprisingly perhaps, the most shameless advocate of this position is Paul Willis himself in his later books *Common Culture* (Buckingham: Open University Press, 1990) and *Moving Culture* (London: Calouste Gulbenkian Foundation, 1990). Entirely absent from these texts is Willis's earlier sensitivity, in *Learning to Labor: How Working Class Kids Get Working Class Jobs* (New York: Columbia University Press, 1977), to the means by which hegemonic social processes effectively incorporate creative forms of resistance.

108 Hall, 'The Culture Gap,' in *The Hard Road to Renewal*, 215.

109 Hall, 'The Meaning of New Times,' 234.

110 Ibid., 233, emphasis added.

111 As an example of both Hall's and Hebdige's overoptimistic reading of acts of cultural politics, see their respective analyses of the Live Aid and Band Aid musical concerts for famine relief. See Hall, 'People's Aid: A New Politics Sweeps the Land,' in *The Hard Road to Renewal*, and Hebdige, *Hiding in the Light: On Images and Things* (New York: Routledge, 1988), 213–23.

**5: Articulation and the Commodity Form**

1 For a useful overview of the evolution of this concept in cultural studies, see Jennifer Daryl Slack, 'The Theory and Method of Articulation in Cultural Studies,' in *Stuart Hall: Critical Dialogues*.

2 There are some notable exceptions to this trend. See, for example, many of the essays collected in Ian Angus and Sut Jhally, ed., *Cultural Politics in Contemporary America* (New York: Routledge, 1989); Susan Willis, *A Primer for Everyday Life*; Robert Miklitsch, *From Hegel to Madonna*; Andrew Wernick, *Promotional Culture: Advertising, Ideology and Symbolic Expression* (Newbury Park, CA: Sage, 1991); and Agger, *Cultural Studies as Critical Theory*.

3 John Fiske, *Understanding Popular Culture* (New York: Routledge, 1989), 177.

4 Chambers, 'Waiting on the End of the World?' 202.

5 Miklitsch, *From Hegel to Madonna*, 16.
6 Ernesto Laclau, *Politics and Ideology in Marxist Theory* (London: Verso, 1979), 99.
7 Jean Laplanche and J.B. Pontalis, cited in ibid., 93. The original is from *The Language of Psychoanalysis*, 82.
8 Laclau, *Politics and Ideology*, 173.
9 Hall, 'On Postmodernism and Articulation,' 141–2.
10 Hall, 'The Toad in the Garden,' 49.
11 See the discussion in Hall, 'On Postmodernism and Articulation,' and his remarks in *The Hard Road to Renewal*, 10–11.
12 Stuart Hall, 'The Rediscovery of 'Ideology': Return of the Repressed in Media Studies,' in *Culture, Society and the Media*, 84.
13 Hall, 'The Problem of Ideology,' 43.
14 Grossberg, 'Toward a Genealogy of the State of Cultural Studies,' in *Bringing It All Back Home: Essays on Cultural Studies*, 283.
15 Ibid.
16 Cited in Grossberg, *We Gotta Get Out of This Place: Popular Conservatism and Postmodern Culture* (New York: Routledge, 1992), 49. The original is from 'Truth and Power,' in *Michel Foucault: Power, Truth, Strategy*, 33.
17 Grossberg, 'Experience, Signification and Reality: The Boundaries of Cultural Semiotics,' in *Bringing It All Back Home*, 84.
18 Grossberg, 'Cultural Studies Revisited and Revised,' in *Bringing It All Back Home*, 170.
19 Grossberg, *We Gotta Get Out of This Place*, 54.
20 Jameson, 'On Cultural Studies,' *Social Text* 34 (1993): 32.
21 Grossberg, 'The Circulation of Cultural Studies,' 236.
22 Grossberg, *We Gotta Get Out of This Place*, 82.
23 Ibid., 105.
24 Ibid., 79.
25 For a fascinating discussion of affect and potentiality, see Brian Massumi, 'The Autonomy of Affect,' *Cultural Critique* 31 (Fall 1995).
26 Grossberg, 'Another Boring Day in Paradise: Rock and Roll and the Empowerment of Everyday Life,' *Dancing in Spite of Myself: Essays on Popular Culture* (Durham: Duke University Press, 1997), 31.
27 Grossberg, 'Is Anybody Listening? Does Anybody Care? On "The State of Rock,"' in *Dancing in Spite of Myself*, 115.
28 Grossberg, 'Rockin' in Conservative Times,' in *Dancing in Spite of Myself*, 261.
29 Grossberg, *We Gotta Get Out of This Place*, 221.
30 Grossberg, '"It's a Sin": Politics, Postmodernity, and the Popular,' in *Dancing in Spite of Myself*, 245.

31 Grossberg, 'Cultural Studies Revisited and Revised,' in *Bringing It All Back Home*, 169.
32 Grossberg, *We Gotta Get Out of This Place*, 305.
33 Grossberg, '"I'd Rather Feel Bad Than Not Feel Anything at All": Rock and Roll, Pleasure and Power,' in *Dancing in Spite of Myself*, 80. The latter quote is from M. Safouan, *Pleasure and being*, 235.
34 See Freud, 'Beyond the Pleasure Principle,' 283–310.
35 Horkheimer and Adorno, *Dialectic of Enlightenment*, 109.
36 Grossberg, 'Cultural Studies in/and New Worlds,' in *Bringing It All Back Home*, 366.
37 Naomi Klein, *No Logo: Taking Aim at Brand Bullies* (Toronto: Knopf Canada, 2000), 157.
38 For a useful account of this process and some interesting speculations on its broader social effects, see Robert Goldman and Stephen Papson, *Sign Wars: The Cluttered Landscape of Advertising* (New York: Guilford Press, 1996).
39 For specific examples that trace the effects of marketing upon product design see Hebdige, 'Object as Image: The Italian Scooter Cycle,' in *Hiding in the Light: On Images and Things*, 80–118; and Wernick, 'Imaging Commodities,' in *Promotional Culture*, 3–20.
40 Andrew Wernick, *Promotional Culture*, 190. For a particularly incisive and detailed ethnographic study of the microscopic penetration of commodification into the labour processes through which culture is produced, see Ryan, *Making Capital from Culture*.
41 Grossberg, 'The Context of Audiences and the Politics of Difference,' in *Bringing It All Back Home*, 323.
42 Grossberg, 'Cultural Studies: What's in a Name? (One More Time),' in *Bringing It All Back Home*, 260.
43 Grossberg, 'Cultural Studies Revisited and Revised,' 169–70, emphasis added.
44 Benjamin, 'Left-Wing Melancholy,' in *Selected Writings*, 2: 425.
45 Grossberg, 'Postmodernity and Affect: All Dressed Up with No Place to Go,' in *Dancing in Spite of Myself*, 154.
46 Grossberg, 'Postmodernity and Affect,' 154–5.
47 Arjun Appadurai, 'Introduction: Commodities and the Politics of Value,' in *The Social Life of Things: Commodities in Cultural Perspective*, ed. Arjun Appadurai (New York: Cambridge University Press, 1986), 13, 17. Also see the essay by Igor Kopytoff, 'The Cultural Biography of Things: Commoditization as Process,' in the same volume.
48 Miklitsch, *From Hegel to Madonna*, 88.

49 Grossberg, 'Another Boring Day in Paradise: Rock and Roll and the Empowerment of Everyday Life,' in *Dancing in Spite of Myself*, 35.
50 Ibid., 36.
51 Ibid.
52 Ibid., 60.
53 Clarke, *New Times and Old Enemies*, 102.
54 Cited by Angela McRobbie, 'Looking Back at *New Times* and Its Critics,' *Critical Dialogues in Cultural Studies*, 260.
55 Hebdige, *Hiding in the Light*, 211.
56 For a compelling survey of the encroaching dominance of exchange-relations in terms of their multiple points of impact on the body, see Donald Lowe, *The Body in Late Capitalist USA* (Durham: Duke University Press, 1995). For a well-researched critique of the extension of the market from a liberal, mainstream perspective, see Robert Kuttner, *Everything for Sale: The Virtues and Limits of Markets* (New York: Alfred A. Knopf, 1997).
57 Cited in Guy Debord, *Society of the Spectacle*, trans. anonymous (Detroit: Black and Red, 1983), § 35.
58 Incidentally, Schiller provides a fascinating discussion of how the popularization of this metaphor is actually attributable to attempts by the U.S. government and its supporters in mainstream communication research in the 1940s to justify their own extensive propaganda efforts as a necessary counter to the frightening efficiency of enemy efforts to 'brainwash' American citizens. See *Theorizing Communication*, 53.
59 Horkheimer and Adorno, *The Dialectic of Enlightenment*, 96.
60 Adorno, 'On Popular Music,' 38, emphasis added.
61 Benjamin, 'm (Idleness) [3a,3],' *The Arcades Project*, 804.
62 Marx, 'Manifesto of the Communist Party,' in *The Marx-Engels Reader*, 476.
63 Hebdige, *Subcultures*; Michel de Certeau, *The Practice of Everyday Life*, trans. Steven Rendall (Berkeley: University of California Press, 1984); Fiske, *Understanding Popular Culture* and *Reading the Popular* (New York: Routledge, 1989).
64 Rutherford, 'A Place Called Home: Identity and the Cultural Politics of Difference,' in *Identity: Community, Culture, Difference*, ed. Jonathan Rutherford (London: Lawrence and Wishart, 1990), 11.
65 Stuart Hall, 'The Local and the Global: Globalization and Ethnicity,' 29, 31.
66 Ibid., 29.
67 Antonio Negri and Michael Hardt, *Empire* (Cambridge: Harvard University Press, 2000).
68 Clarke, *New Times and Old Enemies*, 85.
69 Horkheimer and Adorno, *Dialectic of Enlightenment*, 97.

70 Adorno, 'On Popular Music,' 25.
71 On the impossibility of representing utopia, see Jameson's fascinating discussion in 'Of Islands and Trenches: Neutralization and the Production of Utopian Discourse,' *The Ideologies of Theory, Essays, 1971–1986*, Volume 2, *The Syntax of History* (Minneapolis: University of Minnesota Press, 1988).
72 Angela McRobbie, 'The *Passagenwerk* and the Place of Walter Benjamin in Cultural Studies,' *Postmodernism and Popular Culture*, 113.
73 Benjamin, *The Origin of German Tragic Drama*, 175.
74 Stephen Oakes, Broadcast Arts, Interview printed in Richard Ohmann, ed., *Making and Selling Culture* (Hanover: Wesleyan University Press, 1996), 82.
75 The classic account of this process remains Judith Williamson, *Decoding Advertisements: Ideology and Meaning in Advertising* (New York: Marion Boyars, 1984).
76 See the interesting analysis in Henry A. Giroux, 'Consuming Social Change: The "United Colors of Benetton,"' *Cultural Critique* 26 (Winter 1993–4).
77 Wernick, *Promotional Culture*, 35.
78 Adorno, 'On the Fetish Character of Music,' 286–7.
79 See Joseph Turow's *Breaking Up America: Advertisers and the New Media World* (Chicago: University of Chicago Press, 1997) for a useful account of this process.
80 See, for example, the discussion in John Philip Jones, ed., *How to Use Advertising to Build Strong Brands* (Thousand Oaks, CA: Sage, 1999).
81 Grossberg, '"It's a Sin,"' 226.
82 Horkheimer and Adorno, *Dialectic of Enlightenment*, 136.
83 Ibid., 107.
84 Grossberg, '"It's a Sin,"' 228.
85 Adorno, 'Perennial Fashion: Jazz,' 128.
86 Grossberg, 'The Indifference of Television,' 141.
87 Grossberg, 'Postmodernist Elitisms and Postmodern Struggles,' in *Dancing in Spite of Myself*, 173.
88 Incidentally, this enables a rather suggestive critique of Baudrillard's claim that the real has collapsed into the semiotic. According to Grossberg's logic, the difference between the real and the semiotic still exists, but it is a difference in which many people are increasingly unable to invest affectively. The difference between reality and signs no longer matters to them (though it may matter to others and certainly still has an ontological significance). See the discussion in 'The Indifference of Television, or, Mapping TV's Popular (Affective) Economy,' in *Dancing in Spite of Myself*, 141–2. Along these lines, it is interesting to speculate that the current success of so-called

'Reality TV' (i.e., *Cops, Funniest Home Videos, Survivor, Big Brother*) is based on its ability to redefine 'reality' as a site of affective investment, as something that 'matters,' precisely by processing it through the filter of the culture industry. Reality must be mediated through the entertainment industry before it can become a reality that matters.

89 Grossberg, 'The Indifference of Television,' 139.

90 Ibid., 143.

**Concluding Thoughts**

1 Agger, *Cultural Studies as Critical Theory*, 179, 153. Agger is not, however, an unconditional advocate of the Frankfurt School approach. See his penetrating criticisms of Adorno in Agger, *The Discourse of Domination: From the Frankfurt School to Postmodernism* (Evanston, IL: Northwestern University Press, 1992).

2 Tester, *Media, Culture and Morality*.

3 Ian Angus and Sut Jhally, 'Introduction,' in *Cultural Politics in Contemporary America*, 13.

4 Miklitsch, *From Hegel to Madonna*, especially 1–95.

5 See Kellner, 'Critical Theory and Cultural Studies.' For a broader account of Kellner's 'multi-perspectival' model, see Kellner, *Media Culture*.

6 Marx and Engels, 'The Manifesto of the Communist Party,' 483.

7 Eagleton, 'Utopia and Its Opposites,' in *Socialist Register, 2000: Necessary and Unnecessary Utopia*, ed. Leo Panitch and Colin Leys (Suffolk: Merlin, 1999), 34.

8 Hebdige, for example, writes about the importance of 'negative' cultural strategies for postmodernism: 'A "negative" cultural tendency is countered not in "resistance" or in "struggle" (the terms of dialectic) but in a doubling of the same: a "hyper-conformity" or hyper-compliance.' See *Hiding in the Light*, 209.

9 Ernst Bloch famously recalls that 'Benjamin had what Lukacs so drastically lacked: a unique gaze for the significant detail, for what lies alongside, for those fresh elements which, in thinking and in the world, arise from here, for the individual things which intrude in an unaccustomed and nonschematic way, things which do not fit in with the usual lot and therefore deserve particular, incisive attention. Benjamin had an incomparable micrological-philological sense for this sort of detail, for this sort of significant periphera, for this sort of meaningful incidental sign.' 'Recollections of Walter Benjamin,' *On Walter Benjamin: Critical Essays and Recollections*, ed. Gary Smith (Cambridge: MIT Press, 1991), 340.

10 Adorno, 'How to Look at Television,' 137.

11 Adorno, *Negative Dialectics*, 377, emphasis added.

12 Miklitsch, *From Hegel to Madonna*, 143n. For a cogent defence of hedonism from the perspective of critical theory, see Herbert Marcuse, 'On Hedonism,' *Negations: Essays in Critical Theory*, trans. Jeremy J. Shapiro (Boston: Beacon Press, 1969).

13 Adorno, *Minima Moralia*, 97.

14 Ibid., 202.

15 Adorno, 'On Popular Music,' 48.

16 Grossberg, 'History, Politics, and Postmodernism: Stuart Hall and Cultural Studies,' in *Bringing It All Back Home*, 193.

17 Jameson, *Postmodernism*, 47.

18 In *Dreamworld and Catastrophe: The Passing of Mass Utopia in East and West* (Cambridge: MIT Press, 2000), Buck-Morss develops an intriguing response to these questions by looking to images of mass utopia developed in the 1920s and 1930s, mainly in the Soviet Union. In work that owes far less to Benjamin's theoretical methodology yet offers a brilliant if unintentional replication of his basic intent, Mike Davis develops complementary accounts of Los Angeles that liquify the 'natural' physiognomy of architecture and urban planning into the history of social relations and processes, thereby restoring a visceral sense of the various threshold moments in which one particular future was realized from among a wide field of possible choices. See *City of Quartz: Excavating the Future in Los Angeles* (New York: Verso, 1990) and *Ecology of Fear: Los Angeles and the Imagination of Disaster* (New York: Metropolitan Books, 1998).

19 Benjamin, 'N [9a,3],' 473.

# Works Cited

Adorno, Theodor. *Aesthetic Theory*. Ed. Gretel Adorno and Rolf Tiedemann. Trans. Robert Hullot-Kentor. Minneapolis: University of Minnesota Press, 1997.

– 'Alienated Masterpiece: The *Missa Solemnis*.' *Telos* 28 (1976).

– 'Analytical Study of the NBC Music Appreciation Hour.' *Musical Quarterly* 78 (Summer 1994).

– *Critical Models: Interventions and Catchwords*. Trans. Henry W. Pickford. New York: Columbia University Press, 1998.

– *The Culture Industry: Selected Essays on Mass Culture*. Ed. J.M. Bernstein. London: Routledge, 1991.

– 'The Essay as Form.' Trans. Robert Hullot-Kentor and Frederic Will. *New German Critique* 32 (Spring/Summer 1984).

– 'Freudian Theory and the Pattern of Fascist Propaganda.' In *The Essential Frankfurt School Reader*. Ed. Andrew Arato and Eike Gebhardt. New York: Continuum, 1992.

– 'The Idea of Natural History.' Trans. Robert Hullot-Kentor. *Telos* 60 (Summer 1984).

– *Introduction to the Sociology of Music*. Trans. E.B. Ashton. New York: Seabury Press, 1976.

– *Minima Moralia: Reflections from a Damaged Life*. Trans. E.F.N. Jephcott. New York: Verso, 1996.

– *Negative Dialectics*. Trans. E.B. Ashton. New York: Continuum, 1995.

– *Notes to Literature*. Volume 1. Ed. Rolf Tiedemann. Trans. Shierry Weber Nicholsen. New York: Columbia University Press, 1991.

– 'On Jazz.' Trans. Jamie Owen Daniel. *Discourse* 12.1 (1989–90).

– 'On the Fetish Character in Music and the Regression of Listening.' Trans.

Maurice Goldbloom. In *The Essential Frankfurt School Reader*. Ed. Andrew Arato. New York: Continuum, 1992.

– *Prisms*. Trans. Samuel Weber and Shierry Weber. Cambridge: MIT Press, 1981.

– 'Progress.' Trans. Eric Krakauer. In *Benjamin: Philosophy, Aesthetics, History*. Ed. Gary Smith. Chicago: University of Chicago Press, 1989.

– 'The Radio Symphony: An Experiment in Theory.' In *Radio Research 1941*. Ed. Paul Lazarsfeld and Frank Stanton. New York: Duell, Sloan and Pearce, 1941.

– *The Stars Down to Earth and Other Essays on the Irrational in Culture*. Ed. Stephen Crook. New York: Routledge, 1994.

– 'Sociology and Psychology I and II.' Trans. Irving Wohlfarth. *New Left Review* 46–7 (1967–8).

– 'Theory of Pseudo-Culture (1959).' Trans. Deborah Cook. *Telos* 95 (Spring 1993).

Adorno, Theodor, with Hellmut Becker. 'Education for Autonomy.' *Telos* 56 (Summer 1983).

Adorno, Theodor, and Walter Benjamin. *The Complete Correspondence, 1928–1940*. Ed. Henri Lonitz. Trans. Nicholas Walker. Cambridge: Harvard University Press, 1999.

Adorno, Theodor, Else Frenkel Brunswick, Daniel J. Levinson, and R. Nevitt Sanford. *The Authoritarian Personality*. New York: W.W. Norton, 1969.

Adorno, Theodor, and Max Horkheimer. 'The Schema of Mass Culture.' Trans. Nicholas Walker. In *The Culture Industry: Selected Essays on Mass Culture*. Ed. J.M. Bernstein. London: Routledge, 1991.

Adorno, Theodor, Leo Lowenthal, and Paul W. Massing. 'Anti-Semitism and Fascist Propaganda' In *Anti-Semitism: A Social Disease*. Ed. Ernst Simmel. New York: International Universities Press, 1946.

Adorno, Theodor, with Peter von Haselberg. 'On the Historical Adequacy of Consciousness.' *Telos* 56 (Summer 1983).

Adorno, Theodor, with the assistance of George Simpson. 'On Popular Music.' *Studies in Philosophy and Social Science* 9 (1941).

Agger, Ben. *Cultural Studies as Critical Theory*. London: Falmer Press, 1992.

– *The Discourse of Domination: From the Frankfurt School to Postmodernism*. Evanston IL: Northwestern University Press, 1992.

Althusser, Louis. *For Marx*. Trans. Ben Brewster. London: Allen Lane, Penguin Press, 1969.

– *Lenin and Philosophy and Other Essays*. Trans. Ben Brewster. New York: Monthly Review Press, 1971.

Angus, Ian, and Sut Jhally, eds. *Cultural Politics in Contemporary America*. New York: Routledge, 1989.

– 'Introduction.' *Cultural Politics in Contemporary America*. Ed. Ian Angus and Sut Jhally. New York: Routledge, 1989.

Appadurai, Arjun, 'Introduction: Commodities and the Politics of Value.' *The Social Life of Things: Commodities in Cultural Perspective*. Ed. Arjun Appadurai. New York: Cambridge University Press, 1986.

Aristotle. *The Politics*. Trans. T.A. Sinclair. Toronto: Penguin Books Canada, 1981.

Bagdikian, Ben. *The Media Monopoly*. 6th ed. Boston: Beacon Press, 2000.

Barthes, Roland. *Image-Music-Text*. Trans. Stephen Heath. New York: Noonday Press, 1977.

– *Mythologies*. Trans. Annette Lavers. Toronto: Grafton Books, 1987.

– *The Pleasure of the Text*. Trans. Richard Miller. New York: Hill and Wang, 1975.

Benjamin, Jessica. 'The End of Internalization: Adorno's Social Psychology.' *Telos* 32 (Summer 1977).

Benjamin, Walter. *The Arcades Project*. Prepared on the basis of the German volume edited by Rolf Tiedemann. Trans. Howard Eiland and Kevin McLaughlin. Cambridge: Belknap Press of Harvard University Press, 1999.

– *One-Way Street and Other Writings*. Trans. Edmund Jephcott and Kingsley Shorter. London: New Left Books, 1979.

– *The Origin of German Tragic Drama*. Trans. John Osborne. New York: Verso, 1985.

– *Reflections: Essays, Aphorisms, Autobiographical Writings*. Ed. Peter Demetz. Trans. Edmund Jephcott. New York: Schocken Books, 1978.

– *Selected Writings*. Volume 1. *1913–1926*. Ed. Marcus Bullock and Michael W. Jennings. Trans. Mark Ritter. Cambridge: Belknap Press of Harvard University Press, 1996.

– *Selected Writings*. Volume 2. *1927–1934*. Ed. Michael W. Jennings, Howard Eiland, and Gary Smith. Trans. Rodney Livingstone et al. Cambridge: Belknap Press of Harvard University Press, 1999.

– *Selected Writings*. Volume 3. *1935–1938*. Ed. Howard Eiland and Michael W. Jennings. Trans. Edmund Jephcott, Howard Eiland, et al. Cambridge: Belknap Press of Harvard University Press, 2002.

– *Selected Writings*. Volume 4. *1938–1940*. Ed. Howard Eiland and Michael W. Jennings. Trans. Edmund Jephcott and others. Cambridge: Belknap Press of Harvard University Press, 2003.

Bennett, Jane. 'Commodity Fetishism and Commodity Enchantment,' *Theory and Event* 5.1 (2001).

– *The Enchantment of Modern Life: Attachments, Crossings, and Ethics*. Princeton, NJ: Princeton University Press, 2001.

Bennett, Tony. 'Hegemony, Ideology, Pleasure: Blackpool.' In *Popular Culture and Social Relations*. Ed. Tony Bennett, Colin Mercer, and Janet Woollacott. Philadelphia: Open University Press, 1986.

– 'Introduction: Popular Culture and 'the Turn to Gramsci.' In *Popular Culture and Social Relations*. Ed. Tony Bennett, Colin Mercer, and Janet Woollacott. Philadelphia: Open University Press, 1986.

– 'The Politics of 'the Popular' and Popular Culture.' In *Popular Culture and Social Relations*. Ed. Tony Bennett, Colin Mercer, and Janet Woollacott. Philadelphia: Open University Press, 1986.

– 'Theories of the Media, Theories of Society.' In *Culture, Society and the Media*. Ed. Michael Gurevitch, Tony Bennett, James Curran, and Janet Woollacott. New York: Methuen, 1982.

Bernstein, J.M. 'Why Rescue Semblance? Metaphysical Experience and the Possibility of Ethics.' In *The Semblance of Subjectivity: Essays in Adorno's Aesthetic Theory*. Ed. Lambert Zuidervaart and Tom Huhn. Cambridge: MIT Press, 1997.

Best, Steven, and Douglas Kellner. *The Postmodern Adventure: Science, Technology and Cultural Studies at the Third Millennium*. New York: Guilford Press, 2001.

Bloch, Ernst. 'Recollections of Walter Benjamin.' In *On Walter Benjamin: Critical Essays and Recollections*. Ed. Gary Smith. Cambridge: MIT Press, 1991.

Bolz, Norbert, and Willem van Reijen. *Walter Benjamin*. Trans. Laimdota Mazzarins. Atlantic Highlands, N.J.: Humanities Press, 1996.

Brantlinger, Patrick. *Crusoe's Footprints: Cultural Studies in Britain and America*. New York: Routledge, 1990.

Braverman, Harry. *Labor and Monopoly Capital*. New York: Monthly Review Press, 1974.

Buck-Morss, Susan. 'Aesthetics and Anaesthetics: Walter Benjamin's Artwork Essay Reconsidered.' *October* 62 (Fall 1992).

– 'Benjamin's Passagen-Werk: Redeeming Mass Culture for the Revolution.' *New German Critique* 29 (Spring/Summer 1983).

– *The Dialectics of Seeing: Walter Benjamin and the Arcades Project*. Cambridge: MIT Press, 1989.

– *Dreamworld and Catastrophe: The Passing of Mass Utopia in East and West*. Cambridge: MIT Press, 2000.

– 'The Flaneur, the Sandwichman and the Whore: The Politics of Loitering.' *New German Critique* 39 (Fall 1986).

– *The Origin of Negative Dialectics*. Sussex: Harvester Press, 1977.

– 'Review: Walter Benjamin's Aesthetics of Redemption.' *Theory and Society* 13.5 (1984).

Budd, Mike, Robert Entman, and Clay Steinman. 'The Affirmative Character of U.S. Cultural Studies.' *Critical Studies in Mass Communication* 7 (1990).

Budd, Mike, Steve Craig, and Clay Steinman. *Consuming Environments: Television and Commercial Culture*. New Brunswick, NJ: Rutgers University Press, 1999.

Burniston, Steve, and Chris Weedon. 'Ideology, Subjectivity and the Artistic Text.' In *On Ideology*. Ed. Centre for Contemporary Cultural Studies. London: Hutchinson, 1978.

Caygill, Howard. *Walter Benjamin: The Color of Experience*. New York: Routledge, 1998.

Chambers, Iain. 'Roland Barthes: Structuralism/Semiotics.' *Working Papers in Cultural Studies* 6 (Autumn 1974).

– 'Waiting on the End of the World.' In *Stuart Hall: Critical Dialogues in Cultural Studies*. Ed. David Morley and Kuan-Hsing Chen. New York: Routledge, 1996.

Chambers, Iain, John Clarke, Ian Connell, Lidia Curti, Stuart Hall, and Tony Jefferson. 'Marxism and Culture.' *Screen* 18.4 (Winter 1977–8).

Chomsky, Noam, and Edward Herman. *Manufacturing Consent: The Political Economy of the Mass Media*. 2nd ed. New York: Pantheon Books, 2002.

Clarke, John. *New Times and Old Enemies: Essays on Cultural Studies and America*. London: HarperCollins Academic, 1991.

– 'The Skinheads and the Magical Recovery of Community.' In *Resistance through Rituals: Youth Subcultures in Post-War Britain*. Ed. Stuart Hall and Tony Jefferson. London: Routledge, 1993.

– 'Style.' In *Resistance through Rituals: Youth Subcultures in Post-War Britain*. Ed. Stuart Hall and Tony Jefferson. London: Routledge, 1993.

Clarke, John, Stuart Hall, Tony Jefferson, and Brian Roberts. 'Subcultures, Cultures and Class.' In *Resistance through Rituals: Youth Subcultures in Post-War Britain*. Ed. Stuart Hall and Tony Jefferson. London: Routledge, 1993.

Cohen, Margaret. *Profane Illumination: Walter Benjamin and the Paris of Surrealist Revolution*. Berkeley: University of California Press, 1993.

Cohen, Phil. 'Subcultural Conflict and Working-Class Community.' In *Culture, Media, Language: Working Papers in Cultural Studies, 1972–1979*. Ed. Stuart Hall, Dorothy Hobson, Andrew Lowe, and Paul Willis. London: Hutchinson, 1980.

Cook, Deborah. *The Culture Industry Revisited*. London: Rowman and Littlefield, 1996.

Cooper, Harry. 'On *Uber Jazz*: Replaying Adorno with the Grain.' *October* 75 (Winter 1996).

Coward, Rosalind. 'Class, "Culture" and the Social Formation.' *Screen* 18.1 (1977).

Curran, James, Michael Gurevitch, and Janet Woollacott. 'The Study of the Media: Theoretical Approaches.' In *Culture, Society and the Media*. Ed.

Michael Gurevitch, Tony Bennett, James Curran, and Janet Woollacott. New York: Methuen, 1982.

Davies, Ioan. *Cultural Studies and Beyond: Fragments of Empire*. New York: Routledge, 1995.

Davis, Mike. *City of Quartz: Excavating the Future in Los Angeles*. New York: Verso, 1990.

– *Ecology of Fear: Los Angeles and the Imagination of Disaster*. New York: Metropolitan Books, 1998.

Debord, Guy. *Society of the Spectacle*. Trans. anonymous. Detroit: Black and Red, 1983.

de Certeau, Michel. *The Practice of Everyday Life*. Trans. Steven Randall. Berkeley: University of California Press, 1984.

Demetz, Peter. 'Introduction.' In *Walter Benjamin: Reflections: Essays, Aphorisms, Autobiographical Writings*. Ed. Peter Demetz. Trans. Edmund Jephcott. New York: Schocken Books, 1978.

Dworkin, Dennis. *Cultural Marxism in Postwar Britain: History, the New Left and the Origins of Cultural Studies*. Durham: Duke University Press, 1997.

Dyer-Witherford, Nicholas. *Cyber-Marx: Cycles and Circuits of Struggle in High Technology Capitalism*. Chicago: University of Illinois Press, 1999.

Eagleton, Terry. 'Utopia and Its Opposites.' In *Socialist Register, 2000: Necessary and Unnecessary Utopias*. Ed. Leo Panitch and Colin Leys. Suffolk: Merlin Press, 1999.

Farred, Grant. 'Leavisite Cool: The Organic Links Between Cultural Studies and Scrutiny.' *Dispositio/n* 21.48 (1996).

Ferguson, Marjorie, and Peter Golding, eds. *Cultural Studies in Question*. Thousand Oaks, CA: Sage, 1997.

Fiske, John. *Understanding Popular Culture*. New York: Routledge, 1989.

Fiskey, John. *Reading the Popular*. New York: Routledge, 1989.

Frank, Thomas. *One Market Under God: Extreme Capitalism, Market Populism, and the End of Economic Democracy*. New York: Anchor Books, 2001.

Freud, Sigmund. *The Interpretation of Dreams*. Ed. and trans. James Strachey. New York: Avon Books, 1965.

– *On Metapsychology: The Theory of Psychoanalysis*. Ed. Angela Richards. Trans. James Strachey. Markham, ON: Penguin Books, 1984.

Frey, Hans-Jost. 'On Presentation in Benjamin.' In *Walter Benjamin: Theoretical Questions*. Ed. David Ferris. Stanford: Stanford University Press, 1996.

Garnham, Nicholas. 'Political Economy and Cultural Studies: Reconciliation or Divorce?' *Critical Studies in Mass Communication* 12.1 (1995).

– 'Reply to Grossberg and Carey.' *Critical Studies in Mass Communication* 12.1 (1995).

Gendron, Bernard. 'Adorno Meets the Cadillacs.' In *Studies in Entertainment: Critical Approaches to Mass Culture*. Ed. Tania Modleski. Bloomington: Indiana University Press, 1986.

Geyer-Ryan, Helga. *Fables of Desire: Studies in the Ethics of Art and Gender*. Cambridge: Polity Press, 1994.

Giroux, Henry A. 'Consuming Social Change: The "United Colors of Benetton."' *Cultural Critique* 26 (Winter 1993–4).

Golding, Peter, and Graham Murdock, eds. *The Political Economy of the Media*. 2 vols. Northampton: Edward Elgar, 1997.

Goldman, Robert, and Stephen Papson. *Sign Wars: The Cluttered Landscape of Advertising*. New York: Guilford Press, 1996.

Gramsci, Antonio. *Selections from the Prison Notebooks*. Ed. and trans. Quintin Hoare and Geoffrey Nowell Smith. New York: International Publishers, 1971.

Grossberg, Lawrence. *Bringing It All Back Home: Essays on Cultural Studies*. Durham: Duke University Press, 1997.

– 'Cultural Studies vs. Political Economy: Is Anybody Else Bored with this Debate?' *Critical Studies in Mass Communication* 12.1 (1995).

– *Dancing in Spite of Myself: Essays on Popular Culture*. Durham: Duke University Press, 1997.

– *We Gotta Get Out of This Place: Popular Conservatism and Postmodern Culture*. New York: Routledge, 1992.

Gunster, Shane. 'Revisiting the Culture Industry Thesis: Mass Culture and the Commodity Form.' *Cultural Critique* 45 (Spring 2000).

Hall, Stuart. 'Cultural Studies and Its Theoretical Legacies.' In *Cultural Studies*. Ed. Lawrence Grossberg, Cary Nelson, and Paula Treichler. New York: Routledge, 1992.

– 'Cultural Studies and the Centre: Some Problematics and Problems.' In *Culture, Media, Language: Working Papers in Cultural Studies, 1972–1979*. Ed. Stuart Hall, Dorothy Hobson, Andrew Lowe, and Paul Willis. London: Hutchinson, 1980.

– 'Culture, the Media and the "Ideological Effect."' In *Mass Communication and Society*. Ed. James Curran, Michael Gurevitch and Janet Woollacott. Beverly Hills: Sage, 1979.

– 'The Determination of News Photographs.' In *The Manufacture of News*. Ed. Stanley Cohen and Jock Young. London: Constable, 1973.

– 'Encoding/Decoding.' In *Culture, Media, Language: Working Papers in Cultural Studies, 1972–1979*. Ed. Stuart Hall, Dorothy Hobson, Andrew Lowe, and Paul Willis. London: Hutchinson, 1980.

– *External Influences on Broadcasting: 'The External-Internal Dialectic in Broad-*

*casting: Television's Double Bind*. Stencilled Occasional Paper No. 4. Birmingham: Centre for Contemporary Cultural Studies, 1972.

– 'The "First" New Left: Life and Times.' In *Out of Apathy: Voices of the New Left Thirty Years On*. Ed. Robin Archer et al. New York: Verso, 1989.

– 'For Allon White: Metaphors of Transformation.' In *Stuart Hall: Critical Dialogues in Cultural Studies*. Ed. David Morley and Kuan-Hsing Chen. New York: Routledge, 1996.

– *The Hard Road to Renewal: Thatcherism and the Crisis of the Left*. New York: Verso, 1988.

– 'The Hinterland of Science: Ideology and the "Sociology of Knowledge."' In *On Ideology*. Ed. Centre for Contemporary Cultural Studies. London: Hutchinson, 1978.

– 'Ideology and Communication Theory.' In *Rethinking Communication*. Volume 1. *Paradigm Issues*. Ed. Brenda Darvin, Lawrence Grossberg, Barbara J. O'Keefe, and Ellen Warteila. Newbury Park, CA: Sage, 1989.

– 'Introduction to Media Studies at the Centre.' In *Culture, Media, Language: Working Papers in Cultural Studies, 1972–1979*. Ed. Stuart Hall, Dorothy Hobson, Andrew Lowe, and Paul Willis. London: Hutchinson, 1980.

– 'The Local and the Global: Globalization and Ethnicity.' In *Culture, Globalization and the World-System: Contemporary Conditions for the Representation of Identity*. Ed. Anthony D. King. Minneapolis: University of Minnesota Press, 1997.

– 'Marx's Notes on Method: A "Reading" of the "1857 Introduction."' *Working Papers in Cultural Studies* 6 (Autumn 1974).

– 'The Meaning of New Times.' In *Stuart Hall: Critical Dialogues in Cultural Studies*. Ed. David Morley and Kuan-Hsing Chen. New York: Routledge, 1996.

– 'Notes on Deconstructing the Popular.' In *People's History and Socialist Theory*. Ed. Raphael Samuel. Boston: Routledge, 1981.

– 'On Postmodernism and Articulation: An Interview with Stuart Hall.' Ed. Lawrence Grossberg. In *Stuart Hall: Critical Dialogues in Cultural Studies*. Ed. David Morley and Kuan-Hsing Chen. New York: Routledge, 1996.

– 'The "Political" and the "Economic" in Marx's Theory of Classes.' In *Class and Class Structure*. Ed. Alan Hunt. London: Lawrence and Wishart, 1977.

– 'The Problem of Ideology: Marxism without Guarantees.' In *Stuart Hall: Critical Dialogues in Cultural Studies*. Ed. David Morley and Kuan-Hsing Chen. New York: Routledge, 1996.

– 'Recent Developments in Theories of Language and Ideology: A Critical Note.' In *Culture, Media, Language: Working Papers in Cultural Studies, 1972–1979*. Ed. Stuart Hall, Dorothy Hobson, Andrew Lowe, and Paul Willis. London: Hutchinson, 1980.

– 'The rediscovery of 'Ideology': Return of the Repressed in Media Studies.' In *Culture, Society and the Media*. Ed. Michael Gurevitch, Tony Bennett, James Curran, and Janet Woollacott. New York: Methuen, 1982.

– *Television as a Medium and Its Relation to Culture*. Birmingham: Centre for Contemporary Cultural Studies, 1975.

– 'The Toad in the Garden: Thatcherism among the Theorists.' In *Marxism and the Interpretation of Culture*. Ed. Cary Nelson and Lawrence Grossberg. Chicago: University of Illinois Press, 1988.

Hall, Stuart, with Ian Angus, Jon Cruz, James Der Derian, Sut Jhally, Justin Lewis, and Cathy Schwichtenberg. 'Reflections upon the Encoding/Decoding Model: An Interview with Stuart Hall.' In *Viewing, Reading, Listening: Audiences and Cultural Reception*. Ed. Jon Cruz and Justin Lewis. Boulder, CO: Westview Press, 1994.

Hall, Stuart, Chas Critcher, Tony Jefferson, John Clarke, and Brian Roberts. *Policing the Crisis: Mugging, the State, and Law and Order*. London: Macmillan Education, 1978.

Hall, Stuart, and Tony Jefferson, eds. *Resistance through Rituals: Youth Subcultures in Post-War Britain*. London: Routledge, 1993.

Hall, Stuart, Bob Lumley, and Gregor McLennan. 'Politics and Ideology: Gramsci.' In *On Ideology*. Ed. Centre for Contemporary Cultural Studies. London: Hutchinson, 1978.

Hall, Stuart, and Paddy Whannel. *The Popular Arts*. Toronto: Hutchinson Educational, 1964.

Harding, James. 'Adorno, Ellison and the Critique of Jazz.' *Cultural Critique* (Fall 1995).

Harris, David. *From Class Struggle to the Politics of Pleasure: The Effects of Gramscianism on Cultural Studies*. New York: Routledge, 1992.

Hansen, Miriam. 'Benjamin, Cinema and Experience: "The Blue Flower in the Land of Technology."' *New German Critique* 40 (Winter 1987).

– 'Introduction to Adorno, "Transparencies on Film" (1966).' *New German Critique* 24–5 (Fall/Winter 1981–2).

– 'Mass Culture as Hieroglyphic Writings: Adorno, Derrida, Kracauer.' *New German Critique* 56 (Spring/Summer 1992).

– 'Of Mice and Ducks: Benjamin and Adorno on Disney.' *South Atlantic Quarterly* 92.1 (1993).

Harootunian, Harry. 'The Benjamin Effect: Modernism, Repetition, and the Path to Different Cultural Imaginaries.' In *Walter Benjamin and the Demands of History*. Ed. Michael P. Steinberg. Ithaca, NY: Cornell University Press, 1996.

Hebdige, Dick. *Hiding in the Light: On Images and Things*. New York: Routledge, 1988.

– *Subculture: The Meaning of Style*. New York: Routledge, 1994.

Herman, Andrew, and John H. Sloop. '"Red Alert!" Rhetorics of the World Wide Web and "Friction Free" Capitalism.' In *The World Wide Web and Contemporary Cultural Theory*. Ed. Andrew Herman and Thomas Swiss. New York: Routledge, 2000.

Hoggart, Richard. *The Uses of Literacy*. Harmondsworth: Penguin, 1957.

Hohendahl, Peter Uwe. *Prismatic Thought: Theodor W. Adorno*. Lincoln: University of Nebraska Press, 1995.

Horkheimer, Max. *Critical Theory: Selected Essays*. Trans. Matthew J. O'Connell et al. New York: Continuum, 1992.

Horkheimer, Max, and Theodor Adorno. *Dialectic of Enlightenment: Philosophical Fragments*. Ed. Gunzelin Schmid Noerr. Trans. Edmund Jephcott. Stanford: Stanford University Press, 2002.

Horowitz, Gad. *Repression*. Toronto: University of Toronto Press, 1977.

Huyssen, Andreas. 'Adorno in Reverse: From Hollywood to Richard Wagner.' *New German Critique* 29 (Spring/Summer 1983).

Jacoby, Russell. *The End of Utopia: Politics and Culture in an Age of Apathy*. New York: Basic Books, 1999.

Jameson, Fredric. *The Ideologies of Theory, Essays 1971–1986*. Volume 2. The Syntax of History. Minneapolis: University of Minnesota Press, 1988.

– *Late Marxism: Adorno, or, The Persistence of the Dialectic*. New York: Verso, 1990.

– *Marxism and Form: Twentieth Century Dialectical Theories of Literature*. Princeton: Princeton University Press, 1971.

– 'On "Cultural Studies."' *Social Text* 34 (1993).

– *The Political Unconscious: Narrative as a Socially Symbolic Act*. Ithaca: Cornell University Press, 1981.

– *Postmodernism, Or, The Cultural Logic of Late Capitalism*. Durham: Duke University Press, 1991.

Jarvis, Simon. *Adorno: A Critical Introduction*. New York: Routledge, 1998.

Jay, Martin. *Adorno*. London: Fontana, 1984.

Jennings, Michael. *Dialectical Images: Walter Benjamin's Theory of Literary Criticism*. Ithaca: Cornell University Press, 1987.

– 'On the Banks of a New Lethe: Commodification and Experience in Benjamin's Baudelaire Book.' *Boundary 2* 30.1 (2003).

Jessop, Bob et al. 'Authoritarian Populism, Two Nations and Thatcherism.' *New Left Review* 147 (Sept./Oct. 1984).

Jhally, Sut. *The Codes of Advertising: Fetishism and the Political Economy of Meaning in the Consumer Society*. New York: Routledge, 1990.

Johnson, Richard. 'Three Problematics: Elements of a Theory of Working-Class

Culture.' In *Working Class Culture: Studies in History and Theory*. Ed. John Clarke, Chas Critcher and Richard Johnson. New York: St Martin's Press, 1979.

– 'What Is Cultural Studies Anyway?' *Social Text* 16 (Winter 1986–7).

Jones, John Philip, Ed. *How to Use Advertising to Build Strong Brands*. Thousand Oaks, CA: Sage, 1999.

Kellner, Douglas. 'Critical Theory and Cultural Studies: The Missed Articulation.' *Cultural Methodologies*. Ed. Jim McGuigan. Thousand Oaks, CA: Sage, 1997.

– *Critical Theory, Marxism and Modernity*. Baltimore: Johns Hopkins University Press, 1989.

– *Media Culture: Cultural Studies, Identity and Politics between the Modern and the Postmodern*. New York: Routledge, 1995.

Kendall, David. 'Interview.' In *Making and Selling Culture*. Ed. Richard Ohmann. Hanover: Wesleyan University Press, 1996.

Klein, Naomi. *No Logo: Taking Aim at Brand Bullies*. Toronto: Knopf Canada, 2000.

Kopytoff, Igor. 'The Cultural Biography of Things: Commoditization as Process.' In *The Social Life of Things: Commodities in Cultural Perspective*. Ed. Arjun Appadurai. New York: Cambridge University Press, 1986.

Kumar, Amitava, ed. *Class Issues: Pedagogy, Cultural Studies and the Public Sphere*. New York: New York University Press, 1997.

Kuttner, Robert. *Everything for Sale: The Virtues and Limits of Markets*. New York: Alfred A. Knopf, 1997.

Laclau, Ernesto. *Politics and Ideology in Marxist Theory: Capitalism-Fascism-Populism*. London: Verso, 1979.

Levin, Thomas Y. 'For the Record: Adorno on Music in the Age of Its Technological Reproducibility.' *October* 55 (Winter 1990).

Lorrain, Jorge. 'Stuart Hall and the Marxist Concept of Ideology.' In *Stuart Hall: Critical Dialogues in Cultural Studies*. Ed. David Morley and Kuan-Hsing Chen. New York: Routledge, 1996.

Lowe, Donald M. *The Body in Late Capitalist USA*. Durham: Duke University Press, 1995.

McCarron, Gary. 'Pixel Perfect: Towards a Political Economy of Digital Fidelity.' *Canadian Journal of Communication* 24 (1999).

McChesney, Robert. *Rich Media, Poor Democracy: Communication Politics in Dubious Times*. Chicago: University of Illinois Press, 1999.

McCole, John. *Walter Benjamin and the Antinomies of Tradition*. Ithaca: Cornell University Press, 1993.

McGuigan, Jim. *Cultural Populism*. New York: Routledge, 1992.

McNally, David. *Bodies of Meaning: Studies on Language, Labor, and Liberation.* Albany: State University of New York Press, 2001.
McRobbie, Angela, Ed. *Back to Reality: Social Experience and Cultural Studies.* New York: Manchester University Press, 1997.
– 'Looking Back at *New Times* and Its Critics.' In *Stuart Hall: Critical Dialogues in Cultural Studies*. Ed. David Morley and Kuan-Hsing Chen. New York: Routledge, 1996.
– *Postmodernism and Popular Culture*. New York: Routledge, 1994.
– 'The Es and the Anti-Es: New Questions for Feminism and Cultural Studies.' In *Cultural Studies in Question*. Ed. Marjorie Ferguson and Peter Golding. Thousand Oaks, CA: Sage, 1997.
Marcuse, Herbert. *Eros and Civilization*. Boston: Beacon Press, 1966.
– *Negations: Essays in Critical Theory*. Trans. Jeremy J. Shapiro. Boston: Beacon Press, 1969.
– *One-Dimensional Man: Studies in the Ideology of Advanced Industrial Society.* Boston: Beacon Press, 1966.
Marx, Karl. *Early Writings*. Trans. and ed. T.B. Bottomore. Toronto: McGraw-Hill, 1964.
Marx, Karl, and Friedrich Engels. *The Marx-Engels Reader*. Ed. Robert C. Tucker. 2nd ed. New York: W.W. Norton, 1978.
Massumi, Brian. 'The Autonomy of Affect.' *Cultural Critique* 31 (Fall 1995).
Meninghaus, Winfried. 'Walter Benjamin's Theory of Myth.' Trans. Gary Smith. In *On Walter Benjamin: Critical Essays and Recollections*. Ed. Gary Smith. Cambridge: MIT Press, 1988.
Miklitsch, Robert. *From Hegel to Madonna: Towards a General Economy of Commodity Fetishism*. Albany: SUNY Press, 1998.
Morgan, William J. 'Adorno on Sport: The Case of the Fractured Dialectic.' *Theory and Society* 17 (1988).
Morley, David. 'Texts, Readers, Subjects.' In *Culture, Media, Language: Working Papers in Cultural Studies, 1972–1979*. Ed. Stuart Hall, Dorothy Hobson, Andrew Lowe, and Paul Willis. London: Hutchinson, 1980.
– 'Theoretical Orthodoxies: Textualism, Constructivism and the "New Ethnography" in Cultural Studies.' In *Cultural Studies in Question*. Ed. Marjorie Ferguson and Peter Golding. Thousand Oaks, CA: Sage, 1997.
Morris, Meaghan. 'Banality in Cultural Studies.' *Discourse* 10.2 (1988).
Mosco, Vincent. *The Political Economy of Communication: Rethinking and Renewal*. Thousand Oaks, CA: Sage, 1996.
Negri, Antonio, and Michael Hardt. *Empire*. Cambridge: Harvard University Press, 2000.

Nelson, Cary, and Dilip Parameshwar Gaonkar, eds. *Disciplinarity and Dissent in Cultural Studies*. New York: Routledge, 1996.

Nesbitt, Nick. 'Sounding Autonomy: Adorno, Coltrane and Jazz.' *Telos* 116 (Summer 1999).

*New German Critique* 81 (Fall 2000). Special Issue, *Dialectic of Enlightenment*.

Nicholsen, Shierry Weber. 'Adorno, Benjamin and the Aura: An Aesthetics for Photography.' In *Adorno, Culture and Feminism*. Ed. Maggie O'Neill. Thousand Oaks, CA: Sage, 1999.

Nicholsen, Shierry Weber. *Exact Imagination, Late Work: On Adorno's Aesthetics*. Cambridge: MIT Press, 1997.

Oakes, Stephen. 'Interview.' *Making and Selling Culture*. Ed. Richard Ohmann. Hanover: Wesleyan University Press, 1996.

Paddison, Max. *Adorno's Aesthetics of Music*. New York: Cambridge University Press, 1993.

Pensky, Max. *Melancholy Dialectics: Walter Benjamin and the Play of Mourning*. Amherst: The University of Massachusetts Press, 1993.

Peters, Michael, ed. *After the Disciplines: The Emergence of Cultural Studies*. Westport, CT: Bergin and Garvey, 1999.

Pfister, Joel. 'The Americanization of Cultural Studies.' *Yale Journal of Criticism* 4.2 (1991).

Pickering, Michael. *History, Experience and Cultural Studies*. New York: St Martin's Press, 1997.

Pollock, Friedrich. 'State Capitalism: Its Possibilities and Limitations.' In *The Essential Frankfurt School Reader*. Ed. Andrew Arato and Eike Gebhardt. New York: Continuum, 1992.

Robinson, J. Bradford. 'The Jazz Essays of Theodor Adorno: Some Thoughts on Jazz Reception in Weimar Germany.' *Popular Music* 13.1 (1994).

Rodman, Gilbert. 'Subject to Debate: (Mis)Reading Cultural Studies.' *Journal of Communication Inquiry* 21.2 (1997).

Rolleston, James. 'The Uses of the Frankfurt School: New Stories on the Left.' *Diacritics* 21.4 (1991).

Rosen, Philip. 'Adorno and Film Music: Theoretical Notes on *Composing for the Films*.' *Yale French Studies* 60 (1980).

– 'Introduction to Special Issue on *The Arcades Project*.' *Boundary 2* 30.1 (2003).

Ryan, Bill. *Making Capital from Culture: The Corporate Form of Capitalist Cultural Production*. New York: Walter de Gruyter, 1992.

Schiller, Dan. *Digital Capitalism: Networking the Global Market System*. Cambridge: MIT Press, 1999.

– *Theorizing Communication*. New York: Oxford University Press, 1996.

Schönherr, Ulrich. 'Adorno and Jazz: Reflections on a Failed Encounter.' *Telos* 87 (Spring 1991).

Slack, Jennifer Daryl. 'The Theory and Method of Articulation in Cultural Studies.' In *Stuart Hall: Critical Dialogues in Cultural Studies*. Ed. David Morley and Kuan-Hsing Chen. New York: Routledge, 1996.

Slater, Don, and Fran Tonkiss. *Market Society: Markets and Modern Social Theory*. Malden, MA: Polity Press, 2001.

Slater, Phil. 'The Aesthetic Theory of the Frankfurt School.' *Working Papers in Cultural Studies* 6 (Autumn 1974).

Sontag, Susan. 'Introduction.' *One-Way Street and Other Writings*. Walter Benjamin. Trans. Edmund Jephcott and Kingsley Shorter. London: New Left Books, 1979.

Sparks, Colin. 'The Abuses of Literacy.' *Working Papers in Cultural Studies* 6 (Autumn 1974).

– 'Stuart Hall, Cultural Studies and Marxism.' In *Stuart Hall: Critical Dialogues in Cultural Studies*. Ed. David Morley and Kuan-Hsing Chen. New York: Routledge, 1996.

Stallabrass, Julian. *Gargantua: Manufactured Mass Culture*. New York: Verso, 1996.

Tester, Keith. *Media, Culture and Morality*. New York: Routledge, 1994.

Thomas, Calvin. 'A Knowledge That Would Not Be Power: Adorno, Nostalgia, and the Historicity of the Musical Subject.' *New German Critique* 48 (Fall 1989).

Thompson, E.P. 'Review: *The Long Revolution*.' *New Left Review* 9 and 10 (May/June–July/Aug. 1961).

Todd, Jennifer. 'Production, Reception, Criticism: Walter Benjamin and the Problem of Meaning in Art.' In *Benjamin: Philosophy, Aesthetics, History*. Ed. Gary Smith. Chicago: University of Chicago Press, 1989.

Turner, Graeme. *British Cultural Studies: An Introduction*. 2nd ed. New York: Routledge, 1996.

Turow, Joseph. *Breaking Up America: Advertisers and the New Media World*. Chicago: University of Chicago Press, 1997.

Volosinov, V.N. *Marxism and the Philosophy of Language*. Trans. Ladislav Matejka and I.R. Titunik. Cambridge: Harvard University Press, 1973.

Weigel, Sigrid. *Body- and Image-Space: Re-reading Walter Benjamin*. Trans. Georgina Paul with Rachel McNicholl and Jeremy Gaines. New York: Routledge, 1996.

Wellmer, Albrecht. 'Adorno, Modernity and the Sublime.' In *The Actuality of Adorno: Critical Essays on Adorno and the Postmodern*. Ed. Max Pensky. Albany: State University of New York Press, 1997.

Wernick, Andrew. *Promotional Culture: Advertising, Ideology and Symbolic Expression*. Newbury Park, CA: Sage, 1991.

Whitebook, Joel. *Perversion and Utopia: A Study in Psychoanalysis and Critical Theory*. Cambridge: MIT Press, 1995.

Wiggershaus, Rolf. *The Frankfurt School: Its History, Theories and Political Significance*. Trans. Michael Robertson. Cambridge: MIT Press, 1995.

Wilcock, Evelyn. 'Adorno, Jazz and Racism: "Uber Jazz" and the 1934–7 British Jazz Debate.' *Telos* 107 (Spring 1996).

Williams, Raymond. *Culture and Society, 1780–1950*. Harmondsworth: Penguin Books, 1961.

– *Keywords: A Vocabulary of Culture and Society*. Rev. ed. London: Fontana Press, 1988.

– *Marxism and Literature*. New York: Oxford University Press, 1977.

– *Problems in Materialism and Culture*. London: Verso, 1980.

Williamson, Judith. *Decoding Advertisements: Ideology and Meaning in Advertising*. New York: Marion Boyars, 1984.

Willis, Paul. *Common Culture*. Buckingham: Open University Press, 1990.

– *Learning to Labor: How Working Class Kids Get Working Class Jobs*. New York: Columbia University Press, 1977.

– *Moving Culture*. London: Calouste Gulbenkian Foundation, 1990.

– *Profane Culture*. London: Routledge and Kegan Paul, 1978.

Willis, Susan. *A Primer for Everyday Life*. New York: Routledge, 1991.

Witte, Bernd. *Walter Benjamin: An Intellectual Biography*. Trans. James Rolleston. Detroit: Wayne State University Press, 1991.

Wohlfarth, Irving. 'Hibernation: On the Tenth Anniversay of Adorno's Death.' *Modern Language Notes* 94 (1979).

– 'On the Messianic Structure of Walter Benjamin's Last Reflections.' *Glyph* 3 (1978).

Wolin, Richard. 'Aestheticism and Social Theory: The Case of Walter Benjamin's *PassagenWerk*.' *Theory, Culture and Society* 10 (1993).

– 'Benjamin, Adorno, Surrealism.' In *The Semblance of Subjectivity: Essays in Adorno's Aesthetic Theory*. Ed. Lambert Zuidervaart and Tom Huhn. Cambridge: MIT Press, 1997.

– 'The De-Aestheticization of Art: On Adorno's *Aesthetische Theorie*.' *Telos* 41 (Fall 1979).

– *Walter Benjamin: An Aesthetic of Redemption*. New York: Columbia University Press, 1982.

Wood, Ellen Meiksins. *Democracy against Capitalism*. Cambridge: Cambridge University Press, 1995.

Zuidervaart, Lambert. *Adorno's Aesthetic Theory: The Redemption of Illusion*. Cambridge: MIT Press, 1991.

# Index

## CULTURAL SPACES

*Cultural Spaces* explores the rapidly changing temporal, spatial, and theoretical boundaries of contemporary cultural studies. Culture has long been understood as the force that defines and delimits societies in fixed spaces. The recent intensification of globalizing processes, however, has meant that it is no longer possible – if it ever was – to imagine the world as a collection of autonomous, monadic spaces, whether these are imagined as localities, nations, regions within nations, or cultures demarcated by region or nation. One of the major challenges of studying contemporary culture is to understand the new relationships of culture to space that are produced today. The aim of this series is to publish bold new analyses and theories of spaces of culture, as well as investigations of the historical construction of those cultural spaces that have influenced the shape of the contemporary world.



**Books in the Series:**
Peter Ives, *Gramsci's Politics of Language: Engaging the Bakhtin Circle and the Frankfurt School*
Sarah Brophy, *Witnessing AIDS: Writing, Testimony, and the Work of Mourning*
Shane Gunster, *Capitalizing on Culture: Critical Theory for Cultural Studies*